HONOR
AND
BETRAYAL

The Untold Story of the
Navy SEALs Who Captured the
"Butcher of Fallujah"—
and the Shameful Ordeal
They Later Endured

PATRICK ROBINSON

WITH THE COOPERATION OF FORMER NAVY SEALS

MATTHEW MCCABE AND
JONATHAN KEEFE

DA CAPO PRESS
A Member of the Perseus Books Group

This book is based on actual events that occurred when three US Navy SEALs, part of the Special Forces Team that captured Iraq's most wanted terrorist in 2009, faced courts-martial on charges relating to allegations of prisoner abuse. It is the story of those brave SEALs and the subsequent ordeal they suffered, including their courts-martial. As with many such trial proceedings, conflicting accounts of what actually happened were presented. *Honor and Betrayal* is told from the perspective of the defendants and reflects the opinions of the author, who is a devoted advocate for all US Navy SEALs and for these three SEALs in particular. Some names have been changed, and some dialogue has been reconstructed.

Editorial production by *Marrathon* Production Services. www.marrathon.net

BOOK DESIGN BY JANE RAESE
Set in 12-point Dante by Jane Raese

Library of Congress Cataloging-in-Publication Data is available for this book.

First Da Capo Press edition 2013
First Da Capo Press paperback edition 2014

ISBN 978-0-306-82308-4 (hardcover)
ISBN 978-0-306-82352-7 (paperback)
ISBN 978-0-306-82309-1 (e-book)

Published by Da Capo Press
A Member of the Perseus Books Group
www.dacapopress.com

Da Capo Press books are available at special discounts for bulk purchases in the U.S. by corporations, institutions, and other organizations. For more information, please contact the Special Markets Department at the Perseus Books Group, 2300 Chestnut Street, Suite 200, Philadelphia, PA 19103, or call (800) 810-4145, ext. 5000, or e-mail special.markets@perseusbooks.com.

10 9 8 7 6 5 4 3 2

CONTENTS

AUTHOR'S NOTE

Almost a decade has passed since the world first saw those shuddering pictures of the burned bodies of American security officers swinging from the iron bridge over the Euphrates River in Fallujah. It brought perhaps a new dimension to the fiendish cruelty Iraq's jihadists were carrying out in the name of the Prophet.

But, curiously, when a Navy SEAL Team finally went in and grabbed the perpetrator after five years, the aftermath of that event caused an almost bigger sense of outrage. Because the US military authorities decided to court-martial the men who had carried out the raid—for "prisoner abuse."

The US public rose up in protest. Literally hundreds of thousands of people signed petitions. I was among a few writers and historians requested to join the uproar and contribute words and/or cash to the SEALs' defense.

From that moment I followed the scant accounts of the legal process, making notes, tracking the three Special Forces heroes all the way to their respective military trials. And the only thought I ever had was: *these men deserve vindication.* The media did their best, but they didn't bother much to investigate whether the alleged assault actually happened. *Who cares?*

Well, for a start, I cared. And in the spring of 2012 I decided to lay out the complete story, making clear the precise differences between "not guilty" on a point of law, "not guilty" because the case was not proven, and "not guilty" because the crime was never perpetrated in the first place.

I knew that all three of the SEALs were still in the Navy, but I nonetheless reached out to them, trying to find out what really happened.

One of them, a devoted member of the Team, could not reveal very much. The other two confessed that the trials had devastated them and that they would both be leaving the Navy with the utmost sadness.

They had much to say but could not recount anything until they were no longer wearing dark blue. The process was long and sometimes arduous. The iron grip of secrecy imposed on all US Special Forces could not easily be pried open. The reason there are almost no accurate renderings of modern court-martial proceedings is because the military will not allow it. There are massive restrictions on the media, with bans on photographic and recording equipment in the courtroom.

However, even though I say it myself, I have sought the truth. Working closely with the defense lawyers, I have turned this saga into a fly-on-the-wall look at this most notorious court-martial. It's a unique account of how a "politically correct" government works when confronting the inflammatory words, "prisoner abuse."

I've read about a zillion words on the subject of courts-martial, and from this research I present the most dramatic story of a military trial since *The Caine Mutiny*, Herman Wouk's 1951 Pulitzer Prize–winning novel.

Slowly, piece by piece, this sometimes-heartbreaking story of courage, loyalty, and dedication has evolved into a blow-by-blow courtroom drama, in which I take an unprecedented look at what can happen to innocent men when caught up in a system bent on destroying them. And, indeed, what it took to protect them.

I hope I have done the story—and the SEALs—justice and that the US Navy will understand I have tried to be scrupulously fair and have made absolutely sure that no SEAL battlefield secrets have been disclosed.

Throughout the manuscript I have deliberately withheld surnames of many US Navy SEALs and, in some instances, altogether altered their names and, occasionally, ranks. This, of course, applies particularly to those who are still serving.

All actions SEALs have undertaken are classified, and I have meticulously not revealed any strategies or tactics that may prove to be in any way useful, revealing, or helpful to US enemies. Further, in some instances I have deliberately obscured accurate revelations about enemy strongholds or garrisons. This is not detrimental to the narrative, but it does add an extra layer of secrecy regarding US Special Forces' knowledge of various areas.

Only foreign terrorists or other fanatics will concern themselves with these geographic details. But should they decide to mount any attack based on "knowledge" discovered in this book, they will find themselves an impossibly long way from their intended target.

My advisers during the months when I was preparing this manuscript, both of them loyal and patriotic Navy personnel, always stressed they would not tolerate one word uttered against the "SEAL Teams." Neither would they contribute a word that may assist any terrorist with bad intentions toward the United States of America.

I found them to be without rancor or bitterness, though the attitudes of certain members of the Navy High Command did mystify them somewhat. Even more so by the somewhat careless lack of consideration they received from the Army Special Forces High Command.

None of the three accused SEALs will ever quite understand why no one believed their truthful accounts. And none of them will ever understand why they, above everyone else, should have been selected for such ruthless accusation.

Their three "not guilty" verdicts were gratifying. But the scars were too deep to be eradicated altogether; even in the case of Sam Gonzales, who is still in the Navy. Matt and Jon have walked away, much more in sorrow than in anger.

As Matthew McCabe said, "I'm over it now. I'm never going to think about it again."

And, as Jon Keefe once replied somewhat wryly: "Yeah, right. Of course you're not."

—*Patrick Robinson*

PROLOGUE
Open Letters to Admiral Pybus

Rear Admiral Sean A. Pybus
Commander
US Navy Special Warfare Command,
Garrison/HQ
Naval Amphibious Base
Coronado, San Diego

Dear Admiral Pybus,

I formally left the United States Navy this week, after serving for nine years, as a SEAL for the last six of them. You probably heard my name a few times during 2009/2010 when they court-martialed me for abusing a prisoner, failing to protect him, as was my duty, and making a false statement. Not too bad, right? A proud US Navy SEAL, branded a bully, idler and a liar, on the word of a mass murderer and terrorist.

You will understand, as a career SEAL officer, that I could not possibly have been guilty of any such thing. SEALs do not behave like that. Certainly I never met one who did.

I was, of course, found not guilty, after a four-day criminal trial, which, incidentally, almost broke my family's heart, as they watched my humiliation in the courtroom. I was not just found "Not Guilty" by the jury, I was completely exonerated. Mostly because I was completely innocent, but partly because I was represented by one of the finest military lawyers in the world, the former US Marine Lieutenant-Colonel, Neal A. Puckett, of Washington, DC.

Happily, a massive public subscription saved me from financial ruin, but I doubt I'll ever recover from the experience. Because the SEALs were my life. I was Team Leader in the mission which captured the most wanted man in the Middle East. And no one was remotely surprised when he claimed to have been abused. That's what they do. Everyone knows that.

The shocker was, the US military believed him. And essentially, they fell over themselves backwards with political correctness, and hung me out to dry, along with my equally innocent teammates, Navy SEALs Jonathan Keefe and Sam Gonzales, two of the best people I ever met. We were, of course, all exonerated by the courts, every charge dismissed.

Admiral Pybus, I am writing this open letter to you, my most senior commander, only to let you know that I finished with the Navy not for any selfish reason, but for the sake of my "Brothers" in the Teams. After my acquittal, I tried very hard to put it all behind me and I accepted an 11-month deployment to Afghanistan.

But ever since they charged me, I have not been able to sleep. In Afghanistan I was never so sharp, and I could not find the same drive, the same determination. I was not even such a good marksman as I once was. Secretly, I think I was just afraid I might let the guys down.

I don't believe anyone knew I was no longer the warrior of old. But something had gone drastically wrong for me, and, try as I did, I could not recover. It was probably the injustice, that utterly undeserved court-martial; that chilling moment when I read the charge sheet, THE UNITED STATES V. SO2 MATTHEW V. MCCABE. I still wake up thinking about it.

Nonetheless, I still want to thank the US Navy, and especially the SEALs for teaching me darned nearly every worthwhile thing I know: discipline, loyalty, truthfulness, patriotism, courage, skills, and the creed of the team player. I'll never forget those things, and I'll be forever grateful for the opportunity the Navy gave me to be a part of it.

In my mind, I'll always be a SEAL. And, for the rest of my life, I expect I'll be asked, over and over, how long I would have stayed, as an elite American combat warrior, but for the court-martial. And my answer will always be the same: about a thousand years.

> *Yours Sincerely,*
> *Petty Officer Matthew V. McCabe*
> *Formerly Echo Platoon,*
> *SEAL Team 10,*
> *Little Creek, Virginia*

> Rear Admiral Sean A. Pybus
> Commander
> US Navy Special Warfare Command,
> Garrison/HQ
> Naval Amphibious Base
> Coronado, San Diego

Dear Admiral Pybus,

This is a letter of both appreciation and regret. You may perhaps recall that I was one of three members of SEAL Team 10 who faced court-martial in the Spring of 2010, in connection with the alleged abuse of the Iraqi prisoner, Ahmad Hashim Abd Al-Isawi, a killer and terrorist by trade.

Matter of fact, I helped capture him. I was Point-Man in the Platoon that crossed the desert and stormed into his al-Qaeda stronghold. None of us abused him. He was a professional liar, obeying his *jihadist* training manual.

Anyway, after several months of hell, coping with the threat of disgrace and financial ruin, we were all three exonerated in court, Not Guilty, Case Dismissed. I just thought you should, as my superior Commander, be reminded of the dreadful consequences which befall a falsely-accused Navy SEAL.

Firstly, something dies. With me it was the will to strive to be the best, as I'd always done before. My motivation was way down. On training trips I was dragging my feet. I'd simply lost that SEAL ethos, that sense of feeling unstoppable. And I could not get it back.

It's hard for me to write this, because we were all taught in the Teams: never make excuses, only solutions; always be accountable for your own actions; aim for perfection, and never stop learning.

But that court-martial floored me. It forced me into some kind of limbo for months on end. All three of us were outcasts, there was no longer any opportunity for me to better myself. My lofty ambitions to become a SEAL officer were shot to pieces.

Then Matthew McCabe and I both went on that 11-month deployment to Afghanistan. And it was out there, often in real danger, I first realized I was too much going with the flow. I was following orders, and trying my hardest, but not wanting to be noticed.

I was still ready to put my life on the line for any one of my Brothers, as they would for me. But something I could not grab, was missing. The flame which had always burned within me, had dimmed, and if I was not very careful, might die altogether.

It was out there, deep in Taliban country, that I knew I had to go. Because suddenly an average-to-good showing in combat seemed okay. It had never been so before, because I'm a SEAL, and average is *never* okay. SEALs, as you well know, don't do average.

Well, I finally left the Navy last month, and I hope I'll find new paths to follow. And I'll never forget how the Navy straightened me out when I was a kind of goof-ball college drop-out. And I'll never forget the way my character was formed in the discipline of the Teams.

When I look back I hope to remember the good times. The days of triumph, when we were out in force, demonstrating on a daily basis, that we were indeed the front line of United States military muscle.

And yet, the specter of that cruelly unfair court-martial haunts me still. It nearly broke my mom's heart. And when I think of those complacent prosecutors and investigators, deaf to our protests, I'll always feel that rising anger I used to reserve for the enemy.

I can forgive. But I can't forget the brutal unfairness of it all. And would I do it all again? Would I still put my life on the line for my country, for my SEAL Trident?

The question stands stark before me. Looking back, would you risk it all again? Just to have been a United States Navy SEAL, and the hell with the court-martial?

Admiral, the answer will always be, Yes.

Wishing you the very best, in Command of the greatest fighting force the world ever saw.

Yours sincerely,
Petty Officer Jonathan Keefe
Formerly Echo Platoon,
SEAL Team 10,
Little Creek, Virginia

1

THE BUTCHER
ON THE BRIDGE

In the violent, blasted side streets of Fallujah, the demented
Sunni killer Ahmad Hashim had assumed a loose and terrifying
control.

Through millennia the ancient Babylonian city of al-Fallujah has shuddered from violent atrocities and deeply profound mysteries. Did the
Persian hordes really slay the teenage Emperor of Rome, Gordian III,
on the banks of the Euphrates in the year 244? Centuries later, in 1920,
was the English government's envoy, Lieutenant Colonel Gerard
Leachman, truly beheaded with one swipe of a two-handed sword by
Sheik Dhari, right here in the Royal Palace of al-Fallujah?

And who, on the night of March 31, 2004, was directly responsible
for the medieval butchering of four American security officers—all of
them burned alive, dragged through the town, and then strung up
from the old bridge across the Euphrates, turning it into a grotesque
iron gallows, before a roaring crowd of Iraqi fanatics?

The Persians swore that the young Caesar, Gordian III, was cut
down in battle, whereas the Romans, claiming victory, deny it, stating
the gallant Emperor died much later, way upstream.

In turn the Iraqis dismiss the very thought that Sheik Dhari would
have stooped to any such barbarism as murdering a British colonel

with a scimitar. Efficiently, they produce records to show that his son, demonstrating commendable chivalry, shot the colonel in the back.

But the ongoing mystery of who slaughtered the American security officers rumbles on, shaking and shuddering like the bolted iron girders of the old bridge when the heavy US armored vehicles roar daily over the river, west of the city.

This most barbarous act of the twenty-first century, almost eighteen hundred years after the demise of Emperor Gordian III, was more brutal, more primitive, and less human than anything that had ever happened before. And the US intelligence authorities were faced suddenly with near-incontrovertible evidence that another terrorist serial killer was emerging who was even more of a psychopath than the rising "star" of al-Qaeda, the thirty-seven-year-old deranged Jordanian jihadist, Abu Musab al-Zarqawi.

Initially there was little doubt as to who planned the strike against the Americans, who had, after all, been attacked at gunpoint by a gang of armed guerrillas on a main city street and then incinerated, their vehicles set ablaze, while a big chanting crowd stood back and hurled rocks into the flames.

Thereafter things became particularly unattractive. Two charred corpses were tied to cars and dragged through the streets. Body parts were pulled off and hung from telephone wires. Two incinerated bodies were hauled up onto the old bridge and left dangling from the rafters.

All of this seemed somewhat beyond the pale, even for the savagely anti-American al-Zarqawi. And even if it were within the pale, these actions certainly represented a new and grim semitribal low for the apparent successor to Osama bin Laden.

And there was a planned tribal madness to the attack. The Americans all worked for the private security corporation Blackwater and were helping to safely transport supplies for a catering company. But there were more than 150 Iraqis shouting and chanting at the old bridge as the mutilated bodies swung in the light desert breeze: *Long live Islam … Allahu Akbar [God is great]!*

One town official mentioned, unhelpfully, that this would be the fate of all Americans who entered Fallujah. And for several hours the crowd grew and grew, still chanting anti-American slogans. It took the sudden and thunderous howl of a US fighter-bomber, screaming in low from out of the southeastern desert, to finally scatter and disperse them.

And, of course, these four frenzied murders seemed to bear all the hallmarks of the work of al-Zarqawi. Although he was not yet a confirmed member of bin Laden's inner councils, he very soon would be and, indeed, later that year would be proclaimed "Emir of al-Qaeda in the Country of Two Rivers."

But al-Zarqawi required no formal title in order to stand at the pinnacle of al-Qaeda's anointed rogue's gallery. His paramilitary training camp in Afghanistan was revered among all jihadists. In Iraq, however, he became famous for a vast series of bombings—roadside, suicide, and targeted IED blasts. He both planned and carried out hostage executions and beheadings. He masterminded the brutal assassination of the senior US diplomat Lawrence Foley right outside Foley's home in Amman.

Al-Zarqawi was the scourge of the Jordanian security forces, who only just foiled his monstrous plan to slam chemical weapons into the US Embassy, the prime minister's office, and the headquarters (HQ) of Jordanian intelligence. When Jordan's G-men came crashing into the terrorist HQ they seized twenty tons of chemicals, including blistering agents, nerve gas, and sacks containing lethal poisons. In addition to a further five tons of high explosive, there were three trucks with heavy-duty iron plows that had been designed to ram through security barriers in front of the target buildings.

Al-Zarqawi—not for the first time—was subsequently sentenced *in absentia* to death. He was still on the loose, and a few short weeks after the outrage on the old bridge, he showed up, masked, on an al-Qaeda video, cold-bloodedly beheading an American civilian, Nicholas Berg, with a jagged tribal knife.

Everyone in authority knew this was not the only public beheading of an American that al-Zarqawi had carried out; indeed, his pitiless bloodlust appeared to raise the eyebrows of even the icy jihadist monarch, Osama bin Laden himself. In March 2004 US officials credited al-Zarqawi with over seven hundred killings in Iraq, the majority with bombs.

For more than fourteen years the militant Jordanian seemed to prefer to operate his own private terrorist army, which he named al-Tawhid wal-Jihad. There were times when he worked alongside al-Qaeda, but bin Laden was wary of him, troubled that the pure brutality of Zarqawi's methods would do their cause no good and may infuriate the tough Republican president in the White House even further.

Knocking down New York's World Trade Center with a smoothly orchestrated twenty-first-century suicide air attack was one thing, but bin Laden expressed concern over cleaving off a civilian's head with a bread knife on television. Thus, he never allowed a formal partnership between his al-Qaeda councils and al-Tawhid wal-Jihad's bloodstained leader, the most wanted man in both Jordon and Iraq.

In turn, al-Zarqawi was not in any way certain that bin Laden and his Taliban cohorts possessed sufficient fervor to carry out a holy war to the bitter end. His plan was simple: he and his "warriors" would carry on killing US and Western military and civilians until the whole lot of them went home, leaving the Middle East forever. Along this route, he intended to destroy the government of Jordan as part of a strategic master plan, and while at it, at the same time, take Israel off the face of the earth.

For al-Zarqawi, there was no compromise, nor room for maneuver. He possessed the psychopath's messianic belief that there was no other point of view worth listening to except his own. And from the first moment he entered talks with bin Laden, there was dissent and disagreement, differences of opinion both operationally and in terms of doctrine. And the reasons for this were obvious.

Osama bin Laden was a man of religion, a slightly crazed zealot, who believed from his sandals to his turban that the Prophet Muhammad fought in his corner and that all of his actions were justified. Never did al-Qaeda's founder make any kind of speech without invoking the will of Allah and affirming that there was no other God but Allah and that He alone would guide them on the path to righteous victory over the Great Satan.

Al-Zarqawi, however, used Islam essentially as a public relations aid, justifying the most heinous murders by mentioning that the Prophet had approved of the whole exercise and that in the end his troops, every one of them, would cross the bridge into paradise and into the arms of Allah … *DEATH TO THE INFIDEL!*

Despite accepting large sums of money from al-Qaeda, principally to run his training camp, for several years he refused to take an oath of allegiance to bin Laden. Indeed, when the American bodies were strung from the Fallujah bridge, the Jordanian had not yet taken that oath and would not for another seven months.

And even when he did, the two men were never close because of fundamental differences. Bin Laden's objectives were large scale and planned over the course of many months. Al-Zarqawi was too much of a mad dog for the elusive Islamist cleric.

Thus, when the savage events on the bridge first came to light, the CIA immediately assumed they were masterminded and, probably, executed by the mad dog himself. And so the CIA sent the word out immediately that they wanted the crazed jihadist murderer hunted down and brought in, dead or alive.

By this time al-Tawhid wal-Jihad had morphed into al-Qaeda in Iraq, but despite intercepting letters and communiqués of obvious disagreement between bin Laden and al-Zarqawi, the American intel operatives made no distinctions. According to the United States, they were all al-Qaeda, all terrorists and ruthless killers. And this time they had gone too far, way beyond the boundaries of known guerrilla warfare.

The Americans threw a steel wall around the city of Fallujah and prepared for a surge by the US Marines that would last for six weeks, during which hundreds of Iraqi insurgents died. But while the city shook and shuddered to the thunder of artillery and pounding infantry boots through the sandy streets, stealthy CIA agents were uncovering a brand new possibility: al-Zarqawi was nowhere near Anbar Province at the time of the killings, and yet another rising al-Qaeda commander, a man whose methods made al-Zarqawi seem a paragon of restraint, had perpetrated the crimes.

The new field commander was an Iraqi of the blood, born in the city of Fallujah itself, a native son of the old desert trading post and a fanatical killer whose fevered addiction to random murder was becoming a modern fable, even within Arab communities in which violence and brutality had been a way of life for thousands of years.

His name was Ahmad Hashim Abd Al-Isawi. His business was jihadist terror against the citizens and military personnel of the United States and their allies. In Al-Isawi's world there were no holds barred; each "mission" was conducted without a grain of mercy toward anyone. Betrayal in any form always resulted in instant reprisals, with the murder of the suspect's family.

Wives, children, and the elderly were massacred on a routine basis. No desert outlaw, in all the long history of Fallujah's blood-spattered and violent history, had ever been more feared by his own people. He was sheltered, protected, and guarded even by those who trembled at the mention of his name.

Al-Isawi had successfully petrified the populace into becoming his unwilling helpers while also remaining deep in the shadows. He was feared as no other Iraqi commander since Yusuf Saladin, the ferocious Kurdish warrior who captured Jerusalem in 1187. Saladin, however, was famous for never turning his fury upon civilians. Al-Isawi had no such scruples.

His reputation had spread widely on the strange bush telegraph of Iraq, and US manhunts for the man were invariably met with blank stares. The Americans, however—particularly the Marines and the Navy SEALs—were not remotely afraid of Ahmad Hashim Abd Al-Isawi. They were simply unable to find the sonofabitch.

And the entire hunt jumped up about seven notches when the CIA disclosed that the March 31, 2004, murders of the US security men were simply too gruesome to be the work of al-Zarqawi, who had never, even in his most chilling acts of slaughter, resorted to tribal butchery and exhibitionism on this scale.

The burned corpses on the old bridge at Fallujah had brought a new dimension to terrorism in Iraq. And for the first time US and coalition forces were searching Iraq for someone other than al-Zarqawi—a different killer, someone even more deranged.

And they would need to be extra vigilant. Like the US Special Forces in the Middle East, Al-Isawi worked mostly after dark, and as one

SEAL commander stated it: "This bastard will slit your throat before you have time to clear it. But we should bear in mind our brother, Scott Helvenston, a former SEAL instructor, whose body swung from that bridge. We need to track down this Al-Isawi, and do it quickly."

He was right about that. Within hours of the four murders an IED blew up, killing five US soldiers. CIA agents believed this new and local killer had struck again.

The immediate aftermath, conducted during the first week of April 2004, was a heavy-handed US response, with the Marines taking on the insurgents in a five-day battle that saw six hundred Iraqis killed and more than twelve hundred injured. Fighting in the area near the bridge was so fierce that both the Fallujah and Jordanian hospitals were closed. Slowly the city calmed down.

But the insurgents regrouped and attacked again. There was little doubt among the Americans that this new al-Qaeda commander was a tough-minded and dangerous enemy. And for the first time they discovered he did have a quasi-religious side to his character. Marines found several major arms caches hidden in a couple of local mosques—heavy machine guns, AK-47s, several tons of high explosive, RPGs, and improvised homemade bombs.

At this time the name Al-Isawi was being freely mentioned. And, as ever, there was a cruel and sinister edge to any conversation that involved him—reports of civilians being used as human shields and firing on the American troops from inside schools, mosques, and even temporary hospitals.

Local people were forced to help the insurgents build roadblocks; others were barricaded inside their homes. And Al-Isawi's men, as they turned certain city streets into armed fortresses, even roughly ejected some less lucky civilians.

As the month wore on, the situation worsened, despite US efforts to offer terms to surrendering insurgents. In one spectacular air strike US fighter pilots hit a flatbed truck and a following vehicle, both of which exploded continuously for about twenty minutes, shaking the entire area. The Iraqis fled, charging across the street into the shelter of a fortified house.

But the American pilot came screaming in low and fast for a second time, and he hit the house with a missile that blew it to smithereens. More accurately, the building blew itself to smithereens, as it contained literally tons of high explosive.

And this was just the start. All through the year, from the very moment the American bodies were strung up on the bridge, the city of Fallujah, riddled as it was by Sunni insurgents, rallied to the shadowy battle cry of Ahmad Hashim Abd Al-Isawi.

It was now common knowledge that he had been directly responsible for the murders and was equally certain that the infuriated American military was going after him. By the end of 2004 the "City of Mosques" (Fallujah had almost two hundred of them) was wasted. The civilian death toll was virtually uncountable, though Iraqis claimed it was "several thousand." More than eight hundred US troops also died fighting in Iraq that year.

It was an infamous year, sparked by an atrocity, and it concluded with a grand desert city in ruins, virtually wiped off the map. For Al-Isawi, however, the battle for Fallujah had put him well and truly on the map. In the coming years the old warlord al-Zarqawi would be forever looking over his shoulder at the rise of the newly titled "Butcher of Fallujah" as he moved ever forward on his blood-soaked journey to the peak of al-Qaeda command.

All of the above was written with the help of hindsight. But at the time things were not quite so clear-cut, and many CIA agents believed that al-Zarqawi was still at the root of all the evil in the benighted desert stronghold. But back in Langley, Virginia, deep in the "crime laboratories" where events were examined slowly, in infinitesimal detail, analysts definitely believed that the grotesque events at the Fallujah bridge were the work of someone else.

It was the pure public exhibitionism that steered CIA thinking away from al-Zarqawi. Because showing off was not his style. He would strike hard, causing total mayhem, mass death, and injury. And then, often several days or even weeks later, there would be a quiet news leak to Al Jazeera, the Arab television network based in Qatar, that the bombing had been the work of Abu Musab al-Zarqawi.

He had, in the past, hooded and somewhat anonymously, permitted himself a personal television appearance prior to publicly beheading a prisoner. But these events were always in pursuit of a gain for al-Qaeda, such as a reprieve for the prisoner in return for the release of captured bin Laden disciples.

But this public uproar on the Fallujah bridge, demonstrating the barbarity of the terrorist organization, did not ring true to al-Zarqawi's mind-set. The analysts at Langley believed it was out of character. Particularly because television crews turned up at the bridge right on time to film the crowd kicking and stamping one of the bodies. That was not al-Zarqawi's style; he saw himself as too serious to waste time boasting.

They drew the inevitable conclusion: there was a new man on the block in Fallujah, a fiend in desert robes. And as 2004 lurched bloodily forward, he was causing pandemonium in the city.

Al-Isawi had personally started on the rubble-strewn streets the worst close-combat fighting of the entire war. Because for a few weeks in the immediate aftermath of the hangings, the US Army removed the gloves and operated under shoot-to-kill orders against *anyone* standing outside their own private home with an AK-47 or rocket-propelled grenades.

This had the effect of driving the weapons of the Sunni resistance underground. The result was the formation of a tribal hotbed, a kind of Sunni Citadel, determined to fight to the last man. There were wild crowd-control confrontations and endless murders and bombings. The most violent area in all of Iraq was suddenly the blasted side streets of Fallujah, where the demented Sunni killer Al-Isawi had assumed a loose and terrifying control.

But no one, anywhere, had ever reported seeing the man. If they had mentioned such a sighting, their life would not have been worth four Iraqi dinars, and because at the time it took about four thousand of these to buy one US dollar, that would have been a tragically inexpensive life. Al-Isawi habitually took no prisoners. He fixed his own exchange rate down the sixteen-inch barrel of his Kalashnikov rifle.

He was wanted for murder all over the country. But chasing him was to chase the shadows of the desert. In the summer of 2004 the US military was already seeking a ghost. After each new uproar in the city of Fallujah, the SEAL briefings were edged with frustration.

This is a summary of a midsummer briefing by the commander of SEAL Team 4:

Gentlemen, for us there's nothing so difficult as searching for the unknown. But right now, the way it's been for God knows how long, we have only a name for this bastard Isawi. There's no more doubt that he strung up the bodies on the bridge, matter of fact he seems proud of that. But we've never been able to grab him, never been able even to see the sonofabitch. Right now we don't even have a friggin' photograph.

By July 2004 Fallujah was once more in chaos. The insurgents had refused to hand over both their heavy weapons or Al-Isawi in return for a US ceasefire in the city. And despite close US air support, the city fell back under Sunni terrorist control.

But by November the Americans had had enough. They unleashed a full-blooded attack on Fallujah, and this resulted in the fiercest urban combat of the entire war. The US Marines overran the city, darn near flattening it in the process. They got everything and everyone except Ahmad Hashim Abd Al-Isawi.

And then the new year came, 2005, and again there was this uneasy standoff. Attacks continued all through the spring and summer, and on August 1 a car-bomb ambush killed six US Marine snipers in the city of Haditha, a Sunni farming town on the Euphrates. In Langley Al-Isawi was suspected of moving his headquarters temporarily some 140 miles upriver. Suspicions grew even more so when a massive roadside bomb two days later detonated in Haditha, killing fourteen Marines plus their interpreter.

Another blast occurred in the same area on November 19, when a huge IED constructed of artillery shells and explosive-packed propane tanks blew up from under the asphalt, hurling a Marine Humvee into the air, splitting it clean in half, and killing the driver instantly. The rest of the Marines then reported they came under fire from civilian houses, and they immediately responded.

In the end, after a volley of machine gunfire and an exploding grenade, twenty-four apparently unarmed civilians lay dead. And it was six long years before the several Marines charged with assault and murder were ultimately cleared. None of them went to jail. Their defense attorney was Haytham Faraj, a former US Marine officer.

And once again investigators were faced with a situation that bore the marks of Al-Isawi—the particular construction of the bomb as well as the gunfire aimed at Marines that had come from civilian homes, according to the testimony of a Marine lieutenant. This was classic Al-Isawi, who thought nothing of firing at and murdering Americans from schools, hospitals, and mosques.

Winter 2006—Commander SEAL Team 7:

We now know more about this maniac than any other target, except where the hell he is, and what he looks like. ... The one thing we really know is, he's smart, he's an expert in bomb making, and he has excellent INTEL. ... He also has an unusual grasp of military ops, and this suggests he may have served somewhere. His men show up in unexpected places, all over the goddamned desert, and that means he knows a lot about map-reading in difficult terrain, as well as communications, weapons and high explosive. This is no goat-herding Bedouin tribesman. This is a serious operator. And ... the suits in Washington want results.

We got two more missions tonight. Both based on new Intelligence. One in the city, one somewhere out in the desert. I don't like the sound of either of 'em much. So be darned careful. ... Even if Isawi doesn't show up, there's a couple of other al-Qaeda guys we really want to locate. That's all.

All of these operations were and still are strictly classified by the US Navy. They are as significant today in Iraq and Afghanistan as they were in 2005. For that reason they are incomplete so that no material confidential to US military intelligence should be made public, not even to an American audience, because to do so achieves nothing but to alert the enemies of US armed forces.

Iraq has always been an extremely "leaky" spot in which to conduct any form of warfare. For instance, even the fighter pilots flying off US aircraft carriers in the Gulf and headed for the forbidden air space above the US-imposed No-Fly Zone were often astounded at how regularly Saddam Hussein's rocket men, hidden in the desert, were absolutely aware of US flight-wing arrival times in Iraqi airspace.

It's a country where no one could be trusted. No one living there understood who was al-Qaeda and who was a mere tribesman. Some Iraqis used every subversive trick in the book, with their hot cell phones, utter lack of loyalty, and propensity to sell information to the Americans for money and to the terrorists out of fear—Al-Isawi's speciality.

Confronted by advancing US troops, insurgents knew how to get rid of their weapons faster than any stage magician. Men who had, moments before, been blazing away with the AK-47s were suddenly unarmed, hands held high, appearing utterly bewildered as to why they had come under suspicion.

They knew the US Rules of Engagement (ROEs) better than the American themselves. And they really knew the one about not firing on the enemy until fired upon. They knew exactly when to stop, often stranding advancing American troops in some kind of no man's land in which Americans might get shot but were not permitted to open fire. As the months went by, Al-Isawi became a global authority on the US section of urban guerrilla warfare.

To the American soldiers it often seemed they must wait for someone to take a bullet in the head before they were legally permitted to fire.

The year 2006 wore on, and the insurgent attacks on US forces continued. Wave after wave of Navy SEALs crossed the ocean from Coronado and Virginia Beach, joining vast legions of US Marines in the fight to bring Iraq under control.

And night after night small groups of these Special Forces ventured out into the dark of the desert in search of the "bad guys," the SEALs' all-compassing term for the furtive al-Qaeda killers whose mission remained unaltered: to drive the forces of the West out of the Middle East forever.

The road was hard, but the Americans were winning. Slowly they hunted down the al-Qaeda leaders, grabbing, manhandling, and terrifying Osama bin Laden's field commanders. But they were pursuing an elusive tribe, military intelligence was often sketchy, and sometimes days went by without a significant success.

Early in June 2006, however, Jordanian intelligence made a breakthrough. They alerted the Iraqi authorities that they had some kind of a fix on al-Zarqawi, al-Qaeda's leader in Iraq. And the scene swiftly shifted to the city of Baqouda, capital of the Diyala Governate, situated thirty-one miles northeast of Baghdad and home to almost a half-million people.

In truth the Jordanians were only a couple of gunshots in front of US Navy intelligence, who were simultaneously on the trail of one of al-Zarqawi's main lieutenants as well as his principal spiritual adviser, Sheik Abdul Rahman. They had him in the area of the old Silk Road way station of Baqouda but were still finalizing the finer details.

Heavy-handed US interrogation of al-Qaeda prisoners actually cracked the case wide open for the intelligence agents. Someone finally betrayed al-Zarqawi, and as early as late April, US Joint Task Force 145 was stealthily headed toward a terrorist safe house in a remote area five miles north of Baqouda.

They kept it under tight surveillance alongside Iraqi security forces, which were the first ground troops to arrive. Finally al-Zarqawi showed up for an obvious high-level meeting of the local mass murderers. And US intelligence finally had a bead on one of the worst killers in Iraq since Saddam Hussein was dethroned—Al-Isawi's boss, no less.

The United States wanted no mistakes, and in the late afternoon of June 8 they whistled up a couple of USAF F-16C Fighting Falcons, which identified the house and came screaming in from the north. The lead jet unleashed two five hundred–pound bombs—one of them a laser-guided GBU-12—Lockheed Martin's deadly accurate, finned hunter-killer, PAVEWAY II, made in Pennsylvania and unstoppable once launched. The other was a GBU-38—Boeing's Joint Direct Attack Munition (JDAM) pinpoint targeted, satellite-guided destroyer, utilized here to avoid extensive outer damage.

The GBU-12 blasted the safe house to high heaven, killing everyone in it, al-Zarqawi, Abdul Rahman, and five others, two male and three female, including one of al-Zarqawi's wives and their child.

There was a huge sense of relief in Iraqi government circles, particularly as there had been a marked increase in violent atrocities in the city of Baqouba in recent days. One of them, which culminated in seventeen severed heads being found in fruit boxes, brought forward in intelligence circles the name of the fiendish Al-Isawi once more.

But then there was another mass murder, when masked Sunni gunmen suddenly killed twenty-one Shi'ites, including twelve students pulled from a minibus and shot. That was pure al-Zarqawi, again demonstrating the precise sectarian tendencies bin Laden detested. No one thought the killing would stop after al-Zarqawi's lair was vaporized; Islamist fanatics would swiftly move forward to replace their brethren. But some thought the quality of terrorist commander might decline. The Americans had killed or captured so many of al-Qaeda's top men; surely it would have some effect.

For now, however, the clinical brilliance involved in the total demise of the top al-Qaeda commander in Iraq inspired a grim sense of relief in all the clandestine SEAL bases both east and west of the Tigris and the Euphrates.

Like al-Qaeda, the SEAL Teams constantly required new, young American blood—tough, dedicated men whose sense of idealism and duty matched or surpassed their Islamic counterparts.

That very summer two such recruits were making their separate ways toward the training cauldron of Coronado, home of the fabled BUD/S course, that baptism of ruthless indoctrination designed to answer just one singular question: Are you tough enough for us even to consider making you a Navy SEAL?

Every applicant with ambitions to wear the Trident must tolerate that six-month endurance test on the shores of the cold Pacific in order to even try. And the ancient proverb "Many are called, but few are chosen" understates the rigor of this test. On average, fewer than 12 out of 160-plus men finally make it through. In comparison, Harvard Law School has a higher acceptance rate than the US Navy SEALs.

Matthew Vernon McCabe, a small-town boy with modest high school grades, coming from the outer suburbs of Toledo, Ohio, was the first of the two. The second was Jonathan Keefe, Virginia State swim champion from an even smaller town, near Yorktown. Neither had achieved anything close to their academic potential as students, but both of them had been bound and determined to become Navy SEALs since an unusually young age.

Matt understood perhaps best the iron-clad boundaries of the "Many are called..." proverb, as it was first written in his namesake's gospel. For him, a career in the Navy SEALs was beyond all realms of possibility.

He came from a broken home in Perrysburg, Ohio. His parents' divorce when he was thirteen had the effect of loosening his parental guidelines, first living with his mother and sister, then moving to stay with his father, Martin McCabe, a second-generation proprietor of a prosperous auto body shop who was sometimes inclined to indulge his son.

"Guess that's what kids do," Matt says now. "Head for the area where life will be easiest. Looking back I understand better that my mom was a wonderful lady and laid down standards for me and my sister which could not be changed. She was absolutely certain of her own moral guidelines. And to this day she's always been there for both of us. Hell, my mom worked three jobs to hold the family together after Dad left."

Matt was a gifted, athletic midfielder on his high school soccer team, well on his way to his full five-foot, eleven-inch, 180-pound fighting weight. But the truth was that he was bored sideways by soccer before his sixteenth birthday and wholeheartedly entered another kind of world when his father, from out of the blue, presented him with a second-hand Ford Mustang GT convertible to mark his opening step into manhood.

Generally speaking Matt was happier driving around rural Ohio in his Mustang, accompanied by a veritable platoon of the best-looking girls Perrysburg had to offer, than being kicked and barged into by various schoolboy meatheads whose principal ambitions lay in the pursuit of a round ball.

In any event, his older sister, Megan, a student at Ohio State and a future New York fashion model, had already introduced him to a more sophisticated way of life. So he announced his retirement from the game in order to concentrate his energies on a form of Buckeye *dolce vita*.

"I have to say it," he later recalled, "my dad, a thoroughgoing good guy at heart, let me get away with a few things. My potential college grades were rubbish, and I never took a blind bit of notice of anything my teachers tried to teach me.

"My dad rarely gave me a hard time for anything I did or didn't do. He was kind of proud of me, which put me on the pig's back, and I was loving every hour of it, especially the nights."

And yet there was a ferocious contradiction in Matt's character. At heart, deep in a place no one really saw, he was a hardworking kid, and with his truly moderate high school grades, he went to work locally to make up for his misspent youth, working long shifts as a counter-hand and short-order cook at a pizza chain, with the old Mustang parked out back, all set to go.

"I always worked," he says. "But the longer and harder I did so, the clearer my position became. I'd only been going for seventeen or eighteen years, having a great time, but well on my way, I thought, to a momentous screwup … summa cum laude in partying. Those 2.3 and 2.4 grades from Perrysburg High haunt me to this day. I shoulda been straight As. No bullshit. But only I knew that, and I'm not proud."

That was not the only secret the young McCabe harbored, the other being that he somehow understood the long and historic connection his little town had with the US Navy. Situated right up there in the top left-hand corner of the state, Perrysburg was an early nineteenth-century shipbuilding center, right on the wide Maumee River, which flows into Lake Erie just a dozen miles to the north.

Perrysburg is in fact named for one of America's greatest naval battle commanders, Commodore Oliver Hazard Perry, who not only supervised the construction of the US Fleet along the Maumee but also fought the Battle of Lake Erie during the War of 1812.

In overall command of the US Fleet in the 240-mile-long lake, Commodore Perry faced the British head on, but in the opening exchanges he took a very severe shellacking, with his flagship, named after the immortal Captain Lawrence, almost sinking. The British commander demanded Perry strike his colors and surrender.

But Commodore Perry refused, and in the teeth of the battle and under withering gunfire, he ordered his men to row him to one of his other ships, where he personally fired the salvo that began the rout of the Royal Navy's Task Force. Following the strategy of Admiral Nelson at Trafalgar, he drove forward, in the lee of the wind, and split the British line, pounding them until they surrendered. Altogether the commodore fought nine naval actions on that lake and won them all, and a grateful nation awarded him with both the Congressional Gold Medal and the thanks of Congress.

Still known as the "Hero of Lake Erie," Commodore Perry had a decisive hand in the ultimate US victory in that war. An entire class of modern US frigates was named after him—and there's twenty-four still serving: the heavily gunned anti-aircraft and ASW ships, Oliver Hazard Perry–class, renowned escorts to the US Navy's largest aircraft carriers.

Today a mighty bronze statue of the commodore stands in downtown Perrysburg. Though not many people noticed the young Matt taking a few long looks at it while he was not really bothering with his schoolwork.

But at age eighteen Matt made what he described as the first mature decision of his entire life: he decided to rip one of the opening pages out of the commodore's playbook and join the US Navy. And he kept his thoughts to himself. He did not have the slightest intention of rising to command a warship in battle.

Matt, retired soccer midfielder, secretly wanted to become a US Navy SEAL. Nothing else. And he never told anyone.

Jonathan Keefe's long devotion to the US Navy SEALs began when he was in fifth grade. This was partially because he was born and spent his early years way south into the Virginia Peninsula, where the Atlantic rollers hit the Chesapeake Bay and where America's mightiest warships are both built and stabled in the gigantic Norfolk Naval Yards.

It's impossible not to have at least a passing interest in the US military if you happen to be from those warm, gusting ocean-side lands, which also stand to the north of the wide Hampton Roads, the busiest warship highway on earth.

All around there are signs of the world's only superpower in action—the Langley Air Force Base, the NASA Langley Research Center, the vast shipbuilding yards of Newport News, where they build the colossal fortress at sea, the Nimitz-class aircraft carriers.

Young Jon was brought up watching warships shouldering their way out into the Atlantic and coming home from distant lands. The folklore of the US Navy was instilled deep within him. The Stars and Stripes was always prominent on the flagpole in front of the classy ranch-style house in which they lived, in the overwhelmingly middle-class Virginia country town of Tabb.

Patriotism was not taught in the household of Tom and Dawn Keefe; rather, it was engraved on their hearts from birth. A financial professional, Tom Keefe worked just a few miles away at Newport News Shipbuilding Company, where he was controller and treasurer of its industrial subsidiary, NNI, specialists in constructing and repairing nuclear power stations.

NNI was full of ex-US naval officers, several of whom were buddies with Tom Keefe, the man who controlled the budgets. One of them, a former commanding officer of the Sturgeon-class nuclear attack submarine USS *Lapon,* was Captain Chester "Whitey" Mack, who once silently shadowed a brand-new Yankee-class Russian ballistic missile boat for her entire patrol, an astounding forty-seven days!

Cruising right inside the Yankee's baffles, dead astern, he never got caught and hoovered up enough priceless electronic information to fill a wing of Bancroft Hall at Annapolis. After that the six-foot, six-inch Whitey became a legend in the Atlantic submarine service and later joined NNI in Newport News, where they talk about him still. USS *Lapon* was, after all, built there, five miles from where the Keefe family lived.

Because he grew up in that community, it was little surprise that Jon knew the sights and sounds of US warships before he could recite the alphabet. His father was never in the US military, but, with his strict adherence to rules, sense of order, and punctuality, he would have made a superb naval officer.

The great pride of Tom Keefe's life was being associated with an engineering corporation that built every last one of the US Navy's nuclear-powered aircraft carriers and one half of all of its nuclear attack submarines.

But curiously, his mother, Dawn, was the one who led Jon to the SEALs. She'd been a second-grade school teacher before her sons, Tommy and Jon, were born, and she returned to the profession when the boys were very young. A gifted and natural storyteller, she constantly read to her sons, and when she recounted them an adventure involving a group of men called the SEALs, her youngest was hooked. He was so captivated—and at such a young age—that he actually wrote his fifth-grade career project on the US Navy SEALs.

"I still remember it," he says. "There were a lot of stories, but the ones I always liked most were about those daredevils from Virginia Beach, just twenty-seven miles to the south of the village of Tabb. I made Mom take us down there just so I could see where they lived and worked. Never caught sight of one, though."

And when he was thirteen Jon persuaded his parents to allow him to go to San Diego, California, with a friend to enroll in the US Marines' renowned ten-day "Devil Pups" mini–boot camp youth program on the seventeen-mile Pacific coastal sprawl of Camp Pendleton.

This is the major West Coast base of the Marine Corps, the prime amphibious training grounds for Assault Craft Unit 5 and home to One Marine Expeditionary Force, masters of the sea-to-shore attack.

The course is designed to show students what it takes to become a combat warrior, with the accent on physical fitness, discipline, and devotion to country and the US Marine Corps. The young Jon loved it all, but the part he loved most was when his instructor pointed out in the distance a vast, low, flat grassy wilderness, strictly off-limits and apparently deserted.

"No one goes there," he said. "That's the secret off-limit range BUD/S training, the two hundred–yard rifle qualification."

Jon stood on the edge of his personal heaven. "Can't see anyone," he muttered, staring into the horizon.

"No one ever does," replied the instructor. "But they're out there."

But that was not simply the highlight of the trip for Jon—it was the highlight of his life. He had stood on the sacred ground where the Navy SEALs trained. On this great private enclave of the US military, he had seen the firing range of Special Warfare Command (SPECWARCOM), where they honed their skills. Not so many people had ever seen that, and for him, he now had a bond with the SEALs that would never be broken.

When the "Devil Pup" from the Virginia Peninsula finally returned home, he was utterly determined that one day he would find his way west again, but this time to Coronado, home of the world's most elite warriors.

By now he was growing into a huge frame, headed for the six-foot, four-inch heavyweight he would one day become, with not one gram of fat—pure muscle and bone.

At sixteen he began to understand fitness and what it would take to get a tight control on his physical development. Brought up so close to the sea, he swiftly developed into a top-class high school swimmer, making the teams and powering through the swim-league encounters with kids who were largely older and weaker. Jon won the 2002 Virginia State championship, fifty-yard freestyle, scything through the water in a record-busting 21.18 seconds—a time that stood supreme for three years.

By now his given Christian name, "Jonathan," had slipped away. Young Keefe, the human shark, was simply "Big Jon," and he anchored the Tabb High relay swim team to victory after victory. They weren't always in front when the third-lap man touched the wall, but every last time Big Jon hit the water like a Mark-8 torpedo, and the entire population of Tabb High almost went berserk with excitement as he hammered his way past the leaders. Altogether Jon won seven state championship events.

Unsurprisingly he was awarded a partial scholarship for swimming to East Carolina University, about one hundred miles south, over the border in Greenville, North Carolina. But from there things went even further south for Jon. First he flunked out of college altogether and then he went home to the local community college to study—somewhat ironically, as things turned out—criminal justice.

But, like the best buddy he had not yet met and who was, anyway, busy gunning that Mustang around Perrysburg, Ohio, Big Jon discovered the joys of rural Virginia's *dolce vita* and devoted most of his time to majoring in having a real good time. Like Matt, he went for partying summa cum laude, somehow breaking loose from his old persona of great kid, big military ambitions, and dedicated athlete.

"My parents tried everything to guide me and continued to give me all of their support," he said. "But I guess I was too big, too sure of myself, and a lot too stupid to listen. But after two of the most ridiculous years of my life, finally I woke up and decided to get a grip.

"I resolved to stop wasting everybody's time, drove myself down to the local recruiting office, and joined the Navy. I told 'em straight out I did not have the slightest intention of being in the surface Navy. I was there to become a Navy SEAL. Sea, Air, and Land. Basic Underwater Demolition, right? Special Forces…just point me in the right direction, and get that Trident polished up.

"I didn't actually say any of that. But they were my thoughts. Nearly. You stand right there in front of that recruiting petty officer, I'm telling you, even sitting down he looked about twelve feet tall. He handed me the papers to sign and sent me, *instanto*, to Navy boot camp up on the Great Lakes."

The recruitment officer didn't actually say it, but Jon could tell what he was thinking just by the way he looked at him: *You think you're so damned tough, kid ... then you go right ahead and prove it to us.*

"Matter of fact, I felt a lot less tough when I walked out than I did when I walked in. But I went home and packed, obeyed my orders, the way I always would, just as soon as I pulled on the dark blue uniform of the United States Navy."

Matthew McCabe joined the US Navy, and right after boot camp reported to the San Diego dockyards directly opposite Coronado, on the landward side of the bay. He was assigned to the USS *Belleau Wood*, the forty thousand–ton Tarawa-class amphibious assault ship that had been designed to land battalions of US Marines on distant shores.

She was, in fact, a small aircraft carrier and traveled with forty helicopters and Harrier jump-jets embarked as well as landing craft. Matt, who was not yet nineteen, was never especially interested in the cleaning, polishing, and maintenance routines of the ordinary seaman, as his singular ambition was to join the SEALs, the guys on the other side of the bay.

And as soon it was possible, he filed an application to be transferred to SPECWARCOM in Coronado, California. That application, in the time-honored tradition of huge organizations, became either lost, misplaced, mislaid, or thrown away. Either way, six months later Matt was still a member of *Belleau Wood*'s 930-man ship's company, and still polishing.

Almost every day he watched the SEALs in action, training, fast roping out of helicopters in their wet suits into the ocean, sometimes really close to his ship. Matt wanted so badly to join them that it actually pained him to think about it.

But the Navy does not wait around. The *Belleau Wood*, it was announced, was scheduled for the Gulf at the center of a nine-ship battle group—a six-month deployment that would be conducted in searing heat.

Finally, just before the ship left, a platoon from SEAL Team 2 came on board for two months, giving Matt the opportunity to watch them every day as they trained. No one watching SEALs work is anything less than mightily impressed—their fitness, their strength, their speed.

As always they kept themselves to themselves, barely fraternizing with the crew of this small aircraft carrier. But their presence on board had an effect on Matt like a lightning rod, reaffirming that which he had known for so long: somehow he had to join these guys or die trying.

Once on station, way off the coast of old Persia, there were endless days of temperatures hovering at well over a hundred degrees. The flight deck shimmered as, all day long and much of the night, aircraft thundered into clear blue skies east of Saddam Hussein's old kingdom.

When they returned to base the SEALs were still uppermost in Matt's mind. And Matt once again in search of his application, only to be told that no one knew anything about it. So he filed another, and when that too produced only a kind of endless silence, he marched into the office and, as politely as possible, demanded an explanation.

"What the hell is going on?" he wondered. "You'd have thought someone might have at least acknowledged my request. But I got a very definite impression they just did not especially want me to go to Coronado. I have no idea why. And I asked, 'How did this happen?' And no one knew anything about that either.

"So I just filed again, and one year after my first application I was called in for interview and instructed to report to Coronado forthwith. It was March 2006, three months before my twenty-first birthday, and they sent me to BUD/S Class 259. There were more than 220 of us assigned, and I knew that out of that original intake they would take only a dozen. I have to say it never once occurred to me that I would not be one of them."

By this time Matt had never lost the drive for perfection in terms of fitness. He looked like a highly trained light-heavyweight boxer—a fraction under six feet, devoted to working in the gym, and, weighing in at 180 pounds, light enough to be an excellent runner.

Compact, broad shouldered, and athletically muscled, he was an outstanding skier, having burned up the high slopes all over the place, especially Big Bear in the San Bernardino Mountains, one hundred miles east of Los Angeles.

Since early boyhood Matt had learned the art of downhill skiing in Michigan's cold, hard-packed Boyne Mountains, at the north of the windswept Michigan Peninsula between the Michigan and Huron Lakes. When he finally hit the fast, powdery slopes at Vail, Colorado, it was a minor culture shock. But he soon got the hang of it. And when he did, pine trees swayed.

Matt was as strong as a bull and capable of lifting a 250-pound man and carrying him the length of a football field.

Pound for pound, he stood out, and even in the rarified arena of BUD/S, he could compete with the best of them. Matt did in fact have the perfect build for a SEAL—not too tall and very fast off the mark. Also, he discovered, he was academically as sharp as a tack and swift to memorize lists of facts. There are no dumb SEALs: 75 percent of them have college degrees, and as Matt moved through the early stages of his training, he was plainly up with the leaders in every conceivable discipline.

"New territory for me," he grins ruefully. "I'd never put my mind to academic stuff before. I couldn't believe my lousy high school grades, not after I'd been in BUD/S for a few weeks."

No one "breezes" through this searching, brutal test of a young man's strength, speed, brains, willpower, and ability to absorb pain. It's all too demanding for that. Ask any SEAL about BUD/S and, in particular, about Hell Week, and you invariably receive a kind of stage groan, followed by "Hell Week? … Don't even remind me."

Matt accepts the grueling part but chuckles and remarks, "C'mon … it wasn't that bad." And for him, you sense it really wasn't. His hard-trained skier's legs carried him along the Coronado beach for the four-mile run day after day. He was always a good runner, finishing in the first ten. Same for the push-ups, pull-ups, and sit-ups. Matt had the right build, enormous strength, and all the determination in the world.

But whatever he says about cruising through the course, more than one hundred guys quit in the first six weeks of the action. Twenty of them were gone before they completed indoctrination (INDOC), two weeks before BUD/S starts. Eight of them were outta there before lunch on the first day.

"Tell you the truth, I was just jogging along, trying to get through my tests. I didn't have time to notice 'em much."

Yeah, right, Matt. The whole of Coronado was talking about the DOR rate of BUD/S Class 259 (DOR: dropped on request, SEAL parlance for "I've had enough, and I retire forthwith from this madhouse"). The formal procedure is for the man who simply cannot take it anymore to walk to the office, place his helmet outside with the others, in a line on the ground, and then ring the brass bell.

The chimes of that bell, ringing out confirmation that a teammate has decided this is not the correct career path for him, can be heard down on the beach, where other class members were pounding along the tide line, looking for the firmer sand.

In Coronado there is a ban on ridicule. Anyone caught laughing or humiliating a man who has announced DOR is instantly dismissed, sent back to the fleet that day—wrong kind of person, lacking in team spirit, too self-possessed, too stupid.

A man who has decided the life of a Navy SEAL is not for him may very well make a perfectly fine surface ship commander or a navigator or a submariner. The life of a SEAL is not for everyone, nor is it superior to all other forms of service in the US Navy. But you'd never get one of Coronado's finest to admit that. Not in a thousand years.

Meanwhile Matt was charging along the tide lineup with the leaders, trying to cope with everything the instructors threw at him. He knew how to row and was excellent in the Zodiac boats. He managed to get the hang of the feared obstacle course and eventually worked his way to finish near the top.

His honed and practiced lifting strength saw him through all the work of carrying inflatable boats on his head—the SEAL Elephant Walk. Even the back-breaking effort of lifting logs the size of telephone poles was, in the end, achievable for him.

And to think that once he had been scared half to death to hear the instructors' practiced roar of *"MCCABE, YOU'RE NOT TRYING!—*

YOU'RE NOT PUTTING OUT FOR ME! GET WET AND SANDY! AND YOU ... AND YOU ... AND YOU!"

It took him a week to understand they often picked out men who really were putting out everything, trying with every ounce of strength they had. Because these were the guys the instructors could see were ready to lay down their lives to finish the four-mile races in the top ten. Matt, more by instinct than design, was one of those, and every instructor knew it.

Understanding this, however, did not make it a whole lot better, as he ran into the freezing cold Pacific in full running kit and then came out and rolled in the freakin' sand: *"GET WET AND SANDY!"* Screw that.

By the time Phase II concluded, Matt had only one glitch, and that was underwater in the pool competence section. "Got right back in and nailed it next time," he said. "Half the class blew out on that one."

For strength and athleticism as well as for confidence both in and under the water, Matt was a superbly confident baby SEAL. Always a quick thinker, he concentrated on every last lesson the BUD/S instructors issued. These included the heavy-duty laws of SPECWARCOM—the ones that include moral issues, the standards of behavior expected, the insistence on courtesy at all times to both your commanders and your teammates ... the iron-clad rule of honesty at all times.

Above all there was the sense of being a part of a team, a brotherhood, that binding sense of camaraderie beloved of all fighting forces. But none more than the SEALs—and Matt recalls he sensed that long before the BUD/S course was even halfway over. Even though he was not yet qualified, somehow he knew the high honor of acceptance right here in Coronado, that it was somehow written in the stars for him.

Young McCabe, who had never paid much attention in his school history classes, now found himself captivated by the long and glorious traditions of the Navy SEALs. He was especially touched by the instructors' reminder that no SEAL has *ever* been left behind on the battlefield, no matter how grim the fight.

Matt relished all of this. He had a copy of the new Creed of the SEALs, formalized the previous year, 2005, to clearly delineate the values, duties, and expectations of the world's finest Special Forces.

Matt kept it, and in both hope and determination—and a bit prematurely—he memorized the opening lines:

> In times of war or uncertainty there is a special breed of warrior ready to answer our Nation's call. A common man with uncommon desire to succeed.
>
> Forged by adversity, he stands alongside America's finest special operations forces to serve his country, the American people, and protect their way of life.
>
> I am that man.
>
> My Trident is a symbol of honor and heritage. Bestowed upon me by the heroes that have gone before, it embodies the trust of those I have sworn to protect. By wearing the Trident I accept the responsibility of my chosen profession and way of life. It is a privilege that I must earn every day.

The very words sent a chill down his spine, even though he had not yet passed BUD/S. And never for one split second did he doubt that in the not-too-distant future they would pin the legendary SEAL Trident on the high left-hand side of the jacket of his dress whites.

For the very first time in his life Matthew McCabe had a true purpose to his life. And to this day he recognizes the debt he owes the US Navy. "They straightened me out," he says. "They taught me discipline. They taught me honor, patriotism, and dedication. They even taught me how to study, sent me to a college where, to my amazement, I became a straight-As student. Despite everything, I owe them so much."

Big Jon Keefe joined the Navy in the high summer of 2006 and reported immediately to Recruitment Training Command (RTC), the Navy's one and only boot camp, set in an enormous campus forty miles north of Chicago on the western shore of Lake Michigan, seven miles from the Wisconsin border.

During the two months of basic training they turned him into some kind of sailor, with endless drilling on the great sprawl of the Ross Field Parade Ground, and he graduated on October 16. He took no time for vacation, driving through the gates of SPECWARCOM, Coronado, before the month of October was over.

Somehow Big Jon had been a lot more successful with his paperwork than Matt had been. But that was before the ex-dough flipper from Perrysburg understood he was a potential scholar. Anyway, the swim champion from Virginia was into the BUD/S course before you could say, "Hoo-yah!"

By mutual agreement, the names of still-serving Special Forces personnel will not be used in full in this narrative. And in the case of Jon's first BUD/S instructor, this is just as well.

"He was," recalls Jon, with that touch of old world charm that comes so naturally to him, "the biggest asshole I ever met. Everyone was scared of him. He was an ex-Marine and a full brother to Attila the Hun. But was he ever good at his job!"

That particular instructor was Jon's proctor for INDOC, and he pulverized those guys—running, rowing, heavy lifting, climbing, push-ups, sit-ups, pull-ups—until they thought they'd collapse with exhaustion.

But that instructor instantly made it clear that the SEALs are not remotely interested in men who collapse with exhaustion in the first week. They are interested only in those with the iron will to never quit, men who will drive on through the pain, drag themselves forward even though they have nothing left to give.

Because those guys may become Navy SEALs. And they are always the only ones who count at Coronado. They are the young men who will fight their way to victory because, in their minds, nothing else matters. For them quitting is not even an option. They'd rather die than quit. And Jon Keefe was one of those.

From the very beginning all of his instructors had him pegged to fail. Unlike his classmates—and certainly unlike Jon himself—they understood it was in many ways harder for a very big guy than it was for a medium-size athlete like Matt McCabe.

For a start there's the running. And although nature endows big men with heavier, stronger leg muscles, you don't see many 250-pound marathon runners. Neither do you see that many 250-pound mountaineers, hanging on to the rock face a thousand feet above the valley floor. They usually weigh about one hundred pounds wet through. And as for those real long-distance runners, as the crisply observant Matt puts it: "I've seen a praying mantis heavier than them."

In many of the disciplines a lighter man has a distinct advantage, especially the running. And the standard race for SEALs, each and every morning along the Coronado beach, is over four miles, two down to the hotel and two back, every man timed by the instructors.

The going is difficult. If they run too far up from the tide line, the men run into deep sand, which is murder for a heavyweight runner. Too far down below the tide line, they get their boots wet, which causes the sand to stick, making each foot even heavier. And the sheer bulk of a two hundred-plus–pound body just makes it harder to carry, no matter how fit and how well tuned that heavy-boned male body may be.

The instructors know also that the heavyweight SEAL, with his massive extra strength, is a priceless asset when a platoon is on the move through enemy lands, jungle or desert, mountains or rocks. Someone must carry the heavy machine gun and the ammunition belts, and big SEALs over six foot four always get the job of packhorse. It merely goes with the territory. And there are times when that extra strength may be required in other endeavors.

Jon Keefe, however, had to draw on his last reserves of stamina and determination for these long morning runs and the SEALs' famous obstacle course. And this was, in its way, the worst part of all because of the climbing. The course comprises high rope climbs, the sixty-foot cargo net, walls, vaults, parallel bars, barbed wire, and rope bridges.

Generally speaking it's many times easier for a small guy than for a tall one. And a dozen times easier for light guys than for the heavy dudes. Jon fell headlong into the latter category, but luckily he never fell badly off the ropes, bridges, and walls. Somehow he hauled himself up and over, fighting his way hand over hand up the ropes, gripping with his feet, fingers, and teeth if necessary.

The instructors taught the big boys technique, especially on the cargo nets, which were the same kind they use to embark SEAL Teams onto submarines midocean.

The teachers knew how much they had to put out for these aspiring SEALs. And none of them wanted to lose the big, striving Jon, who'd been trying to be a Navy SEAL since he was about ten years old.

2

—

"WE'RE NAVY SEALS— AND WE *NEVER* SCREW IT UP!"

For each fallen man, a new piece is added to the great mosaic of the Teams—a place where courage and daring are always paramount, but where valor is the unending constant.

The word SEAL is an acronym that stands for Sea, Air, and Land. It has nothing to do with sea lions, walruses, dolphins, or any other deep-diving mammal—not that you'd notice if you ever saw a BUD/S class floundering half-drowned through the Pacific surf trying to land their upturned inflatable Zodiac boat.

Navy SEALs are expected to function in all of the earth's elements, especially fire. They train harder than any other fighting force. Their exercises and physical routines are tougher, heavier, and more demanding.

But even though they never consider themselves a purely water-bound assault force, it is their breathtaking ability to operate in ocean, lake, or river that sets them apart. From their first steps through the BUD/S course to the end of their naval careers, they are taught that, unlike any other warriors on earth, water is always their friend, their haven, and their refuge.

And because the average human being is happier on land, the man who is capable of becoming a Navy SEAL is always a man apart. He alone, among literally thousands of applicants, has made it through— and that underwater section of the BUD/S course would frighten the living daylights out of a blue marlin.

At the start of every BUD/S course a couple of hundred students take their opening plunge into the huge swimming pool in the Coronado training facility. Almost before the ripples have died down, fifty of them will be out of there. This is the most searching test, and the instructors can detect even the slightest sign of weakness.

Kids turn up to BUD/S with no conception of the standards they will encounter. There'll probably be twenty of them gone in the first ten minutes. That's before it gets tough.

Matt McCabe recalls standing on the edge of the pool, talking to an instructor who was watching a student splashing and twisting to get his head up. The student was a really good guy and a friend of Matt's, so Matt turned to the instructor and asked whether he would get another chance.

"I can't do that," he replied. "One day your life may be in that kid's hands. And right here I'm seeing pure panic. We can't risk that happening in a battlefield situation. Sorry, Matt, I liked him too, but he's finished. Guys like that can get everyone killed."

The "pool comp" (pool competency) section of the course needs to be, especially for Navy SEALs, a ruthless examination. And the SEAL instructors ensure that it never falls short. First of all they teach everyone how to swim more like a fish than a human, a special SEAL sidestroke that permits SEALs to make maximum speed with minimum profile and output of energy. Once instructors accept that you can make it up the length of the pool and back without choking or drowning, then they begin the serious action.

Nothing serious. They only rope your hands behind your back, tie your ankles together, and push you into fifteen feet of water, ordering you to drop to the bottom and stay there. If you show the slightest sign of anxiety or distress, you're gone.

The rest must stay calm, hold their breath for one minute, minimum, and then bounce off the bottom back up to the surface for a gulp of air. Each candidate must repeat this exercise over a fifteen- or twenty-minute period. After that every member of the class must swim two hundred yards, still bound, wrists behind their backs, ankles roped together, writhing through the water like a school of angry porpoises.

And that's just the start, just the prelims, to make certain you are worthwhile to proceed. It does, without fail, decimate every class, but no more than the next discipline, which involves pool comp using the breathing apparatus. And right there the pressure builds.

The instructors try everything. They harass each candidate, ripping the airline out of his mouth, tying a knot in it, watching for the strict SEAL procedures to be broken. There's nothing dangerous—the instructors are in the water, swimming around like basking sharks, watching for a foul-up, escorting anyone in trouble to the surface.

Some get another shot. But most don't. Because the instructors are looking for that one in a thousand human beings who is as comfortable in the water or under it as he is on land. They seek men who have no fear of drowning, men who can hide, travel, and fight within its restrictions.

They're looking for guys who can lead through the water, dive under when necessary, and move very, very quickly through it if crisis should arrive. Such a man was Jon Keefe.

The big, amiable, deceptively smart Virginian, suddenly weightless in the one element he could dominate, hit that pool, like a ... well, like a Navy SEAL.

When they finally sorted the class out, they staged the first of the 800-meter races in which students tried out the big SEAL flippers, what they called "rocket fins," to give them even more power. Big Jon rocketed through the water, astounding everyone, including even the veteran pool instructors.

Jon had a theory that although the fins gave you extra kick and a little more speed, they also made you more tired toward the end of the race, which was when he prepared to pounce and steam past the opposition. It was just like old times when the Tabb High faithful were up and cheering. Except no one was cheering Big Jon here at Coronado—they were gaping.

Of course, the instructors were delighted to have a swim champion among their number, and they made careful notes of his technique and approach.

And as the days wore on, everyone got better. The mere question of panic in the water was outlawed, and slowly the men turned into the kind of underwater operators the instructors wanted. The ranks were thinned out, and a lot of good guys had left to return to the fleet or to civilian life. But the few tigers who were left were going to become US Navy SEALs.

For all of them this would be the fulfillment of a dream. For many of them it was a lifelong dream. But no one had dreamed it for longer than Jon Keefe had.

As the reformed college dropout from Virginia continued to perform his now-renowned imitation of Mark Spitz in the Coronado pool, Matt pressed on in his quest to join the most elite force in the US Navy.

Matt had passed BUD/S Phase III before Jon arrived in Coronado. So the instructors knew how tough Matt was. They immediately dispatched him to Jump School, the SEAL parachuting course in which each new BUD/S student learns precisely how to deal with the third letter of the SEAL acronym, air. Because a major part of a SEAL's combat skills may involve airborne insertion—parachuting into enemy territory, way behind the lines.

Matt attended freefall school close to San Diego. He was there for almost two months, having first mastered the proper techniques and protocols of the parachutist and then the basics of landing correctly and absorbing the impact. They get moving from high platforms and complete the course with dozens of fourteen thousand–foot night jumps in full gear. This is compulsory in order to progress. Matt McCabe knocked it out the first time.

Jump School includes combat parachuting, which teaches students how to drop directly into a battle zone, piloting the parachute to a specific location and then concealing it so as to avoid enemy detection.

There's a whole section of the training devoted to Military Freefall Parachuting (MFF), especially HALO (high altitude, low opening). Flying well above the range of anti-aircraft fire or surface-to-air missiles (SAMs), SEALs deploy at enormous heights and wait many, many seconds to open the parachute so as to avoid ground radar.

The major Jump School component is HAHO (high altitude, high opening), when the SEAL cracks open the parachute thousands of feet above the ground, intending to prevent anyone from hearing the snap of the opening. This is a specialist method of covert entry into quiet, guarded terrain. It also enables the parachutist to glide for many miles and then put down in a precise spot.

At the conclusion of Jump School successful students move into another intensive course called SEAL Qualifying, six months of much more advanced training. In addition to his new stratospheric skills, Matt now had the rudiments of land navigation, accurate shooting, mountaineering, stealth, camouflage and patrolling, and weapons proficiency. They also increased everyone's skills in tactical combat diving and underwater ship, pier, and beach attacks.

He could run a fourteen-mile race on the beach, over which he could also attack if necessary, from the surf, burrowing into "hides" (locations, usually concealed or camouflage, that provide concealment and protection from enemy fire as well as maximum fields of observation and fire), above the high-water mark, the dreaded spot where SEAL assault Teams are most vulnerable.

For days on end, in the final phase of BUD/S, they practiced fighting their way out of the water under full combat gear and weapons. And most of the instructors' early impressions proved correct. Every man who had reached the final stage, just twenty of them, passed the BUD/S challenge.

But it was not over. Ahead of them was the long six-month journey around the SEAL schools all over the country, from Florida to Alaska, in heat and snow, learning not just how to be a combat warrior but to become a Team leader, burnishing the skills as a marksman and a sniper, perfecting their abilities in advanced shooting as well as explosives and detonation.

The training and the learning never stopped. For SEALs it never does. And for a determined character like Matt, it all represented some kind of an earthly paradise—the heavy-duty program, which would turn him into the SEAL he had always dreamed of becoming.

He was a good shot, but he needed to demonstrate expertise with not only the M-4 rifle but also the SR-25 semiautomatic sniper rifle and the bolt-action .308-caliber rifle—in fact every possible kind of weapon, including the stuff US enemies use.

As his instructor reminded them all: "One day you may have to grab some foreign bastard's weapon and fight for your life and the lives of your teammates. You must understand thoroughly how someone else's tenth-rate rifle works, because those precious seconds you have may mean the difference between death and survival.

"Remember, we're SEALs. And we don't fuck it up. *EVER!*"

On the day the training ended, fourteen months after Matt had arrived at Coronado, he stepped up to receive his Trident—the proudest day of his life. He shook hands with his commanding officer (CO) and promised faithfully that he would endeavor to earn it every day of his life.

And yet another section of the SEAL creed he knew so well stood starkly before him:

My loyalty to Country and Team is beyond reproach. I humbly serve as a guardian to my fellow Americans always ready to defend those who are unable to defend themselves. I do not advertise the nature of my work, nor seek recognition for my actions. I voluntarily accept the inherent hazards of my profession, placing the welfare and security of others before my own.

I serve with honor on and off the battlefield. The ability to control my emotions and my actions, regardless of circumstances, sets me apart from other men.

Uncompromising integrity is my standard. My character and honor are steadfast. My word is my bond.

No SEAL in all the forty-five years of the Teams was ever more deeply moved by those shining words than Matthew Vernon McCabe.

———

Meanwhile Jon was slogging his way through all of the above, six months behind his future buddy. The long list of skills, which is compulsory learning for all BUD students, contrives to make every member of every Team a composite jack-of-all-trades. This is essential because even SEAL commanders cannot accurately predict battlefield losses, and at any moment, on any mission, a new man may need to take over.

The comms operator goes down ... the Team cannot just be out of communication, either with their teammates or home base command. Someone must take over. The "breacher" goes down—someone needs to grab the sledgehammer and the demolition charges.

The point man goes down, and someone must run forward to take over, and he better be expert in navigating the way to the objective. The SEAL paramedic, the guy with the medical supplies, goes down; he must have a deputy who knows precisely what he's doing.

The number-one sniper goes down; there must be someone just as good or the mission may be doomed. Worse yet, the leader goes down; there must be a number two right there on station, and he needs to know every aspect of the operation.

The simple truth is that every SEAL needs to know everything, and the watchword of both Coronado and Virginia Beach is *preparation*. No Team of a dozen SEALs on any mission sets foot outside that base until every specialist has at least a two-man backup. By design, the position of Team leader is designated on a rotating roster.

No other system works. Any SEAL has the tools to lead any mission. Picking a man and grooming him as a leader to serve on many successive operations is not at all useful. What happens if he gets shot or blown up and no one else has led a mission for months? That's simply hopeless. And certainly not the way of the Teams. They say they are a brotherhood, but what they really are is Knights of the Round Table—equal men who, in the words of their own Creed, "do not seek recognition for their work."

They are forever one for all and all for one. As armed jacks-of-all-trades, as they say, God help the enemy. Because when the bugle sounds, these guys come out fighting, and each man can do it all.

During these long hard months Jon finally returned to his own holy ground, the wide, dusty shooting range at Camp Pendleton, where almost ten years previously he had stood in the distance with the Devil Pups. He'd never forgotten those moments, especially the one with the instructor, when he'd promised himself he would one day return, this time wearing a Trident. He wasn't quite there yet, but, by God, he was closing in.

Like Matt, Jon fought his way through Hell Week and completed BUD/S. Right after that he too made his way around the SEAL training schools. Aside from his remarkable skills in the pool, he could shoot dead straight, and on the mountains his great strength permitted him to overcome the handicap of his powerful physique. He was a fearless parachutist despite traveling downward at what felt like an especially high speed.

In Beach Assault his strength was a definite plus. Under full gear and weapons he came thundering out of that surf, over and over, up the beach and into the hides, hitting the sand as gently as a lotus blossom. Well…almost. But at least the entire shoreline did not shudder, as a couple of instructors had feared. Like many big, athletic men, Jon was deceptively light on his feet. That's on land. In the water he was peerless.

Fourteen months after he entered Coronado, he had become the highly trained, skilled war-fighter the SEAL instructors had hoped he would become. They wished everyone the best and, indeed, took pride in training men to be as good as they were themselves. But Jon was an especially popular guy at Coronado, and at the parade ground ceremony, when they finally pinned his Trident on his dress whites, there was not a man in SPECWARCOM who did not wish him all the good fortune in the world.

It was late in the year 2007 when this happened, and these were serious times. The conflict in Iraq appeared not to be improving, and the weekly reports of American deaths were beginning to irritate Americans back home. Most people understood the place had to be squared away, and the Iraqis trained both to govern and to protect themselves without lapsing into some kind of tribal warfare. But American parents were becoming less and less cool about having their sons and daughters killed in some far-off desert for what they believed was someone else's problem.

There was general disquiet about the wars against the tribesmen all over the United States. And for SEALS there was something else disquieting: there was a feeling that the US military Rules of Engagement were tying their hands, that even the special operators were being hamstrung by red tape.

This was especially true of the rules that insisted US armed forces were not permitted to open fire on known al-Qaeda killers until they themselves were fired upon. The SEALs had a wry interpretation of this: "You mean I'm not allowed to kill him until after he's killed me?"

On top of this, 2007 had bestowed a special sadness on all the Teams when one of the top serving combat petty officers, Clark Schwedler of SEAL Team 4, was killed by enemy fire as he and his platoon laid siege to an al-Qaeda stronghold in Anbar Province.

Trapped in the house were the terrorists the SEALs knew had recently downed a coalition helicopter. But they were heavily armed, and the vanguard of the SEAL assault came under attack as they moved forward. Team Leader Clark Schwedler went down in a hail of gunfire, mortally wounded. His SEAL teammate, Special Operations Chief (SOC) Doug Day was hit fifteen times, his rifle shot from his grasp. Doug drew his pistol and shot three of the enemy as he fell to the ground. Another SEAL, who had also been shot, administered lifesaving aid to SOC Day after the firefight was won.

The death of SO2 Clark Schwedler was one of those tragedies that affected everyone who had known him. SEALs on the far coast from Team 4's HQ in Virginia Beach attended a special service for the ex-Michigan State oarsman, who had served four years as a SEAL.

The son of a US judge, C. Joseph Schwedler, Clark was one of the SEALs' very best battlefield operators, specially selected as combat adviser to the Iraqi Army Second Brigade. Assigned to Special Warfare

Task Unit Fallujah, he took part in 108 combat missions and was credited with being the driving force in the unit's many successes.

Clark's devotion to the SEALs was timeless. He swore by the core values of the Navy: *honor, courage, and commitment*. And now he was gone, aged only twenty-seven. And very few of his friends in the Teams were able to stand by that Special Forces tradition of showing no emotion even under the worst circumstances. Clark's death cast a very long shadow of sadness over the entire brotherhood of SPECWARCOM.

In time they would construct a new building in Team 4's home at Little Creek, Virginia, and name it for Clark. The SEALs' desert base near Fallujah would also be named for him: Camp Schwedler. And no young US warriors, arriving there in the ensuing years, would ever need to inquire about the identity of the fallen SEAL commemorated with such honor. Everyone knew about Clark.

And that would include Matt McCabe and Jon Keefe when they too were posted to these war-torn, cruel, and ancient lands.

But for the moment their paths were diverse. Matt was assigned to SEAL Team 10, the newest of the Teams but one that already enjoyed a fearsome reputation as combat warriors. Team 10 was constantly in the hot spots of the war on terror. Always valorous, they returned from each deployment with fewer warriors than when they embarked. Men talked about the curse of Team 10, and the shocking loss of Echo Platoon in the fatal helicopter attempt to rescue Marcus Luttrell and the Red Wings in the Afghanistan mountains, in June 2005, only escalated this talk.

By the time he reached Virginia Beach, the Team was already deployed, and Matt was immediately posted to Germany for a couple of months. When he returned to Virginia he dug himself into an intense regime of hard training, and in January 2008 Jon arrived, having received his Trident and was assigned to the same Echo Platoon, Team 10.

The commanders took one look at his mighty physique and acquainted him with the SEALs' favorite weapon, the Mark-48 heavy machine gun, which weighed thirty pounds without the big ammunition belts, which the gun depletes by two hundred rounds a minute. When SEALs open fire with this baby, it unleashes shells so fast that its barrel starts to glow red-hot.

Put your head above the parapet when a SEAL master gunner is behind the breach of this thing, and you cannot live. Most of the platoons feel only half-dressed without it, although someone has to carry it on almost every mission. Step forward, Big Jon.

But early days in the Teams are critical times for new men. Everyone wants to impress, and everyone steps up his regime, relentless swimming, weights in the gym, workouts, running, and the countless sets of push-ups, one hundred a time—not much different from BUD/S ... *"PUSH 'EM OUT!"*

In the company of iron men excelling is hard, but everyone tries. No exceptions. You would not be here if you were not that type of man. And already that ethos of self-starting begins to work its way deep into every man's psyche.

"What happens if the guy is unfit and can't lift Jon?" says Matt. "I'll tell you what—I have to go and carry him myself. For a few moments we're in disarray. And disarray is not good where we work. You're coming with us? Get fit, and stay fit. Fat bastards need not apply, because a half-fit guy on ops may be fatal."

The upshot of these unwritten rules means that all SEALs are hair-trigger sensitive to their own reputations and how their teammates perceive their character. The same question is asked of them all: What can you bring to the fight?

Thus, every SEAL is judged by his appearance, and every one of them wants to be seen and admired, as a guy who will "get someone's back" when the chips are down. Every SEAL wants to be looked up to, which is why they are, almost without exception, big, powerful, hard-trained warriors, the very frontline of US military muscle.

Jon "rogered" all of that. And although he never expected to become Inter-Service 100-meter-sprint champion or even make the mountaineering team, he brought an immense competitive edge with him from Coronado. He also knew that his road to true excellence rested in his enormous strength.

And he really saw himself out there in front, smashing his way into the enemy's inner sanctums, battering his way forward with the platoon right behind him, ready to seize their objective.

Big Jon had decided to become a "breacher," the guy who breaks down doors. And although this may sound like a perfect spot for your pet gorilla, in fact, it is no such thing. It is a highly specialized task that an expert must carry out.

When a Team goes in for an assault on the enemy, they may not yet know what kind of a barricade stands before them. And they may not need to know. Because this is the problem of the breacher, and the SEALs have a special school, an extensive course, to train these men.

The standard tool of their trade is a sledgehammer, with a retractable handle in case they need to make high speed over the ground; a long hammer handle would impede progress. But once that handle is fully extended, a skilled SEAL breacher could cannon open almost any door with one enormous swing of this thing.

Failing that, the breacher carries what SEALs call a "hooly" (short for hooligan—God knows why), which is a long crowbar that will rip the hinges off any door and allow the big man up front to kick it straight in. Tucked into the breacher's harness belt is the inevitable set of bolt cutters plus a heat torch for cutting through steel.

The Teams never know what will face them in terms of security, and the breacher must solve the initial entry, which is always violent. And of course, his last resort is, without exception, C-4 explosive. And because they do not wish to knock the entire building down, that high explosive must be carefully designed.

Thus, the breacher makes his own singular bombs—demolition charges, specially shaped, to blast the doors but not to collapse the house. This stuff never comes prepacked, and an expert needs to prepare it because the SEAL is going to carry in the explosive himself.

Take, for instance, that some reconnaissance pictures have suggested a heavy mud wall to go through. Thus, the breacher may find himself walking through the moonlit desert with a big bomb in his rucksack and upon whom everyone is dependent for entry into the ops area.

The problem is that no imagery can ever reveal precisely how many doors need to be breached for the Team to break in. There may be three, for example, each one more difficult and secure than the last. The breacher cannot possibly say, "Sorry, guys. I don't have any more charges. I guess we better go home."

The breacher needs to have every possible device in his personal armory, ready to blast the platoon into the area. And he better get it right if he doesn't want to become a human bomb.

It's the surprise element and the ability to handle the totally unexpected that makes a great breacher. The sudden appearance of a steel door, a barricaded passage, a door that is barred. There may even be a steel wall inserted into the concrete of a building, and that cannot be blasted out without taking down the whole structure.

Right there the breacher must make fast decisions. And he may have to go to the heat torch to cut the steel. This is hot and noisy and is likely to attract attention, forcing a firefight before the SEALs are even inside.

And then there's the sudden shock of a booby trap, the instant secondary blast, detonating from inside the building as soon as the door rockets inward off its hinges. The technique and skills required of the breacher, the lightning sidestep away from the entrance, inch perfect on the turn, is enough to make a matador gasp with admiration.

And then there's the possibility of running straight into the barrel of a Kalashnikov gun as the door blows into the house. There's probably a split second before the enemy recovers from the inward blast of the breacher's bomb, but no more. And the Team leaders need to move again, with terrific speed, hurling in the grenade with the instinctive reactions of a big-league short stop to first. Nanoseconds matter. Lost seconds might get them all killed.

And there's always the possibility the breacher may go down. He's first in the firing line, and someone has to step up. He must bring an understudy, whose duties would start instantly. If the Team leader arrives at the secondary door inside the building and finds it padlocked or barricaded shut, the number-two breacher must be right at his elbow, with the sledgehammer and the bolt cutters and the C-4. That's the way it works. No mistakes.

The breachers have a quaint name for the high-danger area as they enter; they call it the "fatal funnel," because that's where the enemy will instinctively shoot. That's where the SEALs come under first fire. The role of the breacher requires high courage, and a lot of it. And that was Big Jon's stock in trade. Was he scared? Hell no. They'd taught him to be a US Navy SEAL. And everyone knows they're invincible. Jon loved every last and precious moment of it.

Any time you are privileged enough to see a SEAL Team on television, laying siege to some terrorist stronghold in Iraq or Afghanistan, remember you are watching the maestros of assault at work, banging and blasting their way forward to achieve their mission. You are seeing the results of hours and hours of practice, months and months of training, men whose unquestioning dedication to the American flag is, very simply, without end.

Sometimes they pay the highest possible price. And when these men make their final journey home, the Stars and Stripes always drapes the coffin. A rigid SEAL guard of honor stands motionless at the head for the duration of the journey, no matter the distance, which is often half a world away. No SEAL ever dies in vain. For each fallen man a new piece is added to the great mosaic of the Teams—a place where courage and daring are always paramount, but where valor is the unending constant.

And in the cold January of 2008, Jon stepped into the sharp end of this brotherhood. By year's end he would be a highly qualified Team 10 breacher, and after that would come the unit-level training (ULT), the last few months of fine tuning that everyone receives before deployment, probably to Iraq, possibly to Afghanistan.

Meanwhile Matt McCabe had arrived back from Germany and quickly discovered that the relentless search for perfection had not abated, even in the established Teams. His best friend, Jeff (no proper names for serving Special Forces), had been "rolled back" (sent to retake a course), so the first thing Matt did was to meet and befriend a big powerful new guy from Coronado, Jon Keefe.

Within a few weeks Jeff and Jon showed up in Team 10, in which Matt was in hard training, and the three of them became buddies, traveling out to Reno, Nevada, for a part of a Special Forces driving course. This may sound like a huge amount of fun, but the SEALs treat it with the same grim, hard-eyed proficiency as pool comp.

SEALs need to be able to drive Humvees like stock-car drivers. The day may come when they need either a fast getaway or even (much more likely) a surprise arrival in a combat zone, and they do not want to be looking around for a decent driver.

In those platoons, as ever, everyone needs to be able to do everything. When three regular SEAL drivers arrive in Reno, they are just that—regular drivers. When they return to Virginia Beach they will be world-class experts in rallying—racing over rough terrain, up mountains, down escarpments, and through streams.

SEAL drivers may need to operate at high speed in any war zone. As men may be wounded, it may be necessary to engage in a running firefight from the vehicle, and the nearest man to the wheel needs to get in and move it. He'll need all the steering, braking, and timing skills they taught him in Reno.

All three of them loved it up there on the high slopes of the Sierra Nevada Mountains, as they slid, skidded, and tore up the mountain shale, hard cornering and making high-speed U-turns. And they all passed the examinations. It ended in late March, and they took a long weekend to drive down the Nevada border, crossing the enormous Yosemite State Park and heading for the ski slopes of Squaw Valley, California.

There Matt was the expert, once making an unbelievable Black run down from the rampart of Squaw Peak, nearly eighty-nine hundred feet above sea level, and disappearing at about 100mph down the steep Siberia Slope. "I never thought I'd see him again!" says Jon.

"You know, that's the thing about Matt. He can just do so many things so well, better than most people. But he never goes on about it. Just does 'em. He could win the light-heavyweight championship of the world and forget to tell you. It's what I first liked about him. He was never Mr. Too Cool, like a lot of guys are. He's a real easy character to like, I'll tell you that."

For the record it should be recorded here that Jon forgot to mention for this book that he was one of the fastest high school swimmers on the East Coast of the United States. He even forgot to mention his state championship and longstanding Virginia 50-yard-freestyle record. Someone else told the author.

Reminded, he said, pretty laconically, "Yeah, I guess I could chug along okay some days."

"It's what I first liked about Jon," says Matt. "He never tried to be the coolest guy around. Not even one time when he won a 5.5-mile SEAL swim race in the Pacific out near San Clemente Island. Sonofagun won. I never saw it, but everyone was talking about it. When I asked him, he said it was probably a fluke—he wasn't real sure the others were trying!"

When Matt and Jon reached their Teams, Special Training took a diverse turn. As Jon concentrated on becoming expert at demolishing anything that stood in his Team's way, Matt headed for probably the most cerebral part of SEAL Team missions: the complex business of communications.

For those who would specialize in this slightly secretive section of the dark arts, there was a demanding course in the on-base Comms School. This starts a candidate off right at the basics, which all SEALs must master (just in case), and runs all the way through to advanced satellite communications and space-age battlefield techniques, the ones that ensure no one is out of the loop.

The sheer complexity and myriad chances of the system going down appealed to Matt. Confident now that his goof-off schooldays were way behind him, he had already decided that a career in the SEALs was his natural spot in this world and that, in the long term, an officer's commission was not beyond him.

He swiftly grasped that communications on any mission was the heart and soul of the operation, the mission's critical path. Without top-class comms, there can be only chaos. Every SEAL is obliged to read Marcus Luttrell's *Lone Survivor*, and every SEAL shudders at those terrible moments when the Red Wings' chief comms man, Danny Dietz, could not raise home base to provide help.

And Danny was an expert. A real expert. And he simply could not make the connection. Up there in the high peaks of the Hindu Kush, towering rock faces and steep escarpments that rose above and below them blocked the quivering electronic signal lancing out from Danny's transmitter.

By the time the Red Wings had fallen down two mountains and been shot God-knows-how-many times, Danny's radio gear was history. In the end it was Lieutenant Michael Murphy's final sacrificial action—moving into a bullet-raked clearing and punching in the numbers on his satellite phone—that finally raised a five-alarm uproar on the Bagram Base.

By now Danny had died, and the other three were all badly wounded. Murphy's final act contravened the general practice of not using these special phones unless the situation was dire. And Mike Murphy knew that his situation was as dire as it gets. In the final few minutes of his life, mortally wounded, he made the connection, the very best he could do, which was only to be expected from a SEAL officer of his supreme quality.

Everyone knew the legend of the Red Wings and understood that that disaster, at least partly, involved faulty communications, when they were unable to summon help.

And so Matt went to yet another school as a part of his Special Training course. And right there he became acquainted with the regular SEAL radio that everyone takes on every mission. It's about nine inches long and fits into a special slot in the harness. With its antennae extended, it enables all the operators to talk to each other—probably across distances of five hundred meters, depending on the terrain and line of sight.

The problem is that this radio is encrypted, which although it makes it impossible for the enemy to listen in, it also increases the time required to program the radio and set it up with very complex codes before a mission.

And every step of the way, on any SEAL operation, the unexpected can happen, especially at night, when most Black Ops take place. If, for instance, they meet up with a new group, probably from another

Team, the first thing that happens is the radios must be synchronized, changed, in order to have standard codes, to allow everyone to be in contact whenever necessary.

But the big, heavy central radio transmitter is entirely different. This thing weighs about twenty-five pounds, and the comms operator carries it in a backpack. Matt, when qualified, would assume this duty, hauling the extra load across the desert without a word of complaint. He remembers that even Jon, one of the Team's resident packhorses, was startled when he saw it. "Wow!" said Big Jon, "Sonofabitch looks like a nuclear bomb!"

The sight of it was one thing, but for Matt, learning the areas of modern radio communication from scratch was entirely another.

First there was command and control, the SEAL standard practice of communicating every duty of every man in the patrol, thereby ensuring that even the most minor change was instantly communicated back to the Team leader and then to the Blue Force Picture back at command.

This is the hub of every operation, the one ops room where *everything* is reported and where they know every last detail of the mission, particularly the GPS reading that displays precisely where the Team is in the middle of some godforsaken pitch-black Iraqi desert, probably surrounded by bloodthirsty, tribal cut-throats.

It needs to be right there on the Blue Force Picture, accurate to the finest degree, so that any major rescue or deployment of reinforcements happens instantly, no delays. It's the sole responsibility of the comms operator to ensure that every last vestige of his platoon's information is communicated back to command.

Matt had to master the system of multiple channels. He needed to understand the complications of the SEAL reconnaissance men (recce), the shadowy warriors who operate way out in front of the main force, on their own, working in pairs and communicating back to the platoon their precise whereabouts, the terrain, the dangers, the areas of possible ambush.

This information initially comes back from the recce guys directly to the platoon comms man, who's working closely with the Team leader and helping to make fast decisions. In addition, he must keep them posted on the Blue Force Picture, and all this in the middle of the night, moving behind enemy lines, watching through the green mist of the night-vision goggles.

Then there's the assault itself, the moment the SEALs go in. Everything gets reported: the volume of return fire, if any; the requirement for high explosive, casualties, prisoners, booby traps, and the route back out of the battle zone.

The comms man here is working flat out, probably accessing the satellite, aiming his transmitter, trying not to shout, pretending to be calm—all possibly under fire himself. And everything's still encrypted, incomprehensible to anyone else, and the comms guy is interpreting it, even if the roof's falling in around him.

Right now every single aspect of this wildly complicated process matters. The comms operator is checking that he's still making contact, perhaps giving a fast "satellite shout"—making doubly sure he's on the exact right angle to the heavens where, somewhere, twenty-two thousand miles above the earth, his electronic contact is speeding through inner space, somehow transmitting back to a guy like Matt, confirming the code numbers.

Right here the operator's fingers are flying over the dials on the twenty-five pound heavyweight transmitter. For the moment this is the mission critical, and everything affects the outcome: the atmospherics matter, any radio wave can be disrupted, and the operator needs to keep checking.

And there's a whole load of taboos every operator must remember, the first one being, "For chrissakes, don't key up on the radio if the EOD [Explosive Ordnance Disposal team] is working anywhere close." One wrong electronic pulse can instantly detonate an enemy IED or booby trap, and this may kill or badly wound the front line of the platoon. Don't think it hasn't happened. The SEALs have learned a lot of lessons the hard way.

In addition, the comms man must be on high alert for the need to call for medevac in case SEALs have been seriously hurt and cannot return to base any other way. There must also be constant communication with their close-air support, a heavily gunned aircraft flying a pattern high above them, in case the terrorist opposition is so numerous that they need to be taken out en masse before they do serious damage to SEAL personnel.

In the heat of battle it's not unusual for comms to be monitoring on two different frequencies, and this can make life very difficult. Events happen so swiftly in any assault situation that it's imperative that everything is perfect before the platoon embarks. Which is why any SEAL Team, wherever it is headed, takes the word of the comms operator very seriously.

Thus, Matthew McCabe, formerly of Perrysburg, Ohio, was destined to join this mobile Tower of Babel just as soon as he was relocated to Iraq, which was formerly Babylon and home to the original biblical tower, the base of which, locals say, remains near the city of Hillah in the Babil Governate.

"You'll probably get pretty good reception out there," said Jon, swinging his sledgehammer. "Fallujah's only a couple of hours from where the tower once stood, that's gotta give us great lines of communication, help us do some bad-ass smiting of the al-Qaeda-ites."

So while the teachers in Comms School prepared Matt to become a maestro of the airwaves, Jon was about to begin the longest journey of all SEAL programs—the Team-run ULT. Both men had to complete it, which entailed months of work and travel—from Virginia to Florida, Tennessee, Arkansas, Kentucky, Nevada, and Louisiana.

They perfected their diving skills off Key West. In Indiana they used a run-down four-story lunatic asylum on a miles-long vast campus to practice a SEAL takeover of a building—charging through the old dusty corridors, racing up staircases, perfecting their clearance techniques, and shouting commands.

"[If] anyone from outside had seen us, they'da thought the original residents had never left," recalled Matt.

In Tennessee they attended an intensive course in advanced shooting, as all SEALs must be able to shoot faster and straighter than anyone else. Both men passed with flying colors—the beady-eyed outdoorsman from Virginia and the SEAL from Ohio who was now privately aiming for SEAL leadership as a career.

There was little doubt that long before they were both through with ULT both of them knew precisely how to assault a house or even an entire street full of al-Qaeda or Taliban terrorists. More likely, both. Less certain was their grasp of how to commandeer an entire village without wiping out the populace.

For this, Team 10 sent them to the gigantic sprawl of Fort Knox, Kentucky, the 109,000-acre Army post that lies to the south of Louisville and covers parts of three counties. It also houses the US Bullion Depository.

Matt and Jon found themselves working in a mock city, with its own school and hospital, water tower, soccer field, and every other building you could imagine. The US Army whistles up battalions of civilians and pays them to defend the place. The SEALs don't actually shoot them, but the Army make it as realistic as possible, hiring Iraqis who speak only in Arabic and are ordered to get in the way at all times in order make Team 10 understand what a royal pain in the ass it is when people deliberately obstruct and cannot understand you anyway.

The idea is to get the newest SEALs accustomed to conditions in an Iraqi township, where everyone tries to get in the way and no one even pretends to understand what is being said to them, however politely.

That facility inside Fort Knox is the best of its kind in the United States, providing the most realistic predeployment conditions for a group of men soon to be transported to the frontline of the War on Terror, in one of the world's true hell holes—the ruins of Fallujah and its surrounding Islamist lands.

And all of this was leading up to the final months of pure preparation the SEALs need to undergo. This is Squadron Integrated Training, where they again intensify the tried-and-tested methods of SEAL assault—mobility assault, urban warfare, land warfare, attack from the water. And this time they are working closely with Team 10 veterans, men who have fought in the worst possible conditions, like North Baghdad after the fall of Saddam.

Team 10 contained some of the most expert warfighters in the world, SEALs who had fought in the gigantic Shi'a slum of Sadr City in northeast Baghdad, headquarters of the feared Mahdi Army. For four years after 2004 the US Army had practically laid siege to this rubble-strewn wasteland of poverty and death.

Thousands of civilians died in Sadr City, wiped out on a daily basis by suicide bombs, RPGs, gunfire, and reckless al-Qaeda attacks. For weeks on end the US troops had been in a backs-to-the-wall situation, only to come charging back, forcing the Mahdis to surrender and ask for terms, over and over.

But it was all to no avail. The fighting always started again. US patrols were repeatedly ambushed as they picked their way through the ruins in search of the senior Mahdi commanders, whose crimes against humanity were boundless and whose military assaults on innocent Sunnis will go down in infamy.

SEALs were especially competent in these nighttime raids, trying to locate and kill/capture the Mahdi gunmen responsible for this age of living misery in Baghdad. Several of Matt and Jon's new teammates had crept through those Baghdad shadows, trying to locate the dead spots, into which the enemy could not see.

These were Team 10 men who'd evaded the deadly al-Qaeda snipers, hidden in the rubble, perched high behind the shells of buildings that had been blasted asunder by the US onslaught. Thus, the serving SEALs had instincts that had been honed in one of the most lethal war zones since World War II.

In battle they'd shot and killed desert tribesmen whose own instincts made them as dangerous as an Apache war party. The Mahdi warriors were grim, furtive fanatics, silent as cats and well hidden and armed. And they asked for no mercy, nor did they offer it, consumed as they were with a profound hatred of America and her allies.

The Team 10 men who had returned from Iraq were expert in urban warfare, and in the great traditions of the SEAL Teams, their duty was to pass that knowledge on to a new generation, highlighting lesson one: it's so much harder to fight through a city that has been hit by high explosive than one that still stands.

Giant heaps of rubble and ruined buildings make perfect redoubts for guerrilla killers. A trained Navy SEAL can take one look down a blasted road in any desert city and understand precisely the spots where the enemy may lurk. He's not *always* right, but that's the way to bet.

And in the long weeks Matt and Jon spent in the United States developing high skills in urban warfare, these vastly experienced Team 10 fighters were on hand to point out the dangers and the opportunities. None of them was especially polite, but all of the new SEALs knew exactly what they meant.

Inserting the words "dimwit," "asshole," and "jackass" into most sentences served, if anything, to make them listen carefully to the training that would prepare them for the dangers they would face when they moved behind proper enemy lines in the not-too-distant future.

And through this final six months, they kept traveling: three or four more trips to California and full mission profiles conducted in Fort Polk, in the woodlands of West Louisiana out near the Texas border.

Part of the objective of all this was to instill in the new SEALs that they may have satisfied the instructors at BUD/S back in Coronado, but they have one further hurdle to clear—the toughest one of all. Because now each man has to be accepted into a Team, one that is already bristling with bloodied SEAL warriors.

These iron-souled veterans are the ones who make the final decisions about whether Matt, Jon, and the very few surviving others were fit and proper candidates to be given the green light.

And once more these seasoned SEALs put Matt and Jon through their paces, making them revisit the skills learned in assembling weaponry, checking that each man's fitness level was still high, that he could, with ease, run four miles under full gear along the sand in under thirty-two minutes.

Even under the most stressful battle conditions, all SEALs must be capable of eight-minute miles on the stopwatch—even Matt, who was hauling the platoon's heavy transmitter. That's an astonishing level of fitness, and nothing else will do. And into this latest regime of physical excellence the veterans threw a water obstacle course, forcing the new men to utilize brute strength and fast, smooth techniques in the pool.

They were made to swing, slide, balance, climb, fall in, get out, and, finally, go like hell for the line. Of course it was always a freestyle race for second place, because the winner was not only the best swimmer; he was also the strongest. And the biggest.

"But you should have been there the day Jon fell off one of the high ropes and hit the water," said Matt. "I thought a killer whale had landed in the pool!"

From moment of entry into Coronado to the moment a candidate is accepted into a SEAL Team, it's nothing less than a war of attrition. So many good men, most of whom will go on to do well in the surface Navy or the submarine force, are unsuited for the world of the Navy SEALs. That's no disgrace; it's just a statement of nature. And even those who collect their Tridents after BUD/S cannot be certain that the regulars who make up the Teams will accept them.

And into this final examination process stepped Matt McCabe and Jonathan Keefe in the spring of 2009. This last stage required them to face up to the challenge alone, each in a separate space, each of them facing some kind of a Spanish Inquisition without any teammates, neither left nor right, to help.

One largely unknown aspect of SEALs is that the ritual of entry to the Teams requires them to formally surrender their Trident as soon as they report. They are then required to earn it over again.

This second ceremony is not so grandiose or public, but in its way it is even more meaningful. Because right here the Trident is represented. It's an old-school tradition, as the veterans gather in the fenced-off platoon hut.

There, in Echo Platoon's private recreation room, with its plain chairs, television, murals of fallen brothers ... and a bar, they call in the future heroes of SEAL Team 10. When each man arrives the veterans already know his specialty, and they grill him relentlessly.

For Matt they demanded that this twenty-three-year-old comms operator from Ohio understood every last nuance of his chosen trade. They bounced him up and down over frequencies, satellite link-ups, and emergency procedures. Making him change the "freqs," contact the recce men, keep the line open to command, aim the transmitter high if there's a sudden change in atmospherics, find the satellite, and check the codes.

These vastly experienced warfighters found no fault in Matt, though they were by no means through. Using a large city map attached to the wall, they next pointed out a major building in the downtown area and informed Matt he was a Ground Force SEAL commander and that his mission was to take that building, coming in from outside the city. How did he propose to do that?

Matt had a pretty well-rehearsed plan to deal with this section, but the vets turned a straightforward leader's response into a diatribe of staccato interruptions, designed to illuminate the sudden unpredictability of a battle zone: *"What about this? What about that? What if this section is fortified? What if the door is barricaded? What if you meet heavy resistance right here? You got a comms hookup to the backup group? Did he get the codes before you left?"*

The interrogation seemed unending. But, as one of the vets mentioned to Matt later, "I might be serving right alongside you in some madhouse in the Middle East—I just need to know you understand precisely what you're doing."

And it was not over yet. One by one these veterans, SEALs who had come back in one piece from the embattled slums of Sadr City, issued a succession of diabolical scenarios from the worst war zones in which they had served—not just Iraq but also Afghanistan, both Kabul and the mountains of the Hindu Kush.

What would you do if … ? If such-and-such broke out, would you attack or find cover? You're pinned down and the transmitter has been destroyed … what now? You got 'em trapped inside, but they have a ton of explosive—do you take out the building, even though there's a bad guy in there and you want him alive?

At the end of it Matt was sent to a room to await the outcome of the other candidates' examinations.

When Jon came in, the vets knew all about him, the swimmer who'd trained to be a breacher. And every man in that room was aware that in the zone everyone relied on the man who carried the big hammer—his strength, his ability to make specialized explosive charges, his speed of reaction, his assessment of the obstacles facing them.

And they bombarded the breacher from Virginia with question after question, probing into how thoroughly he knew his new trade, demanding answers, demanding assessments of when to resort to explosives, when the overwhelming noise is justified over the sudden rip of the "hooly" as it splinters the door post.

There's a group of very bad guys behind a steel barricade. They're armed and dangerous. Do you blast the Team in, or take it slower and cut the steel with the heat torch?

Several of the questions fired at Jon required a thoughtful answer, and he provided two or three solutions that required a fast battlefield assessment of the advantages of sudden unstoppable attack over waiting for the enemy to mount a heavy machine gun.

When all the interrogators were nodding quietly in agreement, they switched to the difficult scenarios, informing Jon he was now a Ground Force commander, and how the hell did he propose to capture this downtown building?

Like Matt, Jon knew his assault book backward and forward, and he offered a careful study of his plan of attack, utilizing all of the battlecraft he had had been taught throughout these long months of both practical and written examinations.

At the conclusion this baptismal rite of passage they reached a natural conclusion. And Jon was sent to join Matt and the others to await the verdict of their elders and, almost certainly, betters.

And when, finally, that moment came, all eleven of the Team applicants moved back into the main room. And in the best possible good humor, the veterans reunited every candidate with his precious Trident. There were no more harsh, sneering words or demands leveled at the rookies. Just a few well-rounded insults and rough battlefield humor. Right then they all became drinking buddies.

The plain little ceremony, conducted in the recreation hut, signified once and for all that the candidates, who had been under close observation, were now trained to partake in war. Each man had not only demonstrated his mastery of the vital crafts of battle; he had also nailed down his own specialty, the skilled job upon which every other member of that platoon would, at some point in the years ahead, most certainly depend.

The platoon chief petty officer told them all quietly: "Don't forget. You just earned that Trident for the second time. In the future, like all of us, you must earn it every day. And I know you won't let anyone down."

They'd all expected to be successful, but there was a sense of relief when it concluded at last. Because this had been a ceremony of acceptance, the moment when the senior SEAL combatants stated publicly that each of these new recruits was a true and proper person to serve in SEAL Team 10. They were all accepted into the brotherhood that day, and they celebrated in the time-honored traditions of the Teams on that night—drinks, that is. Heavy.

And as the night wore on, the conversation moved steadily from one of celebration to one of extreme seriousness. Team 10 was going back to Iraq, to Camp Schwedler, which is set into a corner of the enormous US Marine Camp Baharia, close to Fallujah,

There may have been excitement and adventure in the air, but even in 2009 Fallujah was no laughing matter. Attacks on US troops were still legion, and even with al-Zarqawi now dead, there was still a fearless al-Qaeda presence in the ruined city. And the atrocities were still taking place: the hostile killing of both Shi'ite townspeople and, whenever possible, the murder of US troops.

Deployment details are rarely handed out to the Teams until the very last moment, but there was a buzz in the air in Virginia Beach. Team 4 was shortly to return after six months in the Fallujah area, and everyone seemed to know that Team 10 would replace them, that they were going back to the desert.

Matt and Jon had several conversations with the veterans that night, all of which involved the half-crazed fanatical terrorist leader in Fallujah who was still there after five years—never found, never seen, but still killing.

Ahmad Hashim Abd Al-Isawi, the Butcher of Fallujah, awaited them.

3

—

ECHO PLATOON IN BATTLE MODE

A combat operation—so they lashed down the ammo cans in the back of the vehicle, in case they got hit by a hurled bomb, which could blast a gas can into a lethal missile and might easily kill them all.

In his almost twenty-four years Matt McCabe had never had much luck with sandy beaches, at least not in the way that comes with peace, quiet, and relaxation through the gentle lapping of unhurried waters on the shore.

In fact, his limited experiences had been the precise opposite: on the long, white sandy coastline of the Pacific at Coronado, dominated by the shouts and commands of tyrannical SEAL instructors driving men onward to within an inch of their lives.

Including Matt.

Would he enjoy the calm inquiry from an agreeable waiter—"Sir, may I get you a beach lounge, perhaps a drink?" Fat chance. What he heard was: *"MCCABE! GET WET AND SANDY RIGHT NOW! GET IN THE DAMN OCEAN!"*

Virginia Beach, the East Coast home to the SEAL Teams, was not much different: same brutal long runs, same arm-wrenching exercises with the inflatable boats and their paddles, and same kind of commanders, yelling out their usual subtle observations: *"TOO SLOW, GO HARDER! YOU'RE RUNNING LIKE A FAIRY! STEP IT UP FOR ME!"*

Even on his rare vacation time, Matt mostly avoided hot sandy beaches. Any chance he had, he headed for the mountains to ski, just as he had during his teenage years, driving up to the hard-packed fast slopes of the Boyne Mountains in Michigan.

Now, based for months at a time on the Virginia coast, he had found a new playground, just a five-hour drive northwest from the SEAL base: the ski resort of Snowshoe, hidden among the snowy peaks of the Allegheny Mountains, way up there in Pocahontas County, West Virginia.

He'd found a good buddy to join him on the steep westerly slopes of the Appalachian Range—one of the best snowboarders on the base, Petty Officer 2nd Class Tyler J. Trahan, an EOD by trade, a man wedded to the dangerous edge of life, both with bombs and dazzling acrobatic maneuvers on his snowboard.

Whereas Matt stuck to the hard-eyed high-speed runs of the downhill skier, Tyler was leaping and cartwheeling on his wide single board as ever out there on the edge. And this was a hell of place to be on the edge. One of the runs, chillingly named Shay's Revenge, has a fifteen hundred–foot vertical drop, the highest in the mid-Atlantic.

The highest elevation was almost five thousand feet, and the trails—Grab Hammer, J Hook, Ball Hooter, and Skidder—were named for the old steam locomotives that once hauled logs over the vast Appalachian Range.

Both of them loved it up there, especially Tyler, who was always seeking the most challenging snowboard runs. He was a special guy: an outstanding high school football captain and quarterback, inducted into the National Honor Society, and at the US Navy Boot Camp had marched at the head of the parade, holding the golden sword awarded to the class leader.

As a deployed EOD expert in Iraq, the twenty-two-year-old Tyler was regarded as one of the most valuable young explosives technicians attached to the Teams. He and Matt shared not only a love of the mountains but also an unusual devotion to high patriotism and training.

Either of them would tackle any mission, no matter how danger-ous. But not many people understood they were among the winter kings up in those snowy Allegheny trails, riding high and sliding fast. Real fast.

It was therefore doubly surprising to find Matt sitting on warm sand in late February, before they even took off for Iraq two weeks hence. He had turned up in the northeast corner of Mexico's Yucatan Penin-sula with his girlfriend at the time, Danielle, on a hotel beach outside the city of Cancun.

After a few days' practice he was just getting the hang of relax-ation—no one was yelling at him to get wet and sandy. The turquoise waters of the western Caribbean were superb for swimming and div-ing, and the drinks were as good as those in Squaw Valley.

It was not a long vacation. And like Jon Keefe, Matt was soon headed back to Virginia to pack up for Iraq. Jon was off base at his par-ents' home, packing and saying good-bye to Tom and Dawn. When SEALs prepare for deployment, every parent understands the honor, the trust, and the responsibilities that have been bestowed upon their sons by the US Navy. And every parent understands the innate pride deep inside the heart of every serving Navy SEAL.

But the unspoken dreads are always there: *What if I never see him again? What if he dies at the hands of some half-crazed tribesmen? What if he hits a roadside bomb? Will I understand what he died for? How could I ever get over it?*

SEAL commanders do not allow the waiting time to go on for long. Jon and Matt were due to leave just twenty-one days after they were initiated into Echo Platoon, and Matt was back from Mexico with just a few days to pack and be on the tarmac by March 2.

Early that morning he was outside his house, just beyond the perimeter of the Virginia Beach base. Jon arrived in a blue truck, driven by his brother, Tommy, who dropped them both at the airport before they set off for one of the most dangerous places on earth.

If one of the Teams is leaving, the situation must be truly danger-ous, otherwise the SEALs would not be involved. And this was re-ported to be Fallujah. How could anything be worse than that?

Jon's most difficult farewell happened at home, when he said good-bye to his childhood girlfriend and future wife, Krista Hedrick. Jon had known Krista since second grade, and she understood as well as anyone where he was going and that there was a possibility she may not see him again.

But Krista was from a very special area of the United States, this enclave of the Virginia Peninsula, where the vastness of America's Navy and military were an ever-present fact of life.

Right here, in the beating heart of the US defense system, close to the gigantic aircraft carriers, the guided-missile destroyers, the Marines, and the SEALs, a brave face was compulsory for everyone. Thus, there were no tears at Jon's family home at Yorktown. Well, not that many.

Tommy Keefe, an Air Force combat controller stationed at Fort Pope on the Fort Bragg Army Base, had driven up from North Carolina for a few days with Jon. And now he was driving his kid brother away, bound for Iraq. It was shortly after 0400 and still dark when they picked up Matt at Virginia Beach and was just as dark when they arrived at Norfolk Airport fifteen minutes later.

On the tarmac was one of the biggest military aircraft in the country, Boeing's gigantic C-17 Globemaster III, the prime transporter for the rapid strategic airlift of troops and cargo to US forward operating bases throughout the world. This thing is 174 feet long and 55 feet off the ground at the tail. Its cargo hold is 88 feet long by 18 feet wide by 12 feet high. It can whisk a half-dozen M1 Abrams main battle tanks anywhere in the world without the slightest stress.

Right now the SEAL transporter was under full load-out for deploying Team 10's Echo Platoon. Because when SEALs travel they assume nothing is available where they are headed. Every conceivable item they might need in any war zone is transported with them, including Zodiac boats, engines, paddles, scuba gear, wetsuits, rocket fins, and goggles—despite the fact that Arabian deserts received about a quarter inch of rain every six thousand years.

So much of the equipment that would go with them would never be used. But for SEALs this is not the issue. What if they were suddenly rerouted to the Gulf? What if they were moved on from Fallujah to al-Basrah? What if someone wanted them to cross the wide Shatt al-Arab to Iran and they did not have their beach assault gear?

It's a Special Forces mind-set. Great Britain's SAS are precisely the same. Deployed, they take everything but the kitchen sink.

The T-tailed Globemaster III would not be overwhelmed with passengers. Built by McDonnell Douglas to hold 236 personnel for instant troop movement, today it would carry only eleven SEALs and a three-man crew—pilot, copilot, and loadmaster.

The rest of the space, right down the middle of the aircraft, was occupied by big metal containers, loaded with every last one of the platoon's weapons, rifles, machine guns, combat knives, pistols, all of the breaching tools, and dozens of ropes, heavy and light as well as fast ropes (30 foot, 90 foot and 120 foot).

There was climbing equipment, including ladders, for urban assault and the possibility of scaling buildings. There were computers, cables, monitors, and flat-screen TVs—everything to set up an instant SEAL platoon ops room, no matter where. All the comms equipment, radios, antennae, backpacks, and GPS were packed.

All of their personal operations gear was packed and stowed. Every item of medical equipment SEALs take on patrol was in there. The SEALs support staff had taken care of everything. It was perhaps the first time either Jon or Matt realized precisely the high regard in which the Team members were held. By everyone.

Because everything that could be done for them had been done. They were required to present only themselves, with their handheld ready bag, which holds each SEAL's M-4 rifle, body armor for Iraq, plus night-vision goggles, a combat knife and Sig-Sauer pistol, helmet, and medical blow-out kit.

The ready bag contained all the essentials in case they ran into what they quaintly describe as an "Oh shit! scenario." As the enormous Boeing freighter commenced its final flight path, helmets and body armor would be pulled on, with rifles ready. No SEAL would disembark through that aircraft door unless the platoon was prepared as a fighting unit to engage the enemy.

One by one they embarked the aircraft, climbing the boarding stairs in the early morning darkness of Virginia's Atlantic coast. When they were inside and all together, the CO reminded them for the last time on American soil: "This is a very serious SEAL deployment. We are going to an extremely dangerous place, and every one of you needs to remember every last lesson you have been taught. Might as well start right now and put on your game faces. Because that's the way it's likely to be from now on."

Matt recalls that this was a departure like no other they had ever experienced. There was not one iota of levity—no laughs, no jokes. Like so many valorous young men in the past, all of them holders of the legendary SEAL Trident, they were leaving for a war zone. And not everyone comes back.

In silence they each sought out a spot on the aircraft, slinging their hammocks between the great steel packing cases that were stacked high to the ceiling. They cleated them off about ten feet above the cargo floor, some fastened to the high freight palettes, others to the heavy nets that covered the weapon cases.

And everyone felt the faint shudder down the interior as the four giant Pratt and Whitney engines were fired up—special military designation: Globemaster III—F117-PW-100, over forty thousand pounds thrust on each one—seventy-two tons of raw turbo-jet power to hurl them skyward.

They set off into a gusting March wind, the twenty wide wheels of the undercarriage rolling hard through the first revolutions of a journey that would put both Matt McCabe and Jon Keefe through some kind of a living hell. But not yet.

The C-17 thundered southwest, rising off the runway and banking left over the myriad of bays behind the SEAL base. Climbing north up the Atlantic, they left the long finger of Virginia's eastern shore to portside and pressed on along the eastern seaboard over the deep waters off New Jersey, staying well out to sea as they made for Nantucket Island and then the coast of Nova Scotia.

The nine men who traveled with Matt and Jon were a highly diverse group—the most important of them was almost certainly the experienced Sam Gonzales, from Blue Island, South Chicago, a Special Operations petty officer 1st class, aged around twenty-nine and a highly decorated SEAL, including a Bronze Star with valor. Sam had been in the Navy since 1999 and a SEAL since 2006.

He was one of the most popular SO1s on Team 10, a very smooth operator of the comms systems and a joint terminal attack controller (JTAC). And on top of all that he dealt with the onerous duties of the leading petty officer. He stood only five feet seven inches tall, but he found a way to look like an offensive lineman for his local Chicago Bears.

Also on board was a highly amusing twenty-nine-year-old petty officer 1st class from South Carolina, a SEAL who had served in Yemen and Baghdad. He was a breacher by trade and went by the colorful name of "Greens."

Next to Jon on the flight was another exquisitely named Navy SEAL: Carlton Milo Higbie IV, a twenty-six-year-old petty officer 2nd class. Carl, as he was usually called, was the son of a wealthy financier, based—where else?—in Greenwich, Connecticut.

This six-foot, 240-pound SEAL had always known he would greatly prefer some bomb-blasted landing beach or the rubble of the Fallujah ruins to an office on Wall Street. Carl was a big boy, in terrific shape—the consummate SEAL noncommissioned officer. As a JTAC, his job was to stay in touch with the overhead aircraft on all missions. Jon was one of his main weight-lifting buddies.

Another petty officer 1st class on board was Eric, the platoon's top medic and lead sniper. He was an excellent swimmer and runner, and he competed in triathlons. He was very, very fast across the sand. Slightly unusually for such a dedicated athlete, Eric was also the platoon intellect, a graduate of Georgia Tech, which NASA now recognized as the aerospace capital of all US universities.

Echo Platoon called him the rocket scientist. And although he could most certainly find his way through outer space, Eric was equally adroit at navigation on planet Earth. He spent a lot of time studying maps, and this made him, in SEAL parlance, the point man, out in front of the others, leading the Team from waypoint to waypoint, checking the ground contours, watching the compass and the GPS.

Eric was, invariably, the reconnaissance leader, exploring the lay of the land, reporting back from his forward position. He was experienced, too, and had already been on two combat deployments, one of them to Baghdad at a very bad time. Every man on the C-17 was pleased to have Eric in the platoon.

The other five SEALs who traveled in the C-17 have remained in the US Navy, and their names will not be revealed. Meanwhile the mighty Globemaster III, jammed to the gills with SEAL equipment, thundered out over the North Atlantic, making its crossing just to the south of Greenland.

It was an eight-hour journey, and the men mostly slept, waking when they entered Europe and crossed the Scottish borders before flying high over the rough, gale-swept North Sea. They made their mainland Europe landfall just north of Ostend, Belgium, and then descended over tiny Luxembourg and into the American Air Base at Ramstein, Germany.

They touched down shortly after 1900, and it was as dark as it was in the United States when they took off. This was a two-hour refueling stop for the C-17, which took on board about a zillion gallons of gas and, for the SEALs, a few dozen cheeseburgers.

Surrounded by fifty-three thousand Americans—the largest overseas population of US citizens in the world—the guys from Echo Platoon were mildly surprised at how isolated they immediately became. It seemed that no one felt sufficiently confident to come over for a chat.

But Ramstein is a massive military base, home of the 86th Airlift Wing, headquarters of US Air Force in Europe. Everyone knows the unwritten rules of the Special Forces: basically, leave them alone, because their work is always top secret and ought not to be discussed with anyone.

Matt had firsthand experience of this military form of *omertà*, their own code of silence. "The SEALs operated with the Marines for a couple of months while we were in the Gulf," he recalled. "I never once spoke to any of them. It's just the way it is with SEALs. They always seem pretty quiet, and everyone keeps their distance."

Slow on conversation but outstanding at cheeseburgers—that was more or less the SEAL verdict on this little corner of the US of A right here in the Rhineland.

And by 2100 they were back in the aircraft, settling down for another long journey, seven more hours in this flying warehouse. Their route would take them south as swiftly as possible, as all US military transporters avoid flying over the old Eastern European states, preferring to run down the Adriatic Sea, east of the Italian coast, and then angle even more easterly across friendly Turkey before cutting south again over northern Iraq and down toward Baghdad.

During this time most of the SEALs were asleep, but those who weren't sipped iced water and laughed at the endless anecdotes Carlton Milo Higbie IV offered as he outlined his plan to retire one day from the SEALs and write a political book.

The final destination for the C-17 was al-Taqaddum Air Base— known as TQ in military slang—which was fifty miles west of Baghdad and operated by the US Marine Corps. With its two giant runways, both of them more than two miles long, TQ stands on a pancake-flat desert plateau on the shores of Lake Habbinaya, south of the Euphrates. It's around halfway between Fallujah and Ar-Ramadi and was the main US air hub for men and materiel moving into Anbar Province for Operation Enduring Freedom.

The SEAL transporter came down through clear skies and landed just before 0700, local time. The sun had already risen above the shimmering horizon of the Syrian Desert, with its parched and dusty wadis.

By the time they came to a halt the SEALs were wearing body armor and helmets. There was, as yet, no sign of an "Oh shit! scenario," and they disembarked into a hot, silent wasteland, dead flat, with, as far as the eye could see, no trees or any kind of vegetation. Also, it was hotter than hell.

Worse yet, it was likely to be home for the next six months. "Holy shit," said Matt. "Perrysburg suddenly looks like paradise."

And he had been there before, briefly, with Carlton, for just a couple of weeks after their training in Stuttgart in October 2007. But he'd forgotten how diabolical it actually was, this colossal sweep of flat, unbroken land, without a rise, a hill, or even a decent gradient. They'd been on the ground for all of four minutes and could all see that desert heat shimmer on the aircraft's fuselage.

All they knew about this place involved its population of thousands of frantic tribesmen who were happy to kill each other over some religious differences but would much prefer to kill American military personnel for no reason whatsoever.

"Is this it?" said Jon, staring at the horizon and shoving back his helmet. "Does anyone actually live here?"

On the tarmac to meet them was their officer in charge Lieutenant Jimmy and his veteran chief petty officer, Gibby, a great bull of a man, aged thirty-four, platoon chief.

The biggest man there was Petty Officer 1st Class Rob, a natural-born breacher if ever there was one. This was one smart Navy SEAL. A former second-choice offensive lineman for Penn State, Rob weighed in at 289 pounds and stood six foot five inches in his game socks.

He was, as his fast mobile position on the Team suggests, a light-footed tiger out there in front of an advancing SEAL Team. And when he swung that sledgehammer at an unsuspecting, barricaded door, the foundations shuddered. He would likely cave in not only the door, its frame, and half the mud wall but also the roof with it. Petty Officer Rob had to think hard to control his own power. His teammates loved him.

And there they stood, blinking in the dazzling desert light with a hot wind from the south drifting past, blowing little dust storms across the runways. There is nothing more foreign to an American than the Arabian Peninsula.

Except for the vast oil deposits, much is unchanged since biblical times. Tribal laws have survived down the centuries. You can sense it, feel it, this inner soul of martyrdom, where the residents will go to war—a real, hot, shooting war, red in tooth and claw—over a difference of religious opinion. And not even much of a difference.

There is a brutality here, where one group of Muslims will think nothing of blowing up an entire marketplace, killing, maiming, and blasting women and children, because the shopping group believed in some variation of the Koran.

And although US troops tried to bring sanity to Iraq, nothing really worked. They are who they are: a couple of paces in front of the ancient Bedouin tribes, but not much more. And now Matt and Jon were in the heart of the War on Terror on the edge of the Syrian Desert, ready to play their part in hunting down the commanders of this weird and secretive killing society, al-Qaeda in Iraq.

And now a line of US military trucks was advancing to transport the men from Echo Platoon to their new base, Camp Schwedler, a custom-built Navy SEAL stronghold set in the corner of the US Marine Corps' Camp Baharia. As Marine camps go, this one was in the heavyweight division. Twelve miles around, with a lake that was six miles around, it was home to thousands of troops.

It was a ninety-minute journey for the SEALs, now sweltering in their body armor but under orders not to remove it. It was, for Jon and Matt at least, a first glance into the accepted method of driving through the Islamic Republic of Iraq: floor it, and keep it right there.

Those trucks bumped, lurched, and rattled as they sped along the road that led up to Baharia. There is no other way for US troops to move about, so cunning and full of hatred are their enemies. A roadside bomb, an IED placed under the asphalt, a rocket-propelled grenade, explosives, raking fire from an AK-47—the insurgents were everywhere: lean, bearded terrorists, awaiting their chance.

But hitting a huge truck meandering slowly along a desert road is one thing. Hitting a high-speed military vehicle hurtling along at 70mph plus, packed to the gunwales with armed Navy SEALs—that's quite another. And the al-Qaeda "warriors" have always been specialists in the sneak attack, not full-on confrontation with US fire and steel.

Timing a bomb accurately is almost impossible if the target is moving fast, covering one hundred yards of ground every three seconds. And these Muslim IEDs, though lethal, are famously inaccurate. "Abdul the bomb maker" probably was not trained at Textron Defense Systems in Massachusetts. At least he better not have been.

And so they charged forward, making fast time up to Camp Baharia and, finally, into their new home, named after the fallen Spartan of

SEAL Team 4. Camp Schwedler was approximately two hundred yards by two hundred yards, surrounded by four-foot-thick concrete walls that were fifteen feet high and topped with rolled razor wire. Guarding the entrance was what Matt described as "a big-ass two-ton steel gate," which not even Rob and Jon, both slamming away with their sledgehammers, could possibly have taken down.

Inside the small desert fortress everything was built purposefully. There were a couple of temporary detainee holding cells that were quite close to the recreation room known as Danny's, with its video games, movies, and television. Outside there was a barbecue pit, tables, and chairs. Danny's, for the record, had profound SEAL Team roots, named as it was after the legendary bar on Orange Avenue close to the Coronado base, second home to generations of Special Forces.

Schwedler had four lines of huts to house the SEALs and support staff, with SEALs on the front end, facing a line of massive heavily armored vehicles in case they had to move fast. Fifty yards further in front, was a long line of smaller military vehicles, all of them ready to go at a moment's notice. The big mechanics' workshop was right there.

At the far end of the compound was the excellently equipped medical room next to the gymnasium and weight room, plus the briefing room and the ready room. Between them was the tactical operation center (TOC), where the senior commanders plotted and schemed the SEALs' missions.

Matt was given a hut in the second line, two doors from his buddy Tyler. Jon was right in front of the ace snowboarder, one hut from Sam.

The camp was on a hair trigger of operational readiness, and the volume of intel coming into the TOC every day never let up. Because half the country wanted the US and coalition troops out of the Middle East forever, this was scarcely surprising.

A SEAL platoon on active duty is there for a purpose, in this case to capture or kill known al-Qaeda operatives who were against the new Iraqi government and insane with dislike for the American military, which was attempting to put the place back together after the carnage that the late Saddam Hussein caused.

The idea was never to kill squads of al-Qaeda personnel but rather to capture their top people and interrogate them. SEALs call them the HVIs (high value individuals), these commanders and planners were the ones the SEALs went after—bin Laden's far-flung henchmen and men with cell phones and Internet connections, not bands of trigger-happy gunmen. The philosophy was quality before quantity.

And the wanted list grew almost by the hour. Not just the jihadist bomb makers who had been responsible for so much destruction but also the bomb distributers—men who journeyed through the night across the desert, delivering high explosive designed to blow young Americans to pieces. There was a vast network of al-Qaeda staff involved in their planning and operational procedures.

And every day American intel field officers either tracked them down or received tip-offs or evidence of sightings, all of which needed to be followed up, checked, and then hit, and hit hard. That's what the SEALs were there for, but great caution was required, because they were always headed directly into harm's way.

And although all SEAL platoons are essentially fearless, their commanders are strongly averse to sending these highly trained special forces on what might become suicide missions. The TOC in Camp Schwedler would need a lot of cast-iron facts before unleashing the might of Echo Platoon onto the local suspects.

The procedures for setting up and then executing a Special Forces attack was time consuming and almost unbearably thorough. And the SEAL senior commanders were relentless in ensuring that the guys had a fighting chance of hitting their target, getting out, and getting home, with their HVIs either dead or alive.

The very first step was almost as dangerous as the last, because the Americans were working under strict rules. For every SEAL on any mission they had two Iraqis working alongside. That was Iraqi Special Weapons and Tactics (ISWAT) in action, trained by the SEALs as decreed by Foreign Internal Defense (FID).

And no matter how urgent the mission, the SEALs were required to first obtain warrants of approval from the Fallujah police headquarters, situated way downtown in this poisonous, bomb-blasted hotbed of insurgent anger.

Broadly, that meant the SEALs had to risk their lives to get permission to risk their lives again. The first time Jon made the journey to collect the warrants he was stunned by the security that surrounded the police HQ; the whole building was barricaded and guarded against the world, the result of years of al-Qaeda attacks on police premises all over Iraq.

The fact that they sent SEALs on what appeared to be a mere errand was a measure of the danger involved. But sending anyone into Fallujah who was less than a combat warrior was impossible. Not if you wanted to see them again.

The SEALs took characteristic precautions from the very start of each downtown journey, which were now regarded as so menacing that they were formally classified as a combat operation. They started by lashing down the standard ammo cans in the back of the vehicle in case they got hit by a hurled bomb or an RPG, which could blast a standard can into a lethal missile that might kill them all, especially if it were full.

Comms systems were primed, seatbelts were fastened with five-point harnesses tight, and machine guns were ready. At least two vehicles would conduct this operation, with four armed SEALs in each—weapons drawn, always in attendance.

And three miles outside the town, the drivers hit the accelerators, and with eight miles to go—five of them through treacherous enemy territory—according to Matt, we "hauled ass every yard of the way."

They braked and swerved, shot up onto the sidewalk and back down again, and never gave the enemy one moment to set up. They howled through street markets, horns blaring, scattering chickens, and terrifying goats. They shoved cattle out of the way, occasionally camels, as they dodged oncoming traffic.

Shoppers in the markets moved aside and vendors retreated into baskets of fresh vegetables as the US Navy SEALs sped their way through town, weaving and bumping, and God knows what else. Just keep going—fast. That's all.

"It wasn't any fun either," recalled Jon. "And no one was laughing. This was hostile territory, and we half expected a friggin' bomb to land right behind the driver. Screw that."

When they arrived at police HQ they left two guys on guard, weapons drawn, and the other two raced to the bolted and barred front door, where guards let them in. The warrants were sometimes waiting, sometimes not, but they eventually were signed, issuing Iraqi approval for American action against their joint enemies in al-Qaeda.

There was always a quick handshake and a polite greeting for the local police chief, and then the Americans raced outside, scrambled back into the vehicle, and burned rubber on the rough sandy ground as they sped back the way they had come—through the five miles of alien streets, where everyone hated them and where death might await around any corner as it had for so many other members of the US armed forces.

This entire business of driving through unfriendly Arabian streets was a thoroughly nerve-wracking experience. This was like Bahrain, 2005, at another forward SEAL base south of the capital, Manama. Any time those SEALs were going anywhere from out of the US Air Base at Muharraq Island, they had to go through the middle of town. And back then it was darn near as bad as it was in Fallujah—at least it was in spirit if not in active high explosive.

The citizens of Manama were fed up to the back teeth with the American military, and there were even areas where the locals hung out black flags from homes and shops signifying *Americans not welcome.* It was similar in Yemen, not quite so intense in Saudi Arabia, but again very obvious in areas of Damascus in Syria and certainly worse in Gaza City, Israel.

Fallujah never needed those black flags. Every house was a black flag. The SEALs saw the whole place as one massed enemy redoubt. And every time the Camp Schwedler intel guys thought they'd located a possible target, the SEALs had to race straight through the middle of this hostile city to get Iraqi permission to attack ... huh?

That was just the way it was. And in fairness to the Iraqi police, they rarely if ever refused to sign the warrants because, of course, they were under attack as well. And they were granted a major voice in finalizing who should be taken down. But when push came to shove US Navy SEALs carried out the actual operation.

When Echo Platoon first arrived there were heavy briefings day after day, lecturing the men on Iraqi customs, the likely tactics of their enemy, and the standard SEAL operational procedures to deal with every conceivable occurrence.

They were shown lists and photographs of the most wanted terrorists and reports of previous attempts to detain them, both successful and unsuccessful. Like all US military postmortems, they were searching in the extreme, trying to pinpoint what had worked and what had failed. Many lessons had been learned, but some of these al-Qaeda commanders remained on the loose, several for many months.

There were two or three still free after several years. And one of these was the murderer Ahmad Hashim Abd Al-Isawi, the Butcher of Fallujah, who had been evading capture for almost five years. There were others too. Matt recalls reading up on one al-Qaeda tribesman who they'd gone after twenty times and had still not located—not because the SEALs had been outfought or outwitted but simply because the villain was not where he was supposed to be.

The al-Qaeda networks had become more and more efficient. And the reason for this was not only obvious; it was god awful. The Americans and their coalition partners were forced, politically, to reveal almost all of their plans to the Iraqi police in order to get the agreed warrants signed.

This was, in one sense, a reasonable method of ensuring mutual cooperation, but in another sense it was like standing up on your hind legs and begging for a betrayal. No one knew what the hell was going on inside those barricaded police buildings. And yes, most of the Iraqi personnel genuinely wished the US security forces well.

But in the shady world of espionage, be it in rain-swept night streets of Moscow or the hot and sandy terrorist enclaves of the Middle East, it still takes only one mole. Just one solitary person working quietly, listening to his superiors, or copying down those warrants for the whole thing to come unraveled.

For the SEALs finally to capture or kill one thoroughly dangerous member of al-Qaeda, any scheme will simply flounder if someone tells him the Americans are coming at this time, in this place, with this intention.

Of course US intel was keenly aware of the problem, but nothing could be done—not against politicians who had made up their minds that US-Iraqi relations were always more important than mission secrecy.

From the SEALs' point of view this was doubly bad. Not only were their missions likely to come up empty, but the risk of enemy ambush was plainly heightened. The dread of a heavily armed terrorist fighting force actually waiting for your arrival is not much fun.

But it was a daily fact of life for the residents of Camp Schwedler. And it always meant intensive briefings, maps, charts, warnings, black spots, and long walks into the zone under full gear and weapons because the noise of car or aircraft engines was always too loud and too risky in the silence of the desert nights.

Like most terrorist operations, it was a guessing game. Hard facts were rare, but the one that stood out over long periods of study were al-Qaeda and Taliban attacks on Iraqi police personnel, attacks in which the staff were targeted, usually so well that it must have been conducted with inside information. It took Matt and Jon very little time to view the police HQ in downtown Fallujah with consummate mistrust.

Meanwhile Echo Platoon was moving into battle mode. There was intensive training in stealth, marksmanship, and navigation across the burning sands, where temperatures sometimes reached 115 degrees.

When the operations began they were, like most SEAL missions, conducted at night. And the objectives were often simple—at least they were to the guys who were not actually out there. The orders mostly involved a long walk in, through the night, before busting into a building, locating this or that al-Qaeda terrorist, grabbing him and his immediate cohorts, and bringing them in for questioning and incarceration. If there was heavy armed resistance, the SEALs were to shoot them.

And no chances were ever taken with these killers, who would slit a SEAL's throat or knife him in the back as soon as they looked at him. Procedures for capture were subsequently harsh: grab him, search and disarm him, then get him on the deck fast—either the easy way or, if necessary, the other way. Hold him down, get the cuffs on him, and tell him to shut up.

None of this could be described as subtle. But this was not a subtle business. At best it was lethal. And the greatest care needed to be taken at all stages of the mission. Matt and Jon had effectively been in strict training for this since they arrived in Coronado three years previously. And now they were judged to be ready to step forward into the footprints of so many heroic young Americans who had gone before them.

Matt remembers the briefing in the evening before they left on an operation—the thoroughness, the maps, and the details of the journey in. It was scheduled for a small town maybe twenty miles outside the base, and the Iraqi security men who were accompanying the platoon were already inside the walls of Camp Schwedler.

A Team leader had already been selected on the rotating basis, a system that would last throughout their tenure in Iraq. Everyone would take night-vision goggles and silenced rifles. The man the SEALs were after was a highly dangerous and known terrorist. The commanders saw no reason to get involved in a firefight when there was a good chance of grabbing him quietly after advancing through the town with the utmost stealth.

Matt would carry the heavy radio; Jon would handle the breaching gear: sledgehammer, bolt cutters, and demo charges. They left on time and drove to a point three miles out from the town. Right there they silenced the engines and then proceeded on foot, making their way to the outskirts.

Staring through their "green eyes," they found their target house, and Jon ripped off the door by its hinges, using the hooly. They found the bedroom door and opened it more softly, with four of them moving into the room for the immediate surrender they correctly expected when the terrorist woke up, when he found himself looking down the barrels of four assault rifles leveled at him by huge masked men.

He allowed himself to be handcuffed and taken into captivity and back to Camp Schwedler, where he would be held and then transported to Baghdad for interrogation by the US military.

The opening assault by Echo Platoon had gone off in textbook style, but in the coming weeks not every mission would be so flawless. Several times they were betrayed, and the HVI was not in residence when they arrived. Once there was an absolute uproar in the middle of the night when the target was missing, but several of his wives were at home and asleep. The women went berserk with fear when Echo Platoon came calling. Woke up half the town.

And the fact that the SEALs suffered no casualties on their opening missions did not mean the danger was suddenly less. They got out without losing anyone because of their supreme attention to detail, never doing anything carelessly, standing by the rules of the most demanding playbook in the world. No mistakes.

On April 30, however, the whole game changed, and the real Iraq, with all of its seething hatreds, wanton killings, and loathing of Americans, flashed into very sharp focus. Tyler Trahan was killed in action in Fallujah, two days before his twenty-third birthday.

It was a roadside bomb, an IED, ironically, that did it. The bomb appeared safe when it suddenly exploded. Two others died with the young bomb technician, and the incident brought great sadness to everyone at Camp Schwedler, especially Tyler's skiing buddy, Matt McCabe, and his next-door neighbor, Jon Keefe.

Back in Tyler's hometown in rural Massachusetts near Fall River, news of his death was greeted with disbelief. The little New England town's favorite son was gone, and when his flag-draped casket was finally brought home with a full Navy honor guard, literally thousands filed past to pay their respects—family, friends, and legions of local people who just knew about him and his too-short but exemplary career in Dark Blue.

The funeral home stayed open four hours later than planned, until almost midnight, and the funeral mass was no different. The five hundred–seat Catholic church at East Freetown, the church where Tyler was baptized, was filled to capacity one hour before the service began.

There were as many people outside as there were inside, where several Navy SEALs and EOD technicians who had served with Tyler were seated, plus the governor of Massachusetts, Deval Patrick, and US Senator John Kerry. Throughout the mass Tyler's own baptismal candle flickered softly beside the coffin. It was the saddest day anyone could ever remember.

After the mass a military procession more than a mile long followed the coffin to Massachusetts National Cemetery, located in the village of Bourne, adjacent to Otis Air Base. Tyler was laid to rest with full military honors.

Nearly seven thousand miles away in hot, dusty Camp Schwedler, a less grandiose but perhaps even more poignant ceremony took place for Petty Officer Tyler Trahan. The memorial service was held outside and attended by about one hundred US Navy SEALs and their back-up staff, every last one of whom knew him, worked with him, lived close to him, and saw him almost every day. This was his other family.

All four platoons were represented, plus Marines who had worked with him. And for Tyler's teammates this was an extremely emotional day. The sudden loss of his ski buddy had placed Matt closer to the finality of death than he had ever been. He had also never been more upset.

And almost everyone shared his grief. Because every serving member of the Special Forces understands what they all owe to the bomb disposal experts. These sophisticated explosives technicians have saved countless lives, more than anyone can calculate.

And every last time they achieve their objective, they have put their own life on the line. There is nothing—repeat, nothing—more upsetting for a Navy SEAL than the death of one of these iron-nerved bomb experts, blown up in the line of duty.

It's a way of life, and a darned hard one at that. Because IEDs in Iraq are all over the place. SEAL Teams working at night may discover one, hidden as a booby trap. They cannot go forward, right past it, and they sure as hell cannot just leave it there for others to be blown to pieces.

Step forward the EOD, men like young Tyler, with their soft tread, ultrasensitive stethoscopes, wire cutters, and steady fingers as they try to identify the detonator and listen for the electronic pulse that will betray its timing. Everyone stands back while he works. No one's heart even pretends to beat. Scarcely a breath is drawn.

And then there's the soft click as the EOD cuts the electronic wire. And everyone braces for the blast—flat to the ground, with heads down or against a wall. When it doesn't come and guys like Tyler move back, sweating, they're usually grinning cheerfully. Especially Tyler. He was always laughing, particularly when he'd just saved everyone's life.

A naval chaplain flew up for his service. The guys from the long rows of huts had organized a system to play hymns throughout the base, and they also played a video of Tyler, one last glance at the life of one of the best explosive technicians in the Teams and, by the definition of his calling, a friend to them all.

At the end they all stood up and clapped. It was an emotional round of applause from the toughest men on earth for all that he had done. Tyler Trahan was that good a guy.

Meanwhile the insurgent attacks on the Shi'ite community continued. And once more the name of Ahmad Hashim Abd Al-Isawi moved to the forefront. On May 20 a massive bomb was hurled into a neighborhood takeout restaurant in Baghdad, killing no fewer than twenty-nine people. And once more US military intel suspected the planning at least bore the hallmarks of Al-Isawi, the man they'd been hunting for five years.

The question was: Had he moved his center of operations from Fallajuh to Baghdad? For a while it seemed so, because three weeks later another huge car bomb detonated in a marketplace in the southern desert city of Al-Batha, about twenty-five miles west of Nasiriyah, well over one hundred miles from Baghdad.

This was not the action of some vengeful Sunni individual, lashing out at a known Shi'ite township. This was a well-organized, big, expensive blast that killed at least twenty-nine people and injured seventy others, almost all of them women shoppers and their children.

It blew the entire market to smithereens, and the police immediately blamed al-Qaeda in Mesopotamia, an offshoot of al-Qaeda in Iraq, both of which intended to reignite the sectarian religious war on the lines laid out by the late fanatic Abu Musab al-Zarqawi.

And again both British and US intelligence believed Al-Isawi was deeply involved, becoming near certain two days later when Harith al-Obaidi, head of the Iraqi National Accord, the largest Sunni block in the legislature, was assassinated in a Baghdad mosque along with his secretary and three bodyguards.

That looked like a revenge attack. And then, less than two weeks later, another major bomb, strapped to a motorbike, blew in a market in the Sadr City neighborhood of Baghdad, killing seventy-six people. That happened a few days before all US troops were scheduled to withdraw from Iraqi cities.

But on June 30 a bomb in Kirkuk, 160 miles north of Baghdad, killed another thirty-three people. And Iraqi politicians were considering a major rethink, while every coalition spy in the country was desperately trying to locate Al-Isawi and possibly put an end to this mass slaughter of innocent citizens from one end of Iraq to the other.

Aside from the normal weekly atrocities in Fallujah itself, there were no further national-scale attacks, although SEAL Teams were out there all the time, searching for the al-Qaeda hard men, especially Al-Isawi.

But they never got near him.

As July progressed, so did Al-Isawi's profile, and by now it was widely accepted that he was surrounded by a heavyweight team of bodyguards and an al-Qaeda cell that seemed capable of moving around the country at will, striking where and when they wished.

Somewhere, somehow, they must have left an electronic footprint, but despite a thousand professional leads and another thousand call-ins, they never nailed the terrorists down. And when they thought they were onto something, it always turned out to be a phantom.

"We were seeking him here and seeking him there," said Jon, "but the sonofabitch was always just off the charts."

Al-Isawi was on the move, no doubt about that, but his ferocious reputation and ability to scare people to death with threats against their families continued. And so did reports that he still made his HQ in the teeming ghetto streets of Fallujah.

Was he back in Baghdad on July 31 when bombs went off outside *five* Shi'ite mosques, killing twenty-nine people? No one knew the answer to that, but suspicions ran high. And toward the end of August there was another spate of cold-blooded bombings that again suggested organized, expensive killing—Al-Isawi's specialty.

First, a truck bomb sufficiently powerful to collapse an elevated highway detonated outside the Ministry of Finance and killed thirty-five people. Three minutes later an even bigger truck bomb, probably one thousand pounds, blew the Foreign Ministry asunder, wiping out sixty more people. Individuals could not achieve this kind of heavy-weapon attack because it required substantial financial backing from a proper source, either national or from a wealthy fanatic like bin Laden.

There were other al-Qaeda commanders high on the US suspect list, but none with quite the fearsome reputation of Al-Isawi. Somewhere he was out there. And every time one of these outrageous examples of savage, nondescript sectarian killing took place, the name of the man who had burned four Americans alive jumped right up on every computer screen in US intelligence.

And the question asked but never thoroughly answered was always the same: Where the hell is he? Because Al-Isawi has slipped through a dozen nets, so someone was obviously warning him of approaching danger.

And although it was always possible there was a double agent in the US system, there was nothing quite so suspicious as that Iraqi police HQ in downtown Fallujah, the place where all the warrants were read, signed, and filed in the presence of civilian workers.

But the existence of a double agent remained a worrying possibility. And almost all of the active combat Special Forces noted that only about 10 percent of the warrants, which gave Iraqi permission for the SEALs to go in and capture/kill an HVI with known al-Qaeda connections, were acted upon. The rate of turn-downs that Task Force West, the SEALs' central command located in Ramadi, issued constantly mystified both Matt and Jon.

It was never easy for the support Teams as they tried to gauge what was valuable and what was simply not worth the risk. But so often those signed warrants came back with a blue stamp in the middle: "Not approved."

"In general terms about eight of us or even more had risked our lives," said Jon, "driving right through the worst part of Fallujah to get those signed warrants. And most times we were then told not to bother. Someone knew a lot more than us.

"Right here we'd have a known bad guy, with details of where he'd be tonight. We had Iraqi police approval to go in and get him. But our own guys were forbidding it.

"Now … we're SEALs, and we trust our senior command implicitly because they're always concerned with our safety. But this was a mystery to us. And we concluded they were mostly acting on a negative tip-off, stuff we could not have known—*not to go, ambush being planned, suspect moved on.*

"Whatever. It seemed to us a lot of Iraqis were out there helping the Fallujah Butcher."

And all the SEALs wanted was a chance to get a shot at the little bastard.

4

—

WE WANT THIS MANIAC ALIVE

And Matt, his adrenalin pumping, had his knee rammed into the spine of the most feared terrorist in the Middle East, the Butcher of Fallujah; Echo Platoon's assault Team had captured the mass murderer Ahmad Hashim Abd Al-Isawi. ...

The bombs of August sent a tremble of new determination through Camp Schwedler. SEAL Team 10, already on red alert after Tyler Trahan's death, was now up and ready to go at even the sound of high explosive over the wall at the old Marine base.

And there were plenty of those sounds. Camp Baharia, now closed after the US troop withdrawal, was a constant target for any demented Islamist going for a place over the bridge, where the sound of trumpets would herald the arrival of his personal virgins.

The departed Marines, out beyond the walls of the SEAL compound, used to be expert at avoiding these weekly outbursts of senseless violence, and they conducted dozens of patrols around their sprawling base. It kept Camp Schwedler out of trouble. But with the Marines gone, the SEALs needed to be doubly vigilant for potential attacks on them.

And still there remained one golden target—Ahmad Hashim Abd Al-Isawi. And the SEALs' senior command believed that if they could grab this al-Qaeda killer, everything would calm down, and the danger of being blown up would be lessened for everyone.

At this time there were regular reports coming in, detailing sightings and tip-offs. And by now they even knew what he looked like. They had poor-quality but useful photographs as well as a solid description of his height and build.

They even knew he'd lost the top part of the little finger of his left hand. But whether the half-size pinkie would lead Ahmad to his doom was anyone's guess. They'd been after him for five and a half years now, since the spring of 2004, and he was still ahead of the game.

And many opinions had been revised. Whereas once US intel had been almost certain the Butcher was moving around surrounded by a virtual army of bodyguards and al-Qaeda commanders, they now believed he was operating within a small entourage, somehow managing to stay under the radar. And like Saddam Hussein before him, no one knew where he would spend the night at any given day in the week.

Terrorist commanders in both Afghanistan and Pakistan as well as in Iraq were always ready to phone their friendly newsroom in the Al Jazeera television network in Doha, Qatar. But mostly they seemed to prefer the old tried and trusted ways of their ancestors—sometimes walking miles and miles over the high peaks of the Hindu Kush, pretending to be poor farmers but actually carrying sometimes priceless information in the saddle bags of their camels, beyond the reach of eavesdroppers.

Osama bin Laden himself had almost certainly issued a warning, so infuriated was he at the now-famous intercept when the Israelis hacked into a conversation between his mother in Saudi Arabia and his own mountain cave. These rare recordings were occasionally played to Fort Meade visitors in order to lighten a normally somber subject.

In Iraq, too, this seemed to explain Al-Isawi's silence on the airwaves. The only facts ever came from "contacts"—Iraqi agents being paid by the Americans. It thus seemed increasingly likely that al-Qaeda's messages, plans, and intentions were being carried across the desert and hidden in the panniers strapped to the camels.

It probably was not the fastest thing al-Qaeda had ever done, but at least they could be certain there was not some electronic technician in nearby Tel Aviv, tuning into the frequencies and going for the same intercepts that revealed bin Laden's mother.

And this was how Al-Isawi managed to stay right under the radar, with the main US progress being either from spies or captured illegal combatants who were prepared to betray him for cash. The Americans had been close to their quarry, no doubt of that, but they still knew no one who had ever seen him.

And the entire population was terrified to admit even an acquaintance with him, so formidable was his reputation as a cold-blooded killer who would have a man's family systematically slaughtered for the slightest sign of disloyalty to al-Qaeda's murderous cause. And that fear also applied to the Iraqi police department.

An update was issued every few days, and the senior commanders shared this with the top SEALs, as most of the new information was geographic, involving possible sightings and likely places where the killer might turn up.

The TOC never slept. The place was open at all hours of the night as the major brains in Camp Schwedler pored over the incoming data on their most wanted man. And there was always a special intensity when anyone mentioned a forthcoming manhunt for Al-Isawi.

Everyone knew that one of the burned Blackwater bodies on the Fallujah bridge in 2004 was that of ex-SEAL instructor Scott Helvenston. And that would not be easily forgotten or forgiven. The unspoken pledge was simple: "Scott was one of our brothers. We will, in the end, capture his murderer." So some SEALs gravitated naturally to the Schwedler ops room because the current activities reflected their own areas of expertise.

One of these was Petty Officer 1st Class Eric, the "rocket scientist" from Georgia Tech, point man, and cartographer—the man whose boots might well hit the sand first when they finally drew a bead on Al-Isawi. Eric loved maps, and probably knew more about the ancient trails and wadis of the Mesopotamian Bedouins than anyone since Alexander the Great, three hundred years before Christ.

Petty Officer 1st Class Rob, the ex-lineman from Penn State, was another. Breacher-supreme, he was also a heavyweight in the brains department and was probably born to be in naval intelligence. He loved the subject—loved piecing together mysteries, running his fingers over the charts, measuring distances, working out where the Butcher might and might not be.

Rob was more than happy to work eighteen hours a day in the TOC, studying the data. He also fancied himself as a professional spy and liked to talk to local people, probing for information and listening for a careless remark that might betray the whereabouts of Al-Isawi. He even had a few shots at recruiting people to join the US intel networks in Iraq. Some of them, according to Matt McCabe, were pretty darn clever.

Working alongside Rob was another highly intelligent SEAL, a junior officer with a similar flare for intel, Lieutenant Junior Grade Jason, who in the end left the Navy to go to law school. Looking back, Matt said, "I have to say the heart and soul of this entire operation belonged to Rob and Jason. Seemed to me they hardly ever went to sleep, just stayed right there in the TOC, poring over information, trying to second-guess this Al-Isawi character."

On the burning hot afternoon of Monday, August 24, 2009, with the air conditioning in the TOC burning more gas than a launching space shuttle, the big break arrived. A trusted informer came on the line and revealed precisely where Al-Isawi was going to be on the morning of Wednesday, September 2.

It was a remote and secretive place, way out in the Syrian Desert, west of Camp Schwedler, maybe one hundred miles west. Certainly Matt had never been anywhere near it; no one had. No coalition forces had ever set foot in this lawless place. And Eric's huge fingers were flashing over his computer keys like shafts of light trying to pull up a satellite image, nailing down the GPS numbers.

Matt remembered thinking, "If this Al-Isawi has a lot of sentries or radar or night-vision goggles, it's going to be a tough walk in. And we can't fly in or take vehicles because the desert out there will be absolutely silent. I'll bet you could hear a camel fart at a thousand yards."

Neat turn of phrase, McCabe. But he was right about one thing: the howling twin turbos of the Sikorsky Seahawk, the Navy's version of the Army's Black Hawk, could have awakened the sleeping pharaohs. And Matt's mind raced as he stood with the senior SEAL commanders, trying to visualize the scene as the Seahawks come clattering in to land in that hot desert night, hitherto as silent as outer space.

And there was a reason for Matt's close involvement with the upcoming mission to this apparent al-Qaeda stronghold, miles from anywhere. The young SEAL from Perrysburg, Ohio, was next on the rotation to lead the assault Team on this mission, probably twenty-five men, including the compulsory Iraqi contingent. And their objective would be plain: capture/kill the most dangerous al-Qaeda terrorist operative in the Middle East, Ahmad Hashim Abd Al-Isawi.

Matt stood staring at the map. The target area was almost 150 miles from Baghdad, in the middle of the Al Anbar Desert. So far as he could see there was nothing between the Euphrates River all the way west, 580 miles to Amman, the capital city of the desert kingdom of Jordan.

He could see a tiny village along the one single road that leads across that desert—Ar-Rutbah, situated where the road crosses the Hawran Wadi, about fifty miles further west than Al-Isawi's apparent temporary lodgings.

This place was not coming up on any of the regular Iraqi city maps. There was no record of any commerce or even local government. One military chart suggested Saddam Hussein may have built a few structures out there when he was on the run, but there were no photographs and no map references.

Matt and his buddies could only think it was something like that al-Qaeda training camp that Saddam had constructed north of his hometown of Tikrit. A patrolling SEAL Team had discovered it five years ago, and some of the guys were sure it was a replica of the same camps they'd located in Afghanistan.

Whichever way the situation was examined, Echo Platoon's target area would be as close to Nowhere Central as it was humanly possible to get. This was part good and part bad. The pluses were that with a bit of luck, no one would be expecting them, not out there at the end of the world, where probably no Westerner had ever been.

The less attractive aspect of the assault was that they may run into heavy defenses, set up years ago but still lethal—heavy machine guns, grenades, rockets, and possibly even missiles. Also, they had no way of finding out what kind of bodyguard force would surround this Al-Isawi villain. Finally, they were unlikely to find out who he was meeting with.

The platoon humorist, unnamed here for security reasons, offered, unhelpfully, that ol' Al-Isawi "might just have a hot date with some local belly dancer … you know, Shakira of the Desert!"

In truth, this somewhat relieved the tension, which was inevitably building as the Echo Platoon SEALs pondered the great unknowns of this forthcoming black operation to be conducted on the night of September 1–2.

They worked all through the day and long into the night. The CO named the operation Objective Amber, and designated a twenty-five-man team, comprising only eight SEALs plus the compulsory Iraqis' SWAT to take part. But the local terror of Al-Isawi was such that they did not dare tell the Iraqis who it actually was they were going after.

Otherwise the Iraqis would most certainly have refused to go and probably would not have signed the warrant, not that it would have stopped Team 10 from going in. Not after this long a time.

The senior commander put in a request for further satellite photographs of the area, but even with CIA backing, these requests were difficult because they required specific action at the National Reconnaissance Office in Chantilly, Virginia, from where the United States' space satellite programs are controlled.

Surveillance of desert townships and installations are invariably problematic because everything is similar in color—that kind of scrubland brown, blending with a grayish brown, with hardly any perceptible difference among the sand, the sparse dusty vegetation, and solid concrete or packed mud. At least, not from twenty-two thousand miles straight up.

And this remote and desolate place was likely to be even more difficult than normal to photograph clearly because it had obviously been purposefully built not so long ago specifically to avoid the piercing, prying eye of US surveillance as the satellites passed silently overhead.

If the men of SEAL Team 10 somehow received some clear-cut aerial pictures of this al-Qaeda stronghold, giving them at least a ground map shot from above … well, they'd be darned lucky. And they all knew it.

This would require a major change in direction for the Chantilly satellite lenses that flew over Iraq because they would, logically, be concentrated on the main insurgent cities, like Basrah, Baghdad, and Fallujah. To move them around at short notice to focus on a wide stretch of godforsaken desert—that was a very big request.

Out there, over the dry wadis of outer Anbar Province, there was scarcely one single landmark except the endless road cutting across the sand on the ancient camel route to the northwestern hills of Jordon.

Matt and his teammates figured out that, because of the noise, they dare not bring those Seahawks in any closer than three miles. That would mean a helicopter ride from Camp Schwedler of approximately forty-five minutes and then a three-mile walk over rough sandy terrain in the pitch dark while carrying a lot of equipment.

"That's one and a half hours," said Matt.

"And you can expect a firefight when you get there," said the CO. "They've gotta have defenses ready, with a guy as important as Al-Isawi in residence."

No one argued with any of that. But the prospect of a firefight was bad. Because if they were pinned down by heavy machine gunfire, trying to assault what might be a low-built village, Al-Isawi would have time to make a break for it. Although unlikely, he might even have access to some old getaway vehicle, and if he did, the SEALs would not hesitate to take it out, with a LAW rocket (a light, anti-armor weapon). But that was just one more item to carry.

The main formation of the in-going platoon was of paramount importance because it would almost certainly involve splitting the force and walking in with two columns behind the SEALs who were taking point, as they would be out in front, calling in.

This was because, despite the slender nature of the intel they possessed, they were confident that the main frontal defense of the place faced southwest, the direction in which the SEALs would be approaching the site, and the perimeter was too wide to hit without slamming both ends, where there may be guard towers.

Thus, they swiftly agreed that the right-hand assault force, led by Matt McCabe, would move forward from the helicopter in single file behind recce man Eric, who would be out front testing the ground all the way in.

Immediately behind Matt would be the five ISWAT, pleasant enough combat troops but likely to panic under fire and possibly run for their lives, especially if they found out who the target was. Their actions would not fit precisely into standard SEAL conduct in the face of the enemy.

The tail of Matt's column would walk adjacent to three heavily armed SEALs close up, ready to run forward into assault formation at the first sign of trouble.

Bravo, the left-hand column, would be led by the mighty Petty Officer Rob, with an identical lineup behind him. Jon Keefe would be the recce man on the other side, leading the way for column two and heavily armed, picking his way through the dark desert out in front. He would communicate constantly with Rob and the chief comms operator, Petty Officer Sam, who would be standing in for Matt, the Alpha Team leader.

Between the two columns on the forward march to the al-Qaeda compound would be Carlton Milo Higbie IV ("Carl" to his buddies), marching along with Sam and the mission's forward commanding officer, Lieutenant Jimmy.

The SEALs would be ready to take on anything, no doubt about that. But it was the unknown factor that was so troublesome. They had no idea how big a defensive force they would meet, how well armed and prepared it would be, and how much of an early warning the terrorists would receive—if any.

Worse yet, the Team 10 TOC may not be able to find out, which would mean, inevitably, that Echo Platoon may have to get down and fight it out in the pitch-black desert at least an hour before the Quick Reaction Force (QRF) could even possibly arrive.

If they had to, they could summon their own three Seahawks, capable of carrying Hellfire-guided missiles and heavy machine guns. However, that would provide ample time and diversion for Al-Isawi to make his escape. The last thing Matt and his men wanted was an uproar, which would negate the purpose of the entire mission.

But as the dying days of August passed, one issue stayed solid: Camp Schwedler's "Deep Throat" remained certain of Al-Isawi's whereabouts. On the morning of September 2 Al-Isawi would be right where the informer had stated on August 24—hiding out in that mysterious al-Qaeda "barracks" deep in the Al Anbar Desert.

Team 10's preparations never missed a beat. As leader, Matt did a lot of the legwork, coordinating the finest details, assisting with the communications, and working with Eric on the best route in after they disembarked the Seahawks.

On Tuesday afternoon, September 1, the three SH-60 Seahawks arrived on the landing zone (LZ) at Camp Baharia. They were flown from TQ Air Base and would each carry eight men minimum into the operations zone. The pilots were immediately presented with a thorough briefing inside the ready room at Schwedler.

The helicopters were each armed with an M-240 machine gun and a GAU-17 Alpha, which fires six thousand rounds per minute. All mounted helicopter machine guns were equipped with infrared lasers for night operations. During flight and on landing the helicopter's door gunners would be on red alert.

The Seahawks, though capable of cruising at twelve thousand feet, would fly extremely low on this mission, cruising into the zone at approximately 160mph across the desert. Al-Qaeda defenses would not detect the SEALs flying in low. All SEAL operators would be equipped with night-vision goggles during the flight, as would the pilots and copilots.

Throughout the day the air crew was acquainted with every detail of the mission. As departure time approached, the pilots, copilots, and load masters knew everything there was to know, right down to which way the nose of the helicopter would point when they touched down in the desert. In addition they were given their own battle plan, being told precisely how to attack if Carl called them in for an emergency.

They were also fully briefed with exact details of the escape plan—the three-mile journey across the sand toward the al-Qaeda compound, landing, keeping the engines running, keeping everything prepared for the fastest possible getaway, plus the evacuation of any wounded. And, of course, transporting the HVI who would, by then, hopefully be securely handcuffed and still breathing.

The checklist of equipment was impressive. The heavy-duty gear of the breacher was paramount—the sledgehammer, the bolt cutters, the crowbar, the explosive charges. In this case, the SEALs who would lead the two assault columns, Matt on the right and Rob to his left, would both assume the duties of breacher, leading the guys in just as soon as they reached the entry points. These two, who would walk in with the high explosive, designed and constructed all the charges personally.

The heavy machine guns and their ammunition belts had to be loaded aboard. All the M-4 rifles were silenced, and sniper rifles were also taken, just in case Al-Isawi made a break for it and had to be stopped. They took hand grenades, "flash-bang" grenades, which made an unimaginable noise, as they had been specifically designed to frighten people so much that the sound would stun them temporarily. The special disposable zip cuffs the Teams used on all al-Qaeda prisoners were included with each man's gear.

Every SEAL took his combat knife and Sig Sauer pistol as Petty Officer Sam supervised the communications equipment, personally packing the heavy comms radio he would carry into the zone. He conducted his tests in company with Matt and Rob, the men who would walk at the head of each column and to whom Sam's calm voice might represent the difference between life and death if the men from Echo Platoon came under heavy fire.

For this mission they would take an experienced naval medical practitioner because they would all be operating so far from home base and emergency procedures in the middle of the desert may be required for anyone who was badly hurt. This was in addition to the regular morphine, bandages, and wound dressings that accompany every SEAL operation.

The full medical supply would be carried in the lead helicopter. Their SEAL medical expert, Eric, would go into the zone with the assault Team, accompanied by hospital corpsman 1st Class Paddy, a non-SEAL but a hugely respected and experienced paramedic.

Paddy was also required to stay close to the assault teams and could not be left behind in the comparative safety of the waiting helicopters. That al-Qaeda redoubt may very well become a lethal battle zone, and the presence of both medics, with full equipment, in the heart of any firefight may be critical. Not to put too fine a point on it—life and death.

Rob, leading column two on the walk in, was responsible for the limited data they had for identifying the HVI. He had a small file of photographs and a minibiography containing a description that everyone needed to study: *remarkably tall for an Iraqi, six feet two inches, of slim build.*

The pictures were not great, but they were adequate. Al-Isawi would be recognizable mostly by the twisted scowl on his face, which was probably how he looked when he hanged the burned bodies of the Americans from the old bridge at Fallujah five years previously.

But the key to positive identification (POSIDENT) was that stubby little finger on his left hand. "The guy with the stunted pinkie," as Matt somewhat graphically observed. "That's our target. Because that can't change."

At 2330 hours on Tuesday night, September 1, Echo Platoon was driven out to the three Seahawks that stood silently on the LZ beyond Camp Schwedler. It took less than ten minutes for the twenty-five men to embark. And before the turbo engines rendered the entire place too deafening for conversation, the CO issued one last, somewhat dire warning: "Gents," he said, "stay sharp, and expect a firefight."

At which point the pilots started those big turbo engines, virtually at the midnight hour, and they climbed away from the base to their cruising height. But as soon as they left the lights and the traffic behind and reached the desert, they slipped down to the lowest altitude at which Matt or Jon had ever flown—about seventy-five feet above the ground.

And at that height the Navy pilots accelerated to their 168mph cruising speed and raced through the darkness, SEALs with assault rifles sitting in each doorway, feet dangling outside, and strapped in, left and right. In the lead helicopter Matt was peering through his green-tinted night-goggles when he saw up ahead a hard black line in the desert floor.

At least he thought it was a hard black line, but it was harder than that. "Holy shit!" breathed the Echo Team leader, "TELEPHONE WIRES!"

And he yelled at the top of his lungs, futilely against the howl of the turbos: "BANK RIGHT! ... CLIMB RIGHT NOW!"

He recalled, "I doubt that I called it, the pilot would have done it anyway. But that Seahawk lurched sideways and up. I nearly fell out, and I saw the wires pass right under us.

"The other two helos were staggered at the left echelon, a couple of hundred yards apart, and they climbed too, over the wires. That would have done it, right? If we'd all turned a cartwheel in the middle of the desert and ended up upside down on the sand! Guess we'd planned for every crisis except that—getting brought down by the local phone company."

Regardless, they pressed on, with the huge Seahawk rotors swirling up a sandstorm below them as they hurtled above the flat wilderness of Iraq, where not even Bedouin tribes spend much time these days.

Staring at the charts in the TOC was one thing. But out here in the real world, where it's really happening, none of the SEALs could dismiss the thought that somewhere down below them in the darkness some tribesman was leaning against his camel and phoning Al-Asawi: "Sir, I have just witnessed three of those American airplanes with no wings flying right over my goatherds, and they're heading straight for you ..."

Worse things have happened. One of the great dreads of US Special Forces involved with the War on Terror has always been betrayal by local people, who almost all have cell phones. It was three mountain goat herders who finished Operation Red Wings in Afghanistan in 2005, in the worst day ever for a US Black Operation.

Everyone learned from that, and these pilots transporting Echo Platoon were taking a few wide sweeps, not making a dead straight line for the al-Qaeda compound. Nonetheless, these tribesmen are sure footed and enormously cunning, and they know this land better than any Westerner could ever understand.

Matt and his men may have been well under the radar, but they sure as hell were not above suspicion, not to some desert nomad being scared half to death by six turbo-shaft engines screaming above his head in the middle of the night, shattering the quiet of these biblical lands.

None of the doorway gunners saw anything for the next twenty-five minutes, at which point the pilots assessed they were "ten klicks out"—that's military speak (one klick equals one thousand meters or one kilometer—or .62 of a mile).

So the pilot now assessed they were 6.2 miles out from the target zone. He immediately dialed down the engines, slowing for the landing, and everyone heard the scream of the rotors subside and the so-familiar sound of a Navy helicopter coming into a flight deck, the turbo's lower-tone *BOM-BOM-BOM*.

Carefully they edged down toward the sand, with the pilots letting the landing wheels gently touch down on the surprisingly hard surface before releasing the full eight-ton weight of the Seahawk to settle on the desert floor. In that instant Matt and his gunners hit the release button and charged out of the helicopters, M-4 rifles ready to spit fire.

They took up defensive formation, armed to the teeth, surrounding the aircraft. Any enemy making any kind of advance on those Navy helicopters had approximately four seconds to live. The on-board machine gunners were at their posts, fingers on the trigger until the helicopters took off, rising instantly in the same split second the last man vacated the aircraft and took formation.

Out there on the sand, for several minutes, no one moved, the dust died down, and the night seemed to grow darker. The navigation Team, led by Petty Officer Eric, went into a huddle, checking compass bearing, GPS, maps, and diagrams. Jason and Rob, who would both walk in column two, listened carefully as their communications controller, Carl (call-sign Hammer Zero-Two), tuned into their close air support, which was currently flying a couple of miles above them (they hoped).

This was Boeing's AC-130/U Gunship, known in the trade as Spooky, a one hundred–foot long, heavily armed warplane with four turbo-prop engines. It's capable of swooping in from nowhere and raking surgical fire into a target from its side-firing weapons, all of which are integrated with sophisticated sensor, navigation, and fire-control systems.

The sight of Spooky coming in for the kill is extremely bad news for all illegal combatants who might have raised a hand or a gun against the United States of America. The AC-130 packs an enormous amount of firepower that would crush and devastate any enemy.

And they're excellent in the desert. Spooky played hell with Iraqi troops on the ground during Operation Iraqi Freedom, New Dawn, and Enduring Freedom, often in direct support of US troops engaged with enemy forces.

The onboard infrared sensor and radar systems allow it to identify anything, any place, any time. It can attack two targets simultaneously. Should Carl so desire, big Spooky would be right there, if necessary, to pour in devastating area-saturation gunfire.

Everyone hoped this would not be necessary, as the summoning of the gunship would inevitably mean that a vastly superior force had pinned them down, that they had suffered casualties, and that Al-Isawi had probably gotten loose.

The idea was to move in fast and silently locate the target and then grab him with maximum force and minimum fuss. Nonetheless, Air Comms Chief Carl swiftly had his frequencies tuned in on a direct line to Spooky's flight command, ground to air, and they would stay in touch throughout the night while the gunship flew its holding pattern high above them.

The second radio would keep Carl in constant communication with the two SEAL assault Teams, and he would walk in between the two columns, with Sam and Lieutenant Jimmy, the overall officer commanding.

And now they ordered the Iraqi SWAT to take their places in both columns, and still they did not mention the name of their quarry. They also never mentioned the fact that they were headed to a highly classified area. Matt and Rob, the two column leaders, were both nearly certain no coalition forces had ever been out here before. Certainly no Americans had ever been inside the compound, where the latest intel still confirmed Al-Isawi was definitely in residence.

Out on the left the column-two recce man, Jon, began to move well forward of the main group, walking softly into the dark, all alone, wearing his night-vision goggles, with his assault rifle ready and his radio tuned for instant contact with the leaders.

You need steel nerves for this. And every last sense of the big recce man from Virginia was heightened because of the quiet, because of the plain and obvious danger, and because of the unknown. If there's a booby trap, trip wire, small minefield, ambush, or volley of gunfire designed to protect the infamous Al-Isawi, then Jonathan Keefe, son of Tom and Dawn, brother of Tommy, would be the first man to die, right out there on the left flank, all alone.

Out in front of the right-hand column walked Eric. Like Jon, he stepped carefully across the rough sandy ground, peering through the green images of his night-goggles, listening for the slightest sound to betray an enemy. Like Jon, Eric was all alone, segregated from the main assault columns. But he was always within shouting range in case of an emergency.

Behind him, Matt McCabe, carrying the breacher's industrial gear and with his rifle angled forward, led the assault column, followed by his Iraqi SWAT and, in the center, Carl, Sam, and Lieutenant Jimmy, all with their separate tasks, two of them murmuring into the radios.

For more than an hour, under the heavy assault gear, they marched softly across these outer reaches of the Syrian Desert, and as they pressed on, the sand beneath their combat boots seemed to become deeper, no longer hard packed. And the going subsequently got tougher. Jon later said, "It was like moon dust, or snow, and we were sinking in. Hell! It slowed us down."

But then, as they came within a mile of their objective, the ground hardened up. Out in front Jon and Eric were now crossing very rough ground, studded with what looked like bomb craters, like a testing site for army ordnance. And all around Jon and Eric could see wrecked hardware, hunks of metal, smashed trucks, and shells.

"No one," said Jon, "could have reached any other conclusion. This was either an al-Qaeda training camp or a scrapyard. The military decision had to be the former."

And right then a fast message came in from Spooky's crew, high above, watching every move, their eyes in the sky. There was a suspicious car approaching the SEAL patrol, driving across the sand in defiance of the government's all-embracing curfew in this part of Iraq.

Carl came across on the inner-squad radio: *"HAMMER TWO! There's a car two hundred to three hundred yards away coming straight toward us. Find concealment and stand by."*

Moments later some wreck of an automobile came bumping and squeaking straight past them, pretty slow and utterly suspicious. But the driver saw nothing as the SEALs hunkered down in this al-Qaeda junkyard, remaining as deathly still and silent as only SEALs can.

They watched its dusty wake fade off into the night, and then they pressed on forward, into Arab territory in which Jon and Eric needed to be even more careful. They each called their Team leaders and reported they were almost certainly on the outskirts of a terrorist stronghold, a real no-go area. And now they were walking on eggshells, aware that if the two lines of assault troops had been sighted, they could expect opposition.

Slowly they made their way across the jagged approaches to what was an obvious al-Qaeda stronghold. And right there Jon realized they were being watched—not by Iraqi terrorists but by dogs, maybe twenty or thirty of them, surrounding him on all sides, intermittently barking.

Petty Officer Keefe understood that if they attacked, he would be obliged to open fire, and he fervently hoped that if he shot and killed a couple, the others might run. If they didn't, well, that was big trouble and would constitute a total uproar out here in the pitch dark, face to face with a pack of junkyard dogs.

"That was just about the nastiest moment so far," he recalled. "But they were standing off, maybe ten or fifteen yards away, and just barking a bit. I kept going, and none of them wanted to come much closer. But it was real creepy. Some of them were big, like German Shepherds. You could see their eyes glinting."

Jon called back and alerted the Team, but he decided to ignore the canine menace. And up ahead both SEAL point men could now see a line of sand dunes that had been dug and shaped into the outer defenses of a fortified camp.

Through his night-vision optics Jon could now see tall guard towers on the corners. And right now he could not see whether they were manned. He and Eric fanned out and crouched through the dunes until they reached a massive barbed-wire fence, rolled up like the post and wire in front of the German trenches on the Somme in 1915.

They cut the wires and flattened them, creating a gap through which the SEALs could enter. They both recalled making an extra large gap especially for the giant SEAL, Rob. Jon recalls that it still wasn't that pretty watching the man-mountain from Pennsylvania bulldoze his way through between the spikes.

By now both the recce men were certain the guard towers were not occupied, and in a soft voice Jon called in the two assault columns. He stood guard at the gap in the wire until Matt and Rob arrived.

At this point the hot, oppressive cloud-cover was beginning to part, and the moon was rising high above the desert. Seeking the darkest spots, Jon and Eric once more went forward in front of the main group, crossing a perimeter road and heading for a long group of spaced concrete buildings that could have been houses or even low square bunkers, and these formed a defensive line.

In any event Jon and Eric had no idea who was inside them and certainly not who might be looking out. Once more, they crouched low and slipped silently past, finally swinging right to come in between two buildings and through the central walkway into what looked like a small run-down US town. The streets were paved but potholed. There were street lights, some of which were switched on. It was just one of those regular, shabby, Arab townships, more like "the projects" in some fading US-city ghetto.

Jon and Eric hit the radios and once more called in the assault Teams. Deep in the shadows they aimed a pinpoint flashlight at a diagram drawn from a recent satellite image. They checked the buildings they had prenumbered for this very moment of arrival.

Matt led his troops around the corner and joined the recce men in the shadows. Rob brought his Team around right afterward, and the mission's forward commanders took a long look at the geography. All of the buildings had a number, and the ones that mattered were eight and nine. In one of those was the (hopefully) sleeping Al-Isawi.

"Remember, guys," whispered Matt, "they want this maniac alive. So don't, for Christ's sake, shoot him. Not unless you have to."

Right now the SEALs took up position. Jon and Eric, the first men into the outside perimeter of the compound, identified the correct building, locked down on it with rifles leveled, and immediately summoned the assault Team to move up into the critical ground in front of the terrorist stronghold. Lieutenant Jason, with his men already on high alert in the vital blocking positions deep in the shadows, was ready to deal with any threat while the assault Team went in to snatch the most dangerous and wanted man in the Middle East.

Matt and Rob swung off to the right and approached the apartment buildings through a line of bushes—staying low and out of sight of any possible guards in the windows. The dogs were still around, but they were not barking much. And now the assault group closed ranks, moving forward in a tight formation. A stone staircase separated buildings eight and nine, but the intel had stressed that Al-Isawi was in the ground-floor apartment in one of these two buildings.

Matt took the one on the right and Rob headed left, both carrying sledgehammers. And still no one had raised any kind of alarm. Both Team leaders gave the signal to halt, and together they slammed into the doors with the sledges. The noise was shattering, and Matt gave the door one more stupendous thump, and it cannoned inward.

The Echo Platoon leader charged in, conscious of movement on his left. He detailed his troops to secure the apartment as they went, surgically, methodically, like all SEAL assaults. And the first place was a big communal bedroom set behind a couple of stone pillars, with possibly a dozen sleeping Iraqis on the floor.

To the right was a kitchen, and Iraqi SWATs assisted the SEALs as they stood guard, assault rifles raised. Matt went straight ahead until he reached two closed doors, one left, one right. He took the left one and, with a pile driver of a mule kick, almost ripped it off its hinges.

He ducked back to avoid the possible volley of machine gunfire or even a booby-trap bomb, and then he crashed his way into the bedroom. Flat on the floor, on a mattress, was a tall male figure with a woman beside him. Next to her was a child.

It was dark, but Matt could see a semiautomatic pistol next to the man's right hand. And he rammed his own rifle one inch from the face of the half-asleep figure. This was potential history, and Matt swung around to his Iraqi interpreter, snapping a command and, only half-joking: "Gimme the Arabic words for 'make my day'!"

He ordered him to stand and, to his interpreter: "Tell him to get up right now, and get the cuffs on him."

By now the woman was screaming, and the daughter was shouting. Matt ordered two Iraqis to remove them. Then he slung his rifle around his back, took out his loaded pistol, and stared hard at the handcuffed Iraqi. The height was right—tall for a tribesman. Slim build. That was right too. He pulled out the pictures, and in the gloom it more or less confirmed the identification. But there was one more step.

"Get him back on the floor," ordered Matt, "face down." There were three more Iraqi SWATs in the bedroom by now, and Matt told them to hold the prisoner still.

Then he swiftly knelt down and grabbed the fingers of the man's left hand. Sure enough, the little finger was partly missing.

Matt, his adrenalin pumping, had his knee rammed into the spine of the most-feared terrorist in the Middle East, the Butcher of Fallujah. Echo Platoon's assault Team had captured the mass murderer Ahmad Hashim Abd Al-Isawi.

And Matt flicked on his radio and uttered the code word, which signified that the SEALs' five-year-long search was over.

Exactly forty seconds had passed since he had kicked in the door. "*JACKPOT!*" called Matt.

By this time the initial chaos in the house was gone. The assault Teams were moving quickly, and they'd secured every room, lining up the other residents, separating women and children in one room from males in other sections of the apartment. Military-aged men were grouped together under firm SEAL security.

Matt took charge of the search of one bedroom, and two SEALs held Al-Isawi at gunpoint. Outside there was a blue truck that the SEALs commandeered and disabled. Out where the SEALs had set up a defensive position, four other prisoners were taken because they were "unknown and suspect."

The prisoners had not been harmed—just grabbed, cuffed, and told to shut up. A couple of them found it difficult to comply with this latter instruction, so Jason's guys taped their mouths shut, and now they were under guard. The good news was that no one had yet fired a shot at the SEALs.

Rob arrived with the other assault column and took over the apartment, while Matt took three Iraqis and crossed to the opposite bedroom, the one where he had not caved in the door. He entered and discovered that two of his Team had established the three residents as Al-Isawi's mother and two of his cousins.

He ordered them out, into the holding area, and personally conducted a thorough search of the room, which yielded two bundles of US currency, totaling $6,000. Each bill had a little blue tracking stamp on it, which suggested Al-Isawi's henchmen had somehow stolen it from a bank. Either that or it was counterfeit.

There were also several passports in his name, plus a whole screed of terrorist data, maps, plans, and notebooks. They searched every inch of the place, confiscating computerized maps, hard drives, and documents showing Al-Isawi's movements across the desert and into various known al-Qaeda enclaves.

The "evidence" showed incontrovertible proof that Al-Isawi had been in and out of Syria on a near-weekly basis. And that would be a relief for the SEAL intel Team, as they had always suspected the terrorist commander had been up to no good in Syria but had never quite been able to prove it. No one knew where Al-Isawi was half the time. He could, it seemed, vanish into thin air at any time in Iraq. Right now Matt and his boys knew where he'd been.

"It was," said Matt, "the perfect home profile for a terrorist mastermind who was on the run. Everything in that apartment was shady, not to mention this bearded killer who we'd taken alive, without any violence to anyone. Pretty good job, right?"

By this time the SEALs had fixed the lights, and for the first time they could actually see Al-Isawi's face. Again Matt pulled out the photographs, and the likeness was definite. They had the right man. No more doubt about that, especially with the missing pinkie.

At this point several of the Iraqi SWATs had turned a whiter shade of pale as they finally realized who they had come for. It was a pretty darn good shock for them. This was a killer who would go after the families of Iraqi officials who crossed him. Matt's Iraqis knew that face all too well.

"Several of them really freaked out," said Matt. "They suddenly wanted nothing to do with this operation. They were scared even to let this Al-Isawi character see their faces. Not once they realized who it was we'd grabbed."

The Iraqis were so nervous about their prisoner that Matt ordered someone to put a sack over the Iraqi captive's head just so he could not see or identify anyone. It was this fear of recognition that was bothering the ISWAT guys and the police, several of whom expressed fear for their wives and children. Privately Matt thought Al-Isawi would never walk free again, but under the prevailing rules he now had to hand that prisoner over to the Iraqis.

It was 0300 when Matt and his SWATs finally marched the hooded prisoner out of the apartment, ignoring the hysterical shouting of Al-Isawi's wife, who was loudly demanding the $6,000 back, screaming that they needed that money.

Al-Isawi seemed to accept his fate. He walked quietly, with his cuffed hands behind his back, guided by his Iraqi guards. But this was a highly dangerous part of the operation. Somehow they had to get back into the shadows, and Jon was aware of many figures in the dark windows of the apartments that surrounded the assault group on all sides. They were two hundred yards minimum inside that barbed-wire fence, and Lieutenant Jimmy reported back their exposed position to base command.

There was now a sense of urgency. No one wanted to be out there in front of those plainly hostile buildings with daylight approaching.

Lieutenant Jimmy ordered the guys to reform the patrol. The blocking positions collapsed back into the main group. They took the head count—no one was missing. And Jon and Eric led them all out of there, picking their way through the dark, aiming for the safe areas where they knew no danger lurked.

The patrol was now on high alert, because whoever the hell lived in this godforsaken outpost obviously knew about their presence now. The SEALs constantly looked back, with their M-4 rifles raised, sweeping across the facades of the old buildings to send a clear message that one false move from anyone would cause them to open fire. The fact that someone may get shot in the back as they left, Jon recalled, "kinda concentrated the mind."

But no one dared to raise a trigger finger against the SEAL raiders. And they all kept going, with Carl speaking continually into his radio, summoning the helicopters in for the extract. And now, as they crept between the low stone buildings, they could hear the howl of the approaching rotors.

The pilots, who'd been in a private SEAL stack high above the ops area, were coming in, and Carl was talking them down to land right in front of the sand dunes that guarded the western approach to the al-Qaeda stronghold.

Echo Platoon kept moving forward, headed for the open ground beyond the road. Out in front Matt and Rob were coming through the dunes at a run, staying close to the Iraqis who were hauling Al-Isawi through the wire and over the uneven ground. Everyone else was following them.

By the time they cleared the sand hills, the three Seahawks were prepped and ready to come in. And when they did so, it was impossible to hear anything above the din of the turbos. But SEALs do not need to talk. Everyone knew what to do, and everyone knew where his designated spot was on board the aircraft. They literally piled into the helicopters, with the Iraqis holding Al-Isawi face down on the floor.

Matt was the last man to board, and he took up his position and strapped himself in to the open doorway of the lead helicopter, with his legs dangling outside, rifle poised, night-vision goggles on. They were ready to take off exactly sixty seconds from the moment Matt and Rob had come running in from the dunes.

The three Seahawks clattered into the night sky, reigniting the unimaginable dust storm below. The noise was shattering: "Probably coulda heard it in Baghdad," Matt later said.

On the return journey there was little need for extreme low-level flying. The al-Qaeda enclave had shown no signs of resistance. There was certainly no radar sweeping the approaches, and there had been no rocket attacks or even heavy machine gunfire.

And so they climbed higher and were swiftly beyond the range of anything that might be aimed at them. Each pilot made an easterly course toward Fallujah, heading back to the LZ beyond Camp Schwedler. This was a simple *mission accomplished*. And no one expected special praise.

Behind Matt was the inert, handcuffed figure of the Butcher of Fallujah, a cruel and ruthless jihadist who hated the West but whose reign of terror was over. The SEALs were bringing him in, under guard, stripped now of his weapons and his menace.

Matt could have shot him. Al-Isawi's right hand had been mere inches from his gun, and for most people this would have been a life-threatening situation. But skilled US intel agents wanted to talk to this character in order to interrogate him for information that would significantly decrease the future effectiveness of the al-Qaeda threat.

And Matt—along with the Virginia freestyler, the Georgian rocket scientist, the Penn State lineman, and the rest—had carried everything out strictly by the book, as was only to be expected. There had been intimidation but not one moment of violence. SEAL commanders demand everlasting discipline.

The pilots kept the east-west desert road to Jordan well to their port side all the way across the Iraqi wilderness. And it was still dark when they came in low over Lake Habbinaya and flew on down into their landing zone, right outside the gates of Camp Schwedler. The Team 10 truck drivers were there to meet them, and the SEALs unloaded their heavy baggage, including Al-Asawi.

Lieutenant Jimmy, the officer in overall command, supervised the transfer of everyone back to base, where the prisoner was taken under Iraqi escort to the temporary holding jail cell, which was, in truth, a huge metal box, so big it was really a small room. And right in there they took the Butcher of Fallujah, still cuffed and hooded, and sat him down in a chair.

He would have a four-hour wait on the Camp Schwedler compound, because the Iraqi police, who were supposed to take the captive right away, had contacted the base and said they could not get there until 0800.

At this point Ahmad Hashim Abd Al-Isawi came under the control and custody of a young Navy master-at-arms 3rd class (MA3) of two years experience, Brian Westinson, whose job was now to stay right there and guard that cell no matter what. He was effectively in charge of one of the most high-value individuals ever captured by the US Special Forces, a killer whose reputation rivaled that of Abu Musab al-Zarqawi and Sheik Abdul Rahman.

Meanwhile the SEALs went off to shower and change before reporting to the debriefing room for the standard discussion, presided over by Lieutenant Jimmy with Sam Gonzales, the senior petty officer in backup position. Every SEAL who had taken part in the mission was in there, and they went carefully over the lessons learned. It took only thirty minutes, because Objective Amber had been very nearly flawless, especially as no one on either side had been hurt, but the objective had been achieved.

In the terms of the United States Navy SEALs, it was picture perfect. Echo Platoon was proud of their conduct that night, and this applied especially to the two forward point men, Jon and Eric, who had plotted the way into a secret al-Qaeda stronghold, and to the assault Team leaders, Rob and Matt—particularly Matt, who'd led the charge and carried out the actual capture of the Butcher.

No one said anything, but these guys were going to get decorated for this one.

Lieutenant Jimmy formally thanked them curtly. And the night workers of Echo Platoon dispersed to find some breakfast. Jon and

Matt commandeered one of the four-wheelers, which they all used to get around the base, and headed for the galley. On the way, however, they passed Sam, who wanted a ride.

Picking up Sam proved a serious roadblock in their early morning objective of scrambled eggs, bacon, hash browns, muffins, and orange juice. Jon in particular, who had an appetite like a mountain lion, was slightly vexed, but Sam was the senior enlisted man on the base, respected at all times.

Sam, who had played a critical role in Objective Amber, wanted to pay a short visit to this young master-at-arms and his prisoner, just to check that all was well. So all three of them went, with Jon, starving hungry, steering the four-wheeler painfully past the galley and on to the big metal holding cell.

When they drove into the area, they noticed that Jason and Carl had both been down to take a look at their prize prisoner, but the first thing they really observed was that Brian Westinson was not at his post. They each took a glance at the prisoner around the dividing wall. He was still hooded and cuffed and in his chair. But there was no Westinson. There was no one watching the most dangerous man in the Middle East.

And the three SEALs later said that this breach in discipline frankly shocked them. The responsibility of a naval master-at-arms implies an onerous responsibility. He is, in effect, some kind of super-military policeman.

At least he's supposed to be. The man (or woman) with that MA rank must be a security specialist, expert in force protection, particularly antiterrorism. He is required to exercise physical security and law enforcement "on land and at sea." He's only a naval rating, but his area of duty includes discipline. He belongs to a military police force.

The MA insignia is one single star, like a Wild West sheriff. Westinson, on this hot night, was Camp Shwelder's Wyatt Earp. And he was not at his post.

But after just a few moments he was back, talking outside to Paddy, the SEALs' chief medic on the mission. Here in the timeline there is some confusion, with various slightly conflicting accounts of precisely what took place.

But the man under most criticism for his role in these events was undoubtedly MA3 Brian Westinson. Indeed, both Matt and Jon remember quite clearly that Senior Petty Officer Sam Gonzales said to the MA, very sharply, "What are you doing? Not at your post?"

In the interest of absolute fairness, this narrative will quote from Westinson's own sworn statement made four weeks later and, apparently, regarded as truthful.

By any standards, for the leading law enforcement officer involved, Brian Westinson was not precisely on his game. When the experienced medic Paddy was conducting his medical screening of the prisoner, it turned out that Westinson did not have the necessary forms to be completed.

So Westinson left the area and "walked to my room to look to see if I had the paperwork." Result: he did not, he could not find it. So he walked back, and then Paddy left to gather up the correct forms at his clinic.

Westinson's statement continued: "This was one of two periods where I left the screening facility. When I returned [Carl and Jason] were inside the screening facility. They left shortly after I returned. I left one more time to put my rifle in my room, and to talk to the Intelligence officer about the processing of the detainee.

"When I returned, I saw [Paddy] standing outside, working on his medical paperwork. I looked in and saw [Sam Gonzales, Matt, and Jon] standing near the detainee. I walked in and stood next to them."

In the statement Westinson identifies each man with his rank and proper surname, which this narrative avoids. Also he does not make clear the time and distance between the screening facility and his room. However, no one disputed that Westinson was not at his post when the three SEALs, Sam, Matt, and Jon, turned up on the four-wheeler.

"Look," said Matt, recalling the events of that day, "I didn't write the Geneva Convention, or even the US Military Rules of Engagement. But there are a couple of things I know for sure. ... There is a desk in the room outside the detainee holding cell, behind a wall. The duty master-at-arms is supposed to be sitting right there at that desk, with his rifle, guarding the prisoner. An HVI is not supposed to be left alone at any time, for obvious reasons.

"I cannot understand what Westinson is blathering about. Can't find the papers he *must* have ready for the medic after the screening? ... Then he swears in a statement he went home for a second time to put his rifle back in his room! I mean, what is it with Brian? The rifle is supposed to be with him, at that desk at all times. Me and the guys just risked our friggin' lives to capture this mass murderer, and he's wandering around the base in some kind of a daze.

"By the way, Brian's room is situated at the way far end from the holding cell, in the back line, against the high outer wall, which I guess took him about seven minutes round trip, each time he left, depending on how much time he spent looking, first for his papers and then for the rifle. What kind of a guard is that?"

There is no dispute that Sam, Jon, and Matt's visit to the holding cell was very brief. Matt says between twenty and thirty seconds, no more. When Westinson re-entered the area Sam checked that he was okay, because this senior noncommissioned SEAL officer understood that the nineteen-year-old Brian had never been in sole charge of a prisoner before this—any prisoner, that is, never mind one of this obvious importance. Brian's boss had recently departed.

"Jon and I were there because of Sam's rigid sense of duty, with a bit of curiosity thrown in," said Matt. "We would not have bothered if Sam had not been hitching a ride. And right after that brief stop the three of us left together and drove back to the galley for breakfast. I mean, we'd been up all night. It was just getting light."

It's a SEAL tradition that unless some form of war breaks out, men who have returned from a night mission are given the chance to have a long sleep, perhaps from 0600 to 1600. Kidnapping armed terrorist commanders is tiring work.

And by 0600 on this Wednesday morning, the men of Echo Platoon had crashed thankfully into their bunks before the sun rose above the Iraqi desert. No one had any difficulties sleeping the deep, untroubled slumber of the brave and the just.

Two hours later, however, an unscripted part of the program came blundering into their lives.

Every SEAL who'd taken part in Objective Amber was awakened shortly after 0800 and ordered to report immediately to Danny's recreation room for a full muster, over which Lieutenant Jimmy would preside.

Matt knew immediately this was important. No one awakens an entire platoon of Navy SEALs who'd been up all night unless there had been some kind of a drama.

The SEAL assault leader from Perrysburg knew it could be bad. What he did not know was that the roof was about to fall in on his entire world.

5

—

A PRESUMPTION
OF GUILT

Matt had run a textbook-perfect attack, brought the prisoner in alive and unharmed for interrogation, and was now about to be pilloried by the US Navy for cruelty! "Holy shit," said Matt.

The seven principal US Navy SEALs who had stormed the desert hideaway of Ahmad Hashim Abd Al-Isawi came striding through the Camp Schwedler compound on the double that morning. They walked alone, each man confident that his own conduct throughout Objective Amber had been exemplary. Not one of the seven had the slightest idea what was going on.

One by one they reached Danny's recreation room and sat down opposite a surprisingly grim-looking Lieutenant Jimmy. Danny's, normally a place to hang out and relax, watch television, or play video games, was no place for games right now. Lieutenant Jimmy's angry face said it all. He had always been a balanced, calm man, and right now, according to Matt McCabe, "I'd never seen him that furious. Jimmy was seriously ticked off."

While the Echo assault force had been dead to the world, there had been an unfolding set of truly grotesque circumstances. Shortly before 0800 the Iraqi police had come for Al-Isawi to transport him to their detention center in the nearby city of Al-Karmah, eleven miles north-east of Fallujah.

When Lieutenant Jimmy went to remove the prisoner from the holding cell there was blood on his robe and his lower lip. It instantly became clear to the SEAL lieutenant that the al-Qaeda man was claiming prisoner abuse, that someone had knocked him about.

His bloody appearance should not have been a shock, as the tactic of self-inflicted injuries appears to be a standard ploy in the infamous al-Qaeda instruction book, the *Manchester Manual,* discovered in the year 2000 and so named because it was found in an al-Qaeda "safe house" in England's great northwestern city and Muslim stronghold.

Not only did bin Laden's senior operators write it; it also still stands as the definitive handbook on how a jihadist is expected to wage his holy war, including religious justifications and many quotations from the Koran.

The eighteen-chapter manual had instructed almost every captive in Guantanamo Bay, giving instructions on how to overthrow all "godless regimes" and replace them with the regimes guided by the teachings of Islam. It teaches terrorists about spying and gathering intel; kidnapping enemy personnel, documents, secrets, and arms; assassinating enemy personnel; freeing "brothers" who have been captured by the enemy; and blasting and destroying places of amusement, immorality, and sin—plus embassies and bridges.

Its most significant section, however, deals with the required actions of the brothers after capture. The *Manual* orders them to insist on proving that state security inflicted torture on them. They must "always complain of mistreatment or torture while in prison."

The pure deviousness of this always frustrated former US Defense Secretary Donald H. Rumsfeld. "These detainees are trained to lie," he stated. "They are trained to say they were tortured…their training manual says so."

And that's not all their training manual decreed. In its opening pages were the words: "The confrontation we are calling for knows the dialogue of bullets, the ideals of assassination, bombing and destruction. And the diplomacy of the cannon and machine-gun."

Ahmad Hashim Abd Al-Isawi was a disciple of al-Qaeda, and like the rest of his kind, he lived by the *Manchester Manual*. And right now he was trying to prove he was mistreated while in US captivity. That much was obvious to anyone. All he needed was a lawyer.

Lieutenant Jimmy, Echo Platoon's officer-in-charge (OIC), found himself right in the middle of a dangerous controversy. He had observed the prisoner's lip injury and the blood on his robes, and he had provided a new dishdasha (a long usually white robe traditionally worn by men in the Middle East) before handing him over to the Iraqi police along with the $6,000 Matt had confiscated.

Lieutenant Jimmy had checked that the chief medic, Paddy, had given the detainee a clean bill of health after screening him inside the holding cell, and he'd awakened everyone who could possibly shed any light on the matter.

By 0830 every Team 10 SEAL who had laid eyes on Al-Isawi since he was escorted to the holding cell was called into Danny's, including the rookie master-at-arms.

What Lieutenant Jimmy wanted now was answers. If any one of his SEALs had whacked the Butcher, he wanted to know, because he, Jimmy, was obliged to write and then file a military report on precisely how Al-Isawi came to have blood on his dishdasha—blood and an injury that the Iraqi police had plainly seen.

And he knew his SEALs well. They are inherently unable to lie. They are too well versed in the one rule of the US Navy that is hammered into slabs of polished marble, the one rule that will cause any midshipman to be thrown out of the Naval Academy that day: lying cannot be tolerated.

From the youngest age the issue of truth is paramount. Serving combat officers in a warship that has been hit and burning cannot do anything for anyone except report the truth. There can be no versions, withholdings, or varnishing of the truth. It has to be the plain, simple, shining truth. Otherwise no one knows what the hell to do.

Navy SEALs, equally with battle commanders, have this stamped onto their hearts during BUD/S. No SEAL would dream of lying. All of them innately believe, regardless of whether they admit it, that the

wrath of God would somehow strike them down for lying to an officer or, indeed, to anyone who wears the Dark Blue.

Simply stated, they would be too darned scared. But in the US Navy
fear is not the sole guardian of honesty. The creed of truth at all times
is a part of naval law. It's the bedrock of the silent service. No matter
the misdemeanor, every serving officer knows that when he asks, he
will be told the truth. It's in the DNA of every one of his men.

SEALs, as they must, believe themselves superior to all enemies. For
any one of them to stoop to commit the naval sin of lying would be
to break some kind of a sacred trust. Lieutenant Jimmy knew one
thing above all else: when he asked his men whether anyone had
punched Al-Isawi in the mouth or anywhere else, he would receive an
honest answer.

This knowledge did not, however, lighten his mood. Because, as the
officer in command of Objective Amber, he was empowered to investigate but obliged to report. Senior command would come straight to
him for an explanation of the possible abuse of the prisoner while under the care of SEAL Team 10's Echo Platoon.

Lieutenant Jimmy called the informal meeting to order and briefly
outlined the situation: Al-Isawi had come out of his cell with blood
around his mouth and on his robe, with a minor cut inside his lower
lip.

"Who knows anything about this?" he said. "Because the CO is going to want answers. Prisoner abuse, as you all know, is taken very,
very seriously around here."

The officer gazed around the room. Gazed at his brave and dedicated SEALs, and it was immediately apparent that no one had the
slightest idea what he was talking about. Certainly not the principal
outsider, MA3 Brian Westinson, the duty guard and a non-SEAL who
Matt said was making it clear that he saw nothing, heard nothing, and
knew nothing.

"Brian also admitted he had been absent from his post," said Matt.
"Which, despite the plain implication of wrongdoing, opened up a
window of opportunity—that someone else had sneaked in there
while Brian was absent and attacked Al-Isawi."

But the rest of the SEALs seemed merely bewildered. As indeed was Lieutenant Jimmy, who would very soon confirm that his men had never shown any behavioral issues while under his command and that they were all disciplined professionals.

In that room there was an unmistakable feeling of disbelief that any one of these trusted, supremely responsible servicemen would have done such a thing—and then stood right here and told a barefaced lie to their officer in command, right in front of everyone.

"There was something weird about the whole thing," recalls Jon Keefe. "I just could not imagine any of the guys I worked real close with—you know, Matt, Sam, Eric, Rob, or Jason, and certainly not Carlton Milo Higbie the Twelfth—could have possibly behaved in that way. For what?"

(Jon provided himself with endless amusement by constantly increasing and varying the birth numbers after Carl's name. This was, however, probably the final time he would ever find anything remotely funny about anything even distantly connected with the case of "Who Punched the Handcuffed Butcher of Fallujah?")

No one could help. And for Lieutenant Jimmy this was a matter of extreme concern. Even after the meeting was ended and some of the SEALs stood around talking informally, the officer was given no clues. No one could remember anything that might have shed light.

Lieutenant Jimmy and Leading Petty Officer Sam Gonzales could not even help themselves. In the past hour they had escorted Al-Isawi to the handover and had both noticed that Ahmad Hashim's behavior had changed dramatically when he came in sight of the Iraqi police. He suddenly started moaning and acting as though he were in pain, spitting blood from his mouth.

But this only deepened the mystery. Had someone really punched him? Or had he just braced himself and then bitten his own lip, more or less in accordance with the teachings of the *Manchester Manual*?

At this point it was obvious that Lieutenant Jimmy was most seriously on the hook. Because it was he to whom the high command would look for some kind of an explanation. Any kind. But something. And right now he had nothing.

And the principal military powers in Iraq were still neurotic over the worst military scandal to involve the United States for years: the outrages at nearby Abu Ghraib Jail (2004–2006), involving a whole string of incidents—human rights violations in the form of physical, psychological, and sexual abuse, with reports of torture, rape, sodomy, and homicide of prisoners.

The US Army's Criminal Investigation Command report had led to soldiers of the 320th military police battalion being charged under the Code of Military Justice with prisoner abuse. And the entire catastrophe burst into public awareness with a spate of national television programs and magazine articles.

It made the US military look pretty bad in front of its own people, but it raised hell among the public and was probably the United States' military public relations disaster of the century. The Defense Department removed seventeen soldiers and officers from duty, and they charged eleven soldiers with dereliction of duty, maltreatment of prisoners, and aggravated assault and battery.

Eleven soldiers were convicted by courts-martial, dishonorably discharged, and sentenced to military prison, one of them for ten years. The CO of all Iraqi detention facilities was reprimanded for dereliction of duty and demoted from the rank of brigadier general to colonel.

Never had the US armed forces suffered such humiliation. And the notorious Abu Ghraib Jail was situated a mere eighteen miles from Camp Schwedler, right on the old road to Jordan, which crosses the desert west of Baghdad and meanders across the sand, all the way to Amman.

The sprawling penal center had earned the name "House of Horrors" long before the US military gave it everlasting notoriety. But the incidents, which led to those multiple courts-martial, enraged the Arab and Muslim worlds and caused a huge upsurge in new recruitment to the al-Qaeda armies.

The new buzzword was "prisoner abuse," and the media seized upon it, with the words "Abu Ghraib" immediately following. US military commanders can deal with almost anything, including attack, war, death, and mayhem. But nothing—repeat, nothing—sends them into quite a collective tailspin as the claim "prisoner abuse."

Which was why, essentially, Lieutenant Jimmy of SEAL Team 10, famous for the efficiency of its command and its training and preparation, was right now on the very edge of his nerves as the rumors of prisoner abuse swept through their desert camp.

Meanwhile the men of Echo Platoon were allowed to go back to bed. But not for long. After another couple of hours they were awakened again in response to a report from the Iraqi police that they could not hold the prisoner in Al-Karmah because he needed to be moved to Baghdad.

A few of the more imaginative SEALs put this down to the probable fact that the desert cops were still scared to death of Al-Isawi and everything he stood for, that he might somehow get free and come after the Iraqis' families. They probably would not want him anywhere near them and had come up with some reason to hand him back to the Americans.

Anyway, they all had to drive over to Al-Karmah and collect the prisoner. And this resulted in endless delays while the Iraqis filled out the correct forms. And during those hours, naturally, all of the $6,000 Matt had confiscated went missing somewhere in the police department.

And so the SEALs took Al-Isawi to Baghdad, to the US holding facility, and handed him over. Lieutenant Jimmy signed a similar number of forms to those required for the unconditional surrender of the German army in May 1945.

Finally they were finished and drove back to Camp Schwedler, most of them hoping never again to hear the name Ahmad Hashim Abd Al-Isawi except when someone hanged him for murder. Didn't much matter who.

There is a distinct form of bush telegraph in all military camps. Without one single announcement or phone call, the most outlandish pieces of information somehow drift around among the personnel. People seem to find things out by osmosis. Sometimes things are not even stated, but everyone still knows what's afoot. It was no different in Camp Schwedler.

Jon was possessed of a particular sensitive set of antennae that would always serve him well in combat. And by Thursday morning, September 3, he and Matt both knew something was going on. Lieutenant

Jimmy had asked for "shooter statements," which are individual accounts of Wednesday's events from everybody who had seen the Camp Schwedler detainee after his arrival at the base.

This included almost everyone, because they had all called into the holding cell to catch a glimpse of this most famous terrorist who was then under Team 10 supervision, thanks to their own efforts.

No one knew any details, and no one had read the latest reports from Baghdad. But there were rumors—as ever when dealing with al-Qaeda commanders—that wild accusations had been made, including very definite claims that the prisoner had been abused. That was all standard.

What no one knew, however, was that Ahmad Hashim Abd Al-Isawi, a member of the most flagrantly dishonest "military" organization on earth, had effectively cried *"ABUSE!"* He told US authorities he'd been badly beaten at the Camp Schwedler SEAL base. He said he'd been punched, kicked, hurled to the ground, and had his head stomped on—pounded in the face, chest, body and ribs.

Slightly contradictory to this was the fact that he did not have a mark on him. But it still put Lieutenant Jimmy in one hell of a spot. The bloodied prisoner he'd handed over had made a formal complaint accusing the SEALs of violence against him. No one—least of all Jimmy—had the slightest idea what was going on. But the words "prisoner abuse" were bouncing out of that report like a couple of whizbangs.

Officers in Baghdad, Fallujah, Ar-Ramadi, and Qatar were caucusing, and the old familiar, dreaded words and phrases were being stage whispered all over the desert: *Abu Ghraib, maltreatment, beatings, lies, lack of protection, court-martial, human rights, dereliction of duty, proper care, dishonorable discharge, demotion, loss of rank, military prison.*

There's nothing quite like those two words: "prisoner abuse." And the military, though to a far, far lesser degree than other huge organizations, is not averse to locating of a couple of decoys in order to divert blame from principal executives.

For decoys, read scapegoats—two or three guys to take the rap, that is—because the military hardly dares to claim that no one was responsible or that the prisoner was a liar. That would invite a media on-slaught, alleging a major cover-up or whitewash. And when the media goes into one of those paroxysms of self-righteous innuendo, it makes everyone look utterly dishonest.

In the case of the Battered Butcher, the high command in Iraq would not be unhappy with two or three convictions they could write off as the actions of a couple of "bad eggs"—*not at all like the honorable professionals they really are.* Which is all well and good, unless you happen to be one of the sacrificial eggs.

Still, there was no proof of any crimes being committed at Camp Schwedler. At least that's how it had seemed when the SEALs left to transport Al-Isawi. But the atmosphere was different the next day. There was something accusatory in the air, as if someone had suddenly admitted seeing something or even committed something.

Nonetheless, the SEALs, to a man, said no one had raised a finger against this Al-Isawi, and no one had seen anyone else touch him. He'd passed the medical examination without the slightest trouble, and according to the report in Baghdad, he remained unmarked. This was basically still rumor, but apparently true.

Later that Thursday afternoon, however, things took a sudden and unexpected swerve in the wrong direction. Matt, Jon, Sam, and Paddy were ordered to Camp Ramadi, home of Special Operations Task Force-West. They were ordered to leave almost immediately, and they swiftly discovered there were three vehicles going.

It was no surprise when Lieutenant Jimmy joined them, but the SEALs were all startled to see MA3 Brian Westinson also making the journey. The fact that Brian had all his bags packed and was plainly pulling out of Schwedler for good unsettled them even more.

This was all fairly obvious. What was very much under wraps was that Brian, the MA3 who at least twice had been missing from his post guarding Al-Isawi, had gone to the senior command at Schwedler and claimed that he saw Matthew McCabe punch the prisoner and knock him to the ground while he was in the holding cell.

The presence of Westinson in the same little convoy suggested that something was happening—something that concerned the "prisoner abuse" case. Because Matt, Jon, and Sam had gone into the holding cell together, Paddy had been the examining medic, and Lieutenant Jimmy had been the OIC. Westinson fitted nowhere, unless it was to do with Al-Isawi.

Matt asked Lieutenant Jimmy if he could tell them anything. But the SEAL officer would only say, "I cannot talk. But it's not good."

"At that moment I knew this was all bad," said Matt later. "But I still had no idea what we were supposed to have done. I guess I should have been worried, but I wasn't. I knew only that I had not done one wrong thing. And neither, so far as I knew, had Sam or Jon.

"None of us touched the prisoner. And none of us saw anyone else touch him. Sonofabitch had attacked himself with his wonky front teeth. Any damn fool could see that."

Anyway, they all climbed aboard the vehicles, Brian with his possessions all packed up and the three SEALs with nothing. There was little discussion on the forty-mile journey to the city of Ar-Ramadi, where there was a sizeable US military base and a special SEAL Base, Camp Shark. It was home to the square-jawed SEAL Commander Hamilton, a senior SEAL officer.

This particular naval commander was known to be an absolute stickler for the rule book, and Matt now understood that Hamilton wanted to see all three of the key operators from Objective Amber: Big Jon, who had fearlessly led them in; Matt, the assault Team leader, and Senior Petty Officer Sam, the comms expert who had handled the radio right across the ops area.

Apparently the medic, Paddy, was also required to attend. But his examination of the prisoner had revealed nothing. And all four of them were completely in the dark about what precisely they were doing in Ar-Ramadi in the middle of the night.

When they disembarked inside the camp it became clear that the young master-at-arms, Brian Westinson, was entirely separate. He gathered up his bags, assisted by a guy they did not know, and, according to Matt and Jon, disappeared into the night.

"Wherever the hell he was going," said Matt, "it was nothing to do with us."

At which point Lieutenant Jimmy advised them to hang tight and then left to speak to the commander. This took just a few minutes, and then all three SEALs plus the medic who had walked with them into the desert lair of Al-Isawi were taken two hundred yards away to the commander's office. This was a big room, adjacent to a very large, two-level TOC, about ten times the size of the one in Camp Schwedler, and bristling with flat screens, radar, and computer screens.

And in there they had their first encounter with another SEAL, Master Chief Lampard, the commander's right-hand man. The word "encounter" is used here under advisement from Matthew McCabe and Jonathan Keefe. According to both SEALs, Lampard had already made up his mind about something.

"This was no exploratory chat," says Matt. "This was us four, facing an accuser. This character had made some kind of decision, and he immediately ordered us to be stripped of our weapons, body armor, pistols, and combat knives."

Right here it should be recorded that to strip a US Navy SEAL of his armaments is almost to strip him of his birthright. These men have darn near killed themselves to earn the right to serve their country. To line them up and remove their ever-present combat gear was also to strip them of their dignity, pride, and honor.

The enormously popular hospital corpsman, Paddy, later confided, "I honestly thought all three of them might explode when that happened to them. I had never known anything like it. And none of us had yet been told what we'd done wrong. It was as if that master chief had just pronounced a death sentence on us."

And so they handed over the tools of their trade. As Matt said later: "So far as I could see, we were being accused by some kind of a nutcase and a mass murderer. But no one had yet mentioned precisely what we were alleged to have done.

"The surrender of our combat gear was tantamount to finding us guilty—guilty of something. And for us, there could have been no harsher punishment. We just stood there—me, Jon, and Sam. We were actually in shock."

Having reduced them to a lower form of life, Commander Hamilton ordered the SEALs and the medic to be escorted to a conference room, and there, in company with the master chief, he seated himself at the head of a long table. They were ordered to line up and take their places down one side while on the other sat Brian Westinson, who had suddenly reappeared.

Jon remembers Brian sitting bolt upright opposite him and wearing dark sunglasses in this gloomy room. His folded hands were clad in carbon-fiber knuckle gloves, and on his face there was a strange expression of deadly seriousness, perhaps even defiance. None of them had ever noticed that before. But then MA3 Westinson had never faced three angry Navy SEALs across a table before.

The master chief spoke first. He looked down the SEALs' side of the table and announced: "There have been allegations against the four of you concerning prisoner abuse." He did not mention who had done the alleging, but the motionless Brian was providing an unmistakable clue, sitting on the wrong side of the table, as it were, facing the senior petty officer on the base, Sam Gonzales, who, in the early hours of Wednesday morning, had demanded to know why he was not at his post.

"My advice to you is," continued the master chief, "tell the truth at all times and to cooperate. That way everything will be taken care of. We understand, as you should, that you are all innocent until proven guilty."

Which Matt and Jon both thought was pretty rich, as in the past half-hour they had been treated like common criminals and punished in a way that they believed was unthinkable—stripped even of a reasonable sense of self. In their own eyes, disgraced.

All four of them felt as though they had already been found guilty of some crime. But even now none of them knew exactly what it was.

Matt's mind raced. Every instinct was telling him to stand right up and yell back at these two comedians that he had never done one wrong thing and neither had his buddies. And if some higher authority was going to treat them like this, then someone better be ready to step up and prove their "crimes," right here and now, or shut up. "Even a terrorist has those rights," he nearly muttered.

But his brain won the battle against his heart. This was, after all, the military. And SEAL petty officers do not question commanders and master chiefs. It's all about respect for rank, and this was no place for a row. So Matt decided to shut himself up and get a grip, to stay calm and watchful. His long battlefield training was calling him from afar. Same with Jon and Sam.

Nonetheless it was a perfectly chilling experience. For the first time in their naval careers, Matt, Jon, and Sam felt a cold sense of loneliness, that there were massive forces raging against them, that men who had once seemed senior, strong, and protective were now becoming enemies, answering to a different God.

"Looking back," says Matt, "That was the moment when I suddenly sensed this was more trouble than I could deal with. I sensed they were about to charge us with some god-awful crime which we had not committed. And for the first time in my life I felt helpless. And scared."

It was by now apparent that the "victim" was this Al-Isawi, who all the SEALs had been taught for months was the Prince of Darkness himself. And Matt saw the deep irony of the situation. "I could have blown his fucking brains out," he said. "Shot him dead, right there in his apartment, since he was armed, with a record of crime and violence which would've made Genghis Khan look like Mr. Rogers."

As he says, no one would have cared or questioned his judgment. Instead, however, Matt had run a textbook-perfect attack, brought the prisoner in alive and unharmed for interrogation, and was now about to be pilloried by the US Navy for cruelty.

"Holy shit," Matt later said. Because of the events of the few minutes in that room, he now regarded himself as a military prisoner, unable to leave this building and certainly not this command area. Stripped of his weapons, he assumed, correctly, that he was banned from fulfilling his normal duties. As if in confirmation, the men were formally read their rights. But not Westinson, who, Matt decided, had enough rights already to last him a lifetime.

After that the four "prisoners" were separated, and the executive officer and a lieutenant commander took them to a conference room one by one. There they were each asked whether they were planning to call in lawyers.

Because no charges had yet been leveled at them and no one thought they had anything to defend, they all, quite independently, declined. "Our overall opinion was that since we were entirely innocent," said Matt, "to announce we wanted lawyers would, if anything, make us look guilty. So we all said no, and they very quickly made us sign papers to that effect."

The SEALs had difficulty accepting that someone was somehow trying to hang them. And what about this Lampard? Whose side was he on? Could he be believed? No one had missed his assurance in the CO's office that if they only told the truth, everything would work out.

And now they wanted full statements from everyone, and Matt and Sam had only mild reservations about this. Jon, however, had a very serious objection. "I have already given a written, truthful account of what happened. I will not write a new statement because that's dumb. They must be the same.

"I know nothing about law, but I know you are just trying to find a discrepancy. You want something new from me, and you will not get it unless I have the original statement right next to me to copy."

The big SEAL complied, with the old statement on the desk, confirming that, of course, yes, they had all briefly seen Al-Isawi in the holding cell and that no, no one had touched him or seen anyone else touch him.

Back at Schwedler, other statements had been taken from every SEAL who had wandered in to see their "celebrity detainee." And they all said more or less the same. Several of them also added that they would have been astounded if the serious and efficient Matthew McCabe had suddenly lost it, sneaked down to the holding cell, and punched the handcuffed and hooded prisoner on the nose (or wherever).

Al-Isawi had already said the punch was on his lip, plus face, chest, ribs, and body. Westinson had said it was in the stomach. But the men from Echo Platoon all suggested that no one from the SEAL Team 10 would dream of doing anything so unimaginably stupid as to go down and illegally attack the al-Qaeda commander.

"All I can say," said Matt, "is that if I'd whacked this terrorist in the face, he would have come up looking a whole lot worse than that tiny cut inside his lower lip. As for the suggestion that a group of SEALs knocked him down and then kicked him around on the floor, well, that was just crazy. Because that would have put him in either a coffin or an intensive care unit.

"And the guy did not have a mark on him. Just the lip.

"We're not thugs. We're hand-picked elite troops, and we have enormous responsibilities. Every one of us is conscious of how we are expected to behave, on and off the battlefield. Not just by our commanders but by the American public. We represent our nation, and we are taught to serve with the greatest pride and to treat prisoners as we would hope to be treated should we ever be taken alive by an enemy."

The SEAL statements were taken in the small hours of that Friday morning, and the proceedings were concluded at around 0400. Matt, Jon, and Sam were given a small room together with three beds. And now they realized for certain that they were in lockdown, confined to the base, and sleeping in an area reserved for the Iraqi workers on the base. Ultimately they would do the same work as the Iraqis. It is almost impossible to describe the sense of shame and disgrace this would mean to members of the US Navy's most elite fighting force.

Before they turned in for the night they were told that they were not going back to Camp Schwedler. And here they were—no gear, no washing or shaving kit, no change of clothes.

Their room was no bigger than a cell. They appeared to have no rights whatsoever. They were no longer armed Navy SEALs; some higher authority had condemned them, and they were now at the mercy of people they did not know and who appeared not to care what the hell might happen to them.

As the hours passed, the situation grew worse. The three SEALs were banned from using the same gymnasium as their sister Team 10 Platoon, Foxtrot. They had to train separately from everyone else. There were no arrangements to get them clean clothing. And so far as they could tell by asking around, Westinson and, of course, the monumental al-Qaeda-trained liar, Al-Isawi, provided the only "evidence" against them.

They had not been informed of any of the other sworn SEAL statements, which, incidentally, uttered not one word against them. Lieutenant Jimmy's stated, "I was surprised when Westinson made the allegations against McCabe, [Jon, and Sam] ... they are all level-headed professionals."

The other Objective Amber SEALs, asked by the investigating officer whether they had seen anyone abuse Al-Isawi, all answered with a flat no.

Jason, having confirmed his LTJG rank and top-secret security clearance, concluded his sworn statement with: "I was surprised to hear about the allegations against McCabe, and Keefe, and [Sam and Paddy], these men have been under my command for approximately two years, and in that time I have never had any disciplinary issues with any of them."

At that point Jason was asked, "Did you at any time abuse detainee Ahmad Hashim Abd Al-Isawi, or did you witness any abuse of Ahmad?"

ANSWER: *No.*

The immensely well-respected HM1 Paddy had the following exchanges in his statement:

Q: What was the condition of the detainee at the time of the medical exam?
PADDY: *Fine. No visible deformities or trauma.*
Do you know of any reason why you would lie about the incident?
No.
Do you think someone from your detachment abused the detainee?
No.

Jon added at the foot of his statement: "I am 100 percent confident that the men I work with would never do anything illegal such as detainee abuse."

In his statement Sam confirmed Lieutenant Jimmy's observations: "The only physical thing I saw was the cut on his lip. He was standing upright and showed no physical pain. We then walked him out of the front gate towards the ISWAT vehicles. At that point he began continuously spitting with some blood and moaning. He was also bent over, as if in pain, and speaking to the Iraqis, almost mumbling."

Q: Do you think anyone at the camp abused the detainee?
SAM: *No.*

There were also suggestions in the statements that Brian Westinson was carrying a heavy workload that may have been too much for him. At least one SEAL said the young master-at-arms became stressed out under pressure.

But on the same night the three SEALs made their statements, Brian too put his thoughts into writing, citing events after he returned to his post in the holding cell for the second time, now without his rifle:

I looked in and saw [Sam], McCabe and Keefe standing near the detainee. I walked in and stood next to them. It was at this time when SO2 McCabe struck the detainee (who was standing) and knocked him to the ground.

They saw the reaction on my face and reminded me that the detainee had killed several Americans. Shortly after, I noticed small amounts of blood on the lips of the detainee. ...

Q: Did the three SEALs you saw in the room threaten you in any way after you witnessed the strike?
WESTINSON: *No.*
Q: Why did you wait three days to report it?
A: *I was completely dumbfounded by the incident. I wanted to make sure I wasn't going to make a wrong decision. I talked to two of my immediate seniors for advice and talked to [the lieutenant] shortly after.*
Q: When did you notice he was bleeding?
A: *After I picked him up off the floor.*

Aside from Al-Isawi's claims, Brian Westinson's statement was the sum total of the case against the SEALs. There was nothing else. But it was already obvious that senior command and Master Chief Lampard believed the master-at-arms' words.

By this time, with the combat SEALs stripped of all their equipment, Brian was given his own car to get around the Ar-Ramadi base and was more than once seen in the company of Master Chief Lampard, who was walking with his arm around the young prison guard's shoulders, in a thoroughly buddy-buddy manner.

But the fact was that someone here was lying—either Westinson or every last one of the US Navy SEALs plus the Team's chief medical officer. And it's impossible to dispute the considered opinion of Matt and Jon: someone in a superior position had already made up his mind.

"I can make one statement here which cannot be denied," said Jon. "There was no serving Navy SEAL on that base or back at Camp Schwedler who believed we were guilty of anything. And a lot of them did everything they could to help and have these accusations overturned.

"The guys at Schwedler drove up here with our clean clothing. They brought us toothpaste, toothbrushes, soap, socks, and deodorant. Because of our training, SEALs are among the most loyal and dedicated patriots in the country. Thus, for the moment at least, true anger was kept under tight control."

Sometimes the three of them slipped quietly over to the other base where the Team 10 guys of Foxtrot Platoon were. They were officially banned from doing this, but we must understand the full scale of their position: they were somehow in disgrace, and they had no one to speak to and no lawyers to help them. Those night sorties to confer with their brothers were their only source of information and support.

And the words of Lampard remained strong their minds: "Don't let us catch you over there."

But the semi-incarcerated SEALs badly needed to speak to men of their own kind. And the Foxtrot petty officers were sincerely worried about them and anxious to help. And a few of them were plainly angry that Matt, Jon, and Sam were somehow banned from seeing their closest brothers.

That unseen bond between Navy SEALs is unbreakable, and the resident SEALs at Ar-Ramadi made it very clear that they did not approve of what was happening to the Echo Platoon three, and someone had better start proving something real quickly or else a lot of very smart and very tough men would want to know why.

On Sunday, September 6, Matt was ordered to report to Naval Criminal Investigative Service (NCIS), where Special Agent John Stamp was waiting. He videoed Matt and took fingerprints and a new statement based on the two previous ones.

Then the agent read Matt his rights and told him he was being accused of the assault of a detainee. This was all recorded, and Matt, still fully cooperative and somewhat in disbelief at what was happening to him, took the pen and signed it.

There was now no doubt in his mind: Westinson had concocted this whole bizarre story and, for some reason, was sticking to it. And Matt was within a whisker of being charged with a military crime that would surely end his career as a Navy SEAL. If found guilty, he might be incarcerated in prison.

Jon and Sam were also called into the NCIS. They were not accused like Matt was, but the agent wanted new statements, and Jon was very unhappy with this procedure and asked for stuff to be crossed out. He told them he had never said those things. He told them he would not sign anything until it was accurate, and they eventually acceded to his wishes.

He recalls that they kept telling him he need not worry about these minor details. They didn't matter, they said. Big Jon, however, disagreed strenuously. He said they did matter, at one point even telling them he'd never heard of legal people saying details did not matter.

One detail, which escaped no one, came when they were separated and then asked independently whether they were prepared to take a polygraph test, one that would demand them to answer, categorically, whether Matt had punched the prisoner and whether the other two had seen him do so.

Matt replied, "Absolutely. But only if Westinson takes one."

A little later Jon agreed, telling them: "Of course I'll take it. Any time you like."

Sam also responded, "No problem. I'll do it right here."

They were, even by the standards of Camp Ramadi, scarcely the responses of guilty men. And for the record, Westinson was never required to take the polygraph.

The polygraph (lie detector) team would be arriving in a few days, and all three SEALs signed a paper confirming they agreed to undergo the test.

Back in their room they also agreed that this could really get out of hand. Sam said it was plain that these superior officers did not believe them. Westinson had made an insane accusation, and the senior naval authorities believed him. They did not believe the SEALs, collectively or singly, and this was why they were about to wheel in a polygraph machine.

Matt later guessed it was entirely possible that Westinson had made his wild remarks to deflect attention from his own eccentric behavior that night—deserting his post and mislaying the medical forms.

Looking back, Jon, trying to think of a reason why Westinson said what he said, thought that maybe "he just blurted it out, saying Matt had whacked this nitwit jihadist and then found it impossible to retract because that would make him a grade-one liar. He just kept on saying it—probably in the end believing it."

At 2100 they were summoned to Master Chief Lampard's office and informed they were being detailed to "busywork" under his command. And they all knew what this meant: three-hour watches twice a day, cleaning up the cafeteria at the special operations task force headquarters (SOTF-HQ). SEALs call it bitchwork. It represents the most heinous of punishments, bad for any military personnel but some kind of living death for Navy SEALs, each of whom cost millions of dollars to train.

Jon managed to prevent himself from shouting out: "Busywork! You bastard. You must be joking. I'm a US Navy SEAL. ... I'm one of the most trusted combat warriors in the US armed forces—and I haven't done one wrong thing. You cannot do this to me."

The problem was that Master Chief Lampard could, and did. As far as Matt, Jon, and Sam were concerned, this was the day hell froze over, as they were separated from their brothers, the final humiliation—three SEAL petty officers just back from a major direct action mission, about to be presented with buckets and mops and ordered to wipe tables. They would have to pick up food from the galley and bring it back to Lampard and his staff.

And running through Matt's mind was one thought: *If we'd had lawyers, this could never have happened.*

The trouble was that the SEALs were so certain of their innocence, so trusting of the US Navy and their SEAL commanders that they never dreamed they could possibly need lawyers. They had always cooperated. "We were guilty of *nothing*," said Matt. "And we never even suggested we needed lawyers, as any guilty person might. We never did."

The inescapable truth was that they had already been found guilty of something. After all, they were already being punished in what they believed was the most severe way. "That master chief had told us we were innocent until proven guilty," added Matt. "Yeah, right. They hadn't yet hanged us, but they sure as hell had hung us out to dry.

"And they can repeat that 'innocent til proven guilty' refrain for a thousand years, but it did not apply to us. We had already been judged guilty and punished. Jesus, they were punishing us all day, half the night, and every day. And doing it in the harshest possible way. They were systematically trying to break us, I think, to get some kind of confession."

The naval authorities had time to give that a great deal of thought that morning, because shortly before 0922, a massive one thousand–pound bomb detonated on the other side of the Euphrates River, which ran right past the outer wall of the camp.

It was a suicide car bomb, pure C-4 explosive, and the thunderous blast shuddered the entire camp, shook every building. The ground trembled, and the waters of the Euphrates rippled. That bomb had blown at an Iraqi police checkpoint, killed seven policemen, wounded fifteen others, and sent a giant mushroom cloud right over the base.

"You couldn't see anything but dust," said Jon. "Sam was four hundred yards away. All we could hear was heavy machine gunfire, but we had no idea who was firing at who. Our bunks were shaking from the impact, we had no heavy weapons, and the base was under attack."

Jon and Matt charged out of bed, raced across the base to the SOTF-HQ, and came hurtling through the door to find everyone terrified, huddled together—mostly support guys, plus Westinson.

They could hear people whimpering, "Help us," and they knew that front door could be cannon-blasted in any second and a group of armed tribesmen would bust in with machine guns or another bomb. Outside there was continuous gunfire.

Right then Sam came running through the door, demanding his rifle and armor. "And Matt reacted like a true SEAL," said Jon. "I remember he said, 'Tell these people to get out of our fucking way, and let's get to the roof.'"

At which point he yelled at the top of lungs: *"FOR CHRIST'S SAKE, GIVE US BACK OUR GEAR—RIGHT NOW! THIS BASE IS UNDER ATTACK! WE GOTTA GET TO THE ROOF!"*

Someone went to the TOC's armory and pulled out the equipment the three SEALs needed. And the Echo Platoon men pulled on their body armor, loaded their rifles, and headed for the ladder that led to the roof. Someone yelled, "Can you save us?" and Matt yelled back, a tad ungraciously: "We're gonna try—somehow—to protect you fucking pussies."

No one joined them. Everyone in that TOC building, including a lot of military guys, were just cowering. People were under desks. And Jon, Sam, and Matt, ramming new magazines into the breach of their rifles, pounded up that ladder and onto the roof, not knowing whether to expect an RPG or just sustained gunfire from across the river.

Whatever it was, that enemy would quickly know it was now in a very serious fight. Three armed SEALs are enough trouble for any al-Qaeda force. They reached the edge and spent a few minutes scanning the far river bank. And now they took up their defensive positions, leaning into the parapet, with rifles aimed at the river's edge where police and ambulances were arriving.

"We never opened fire," said Jon. "Because they were not yet crossing the river to attack us with ground troops. But we were ready for 'em, and if any of them chanced their luck, those bastards were dead men. We'd have shot anyone who as much as raised a rifle at the walls of our base."

Finally Commander Hamilton came up to the roof and asked for a situation report (SITREP), which Sam provided. He assured the CO there was no possibility of any force advancing against them. Not without getting killed. They said they were happy with their defensive position. It was classic Navy SEAL, the highest ground, with a clear attacking zone.

Matt recalls the commander remained taciturn. "He left, and we stayed up there for an hour," recalls Jon. "And when the far bank of the Euphrates was finally quiet and the uproar had died down, we climbed back down the ladder, where some people did in fact thank us. Many of them had believed they might die. That huge blast shook the entire camp and a lot of people with it."

What happened then? Had the SEALs' action been sufficiently brave and loyal to be issued with a total reprieve, with any and all pending charges against them dropped? Not quite. They were told to hand in their body armor and weapons and to continue as before.

So they went down to the Marine chow hall and collected lunch for the people they'd just rushed to defend. And then cleaned up after them.

And the psychological attacks on them continued. That same day, quite late in the evening, Master Chief Lampard hauled them into a conference room, a bleak little place with bleacher seating, and delivered an almost laughable lecture.

It was about honor and integrity in the Navy. Jon recalled that the chief told them he had personally been investigated several times and that if they just told the truth, it would all work out.

Jon recalled that the chief then told them what they already had figured out: he had made up his mind and knew who the guilty party was.

He was staring straight at them. "And you could see the pure malice in his face," said Matt. "I felt like saying, 'Oh, thank you, God, Master

Chief God, who knowest all—but in our case knowest nothing, vicious, smug bastard.'"

At the conclusion of his sermon Master Chief Lampard added that no matter what happened to them—loss of rank or getting discharged from the US military—at least they're "still Americans."

Oh, thank you Master Chief God, for not turning me into a Pakistani or a Moroccan, thought Matt, who only rarely lost his sardonic sense of humor. And now Mr. Lampard had taken him to the limit.

At 10 A.M. on Wednesday, September 9, the master chief stopped Jon and asked him what he knew about the case. The big breacher replied, "Sam has told us the investigation was complete and that we were being sent back to the States, and the entire issue would be dealt with on home soil."

Jon says Lampard shook his head and smiled, then told him that the Iraqis wanted answers and were demanding justice—right here in Iraq.

"You mean a trial in an Iraqi court?" said Jon quietly. "Me and Sam and Matt?"

"Very possibly."

"But, if it goes against us, not an Iraqi jail, right?"

"It's a possibility."

That scared Jon worse than he had ever been scared in his life. "An Iraqi courtroom, an Iraqi judge?" he recalled thinking. "For me, who'd played a major role in the kidnapping and incarceration of this Sunni hero and al-Qaeda commander?"

Standing there, face to face with the hard-faced, stocky master chief, Jon found himself shuddering, almost certainly with fear. "He'd just mentioned what could be a death sentence for me," he says. "Can you imagine? An American Special Forces operator getting justice in Iraq? And then being thrown into a Baghdad correctional institution? My life would not have been worth two bucks."

Looking back Jon now believes the master chief was just trying to scare him. "And he sure as hell managed that," he says. "To this day I'm not sure whether Lampard was merely a sadist or whether he would just have done anything in this world to get us to admit to something, anything.

"He plainly wanted Matt to sign something saying he had knocked the living hell out of Al-Isawi. He also wanted Sam and me to admit we had stood by and watched this. And then confirm the pair of us had told a pack of lies to cover up what Matt had done and what we had witnessed.

"Like Westinson, Lampard had jumped very quickly onto the wrong side of this one, and I thought at that little encounter, he'll get his false, untrue confessions over our dead bodies. Screw him."

That was probably the day the game changed. And the first evidence it had really changed came at noon on Saturday, September 12. Jon and Sam were ordered to report separately to NCIS, where their rights were read to them. The officer said that Jon was being charged with two articles that contravened the Uniform Code of Military Justice (UCMJ).

He was then told to sign his formal acceptance of these charges, one of which was dereliction of duty, the other that he had made a false official statement. "It was," he recalls, "the most shocking, untrue allegation which had ever been made against me by anyone, anywhere, or any time. And that includes when I flunked out of the University of East Carolina and was widely regarded at the time as a total deadbeat."

Sam was also asked to sign an acceptance form confirming the charges of dereliction of duty, false official statement, and impeding an investigation.

"How about that!" said Jon, "Sam! The senior petty officer on the base, who had just seen us safely through such a dangerous mission and then went at 0500 to check Westinson was okay, as he knew he was having one or two problems and might need help. Dereliction of duty! I thought then, as I think now, the Navy's system of justice has actually gone off its rocker."

Jon flatly refused to sign anything until he had a lawyer, and this took the NCIS by surprise. He was out of there in under two minutes.

Matt also said he was signing nothing until he had a lawyer. And then he noticed that the papers in front of him confirmed that the US Navy was about to throw the book at him. He was being charged with assaulting the detainee, dereliction of duty, making a false official statement, and failing to safeguard a detainee.

With the lawyer issue apparently hanging in the balance, all three of them stood by for a few days. And their requests for legal assistance were not yet acted on. But then on Friday, September 18, Jon received a truly encouraging piece of news.

One of his fellow SEALs found him, and informed the Echo breacher that Special Agent Stamp, who had taken the statements and conducted the biggest part of the investigation, had filed a report that stated there was insufficient evidence for any further proceedings. The SEAL was a member of Foxtrot Platoon and had seen the report himself.

For a while this was enough to sustain the three SEALs, and their hopes for exoneration were high. But they still had no attorney, not one between the three of them, and they were still prepared to cooperate in any way they could, despite the charges now leveled at them. In a way none of them believed there could possibly be this much unfairness in all the world, never mind in a SEAL base.

And perhaps in confirmation of the Navy's very weak case against them, their brother SEALs across the way in Foxtrot Platoon reported an incident that the high command had become totally exasperated with the dogged refusal of the Team 10 personnel to admit anything nor to condemn anyone else.

In what seemed to be a fit of pique, they arrested *everyone* who had been on Objective Amber, including the OIC, Lieutenant Jimmy, and sent them all to Ar-Ramadi, each man with a charge sheet accusing him of conspiracy. As a legal tactic to make one of these men crack, it was on the crude side. And it backfired badly when it was discovered that one of the SEALs had a high-ranking Washington lawyer for a father who took a poor view of the treatment his son and all of his son's friends were receiving.

According to Foxtrot Platoon, this lawyer placed the entire law firm on high alert to defend the boys at a moment's notice. The Navy was informed of this, and the charges were dropped en masse within twenty-four hours. Except for those against Matt, Jon, and Sam. Those charges stayed in place.

Furthermore, the naval authorities appeared to have decided to put more pressure on all three of them. That same Friday night, at 0130 in the morning, Matt, Jon, and Sam were called into the command office, where Commander Hamilton's deputy, an acting CO, sat in the big chair.

They stood rigidly to attention and were told, "Your actions have given the Naval Special Warfare Community a black eye and stained the reputation of the SEAL Teams which have gone before. You have ruined SEAL Team 10's deployment." He also told them they would be flying on to Al-Asad to meet up with the commander and the master chief. From there they would proceed to Qatar to meet with the general and receive a letter of caution.

This at least settled one issue: they were definitely considered guilty—no ifs, ands or buts. "We were not quite sure who had found us guilty," says Jon. "But someone had, and there seemed no further doubt in their minds. Jeez, you could just tell how upset they were— this new guy and, presumably, his boss, Commander Hamilton, hated us."

By this time there was a fusillade of paperwork flying around, and just about every one of several hundred sheets was headed "US Naval Criminal Investigation Service." And the word "Criminal" leapt off that page every time these three decorated SEALs were shown anything.

That word was so upsetting to Jon that he was afraid even to tell his parents. But he did take time to read up on that basic bedrock of all US, British, and Roman Law that deals with the presumption of innocence.

Because this presumption of guilt was so worrying for the SEALs. "Whichever way you looked at it," said Jon, "they were treating us as if we'd been found guilty already. We had not even walked up the steps of the courtroom, never mind been found guilty of anything. And they'd seen fit to strip us of damn near everything, including our regular SEAL Team gear and possessions not to mention our freedom and, worse yet, our pride and honor.

"It was pretty darned awful for Matt, who had never raised a finger against the prisoner. But for me it was almost worse. All I'd done was say I never saw him or anyone else strike anyone. And now I was being told that was dereliction of duty or conspiracy or God knows what else.

"I mean what is it with those guys? What do they want from me? Am I supposed to make up some lie that I'd seen Matt or Sam wallop this Al-Isawi? I know it sounds crazy, but by now this was getting kind of sinister."

The first leg of their journey to Qatar, up to Al-Asad, went particularly badly. Jon, Matt, and Sam were ordered to report to Commander Hamilton, who, they could immediately detect, was seriously angry with them.

He broke the stunning news that the master-at-arms, Brian Westinson, had gone missing. At first the implication was that the three men plainly knew where he was. Then, according to Jon, it became obvious that the commander and the ever-present Master Chief Lampard believed they had kidnapped him, like a couple of Mafia dons dealing with a key witness in a mass-murder trial.

Commander Hamilton flatly accused Jon, Matt, and Sam of knowing where the vanished Brian was. And Lampard talked to them as though they might have murdered him, making it clear he believed nothing any of them said. And of course the SEALs denied it, stating that none of them had the slightest idea what had happened to Westinson.

Unhappily for the master chief, Brian eventually turned up, having been a mile away in protective custody at his own request under the auspices of NCIS, who apparently forgot to inform the CO of this preventive action.

Outside Commander Hamilton's office, Lampard, for whom this had not been his finest hour, covered his rage with insults. He pulled all three of them aside and told them they were unacceptably scruffy—his phrase was, precisely: "all fucked up." He told them to get ironed, pressed, and sharpened up, even though he knew they had been unable to get new clothes.

He yelled at them relentlessly for several minutes, knowing, of course, that they could not answer him back. Then he confirmed his real feelings, informing them formally that "You guys are a disgrace!" And, he said, he was writing to the senior master chief on SEAL Team 10, to tell him: "Thanks for disappointing me one more time."

Said Jon later, rather sardonically: "All things considered, he was possibly the most unpleasant man I ever met."

Certainly, Master Chief Lampard, working directly for Commander Hamilton, was one of the driving forces in this potential legal battle as it steadily forged its way forward, moving to higher and higher authority. And now Matt, Jon, and Sam were informed they were on a three-day standby, right here on this remote but enormous desert airbase, waiting for Major General Charles T. Cleveland's private C-17 Boeing, which would take them to Al-Udeid Air Base in Qatar.

The principal Middle East office of Special Operations Command Central (SOCCENT) was located there. This effectively put two kingdoms side by side on one Arab Peninsula—that of the absolute monarchy of Sheikh Hamad bin Khalifa Al Thani, Emir of Qatar, the richest nation on earth, and that of General Cleveland, commanding officer of SOCCENT, a man unaccustomed to being interrupted, never mind argued with. He would stand in ultimate authority over Matt, Jon, and Sam.

In Ar-Ramadi there had been a strong suggestion that this would end in a letter of caution for the SEALs, who would then be sent on their way with only a mild slap on the wrist. In the Navy, however, there is a major difference between a "caution" and letter of reprimand, the latter of which can be a career killer.

The "caution letter" traditionally has no impact whatsoever on a man's career, and despite their certainty that they were 100 percent innocent of any and all charges, the SEALs would have been inclined to accept that should it have been offered. At least then Commander Hamilton and Lampard might possibly stop treating them like escaped convicts.

During their days at Al-Asad there had been indications that the Navy was as anxious as they were to dispense with the entire matter and to agree that there was, at the very least, an element of "reasonable doubt."

So far as the SEALs were concerned, in these utterly tenuous cases against them "reasonable doubt" was approximately the size of the Grand Canyon.

"I hate to say it," says Matt, "but we'd have been better off in the Lubyanka, Article 49 Russian Constitution, right? Innocent until proven guilty. Everyone except for us."

6

—

SCAPEGOATS
OF EMPIRE

The barbarities of war ... are committed in situations where the
ebb and flow of everyday life have departed, and have been
replaced by a constant round of fear and anger, blood and
death ... soldiers at war are not to be judged by civilian rules.

The one hundred–mile-long peninsula of Qatar juts upward like a giant thumb from Saudi Arabia into the Persian Gulf. There were, however, no thumbs-up for Matt, Jon, and Sam when they finally left Iraq
and arrived in yet another ancient Arab land.

After three almost unbearably frustrating weeks, their questions
came raining in to anyone who'd listen: *And how about the letter of caution? Where do we stand with complete exoneration? Is this Westinson guy
still making these accusations? Do we have a lawyer yet? Right now we'd take
an out-of-work Bedouin.*

But no one was listening. In the kingdom of Major General Cleveland military politics and the dreaded "politically correct" was elbowing its way to the front.

The case, which had begun before sunrise on September 2, when
the blindfolded Ahmad Hashim Abd Al-Isawi had complained that a
mysterious punch to the stomach had made his lower lip bleed, was
now moving inexorably toward a courtroom.

On their first morning in Qatar the three SEALs were led into an office of the legal department, where a senior officer awaited them—a naval commander, legal assistant to General Cleveland. In turn a paralegal Army sergeant assisted him. According to Jon, this now made fifteen people who were all lined up alongside General Cleveland to help.

"We, on the other hand, had no one," said Jon.

They were then taken to another room, where the sergeant placed one piece of paper in front of each man. It stated that Matt was charged officially with assault, the other two with dereliction of duty and making a false official statement.

"This was the first time," said Matt, "any of us had seen the charges all written down, complete with references to Article 128, and 92 [dereliction of duty]."

Now it should be noted that there could not have been one living person who had breathed the desert air anywhere around the SEAL bases who was not acutely aware that all three of them were denying the charges vehemently.

And here were these three pieces of paper being thrust in front of them, with a total stranger demanding they each sign them, here and now, admitting their guilt.

"I'm signing nothing," said Jon.

"Sign there," repeated the paralegal, pointing to the signature space on Jon's document.

"None of us are signing anything," said Matt.

"You guys are being charged with these violations," he replied. "That's where you sign."

Matt's mind was in overdrive. He recalled the many conversations they had sat through in Ramadi, especially the one in which the authorities had seemed to accept that there was an element of doubt here that would almost certainly end with a letter of caution—not even a reprimand.

All three SEALs had intimated they would accept the mild rebuke of a naval caution letter, despite being completely innocent of everything. And now, here was this Army sergeant effectively throwing the book at them, leveling charges of the most damaging nature against them and trying to slide the gravity of the matter right past them, almost by sleight of hand.

"Just sign the papers, right where I instruct," he repeated.

And quite suddenly the pure subterfuge of the military case against them and the methods being utilized in order to lead them into a trap stood starkly before all three SEALs. Jon, Matt, and Sam were suddenly very frightened. And they turned and looked at each other. Their lifelong goodwill toward the US military system of justice and fairness seemed to crumble away.

Simultaneously, they all recall, they knew they were up against a big and all-powerful enemy who would stop at nothing and would say anything in order to put them behind bars. Promises meant nothing. In the future innuendoes must be ignored. This new pressure point was a game changer.

Jon said simply: "They were trying to trick us. I don't know why. And I never will. That Army guy just wanted to get us into a corner, where we were trapped, not able to escape. They were trying to deceive us, trying to pretend this was all routine stuff, just three little signatures. That was all they wanted.

"Three little signatures, just a little paperwork formality to them. No big deal. Yeah, right. Those signatures would have been a death warrant to us. And they knew it. But we knew all about signed warrants and how they signified life and death. There was nothing we didn't know about signed warrants. And we refused to comply."

"Sign here," repeated the sergeant.

"Why don't you go fuck yourself," Matt almost growled. But instead he said, "We were told in Ramadi by the acting CO we were being given a letter of caution. Not a reprimand. And certainly not a charge, or a General's Mast."

Matt's words were delivered with that straightforward respectful sense of protocol all SEALs are taught to employ when dealing with their superiors. But deep within Matt, as a direct result of this latest encounter, there rose a sudden and unmistakable iron curtain of pure defiance—battlefield defiance. SEAL defiance: *I am never out of the fight. I will get back up every time.*

Sam and Jon experienced the precise same thing—a kind of rising anger at being knocked back, over and over, by an enemy who was indifferent to their plight and cold to their helplessness.

"It was as if they were trying to rush the formalities as fast as possible before we got lawyers," said Jon. "Because they knew we'd had no legal advice, no help from anyone. And I guess they understood that if we ultimately did hire lawyers, we would suddenly have a whole new set of legal rights."

The sergeant said that he knew nothing about letters of caution nor anything about what had been said in Ramadi. But he would check that out right away.

When he returned he declared, "There's nothing of that on the record. You guys are being charged, and you are to sign these sheets of paper right here."

Again all three SEALs refused, and the sergeant retreated, leaving the three accused men in the room.

For a full minute they sat together in silence. A thousand thoughts swept through their minds, but not a word was spoken. "I guess we knew right there," said Matt. "We were suddenly in a fight to the death against the high command of the United States Armed Forces. They were prepared to smash our lives to avoid accusations of US military bullying and prisoner abuse.

"All we wanted was to prove our innocence beyond all doubt and to regain our honor. Because that's a big thing in the SEAL Teams. Every class had its honor man. That's what we're taught. And we had done *nothing* to deserve anything less."

At midafternoon in the burning heat of the Qatar Air Base, 480 miles closer to the equator than the city of Baghdad, the SEALS were again summoned to a room adjoining the legal offices. This time the tactic was to speak to them individually and separately. Master Chief Lampard was now working with General Cleveland's senior enlisted adviser, Master Sergeant Bob, and there was an unusual attempt to make this a more friendly atmosphere. Cans of soda and candy bars were laid out, and it began with just a general discussion about the case.

Matt has a vivid recollection of the day. "I allowed myself a cold Dr. Pepper," he said. "And I was told that if I admitted my 'crime,' I would be helped. There would just be loss of rank and pay. However, if my Team 10 command wished to take away my Trident, these guys, Lampard and his Army cohort, would fly home on their own time and stand character witness for me, stating that I was a stand-up kind of a guy.

"Huh? Right about now I thought the whole place had gone crazy. For the past three weeks I'd been treated as if I was a murderer or something, now I've got a general's senior assistant claiming that he'll fly halfway around the world to swear to God I'm a good guy. Really!? What is it with these people?!

"I was not, however, fooled by this. Because I knew that Abu Ghraib had reared its ugly head all over again."

Petty Officer McCabe knew as well as anyone that the alleged punch that felled Al-Isawi was not yet public nor was the al-Qaeda killer's allegation of prisoner abuse. But these kinds of military secrets never stay secret for long. And when these allegations finally hit the airwaves, almost certainly through the Al Jazeera television network, the liberal press in the United States would jump all over it—on the side of the detainee, no matter what his background.

And the Pentagon would have one overriding desire: to have their spokesmen assure everyone the matter had been sternly dealt with. Heads had rolled.

"What they wanted," says Matt, "if this went ahead, was moral righteousness, a confirmation that they disapproved of US bullying in Iraq. They wanted headlines that would state,

NAVY SEALS STRIPPED OF RANK
DISHONORABLY DISCHARGED FOR IRAQI PRISONER ABUSE

Lack of discipline will never be tolerated in the US Armed Forces.
—*General Cleveland*

"We, of course, agree with the general," Matt said. "But there was still no reason to treat us as they had done so far. You can't get better people than Jonathan Keefe or Sam Gonzales, and I hope they would say something similar about me.

"There was not one thing in our actions or backgrounds which could be held against any of us, nothing to justify this vicious assumption of our guilt. I could only conclude the authorities had their own agenda, and they were happy to make us sacrificial lambs."

Sacrificial lambs have occasionally been slaughtered in various militaries down through the years, perhaps the most celebrated being the three Australian lieutenants in the Bushveldt Carbineers, all charged with murdering prisoners in the second Boer War (1899–1902).

The British Army's chief of staff, Field Marshall Lord Kitchener of Khartoum, intended to bring the war to an end with a peace conference. But when it became public that Boer prisoners had been shot, Lord Kitchener provided a demonstration of his willingness to judge his own soldiers harshly if they disobeyed the rules of war.

He ordered a court-martial of the Australians. And he wanted a guilty verdict—no ifs, ands, or buts. Harry "The Breaker" Harbord Morant, Peter Handcock, and George Witton were doomed before they set foot in the courtroom.

In the 1980 film, *Breaker Morant*, there is a poignant exchange when Kitchener's second-in-command explains to the Australian defense lawyer that the execution of his three clients would be a small price to pay for ending this long and bloody conflict on the hot plains of the Eastern Transvaal.

"Yes, I suppose so," replied the lawyer, "Unless of course you happened to be one of the three Australians."

"That was precisely how we felt," said Jon. "Just because it seemed that no matter what we said or how many of our teammates verified our statements, there was a separate agenda, known only to the military high command, which deemed us guilty."

There was also a quiet unease in the Iraq-based SEAL Teams that their brothers were being treated as though this was a civilian world, which it most certainly was not. And once more the words of Breaker Morant's defense counsel, Major James Thomas, echoed down the years:

The barbarities of war ... are committed in situations where the ebb and flow of everyday life have departed, and have been replaced by a constant round of fear and anger, blood and death ... soldiers at war are not to be judged by civilian rules.

Those three Australians were not denying the killing of the Boer prisoners; rather, they were disputing their orders, and their defense was formidable. But it was all to no avail. Harry Harbord Morant and Lieutenant Peter Handcock were found guilty and swiftly executed by firing squad within days of the trial, outside the fort in Pretoria at sunrise, at six o'clock on February 27, 1902. Lord Kitchener personally signed their death warrants.

Both men declined a blindfold, and the Breaker's last words were shouted, "Shoot straight, you bastards! Don't make a mess of it!"

The younger Lieutenant George Witton was also found guilty but was released after three years in an English jail and returned to Australia, still heartbroken, to write the book, *Scapegoats of Empire*, which inspired both the stage play, the motion picture, and many, many books on the infamous court-martial.

Apparently blind to the inevitable surge of public outrage when SEALs of any rank are subjected to any kind of criticism or persecution, the military continued to go after Matt, Jon, and Sam. And one by one they sent them into that room with the soda pops and bizarre promises.

Jon's memory of the proceedings casts the gravest doubt on the motives of General Cleveland's staff. "They weren't all that subtle," he recalled. "They wanted me to say that Matt had hit the dude, and they didn't seem to care much whether it was true, false, or made up. They just wanted me to say it and sign a paper that Matt was guilty of assault and that we were both guilty of dereliction of duty and accepted all charges."

He was told, "Jon, this is not an interrogation. You can waive and revoke your rights. Then you can tell us off the record, if you like."

"I just stood there," said Jon. "And I was thinking, *Do you guys think I'm that dumb, that I will just stand here and tell an outright lie about my buddy and teammate?* I had nothing to say to them. So I said nothing."

Jon was then warned this could go to "four-star level." And he knew that meant to General David Howell Petraeus, the tenth commander of US Central Command, former commander of all multinational forces in Iraq, and future commander of US forces in Afghanistan.

"That was kinda big," said Jon. "I simply could not believe how this thing had gotten utterly out of hand. *Four-star level!* What the hell were these comedians talking about? The punch that never happened on the lip of a lying little jihadist killer, who never had a bruise on him? And they're calling in the head of the US Army? Someone, anyone, give me a break."

It is not possible to exaggerate the effect all this had on Jonathan Keefe. His parents were God-fearing people, and his mother, Dawn, was proud of the fact that Jon had attended the same local Catholic church, Our Lady of Mount Carmel, in which he was both baptized and made his first Holy Communion a quarter of a century earlier.

That long religious upbringing in a family of strict moral codes was an important part of the young SEAL's character. And, of course, there had also been the strict US Navy doctrine of the truth, the whole truth, all of the time. Lying was pure anathema to him: his parents, his parish priest, and the US Navy had combined to outlaw in his mind the very concept of lying.

This was a genuine stand-up guy. Like Matt and Sam. Ask either of them a question, you'll get a straight answer. And now here were these uniformed legal eagles almost imploring Jon to tell a deliberate, Southern-fried, copper-bottomed whopper: that he had indeed watched his best buddy whack Al-Isawi.

Jon stood before his inquisitors, unblinking, shoulders back, and silent. And through his mind raced the phrase, *They're asking me to tell a lie.*

And now he remembered Master Chief Lampard telling Jon that he had personally been investigated seven or eight times and had always manned up and taken the punishment. Lampard had added that he had known SEALs in trouble who had run up legal bills of $40,000 and still been found guilty.

"We know you have loyalty to your team," he added. "But if you'll just tell us the truth, that the allegations are correct, no one will get into trouble. All you need to do is to stand in front of General Cleveland and confirm what Matt did."

Jon said nothing. Like Matt and Sam, he knew perfectly well that this was no longer some kind of a softball sparring match. This was hardball, and these guys were trying to get him to comply with their wishes, and he was damned if they were going to succeed.

They again assured Jon that he could revoke his rights and tell them off the record that Matt had struck the prisoner. "No paperwork will be necessary," they said. They then went further than that and said he could re-invoke his rights and get back on the record.

Jon had not spent time at law school. He understood little of the finer points of trials and justice. But even he understood this was utter rubbish. Revoke his rights? Off the record? Re-invoke your rights? No paperwork?

Jon refused to answer.

And once more his inquisitors swerved onto a slightly different tack, urging him to accept what the US Army refers to as Article 15. The Navy has its own procedures for lower-level punishment, dating back to the days of sail. It's called a Captain's Mast, a method of non-judicial punishment (NJP) in which a sailor who has committed an offense appears before his commanding officer on board a warship and may be reduced in rank or pay or even discharged. He will not, however, face really serious punishment like jail or, in days of yore, the lash.

These days there is more often a procedure called Admiral's Mast, in which an alleged offender may appear before a fleet commanding officer and admit the error of his ways. Again, the process is more or less unchanged—nothing as serious as court-martial but still requiring an admission of guilt. For whatever reason, in the US Marines, their NJP procedure is always called Office Hours.

US naval personnel only rarely refer to the Army's very similar Article 15 because it only rarely affects anyone wearing dark blue. But in the case of Matt, Jon, and Sam, something very significant had happened. The case had moved over from naval jurisdiction to that of the Army. Those who mattered now were Major General Cleveland and his staff. And there was now a rumor that General Petraeus himself would be involved and, indeed, may be obliged to give the green light to any judicial matters involving the three SEALs.

Faced with the silent Jon Keefe, the inquisitors now urged him, over and over, to take Article 15, effectively the General's Mast. They told him an admission of guilt would be ideal, all three SEALs could renege on previous statements involving the nonstriking of the jihadist, their "lies," "dereliction of duty," "false statements," and so forth.

Instead, they should throw themselves upon the mercy of Major General Charles Cleveland. They again gave Jon reassurance that if he admitted he had seen Matt punch Al-Isawi, his own part in the debacle would be glossed over.

"Do you have any questions?" they asked him.

"No," replied Petty Officer Keefe. It was the only word he uttered throughout the entire interview.

As he left the room Jon had only one thought in his mind: *These people would do anything, say anything, promise anything, or, if necessary, threaten anything in order to get a confession.* Obviously Jon had not been in the other rooms while Matt and Sam were being "persuaded," but he had a pretty good idea they too were being lied to, tricked, and otherwise hoodwinked, not to mention humiliated.

This day had been a game changer, and now the gloves were off. There would be no more trust, no more cooperation, no more nice guys. From now on the three SEALs would fight tooth and nail to the bitter end—a state of mind in which they were all hard trained. There would be no surrender inside or outside the courtroom.

Jon, for the twelfth time, requested a Navy lawyer to help him, as had the other two. At this point, however, only he understood, after his third-degree going-over by General Cleveland's legal staff, that this was all headed for the highest level of the military judicial system. Jon already knew he needed an expensive civilian lawyer, a ruthless courtroom operator who would protect him and get Westinson on that witness stand to tear his "evidence" to shreds.

The three SEALs regrouped and exchanged updates, agreeing among themselves that they had to get top-class civilian attorneys, skilled advocates who could punch holes in all the lies and distortions being leveled at them.

At this stage the authorities seemed to consider Jon an easier target than Matt. At least they apparently thought it might be easier to get him to say that Matt had whacked Ahmad Hashim than it ever would be to persuade Matt to admit to having done so. Wrong. Jon was as determined as any man could be. He would never even consider surrender.

There was also the slightly uneasy situation with Sam Gonzales, who was very senior, very highly regarded, and very important on the SEAL base. His evidence would certainly prove damning to the prosecution, as he had been there or thereabouts throughout all of the critical hours and encounters.

He would hear not one word against Matt or Jon nor against any other SEAL Team member. He had dictated a sworn affidavit that the men were completely innocent. He had been there with them at the holding cell and had seen everything there was to see. Also, he was taking a somewhat skeptical, sideways look at Westinson, who he thought was acting pretty "stressed out."

Looking back, it was quite possibly the presence of Sam that was generating such urgency when questioning Matt and Jon. The military legal team was anxious to deliver a confession to their masters simply to avoid a trial, at which SEAL Petty Officer 1st Class Sam Gonzales was perfectly capable of blowing them all out of the water. Judge, jury, naval officers, courtroom guards, stenographers, and clerks—they would all believe him.

The trick was either to get Matt to admit his "crime" or for Jon to say he saw it as an eyewitness before the matter ever got to a court. They could then hang Matt out to dry in front of the general. And the Pentagon would have its headlines when the media had liftoff. A spokesman for the Navy would quietly confirm that they had dealt with the matter in the severest possible way. As was only to be expected.

Meanwhile the pace quickened. Within the hour the SEALs were once more summoned to the US Army's legal offices. Matt was escorted into a different room and found himself again face to face with Master Chief Lampard and the army sergeant major, General Cleveland's senior enlisted adviser.

And there, for the first time, he was formally told the assault charge was by no means the only accusation he faced. He was also being charged personally with dereliction of duty and false statements. No one had ever told him he would be arraigned on three counts, that he had three very serious, almost criminal charges lined up against him.

Matt stood tall, ramrod straight, facing his accusers, every inch a US Navy SEAL Team leader who only one month previously had courageously smashed his way into the armed headquarters of Iraq's most dangerous terrorist and grabbed and "cuffed a wanted killer who had evaded capture for almost five years" but now found himself on the wrong end of Matt's M-4 rifle.

"I suppose none of that counted anymore," he said later.

And for the umpteenth time on this day Lampard and the sergeant major verbally tackled Matt, asking him twice more to confess.

Matt refused to answer. He just stood there, staring straight ahead. And for some reason his accusers thought his silence signified submission, and they were plainly expecting him to request clarification, maybe even advice about his chances before the general if he took Article 15.

What lenience could he expect? Did he need to admit all three crimes? Would he risk losing rank? Could he count on some senior character witnesses, men who would stand up for him in court, citing his impeccable record? Above all else, would they take away his Trident?

Never have two legal military interrogators been more widely off track. Matthew McCabe, like all of his kind, had an inner core of pure steel. He never flinched and never spoke.

Finally, Master Chief Lampard, fully expecting a climbdown, asked him persuasively whether he had any questions.

"No," snapped Matt.

"And," Matt recalled, "they both looked absolutely astounded. And I just left the room."

It was precisely the same for Jon and Sam. Both men were given details of the newly written charges against them.

Jon was asked: "Questions?"

"No."

"None at all?"

"No."

"We'd all had quite enough of their lies, tricks, glibness, and threats. Not to mention their stupidity," he said. "None of us had anything to say, at least not to them."

All three men had by now requested, over and over, the assistance of a Navy lawyer, just to have someone for the first time standing in their corner. They all knew this was a standard right for any naval personnel accused of anything. Jon had asked for Lieutenant Paul Threatt, who was based in Norfolk, but so far he had heard nothing.

Day after day Jon, Matt, and Sam heard nothing. And they were as alone on these days as they had been throughout their ordeal. Hour after hour they had faced experienced inquisitors, men of a higher rank who, so far as anyone could tell, had pulled just about every trick in the book to persuade them to make confessions—to sign admissions of guilt.

These were unfailingly presented as "no-big-deal formalities." But these three smart Special Forces operators, though young and inexperienced in the guiles of martial law, knew instinctively their signatures would almost certainly prove fatal. Thus, they had not given way. And they had treated the offered pens and paper as bomb disposal men treat a ticking roadside IED.

And then their accusers summoned Jon to face a gimlet-eyed Army staff sergeant who thrust three legal documents in front of him.

Jon perused them swiftly and noted they dealt with three separate subjects. "They could hardly have appeared more legal," he remembers. "Kind of papers you'd expect for the trial of a mass murderer like Al-Isawi, not me."

The staff sergeant told Jon to initial each page where he indicated and then to sign them.

"I'm not signing anything until I have legal counsel," replied the heavyweight SEAL breacher from Virginia.

The sergeant paused and stared hard at Jon, and then he softened a bit and continued, "You *must* sign them. And when you've done it, you can speak to a Navy lawyer in Norfolk."

Jon just stood there, entirely alone, and flatly refused. But the staff sergeant came back, again and again, first cajoling, then persuading, then threatening. But Jon stood firm. "I am signing nothing," he repeated, "not until I have counsel."

Finally, when it was clear that this was going nowhere, the sergeant left and returned with General Cleveland's head legal counselor, another member of the Judge Advocate General's Corps (JAG), who selected one of the three sheets and removed it.

This left just the two charges, and for the last time, the sergeant told Jon to sign them, confirming the third one had gone.

And Jon, still patient and polite but nonetheless very scared, uttered the same phrase he had uttered so many times before: "I will sign nothing."

At which point he was left alone, and after a few minutes the phone on the desk suddenly rang. Jon answered it, and a voice said, "I'm calling you from US Naval Base, Norfolk, this is Lieutenant Paul Threatt. I'm a Navy lawyer, and I'm here to help you."

A tidal wave of relief swept over the big Virginian. It was the first time anyone in the world had stepped up to offer help to any of the three of them. Paul Threatt was the lawyer Jon had requested. One of his SEAL brothers had strongly recommended the attorney because he was a stern intellectual moralist and, if necessary, a courtroom brawler.

"It was as if my prayers had suddenly been answered," says Jon. "For a few moments I couldn't even speak."

When he did he just blurted out his profound thanks and then told the JAG officer from Norfolk about the two legal sheets of paper he had been told to sign.

Very carefully, Threatt asked Jon to read the words out to him slowly. And it was clear to Jon that the lawyer was listening with rising anger. At the end of the section he snapped, *"DO NOT SIGN THAT."*

Right here Threatt had some kind of sixth sense, because he could feel that the SEAL was very tired, mentally beaten down by days of questioning and persuasion. "There was a weariness in his voice which I did not like," the lieutenant recalled. "Of course I did not know Jon.

But even at that distance I could tell he'd taken some kind of a battering. I needed to be stern and very definite. Jon Keefe did not want to hear vacillation."

And he repeated the phrase, *"DO NOT SIGN THAT,"* again and again, as Jon worked his way down the pages, dictating the accusatory words halfway across the world to the headquarters of the US Navy (legal department), where Lieutenant Threatt sat almost in disbelief at the cruel and ruthless way this Navy SEAL was being treated.

"I am afraid I had to be harsh with Jon," he remembered, "Short with him. Staccato, rude. But I had to keep him focused. I did not want him to relax. And I just kept going, making sure he could never lose concentration. He probably thought I was some kind of ogre. But I never lost him, and his determination stayed high."

Lieutenant Threatt later told Jon: "I knew from those initial moments that you were tired but completely innocent. How did I know? Don't ask me. I just did."

For the next forty-five minutes the two men talked, with Threatt explaining to Jon, chapter and verse, what it would mean if he accepted the General's Mast (Article 15) and agreed to stand before Cleveland and confess that he had indeed lied to the authorities and been derelict in his duty of care to a captured prisoner.

"If you do that, it is very likely you will receive nothing much worse than a reduction in rank and pay and that your loyalty to your teammates will be taken into consideration."

"I cannot do that," Jon told him. "I have not lied, and I cannot say I did, because that wouldn't be true either. They've already asked me to lie about a dozen times, and I can't do it."

Seven thousand miles away, Threatt smiled the smile of the legal predator. Rarely had he interviewed an accused man so plainly not guilty.

"Well, Jon," he said, "Article 15 is the easy way out for you, the path with the least risk to you personally. The other way is court-martial. And that's considerably more serious, because that can very easily involve jail. For Matthew, on an assault charge, that could mean five years, if the three of you were found guilty."

"I cannot do anything which requires me to admit any wrong-doing," replied Jon. "Either by my teammates or by myself. None of us is guilty of anything."

"And that," said Threatt, "leaves us with the courtroom. And there you will be given a clear opportunity to defend yourself, and your legal counsel will cross-examine the prosecution's witnesses."

"So if we want to fight it, we elect to be court-martialed?" Jon had swiftly grasped the situation.

"That is correct," said Paul. "It's a dangerous course of action because of the obvious downside with a guilty verdict …"

Jon remembers interrupting: "Paul, there can be no guilty verdict. All three of us are one hundred percent innocent. Every SEAL Team member will stand up in court and speak for us. We already have those assurances. The prosecution has nothing except the word of the master-at-arms kid who deserted his post at least twice during that evening. And he's a nervous wreck. I wouldn't believe him if he told me it was daylight."

Threatt calmly warned that "trials can go wrong, and innocent men have been found guilty …"

"Yeah, but no three people in the history of the US Navy have ever been as innocent as us," replied Jon. "Matt McCabe never laid a finger on that little Iraqi creep. Neither did Sam, and neither did I. Matt didn't lie, Sam didn't lie, and I didn't lie."

He added that this Westinson character had been wrapped up in cotton wool and protected, encouraged, and even guarded from the very beginning, "ever since he came out with that cockamamie story about Matt," said Jon. "No one has corroborated it, and no one with a lick of sense believes it. That's all they've got, Lieutenant Threatt. Nothing else."

"Then, Jon, it's my duty to advise you to go to court-martial. And there I will do everything in my power to defend you. I will come to see you as soon as possible, and you should consider the possibility of retaining a civilian lawyer as well."

Jon knew nothing about legal expenses in the civilian world. He did, however, understand that it was unlikely to be cheap. "Are we talking $50,000, maybe $100,000?" he asked.

"Very possibly," replied Threatt.

"Well, my family does not have that kind of money to throw around, and I really do not want to involve my family. The shame of my situation would be bad enough."

"In this case it's possible the money may come from somewhere unexpected," said the naval lawyer mysteriously. He would elaborate no further. But already there was a seed planted in his mind.

Somewhere deep within him, Threatt knew the American public was capable of rising up in fury when they heard that three heroic Navy SEALs were being court-martialed in Iraq for allegedly punching the local mass murderer—the same man who in 2004 had publicly strung up the bodies of four US citizens after having shot and burned them alive—the Butcher of Fallajuh, no less.

Jon hung up the telephone and waited to consult with Matt and Sam. By the time they met, all three of them had spoken to naval lawyers, and it was decided they should make one last-ditch effort to get out of all this with a plea to the highest authority.

They each requested a General's Call—a far less serious meeting with General Cleveland than Article 15. This was a meeting at which they could once again protest their innocence without signing a written confession, which was, in truth, abhorrent to them all—to Matt, because he had not whacked anyone, to Sam who knew darned well Matt had not whacked anyone, and to Jon because of the lies.

But all of this swiftly became irrelevant, because the request to plead their case in front of Major General Charles Cleveland was refused. And that concluded phase one of their ordeal. On the night of September 25, 2009, the three SEAL petty officers, Matthew Vernon McCabe, Jonathan Keefe, and Sam Gonzales, formally requested courts-martial, a drastic step in anyone's fight to establish innocence.

A court-martial was the only avenue left open to them, as Major General Charles Cleveland would neither listen to nor even see them. And thus far the only intellectual drift any of the SEALs had seen from the General's henchmen was either accusatory, disbelieving, manipulative, or occasionally scornful. A meeting with Cleveland was a dead end.

For the first time Jon, Matt, and Sam understood they must go to trial and plead their case in a room of strangers, before a judge and/or jury.

Still, at least the strangers would be neutral, which was a sight more than anything they had encountered thus far. And certainly they realized that a naval court-martial was an extremely serious matter, its origins stretching back to the days of sail, to the eighteenth century, when it adopted procedures from the 1749 British Naval Code.

Since 1865 there have been US naval officers belonging to the Judge Advocate General's Corps. And today there is a worldwide organization of 730 JAGS providing legal and policy advice to the secretary of the US Navy in all matters concerning military justice.

The JAG Corps' official insignia incorporates a silver "mill rinde," the ancient French symbol of justice for all, under the law. Its purpose was to keep the great stone wheels of the flour mills separate and even, and thus it represents the fine balance the law must observe between the accused and the accuser. The English law also adopted the old iron mill rinde as a symbol of even-handed judgment.

Which all sounded excellent to Jon, who, right now, had his own JAG. Even in their short phone conversation, Threatt had made it very clear that he believed in his client's innocence.

But Matt was scared. He had now been told how dangerous it was to appear before a court-martial on a charge that could lead to prison, but he saw no way out. He understood he may need a substantial amount of money to fund his own defense and did not have the slightest idea where to turn.

The fact was he had no one. And he might very shortly owe a law firm $100,000, which he did not have and, in the foreseeable future, had no way of getting. He did, however, understand he could not go into a courtroom charged with beating up a high-profile Iraqi prisoner without a civilian attorney in his corner.

In desperation he called his father and explained what had happened. He had no idea whether his grandfather had anything close to sufficient cash, but he had to start somewhere. He did not know whether Jon might somehow come up with the money, but the Mc-Cabes almost certainly could not. Of that he was sure. Neither could Sam's family. Matt had no idea what he and Sam would do.

"So far as I could see," he recalled, "I either found a way to raise tens of thousands of dollars or I might end up in the friggin' slammer. Beautiful, right?"

Matt's grandpa said he would, of course, help, but he could not raise anything like $100,000. And all three of the SEALs now understood the gravity of their situation. They tried to find details of the court-martial procedures on their computers, but it was not easy.

They did, however, discover there were three types of court-martial: summary, special, and general, the last being easily the worst, as it could not only impose dishonorable discharge, imprisonment, or even have officers fired, but it could actually sentence a man to death for certain offenses.

The summary court-martial was for relatively minor charges of misconduct and usually involved either a reduction in pay or a month in jail. The three SEALs had indications that their own case was anything but minor. The military was regarding it as a potential Abu Ghraib all over again, and the prospects were not pretty.

None of them thought they'd be whisked through a summary court-martial, but they did think they might land the special court-martial, the intermediate level–trial system. This involves a military judge, trial counsel (prosecutor), defense counsel, and a minimum of three officers forming a jury. This court could remove two-thirds of a man's pay for a year but, on the bright side, was not empowered to impose a sentence of longer than one year's confinement.

What they did not know was that their request for a court-martial trial had sent a chill of apprehension through the upper reaches of the US High Command in Iraq, both Army and Navy. The words "prisoner abuse" doubtless caused obvious consternation.

And there was plenty of consternation, as seen when General Cleveland's staff did everything they could to persuade the SEALs to change their minds. But there was no trust there any longer. Matt, Jon, and Sam believed they would be cajoled and lied to. Essentially they had had enough. And the Army command at Qatar had little option but to allow the case to roll ever upward.

There's no point in allowing such a matter to take any other course; sending it upward takes the responsibility with it. Which was why, only four days later, an official communiqué was transmitted to General Cleveland's office, "pursuant to his request to dispose of the allegations of misconduct by SO2 Jonathan Keefe, SO1 Sam Gonzales, and SO2 Matthew V. McCabe."

It read,

> I release jurisdiction to you, and authorize you to dispose of these matters in any manner you deem appropriate. This includes the authority to convene courts-martial at any level, up to and including General Courts-martial, and to refer charges concerning these individuals to any court-martial.
>
> *Signed: David Petraeus, General, US Army*

"Four-star level, right?" said Matt, a touch sardonically, when he was informed. "No bullshit. From a phantom bang in the guts, straight through to the death penalty. That's what I like about the Army—no half-measures."

Three days later the critical document was sent from Special Operations Command Central, MacDill Air Force Base, Florida. It was headed, SPECIAL COURT-MARTIAL CONVENING ORDER 1-09. And it was signed by Charles T. Cleveland, Major General US Army, Commanding:

> A special court-martial is convened and may proceed at Naval Base Norfolk, Virginia, or any authorized place as directed with the following members:
>
> Captain G. O'REGAN, U.S. Navy; President;
> Commander J. TORRES Jr., U.S. Navy;
> Commander K. L. ICARIUS, U.S. Navy;
> Lieutenant Commander C. R. LARSON, U.S. Navy;
> Ensign B. J. BEYER, U.S. Navy; and,
> Chief Warrant Officer 4 A. D. BOWER, U.S. Navy.

The Army might have taken over the reins of the proceedings, but it remained a US Navy issue. The exchange of letters between Generals Cleveland and Petraeus had nailed it all down. Matt, Jon, and Sam would stand trial in a naval courtroom, and if recent events were any guide, they would probably be tried separately.

That meant three separate courts-martial, at withering expense. But expense was no object in this case, not in the military's relentless search for political correctness, for being seen publicly to have done the right thing—protecting a prisoner's human rights—and being seen to have punished the "miscreants." Which is all very fine if they are indisputably guilty.

But if they are not, that search for political correctness may prove catastrophic. Especially if Threatt's instincts proved correct: the American public and media would loudly disapprove of heroic US Special Forces being dragged through the military justice system on the word of a notorious al-Qaeda terrorist.

That kind of uproar could cause lasting humiliation for the men who had elected to charge the three SEALs. And in the fullness of time, it may prove to be a thoroughly regrettable course of action, from which it might take years to recover.

Meanwhile it all remained a deep secret inside the confines of the military. And the only humiliating that was going on was directed squarely at Matt, Jon, and Sam.

The day after General Cleveland's court-martial letter was delivered, SEAL Team 10 vacated Camp Schwedler and embarked the aircraft for home, Virginia Beach, with their tour of duty in Iraq completed. The three SEALs facing court-martial did not go with them, however, and this caused their families to be very concerned.

Instead, the three men were ordered to continue their back-breaking menial tasks on the Qatar base, one of which was to load by hand several tons of old furniture onto dump trucks. "That was a bit of a killer, four hours at a time in 130-degree heat," said Matt, who added wryly: "But the really great part was the US Army never once made us work with a ball and chain around our ankles."

The truckloads of furniture were not all. There was, on the base, a gigantic warehouse, the size of two football fields, and the three SEALs were made to sweep it out, by hand with brooms, from end to end until it was free of dust and sand.

They were then transferred to the gymnasium and made to clean and sanitize the equipment. They cleaned bathrooms and laundry rooms—"stuff that had not been done in a year," said Matt. "Just for the record, we completed the lot in one week. I mentioned before, no one can do anything better than us."

Long days of this kind of punishment were interspersed with regular sessions of lectures, as the Army's legal men tried to persuade them to accept a General's Mast. Apparently General Cleveland was prepared to see them only under these circumstances, when they would, of course, be required to "confess their crimes." But the SEALs refused to answer, saying nothing and remaining stubbornly righteous to the end, while everyone waited for the court-martial papers to come through.

This happened on October 5, and at last, a few days after their teammates, Matt McCabe, Jon Keefe, and Sam Gonzales were released to return home. They flew commercial from Qatar to Washington and then down to Norfolk. They were under strict orders not to discuss the case with anyone.

But they did talk to their parents, who had no idea what had happened or why Team 10 arrived back without them. This was not a joyful reunion, and the atmosphere of gloom and dread would remain with them all for the next six months.

Shame affects everyone, especially a young serviceman whose honor has been challenged. It happens very rarely, but when it does it's an insidious thing: *My son is accused of assault and lying ... My son is accused of dereliction of duty ... Can he be guilty? ... Why would the US Navy do this to him if he were innocent? ... Can there be this much smoke without fire?*

In these three cases the friends, relatives, and, especially, family members were dumbfounded. Matt, Jon, and Sam were such obviously upstanding people—the charges against them were unthinkable. No one was supposed to say anything about the forthcoming trial, but the rumors were rocket boosted as soon as Team 10 arrived home without them.

The families had been assured they were not dead, injured, or missing in action, but this served only to deepen the mystery, which then had about four days to burgeon into a cauldron of speculation, wild guesses, and despondency. The military is extremely competent at keeping a lid on things, and thus far, despite the breathtaking "news value," not a word had leaked beyond the Virginia Beach and Norfolk Bases.

As the mystery for the families deepened, inside the Pentagon there was growing dread that the Army was about to hurl the Navy into the worst possible light, led by the convening major general, Charles T. Cleveland.

And those growing dreads grew more realistic every day. And the arrival of the court-martial papers in the first week of October effectively cast the one-month-old saga into stone. There was no going back now. All three SEALs were in the process of hiring civilian lawyers. The high command of the US Army temporarily sidelined the Navy.

The official papers were arriving almost hourly—statements, affidavits, and, worst of all, charge sheets. Jon was almost physically sick at the sight of them:

In that Special Operator Second Class Jonathan E. Keefe, SEAL Team TEN, Naval Amphibious Base Little Creek, Virginia, US Navy, on active duty, who should have known of his duties, at Camp Schwedler, Baharia, Iraq, on or about 1 September 2009, was derelict in the performance of those duties in that he willfully failed to safeguard a detainee, Mr. Ahmad Hashim Abd Al-Isawi, as it was his duty to do.

That was Jon's violation of Article 92 (UCMJ). The violation of Article 107 was worse, alleging that

with intent to deceive, made to Special Agent John Stamp, Naval Criminal Investigative Service, an official statement, to wit: "I did not see anyone abuse or mistreat Mr. Al-Isawi" or words to that effect, which statement was totally false and was then known by the said Petty Officer Second Class Keefe to be so false.

They hit Matthew McCabe with those exact same charges and then added his alleged violation of Article 128:

In that SPECIAL OPERATOR SECOND CLASS MATTHEW V. MC-CABE SEAL TEAM TEN ... on active duty, did at Camp Schwedler ... same date ... unlawfully strike Ahmad Hashim Abd Al-Isawi in the midsection with his fist.

Matt's accusers were listed as Staff Sergeant Scott K. Ashcraft (US Marines), the man who had first brought in the charge sheet drafts for them to sign, and Commander T. C. Huntley, legal assistant to General Cleveland, the man who had refused to listen to one word of their protests of innocence and who had convened the courts-martial.

Those charge sheets represented the drawing of battle lines. In the coming weeks of October Jon hired the famous Virginia Beach no-holds-barred attorney Greg D. McCormack as his lead defense counsel in addition to the Navy JAG Paul Threatt.

McCormack had the reputation of a formidable court-martial trial advocate. He was himself a former member of the US Army's JAG Corps, serving first as a military prosecutor and then as a defense counsel for three years until he left the Army in 1982.

McCormack had over thirty years experience of litigation and was licensed to practice law in all military appellate courts. His acknowledged expertise has always been in criminal cases, where his fast, adversarial manner has helped win the release of many, many falsely accused men.

And like Paul Threatt, McCormack made up his mind very swiftly about Jon. He would later state that from the very first he found it utterly impossible that the big Virginian would have dreamed of lying to the SEAL authorities or that he had seen his teammate Matt punch the blindfolded prisoner.

For McCormack it did not add up. Jon was about as blameless as any serviceman he had ever defended. And when the renowned courtroom aggressor felt like that about any accused man, he would go to the ends of the earth to protect him, if necessary. And that included Iraq.

Matt too made a major move toward hiring the very best legal assistance. He went to the former US Marine Lieutenant Colonel Neal A. Puckett, a thirty-five-year courtroom veteran, having been a former JAG and military judge with a towering reputation for combative court-martial expertise.

Puckett had represented the accused in a series of high-profile military cases. But the one that propelled him into national recognition was that of Lieutenant Colonel Allen West, former battalion commander in the 4th infantry division in Iraq and, later, congressman for Florida's 22nd District Republican Party.

West had been facing charges of detainee abuse in Iraq in 2003 when, admittedly stepping out of line, he had fired a pistol straight past an Iraqi detainee's head and frightened the living daylights out of him during a robust interrogation.

There had been mitigating circumstances—insurgents were plotting to kill West. In addition, the colonel believed the detainee had substantial information about terrorist activity and was determined to get it out of him.

He confessed to losing his temper and equally to taking a few whacks at the prisoner. But, in precisely the same manner as the case against Matt, Jon, and Sam, the entire thing got rapidly out of hand, despite no one having come to much harm. And the gunshot had worked: the prisoner immediately divulged plans for an upcoming attack that would probably have cost many American lives.

His CO, Major General Raymond Odierno, brought down the guillotine on the well-regarded West, immediately relieving him of command, which instantly killed his career. The colonel faced the prospect of resigning his commission just before qualifying for his retirement pension and benefits or facing court-martial, which could have brought him eight years in a military prison.

The colonel acknowledged he had not followed "proper procedures" but insisted that he had acted as he did to protect his men. He stated at his hearing that he would "walk through hell with a gasoline can in my hand to protect any one of them, if need be."

Puckett leapt to his defense. In a memorable exchange with the military authorities he warned them of the rising anger of the American people and compelled them to back down. In the end Colonel West received a letter of reprimand from General Odierno and was allowed to retire from the Army with his pension and rank intact. In turn, people both within and outside the military congratulated Neal Puckett. And when Petty Officer Matthew McCabe walked through his office door in Alexandria, Virginia, Puckett could not help but draw sharp comparisons between the two cases, the main difference being that Matt had done nothing wrong in the first place.

Major General Odierno, promoted under Bill Clinton, had plainly shot himself in both feet, not the least of which for arousing enormous public fury at the cruel way he had tried to force an outstanding officer to forfeit his entire pension when he was just seventy-two hours short of qualifying.

The general should, of course, have just let the clock run out over three days and then quietly sent the colonel home with a letter of reprimand, with his pension for a lifetime of service intact. Instead, however, in the interests of "human rights," and "being seen by the terrorists to be fair," he had caused near-riot conditions among the right-wing media and placed the military in a most unfavorable, utterly heartless light.

So far as Neal Puckett could see, this Major General Charles Cleveland was well on his way to doing precisely the same thing if he wasn't very careful.

7

—

SOUND AND FURY
IN CONGRESS

These SEALs are exceptional, having captured a terrorist who
not only killed Americans, but also maimed and mutilated their
bodies. We believe that prosecution of the SEALs will have a
negative impact on others in the military, who risk their lives in
dangerous, often ambiguous situations.

—Congressional petition

The world's largest naval station occupies more than seven miles of
pier and wharf all along the Hampton Roads Peninsula in Norfolk, Virginia, home to some seventy-five US fighting ships and their support.

Given that each one of the two or three gigantic aircraft carriers on
the jetties contains at least two thousand telephones, communication
in this secretive enclave of the US Defense Department is, shall we say,
awesomely effective.

Marginally swifter, however, is the ship-to-shore, jetty-to-quarterdeck, harbor launch-to-ops room, and bush telegraph of rumor, report, buzz, and speculation. There are other places in the world with
standard rumor operations and half-witted publications to project the
type of drivel that Hollywood show business adores, but when even a
whisper of something truly major breaks out in the US military, that
sprawling Norfolk Navy yard is atomic by comparison. And if you

really want to set the lines of communication vibrating, just start arresting US Navy SEALs who have just returned from a highly dangerous and successful combat mission.

US Navy personnel are masters at short, terse, signals that convey everything very, very quickly: *Hear they're planning to court-martial three guys from SEAL Team 10? That's Echo Platoon, right? ... The guys who grabbed that killer, what'shisname? Al-Isawi? You have to be kidding me! You could start a civil war doing that! I hear a lot of the guys are very upset. Not half as upset as the American public when the friggin' media gets ahold of it!*

And this was not mere gossip among the rank and file, although the yards were buzzing with speculation about the three SEALs who did not come home with the rest of Team 10. This was also rapidly making its way into the upper reaches of the military citadel across the Potomac from Washington, DC.

Senior officers, at least those with a semblance of recollection about the world beyond the five giant outer walls of the Pentagon, quietly considered the actions of Major General Cleveland and found them to be about as ill advised as they could possibly be.

The Navy had somehow jumped all over an unreliable statement from a stressed-out kid in one of the SEAL bases in Iraq and taken the colossal step of believing it and then acting as though a heroic SEAL platoon did not have an honest man among them.

They were effectively branding the SEAL Team leader a bully and a liar, the senior enlisted man of the entire base both a liar and guilty of dereliction of duty, and, perhaps the bravest of them, the mighty breacher from Virginia, the God-fearing Jonathan Keefe, a liar and a disgrace to the SEAL uniform.

If anyone truly had an ambition to denigrate the US Navy and open a veritable Pandora's box of universal contempt for the service, this was a pretty good way to start. Any junior copywriter in the public affairs department could have forecast a firestorm of criticism via radio, television, newspapers, tweets, blogs, Internet, World Wide Web, and God knows what else.

And for what? Did these senior officers really wish to turn against three of the SEALs' finest on the word of a wanted mass murderer and terrorist and a young serving sailor who was caught absent from his post—twice—and who was reputed to be a stressed-out kid?

Like it or not, the American public *loves* the SEALs. They see them as the bravest of the brave, the hard men the US military sends in when the going gets tough. They are regarded as the frontline of US military muscle, the American warrior class who will charge in where others fear to tread, the inevitable spearhead when defeat is unthinkable. They make America proud. And when they die in combat this makes the nation sad. And when they come home in body bags the nation quietly mourns.

If you pick a fight with these guys, you better know precisely what you are saying. Because no one's going to think much of you if you start a fight with the beloved SEALs. And there are two rules to remember: (1) anyone saying anything bad about them is an unprincipled bastard and (2) the SEALs have collectively told fewer lies than General Washington, and if you plan to disbelieve them publicly, you're on the wrong side before you even get out of the starting gate.

In cases such as these, the force of public bias must be carefully taken into consideration. The military is always the loyal servant of the US government, and in turn, the government is elected by the people. And any time either the military or the politicians decide to press ahead against the wishes of the populace, alarms should sound.

Because the public does not like it when high-ranking military officers—whom they trust cautiously—pillory Navy SEALs, whom they trust implicitly. And in this case, it is inconceivable that dire warnings were not heard all over the US Navy's inner sanctums not to mention the Pentagon, the Army, and anywhere else the shrewdest minds were active.

We now know that in the months leading up to the courts-martial senior US Navy legal officers were voicing unease about the forthcoming debacle. In the Naval Legal Service Office (NLSO), Mid-Atlantic, in the Norfolk Yards, wise words of warning were frequently heard.

But the trouble was not only ahead; it was also all around, and the senior officers, doggedly pressing on with the charges against probably innocent men felt that turning back now was impossible. In hindsight nailing the real problem is simple: the Navy authorities had, with lightning speed, jumped onto the wrong side of this conundrum, believed entirely the wrong people, and found themselves stranded—no retreat. And with every passing week the situation worsened.

It was now edging toward mid-October. And there were not only naval JAGs involved, wanting documents and demanding discovery, but there were also civilian lawyers, men like Neal Puckett and his staff as well as Greg McCormack and his paralegals, who were demanding the statements both from the SEALs and their accusers, requesting the information right now, insisting that everything be made available to the legal teams.

This was clearly enough to put the fear of God into the Navy's legal services, and the delays became legion, particularly as the reliability of the prosecution's star witness, Brian Westinson, was so plainly vulnerable to attack. The prosecution's only other "witness" was the transparently dishonest, world-class liar and murderer, Ahmad Hashim Abd Al-Isawi.

For the first few weeks following the initial requests, there was a kind of Mexican standoff, with the military playing an unrelenting defense, pointing out that the statements of SEAL Team 10 were classified and that the process of declassifying them was long and detailed. And this brought any forward movement to a virtual standstill.

By now there were dozens and dozens of pages, all sworn to, signed, and re-signed by every Navy SEAL who had been anywhere near the prisoner's holding cell in the early hours of September 2. And every one of those written statements declared that no one had hit Al-Isawi, no one had seen anyone else hit Al-Isawi, no one could even imagine a SEAL hitting Al-Isawi, and, yes, each and every one of them was prepared to stand up in a military court and swear to God that their combat brothers, Matt McCabe, Jonathan Keefe, and Sam Gonzales, were innocent of any wrongdoing.

But to the defense teams, the statements remained unavailable. And because no trial or court-martial under US law could proceed without due discovery afforded to the defense, there could be no trial, no setting in which the accused can challenge his accuser. Right now the defense had no means of examining the evidence offered against their clients. This alone would be quite sufficient to impel any self-respecting judge to throw the entire thing out or, to use judicial language, to abate the court-martial (postpone it indefinitely).

On the one hand, the US military was very obviously nerve wracked about the paucity of their evidence and feared that the civilian defense counsel would rip apart their witnesses, Westinson and Al-Isawi, in cross examination. On the other, they could scarcely withhold the documents for fear that the judge would cancel the court-martial.

There is no record of the personal hopes and demeanor of Major General Cleveland during this time. But there have been suggestions that he was not alone in his quagmire. Perhaps the general was certain in his own mind that the SEALs were guilty and that Westinson and Al-Isawi were men to be trusted.

But it appears more likely that political pressure was being exerted, that the White House was prepared to do anything in its power to avoid another prisoner-abuse scandal on the scale of Abu Ghraib. And this Al-Isawi character was an extremely high-profile character. President Obama had already made it clear that the United States would not shrink from its obligations to act with fairness and justice for all, no matter the nationality or circumstances.

Excessive violence would not be tolerated, and those guilty of unreasonable force against a captured detainee would be brought to task. It would not be unfair to mention here that some people thought President Obama was somewhat obsessed with detainees' rights.

Hauling three SEALs with impeccable military records before a court-martial might cause a local public uproar, but that would not be comparable to an international condemnation of US tactics on foreign soil. That would indeed make life very difficult for the US president and might even cause a demand for a US apology to the Iraqis and the universal anger of the entire Middle East.

Throwing Matt, Jon, and Sam to the wolves would be a small price to pay on an international scale of US humiliation. Unless, of course, you happened to be Matt, Jon, or Sam. In this case the perspective from the Oval Office might very well have been different from that of most Americans. And there is much to suggest that Major General Cleveland may have found himself caught up on the horns of a very tricky dilemma: to obey the wishes of his commander-in-chief or to sink these tenuous courts-martial without a trace.

The trouble was that it had all gone too far, and now there was no turning back. These SEALs had *demanded* courts-martial because it was the only way for them to clear their names, to prove their innocence in a court of military law. And they had that right. No one could take it away from them.

Nonetheless, there was disquiet down in the NLSO Mid-Atlantic headquarters on Maryland Avenue, deep inside the Norfolk Base. But that disquiet was surpassed in the branch offices in Little Creek's Naval Amphibious Base and NAS Oceana in Virginia Beach. Because men of Special Warfare Command surrounded these legal offices, and as the month of October proceeded there was a rising anger among the SEAL community that they were somehow being betrayed.

Senior legal counselors, some of whom had spent a lifetime in the US Navy, firmly believed that even if the prosecutors were correct and Matt had given this captured murderer a bang in the slats, the American public, with its irritating surfeit of common sense, would say, "So what?" And then: "At least Matt McCabe didn't cut off his head or shoot him or burn him alive in a car and then mutilate him and drag his body through the streets before hanging him from the Hampton Roads Bridge. What do we care if he gave him a short punch in the guts that never even left a mark? And now you want to court-martial Matt, the assault Team leader that captured the terrorist? Are you out of your minds?"

Over and over senior lawyers warned of the dangers the prosecutors faced. Even if they were right (hugely doubtful), they were in a no-win situation. If the court found the three SEALs not guilty, the Navy would be subject to utter ridicule. If they were found guilty and punished, there could be riot conditions all over the country.

However, in the minds of several Navy JAGs there was one great hope: Robert M. Gates, the twenty-second US secretary of defense, appointed by President George W. Bush in December 2006 and still serving under President Obama.

Secretary Gates, former director of the CIA and deputy national security adviser to President George H. W. Bush, was renowned for his capacity to make balanced, fair, and reasonable judgments. Some people believed he was the best defense secretary in the history of the United States and that there was no way he was going to allow the US Navy dragged through the mire on this one. If he wished to, some thought he could overrule and order the court-martial proceedings to stop.

Secretary Gates had vast experience in making sound judgments. He was a former president of Texas A&M University and had served under James A. Baker III, President Reagan's former chief of staff who also cochaired the Iraq Study Group (ISG) in 2006, which had prepared the most important documents on the Iraq War. Gates knew the country along with its endless difficulties. He also understood the criminal brutality of men like Ahmad Hashim Abd Al-Isawi. Many naval lawyers were confident Robert M. Gates would not tolerate these almost-farcical courts-martial.

But inside the Pentagon there was already the beginning of an enormous dichotomy involving the office of the secretary of defense. Even as early as mid-October there were few legal officers in the Pentagon who were not acquainted with the burgeoning uproar surrounding the phantom whack in the stomach Matt McCabe had not delivered.

Although technically the secretary of defense could intervene, no one could recall that ever having happened before. If he did step forward and overrule the lower commanders, he would probably need to take control and claim full authority before convening his own military court. He could not, however, dismiss the current charges out of hand, but he could most certainly encourage others to do so.

Basically Secretary Gates would have to jump through a whole lot of hoops, and that would probably contribute to a bigger public outcry than the one already anticipated as soon as the media got ahold of the story.

The fact was that there were very definite legal obstacles standing between the military boss and the potential action of overturning decisions made by the lower-level commanders, who preferred to proceed with the prosecution.

There was a court-martial rule that prevented intervention under the heading of "unlawful command influence." This rule stated that no high-ranking commander may interfere with a court-martial conducted by lower-level commanders regarding the "functions of … such persons in the conduct of the proceedings."

Secretary Gates could, however, step in after the court-martial to reduce penalties. But in this case the secretary's lawyers would doubtless advise against this. It was the "unlawful command influence" that really stood in the way. For the high command to start telling lower commanders to do this, that, and the other in a court-martial case, would, strictly by the book, be illegal.

The military legal process in the case of judicial punishment is commander- not prosecutor-driven as it is in the civilian legal process. During the very early discussions the highly influential Frank Gaffney, former assistant defense secretary in the Reagan administration, stated that in his view the problem stemmed from an early policy decision by the Obama administration.

"I cannot," he said, "imagine anyone in uniform, JAG officers included, supporting this prosecution." Gaffney thought that the whole issue was "not inconsistent with the Justice Department's decision to try 9/11 terrorists in US civilian courts, with full constitutional rights."

He added that some people may need reminding that "these terrorists are killers." Capturing them may bring vital intel, which may save American lives. "If we cannot get the intelligence out of these people," he said, "that may *cost* American lives." It was, of course, a thinly disguised compliment to the SEALs' desert mission, led by Matt McCabe.

All of which left the Republican Robert Gates in a somewhat awkward spot. And all the while the requests for the documents of discovery poured relentlessly through the doors of the Navy's legal department. And no one appeared to know what to do—whether to hand them over to the lawyers or hold back and hope something might break in the prosecution's favor.

And all through these turbulent yet fruitless weeks, Jon recalled driving over to his lawyers' offices several times a week and waiting for the statements to arrive, especially the ones from the SEALs, the ones from "my brothers, who all swore to God we were innocent."

Jon's principal civilian lawyer, Greg McCormack, was standing shoulder to shoulder with the Navy JAG Paul Threatt, demanding to see and examine all the statements made by Brian Westinson, upon whose hesitant words the entire case for the prosecution rested.

The same applied to Matt and Sam—back and forth to Alexandria and Virginia Beach, getting nowhere, trying to stay calm, trying to ignore the possibility of conviction and ultimate disgrace for a crime no one had committed.

In fact the longer this standoff went on, the more certain the defense teams were that the issue was already in front of the highest authorities in the land. It was inconceivable that neither the White House nor the offices of the defense secretary were being kept up to pace with the proceedings.

And this produced a ray of hope—that Secretary Gates would find a way to "discourage" the prosecution from going ahead, even if it were against the wishes of his commander-in-chief.

Because if Gates could not slam his fist on the table and demand an end to these plainly suspect courts-martial of three American heroes, then no one could. And the three SEALs would simply have to try to raise the money and defend themselves against a shockingly unfair world.

Meanwhile, October turned into November, and the miracle was that no word of the forthcoming courts-martial had leaked. The charges were formally issued to all three defendants during the last four days of October, and the pure malice surrounding how these papers were served came as a major shock to both Matt and Jon, despite that they had become pretty accustomed to malice by now.

They were suddenly informed, in the middle of a working morning, that they were to report to the Navy legal offices at the Norfolk Base but that they were not to travel in the same vehicle, as this is banned for personnel on serious charges.

So they went separately and were ordered to report to an enlisted clerk, E3 pay grade, who was standing in the stairwell. Jon went first and was formally handed the charges that threatened to destroy his life. Matt had to wait, and then he too was ordered forward to face this clerk of inferior rank and receive the documents his accusers prepared.

"Once again," said Jon, "we were treated like men who have already been found guilty of something. There was no dignity for us, standing in the stairwell, being summoned to have these disgraceful charges handed to us."

At this point the trials were scheduled for January, with times and places to be decided. And what preceded those trials, through the late fall and early winter, was some kind of daily living hell for the three SEALs, now firmly established as total outcasts from their own tribe. They were restricted to Virginia Beach except to visit lawyers. Each one of them was scared they might lose their homes in order to pay the legal fees, the sum total of which were not yet known.

Returning home after such a tour of duty is traditionally a time for the continuing development of Team members' careers—professional development at the SEAL schools for snipers, JTAC/comms, and breachers. Everybody else was going, but not Jon, Matt, and Sam. They were not allowed to progress through this critical phase of their education, where careers were made and men were raised up to be the best they could possibly be.

Those schools represented a SEAL's gateway to the future. And they were denied to the three accused men. All of the SEAL platoons were trying to help them, writing letters of recommendation their behalf. The commander who ran Troop 3, under which stands both Echo and Foxtrot Platoons, did everything in his considerable power to place Matt, Jon, and Sam in the correct educational strata.

But their status was already being controlled at a two-star level, way above the authority of any SEAL commander, and the result was predictable. Every application was turned down, even though Jon was already slotted to attend sniper school. There were no proper duties for the accused men, nothing until the charges against them were either proven or cast asunder.

But deep inside the Navy legal offices there was already serious consternation about the cases, especially bringing Al-Isawi to the United States to face the men he had so spectacularly accused of beating him.

Every defendant has a right to confront his accuser in a court of law, and the military court is no exception. No one with a lick of sense would believe *anything* Al-Isawi said, and the Justice Department had compounded the issue by granting all terrorists appearing in a US court of law the same rights as a US citizen.

That meant Al-Isawi, if faced with withering cross-examination by attorneys like Neal Puckett and Greg McCormack, would be entitled to identical protection as any American. His own lawyers would be swift to step in: *"With respect, may I remind your honor that Mr. Al-Isawi is not on trial here? And he has the right of refusal to answer that question."*

None of the Navy JAGs looked forward to that, whichever side of the fence they occupied. And the senior command was quickly discovering that Al-Isawi would serve everyone better if he stayed in Iraq, especially for Matt's trial. Neal Puckett would plainly make short work of the unmarked, unharmed Iraqi who claimed he'd received the mother and father of a beating from a big, bad, mean Navy SEAL. After all, the judge might throw it out, right then and there.

Week in and week out, the demands for full discovery came in from the defense lawyers, who so far had received access to nothing. Rumors of this deadlock continued to circulate through the Norfolk Base and the nearby Navy SEAL headquarters. Literally hundreds of personnel were fully aware of the situation, and most of them were not only angry, but they were also aware of the apparent dangers to everyone on active SEAL combat missions.

If it could happen to guys like Matt, Jon, and Sam, it sure as hell could happen to anyone else. And the three Team 10 guys had been forced to hire expensive lawyers—top US advocates who could go into a court-martial and fight for their clients. It did not escape Virginia Beach SEALs' attention that in these early years of the twenty-first century all Special Forces might soon need lawyers, at least they would if they were expected to fight an enemy.

It was merely a matter of time before this seething naval tragedy kicked its way out of the military strongholds of southeastern Virginia and into the public print and airwaves.

———

It finally happened around noon on Tuesday, November 24, 2009. Fox News broke the story nationwide, a tad opportunistically, beneath the headline:

NAVY SEALS FACE ASSAULT CHARGES FOR
CAPTURING MOST WANTED TERRORIST

This was nearly true. But plainly inaccurate. The assault charge against Matthew McCabe was not for capturing the Butcher of Fallujah; it was for allegedly giving him a whack in the stomach several hours after he was brought into SEAL custody.

Still, FoxNews was operating on a leak, and leaks have their own brand of frustration: wonderful information but not enough of it. They are sufficient for a news organization to run with the story but insufficient to lay out, chapter and verse, what actually was happening.

What do we do? Run with scant detail? Or make a few things up, fill in the gaps as best we can, and then stand behind the confidentiality of our source who, plainly, in time-honored journalistic traditions, can never be revealed.

That mind-set was not unique to Fox, which deserves massive credit for getting ahold of the story before anyone else, instantly jumping onto the correct side of the argument, and leading the way for everyone else to follow in their wake.

What Fox did was, as Sherlock Holmes would have concurred, elementary. All of their journalistic instincts told them that the US Navy was a gigantic force to set itself against three guys—hardworking, brave, and loyal patriots. These men were Navy SEALs, America's elite commandoes. So as far as Fox could see, they stood alone against a new foe whose resources were practically limitless.

But not any more they didn't. FoxNews came up with a story with a slant crafted to touch the heart and soul of every American. They wrote it with immeasurable skill. Just the names touched a thousand heartstrings—Matt, Jon, and Sam, proper American boys from Ohio, Virginia, and Chicago: every father's beloved son, every family's quiet hero.

Fox laid it right out. The three SEALs had secretly captured one of the most wanted terrorists in Iraq, the alleged mastermind of the murder and mutilation of four Blackwater USA security guards in Fallujah in 2004, "and now three of them are facing criminal charges."

After just one paragraph the battle lines between the media and the US Navy were drawn. FoxNews understood the American public would *never* put up with this. And once they'd established Al-Isawi's dishonesty, right at the top of the broadcast, they unleashed the cavalry: "Now, instead of being lauded for bringing to justice a high-value target, three of the SEAL commandoes, all enlisted, face assault charges and have retained lawyers."

They listed the charges against Matt, Jon, and Sam and then interviewed Neal Puckett, who stated, "The SEALs are being charged for allegedly giving the detainee a punch in the gut."

Neal proceeded, ingenuously, to add fuel to the FoxNews fire, adding, "I do not know how they are going to bring this detainee to the United States and give us our constitutional right to confrontation in the courtroom. ... We have terrorists getting their constitutional rights in New York City, but I suspect they're going to deny these SEALs their right to confrontation in a military courtroom in Virginia."

Again, this was the image of the unstoppable power of the Pentagon—utilizing the law, crushing the SEALs' rights, and indulging in unfair bullying in the most ruthless possible way. Against their own, no less. Puckett had spread his arms wide, a study in bewilderment and fair play. And this very neatly covered up that hickory-tough seam that runs through the heart of every trial lawyer.

FoxNews was well on top of the situation. Unlike the defense lawyers, they had somehow obtained the official handwritten statement of one of the SEALs, made only three hours after Al-Isawi was captured and was still being held at the SEAL base at Camp Baharia prior to his removal to Baghdad.

The SEAL had confirmed his actions: shower, breakfast, and a quick look at the detainee. "I gave him a glance over and then left," he had written. "I did not notice anything wrong with the detainee, and he appeared in good health."

FoxNews did not know at the time precisely how many similar accounts there would eventually be. And they switched their attack to the Army, connecting to Special Operations, US Central Command, where Lieutenant Colonel Holly Silkman confirmed that the three SEALs had been charged and courts-martial had been scheduled for January.

Central Command would not discuss the detainee, but that was not essential. FoxNews quickly found out precisely who he was and compelled a naval legal source to confirm that the military had been "tracking the guy for some time."

They described the Fallujah "atrocity"—"ambush," "burned bodies," "dragged through the streets," hanging of the bodies on the bridge, all by "Al-Isawi, the ringleader."

They finished with a flourish, reminding the world of the military's nerve-wracked attitude to the words "detainee abuse."

At which point the cat was well and truly out of the bag. Newsrooms, both print and broadcast, all over the country were now on the case. Generally speaking they could hardly wait to highlight the US Navy's "outrageous" conduct in going after their own heroes for possibly taking a swing at a detainee of such obvious evil as Al-Isawi.

And in the very week when all of this was happening—interviews, opinions, experts, solutions, media advice, counteradvice, and counter-counteradvice, the Pentagon continued to move ahead with its prosecution. On December 7 the three SEALs were formally arraigned in a military court in Norfolk.

By some mysterious force the public had found out about the arraignment and somehow gathered outside the gates to the Norfolk Base, hoping, along with the massed ranks of the media, to meet Matt when he emerged. And there Matt found his father, Marty, talking to Donna Zovko, the mother of one of the slain Blackwater contractors. She had driven from Cleveland, Ohio, to stand with the other supporters in the crowd, many of whom were carrying banners.

One of them, a Navy veteran from Virginia Beach, was Richard Berndt, who had been there since 6 A.M. with a sign that read, YOU FOUGHT FOR US—NOW WE FIGHT FOR YOU.

"I just feel I owe these guys everything I can give them," said Richard. "They just need our support."

Matt himself, immaculate in his uniform, looked astonished at the size of the crowd, some of whom wanted to know whether he and his two teammates had really whacked the terrorist.

And he replied without flinching: "No. The answer's no, point blank." And then his father introduced him to Donna, and the SEAL told her: "I can't begin to imagine the pain you have endured for so long. I only hope that the capture of this guy brings a bit of closure."

He stayed for a few minutes, but by then the media were growing restless, firing questions from all angles, and no SEAL wishes to hang around them for long. He just thanked everyone, climbed into a vehicle, and returned to base.

Twenty years ago the media uproar would have been all there was. Not so in the ninth year of the twenty-first century. This was the time of the personalized electronic superhighway, Facebook. And more mysterious forces in highly unlikely quarters were gathering, especially to express the fury of the US public at this apparent betrayal of everyone's heroes, the gallant and unimpeachable SEALs.

Perhaps the eye of this gathering storm was in a leafy suburb of Scottsdale, Arizona, way down in the southwestern Salt River Valley. There, Graham Ware, a thirty-year-old computer technologist and former East Scottsdale High shortstop, was so incensed by the apparent injustice that he charged to his Facebook account and let fly with a hard-hitting blog.

It should be recorded that Graham was a potential Special Forces man himself. Inflamed by the cruel audacity of 9/11, he had made instant moves to sign on for either US Army Special Forces or the Marines. He was young, fit, and highly athletic, as useful on the basketball court as he was on the baseball field. And in the moments following the Twin Towers collapse he had resolved to answer the call of his country.

"In my mind," he says, "the bugle had sounded. Who did these people think they were? The only thing I wanted in all the world was to enlist, get trained, and get after them. I just wanted to help, any way I could."

But his family stepped in. Graham had a younger sister and brother, and no one was pretending that armed service on behalf of the United States in the mountains of Afghanistan was anything but highly dangerous. "Hell, I was young," he says. "And that's where I was headed."

But family pressures increased. "They didn't mean it, but in the end I guess it was guilt they were laying on me. What if I should die, and all that? They didn't realize I was indestructible, at least I thought so, the way the young always do.

"And in the end they won. I never signed on. Then I kinda sat back and nursed my regrets for the next eight years, detesting the Taliban and al-Qaeda, always wondering what would have happened if I'd ridden rough-shod over the wishes of my parents and gone to war anyway. Guess I might have got shot. Like a lot of other guys."

But the plight of Matt, Jon, and Sam ignited within Graham Ware a flame of the purest fire. And there was an immediate response to his Facebook blog. An atmosphere of universal outrage swiftly began to take root. Graham persuaded his local buddy Jason Watts to join him. And with thousands of bloggers jumping on the bandwagon, demanding exoneration for Matt, Jon, and Sam, a new and hugely popular website came into being.

Graham created a dazzling design and named it "Support the SEALs," launching the site in the first week of December. The response was sensational, as the American public rose up in anger at how the three heroes from Echo Platoon, Team 10 had been treated. "At one point," he said, "we were receiving ten thousand pledges of support a week! Not just in spirit but in promises of donations to help with their legal expenses."

Matt himself was on the line to Graham, thanking him with a gratitude so profound that the Scottsdale IT expert admitted, "Suddenly I knew I was not meant to join the armed forces. I was born to do this venture. Not only to line up publicly with the three guys but to set an example, to stand out in front, demonstrate my belief in their innocence. Right here I could really help. And the Internet was my parade ground. I knew it like the SEAL instructors knew the Grinder in Coronado. *Hooyah, Graham!*"

In the coming weeks more than 280,000 people visited the website Graham Ware and Jason Watts had launched. "Support the SEALs" became a rallying point for more than a quarter of a million Americans, all demanding justice for the SEALs—to have the charges against them cast aside, to use whatever vestiges of common sense the military had left to put right this atrocious wrong against the three American elite commandoes.

Graham's skill at operating cyberspace was an enormous factor in the website's success. He had search engines colliding with each other in the stampede to find the place where help for the SEALs actually meant something.

Most people who hit the buttons looking for information on the court-martialed SEALs found themselves reading Graham's words and being guided to where financial contributions would be channeled directly to Matt, Jon, and Sam.

Inevitably it attracted several big hitters, wealthy men who would stand behind those anticipated legal bills on behalf of the three accused warriors. One of them, a wealthy hedge fund financier from Chicago with a heart the size of Wrigley Field, contributed tens of thousands of dollars, the maximum permitted under US tax laws for a gift, and fed the money through to the SEALs' families.

"When he contacted me by phone," recalls Matt, "I just stood there, unable even to blurt out my thanks. I just knew that God was in his heaven and that we had a chance. We'd never asked for exoneration, but we wanted the opportunity to stand up in court with proper help and advice and prove our accusers were totally and utterly wrong. When I took that phone call somehow I knew we'd got that chance."

It was now impossible to miss the avalanche of support building up in cyberspace. Graham and Jason were improving their website every day, and big dollars were pouring in, not necessarily in large bills and credit card donations but sometimes just five- and ten-dollar contributions from ordinary Americans, often people who could barely afford it. But always from people who just could not comprehend why the US Navy had turned their hand against three of its own outstanding people.

And this was indeed a mystery. Because those first couple of weeks in December were bordering on the momentous in terms of the critical path to court-martial and humiliation for one side or the other— the SEALs or the military. The stakes were so high that the Pentagon generals must have had to rethink what precisely they were getting themselves into.

Because it was not just members of the public who were furious at the prospect of these courts-martial. There was also sound and fury in very high places, not least of all in the great hall of the Capitol building, where the US House of Representative sits solemnly (mostly) beneath the Capitol's two thousand–ton cast-iron dome.

And among the many eminent members who sit in this chamber, there was the Republican Duncan D. Hunter of California's 52nd congressional district, son of the Republican Congressman Duncan L. Hunter, who retired after fourteen terms. Congressman Hunter won his father's seat with 72 percent of the vote.

But even more important than his rich Republican traditions, Congressman Hunter was a former captain in the US Marine Corps. He was one of only seven members of Congress who had served in either Iraq or Afghanistan, and he was the first combat veteran of either conflict to serve in Congress.

Captain Hunter was on active duty in Battery A, 1st Battalion, 11th Marines, fighting in Operation Vigilant Resolve when US forces laid siege to the city of Fallujah just four days after Ahmad Hashim Abd Al-Isawi swung the burned bodies from the bridge. Duncan knew of this fiendish action firsthand.

Captain Hunter had commanded his men in those rubble-strewn streets, heard the bombs and blasts as well as the cries and whispers of terribly wounded men. He'd hit back at the insurgents and come through the firefights. And he understood the enemy's fanatical intrinsic evil.

When he first heard that the very SEALs who had finally captured the Butcher were facing courts-martial, he could scarcely believe it. He could not recall ever being so disappointed and angry at the military in which he still served as a part-time captain in the Marine Corps Reserve.

Duncan Hunter was as much a patriot as the men who now faced disgrace. With similar emotions to those of the outraged Graham Ware three hundred miles away in Scottsdale, Arizona, the now thirty-three-year-old California congressman had charged out of his office on the day after 9/11 and joined the Marines.

And now, eight years later, he was looking at an astounding overreaction by the high command, which was marching down a highway that would lead to heaven knows where and probably cost the SEALs some of their best people.

At that moment Hunter was far more than the Marine captain or the US congressman; in his mind he tugged down his treasured camouflaged desert MARPAT (Marine Pattern) combat cap and went straight to work, taking the steps of the Capitol three at a time. This rubbish had to be stopped, and he, Marine Duncan Hunter, was the very guy to get the ball rolling.

He hit the Internet, accessed Graham's website, summoned his assistants to clip the newspaper cuttings, and called for transcripts of the FoxNews broadcasts. He began networking among his fellow Republican Congressmen.

No issue ever raised more eyebrows. Hunter's colleagues, men who would not ordinarily tune in to military matters, reacted as he had— with genuine astonishment.

Matt, Jon, and Sam had just made the leap from the dry and dusty couple of acres of Camp Schwedler to the heart of US government. Congressmen were speaking their names right there in the glorious rotunda of the neoclassical Capitol, where General Washington himself had set the cornerstone more than two hundred years before.

Months later Matt would wonder whether President Washington would have court-martialed his Virginian militiamen for whacking a redcoat. Highly unlikely, he concluded, especially if it weren't even true.

And one by one US congressmen agreed to sign, unconditionally, the petition Hunter drafted that would, in its final form, be forwarded to the highest military authority, urging that the three SEALs be exonerated.

Under the headed writing paper of the US Congress and dated December 4, 2009, it was addressed to the Honorable Robert M. Gates, Secretary of Defense, at his office in the Pentagon. It read,

Dear Mr. Secretary,

We are writing to express our grave concern over reports that three Navy SEALs will face court-martial proceedings over their handling of one of the most wanted terrorists in Iraq. Based on the information we have, we believe that prosecution of these three men is not warranted.

As you are aware, in September, the three SEALs in question captured Ahmad Hashim Abd Al-Isawi [name corrected here], the alleged planner of the March 2004 ambush in Fallujah that resulted in the killing of four Blackwater contractors. We all remember the horrifying pictures showing two of these individuals whose bodies, after being burned and mutilated, were hung on a bridge over the Euphrates River.

Since 2004, Al-Isawi evaded capture. However, in September, Special Warfare Operators 2nd Class Matthew McCabe and Jonathan Keefe, and Special Warfare Operator 1st Class Sam Gonzales undertook a mission that resulted in Al-Isawi's capture. Soon after his capture, an investigation was conducted, based on reports that Al-Isawi had been struck in the stomach by one of the SEALs. As we understand it, there was no allegation of torture or sustained abuse. There was simply just this one alleged act.

Prosecuting individuals for such a limited act seems to us to be an overreaction by the command. As a result of the investigation, the three SEALs refused to accept non-judicial punishment believing, according to one of the defense attorneys, that they are innocent of the charges. If convicted they could face a significant punishment of up to one year's confinement, a bad conduct discharge, forfeiture of a portion of their pay each month for up to a year and a reduction in their rank.

It appears from all accounts that these SEALs are exceptional sailors, demonstrated by the fact that each had recently been advanced in rank. They captured a terrorist who had planned an attack that not only killed Americans, but also maimed and mutilated their bodies. We believe that prosecution of these sailors for such an apparently limited action will have a negative impact on others in the military who risk their lives in dangerous often ambiguous situations.

Again, we strongly believe that these court-martial proceedings are not warranted and would urge that you review this matter.

The letter was signed first by Congressman Duncan Hunter and then by thirty-two others, including the future speaker of the house, John Boehner, who is now third in line to the presidency; he signed, right alongside Congressman Hunter, as house minority leader, the position he occupied at the time.

Then-Minority Leader Boehner was the US Representative from Ohio's 8th congressional district since 1991, the same state as Matt Mc-Cabe. The US Representative from Florida's 10th congressional district, Bill Young, the longest-serving Republican member of Congress, signed his name boldly beneath Boehner's signature.

Below that was South Carolina's Joe Wilson, the congressman who received international attention when he interrupted a speech by US President Barack Obama at a joint session of Congress. He is also the father of four sons serving in the US military.

Bill Shuster, the representative from Pennsylvania's 9th district, also signed, unsurprisingly, as a member of the Armed Services Committee and of the congressional subcommittee on tactical air and land forces.

Randy Forbes, the representative of Virginia's 4th congressional district and Republican chairman of the Armed Services Committee's readiness subcommittee was another prominent signatory. Congressman Forbes is a member of the caucus for Army, Navy, Marines, and Special Operations Forces.

Perhaps the least surprising signer of all was Republican Congressman Robert Wittman, of Virginia's 1st congressional district. That's the one that stretches from the Washington suburbs right down to the Hampton Roads area, home of the US Navy. Congressman Wittman was as mad as Duncan Hunter about the entire court-martial episode, and he had almost certainly heard from several admirals who agreed with him. Rob Wittman was also a member of the Armed Services Committee.

Congressman Mike Coffman from Colorado's 6th district, a former infantry officer in the US Marines, placed his signature right next to Congressman Wittman's. Another Virginia Republican, Frank Wolf, as a former Army lawyer and practicing attorney, was also among the strong supporters of Duncan Hunter's petition.

The Texas congressman, Kevin Brady, was another powerful supporter and did not think the SEALs should be dragged into a courtroom after their exemplary behavior on the mission. In fact, Congressman Brady was possibly not enthusiastic about anyone going into a courtroom, as his own father, a South Dakota lawyer, was shot dead in one when Kevin was only twelve years old.

The Republican Tom Rooney, grandson of Art Rooney, founder of the Pittsburgh Steelers, was another big supporter of Congressman Hunter's petition. A former Army JAG, Rooney taught constitutional and criminal law as an assistant professor at West Point. He served in the famed US Cavalry Division and was a special assistant US attorney at Fort Hood in Texas.

Congressman Rooney knew military law from A to Z. And he believed that Matt, Jon, and Sam were being prosecuted by their own side based on dubious evidence.

The petition was sent by congressional courier directly to the Pentagon. But subsequent events suggest it was transferred from the office of the defense secretary to the convener of the courts-martial, Major General Charles Cleveland, who commanded Special Operations Central Command from MacDill Air Force Base in Florida.

This surprised no one because, as hot potatoes go, this one would deep-fry the palms of your hands. The upshot of all this was that Congressman Hunter was informed that a letter should be sent directly to the Major General because he had been given free rein to handle the courts-martial any way he saw fit.

And so, six days after the first letter, the congressmen went back to work, and this time there were forty-one signatures—eight more influential voices. The new letter read,

Dear General Cleveland,

We are writing to express out strong disagreement with the decision of your officers to pursue first a non-judicial punishment, and now a full court-martial against three Navy SEALs—Matthew McCabe, Jonathan Keefe and Sam Gonzales—on charges of assault against Ahmad Hashim Abd Al-Isawi—at one point one of the most dangerous terrorists in Iraq.

In March 2004, Fallujah, Iraq was a hub or insurgent activity. Four American civilians working as contractors were ambushed and killed; their bodies were mutilated and burned, then dragged through the streets and hung from a bridge over the Euphrates River—one of the most horrific outrages perpetrated on Americans in the last decade. The man widely identified as the mastermind of that attack, as well as other attacks on United States and coalition troops in Iraq, is Ahmad Hashim Abd Al-Isawi.

For over five years Al-Isawi evaded capture until Matthew McCabe, Jonathan Keefe and Sam Gonzales finally brought him to justice. Instead of being hailed as heroes, these brave Americans are being vilified for allegedly assaulting Al-Isawi once he was in custody. First, press reports raise significant doubts about whether Al-Isawi was actually in SEAL custody when his alleged minor injuries occurred.

Second, al-Qaeda's own handbook instructs their operatives to allege detainee abuse if detained by American forces. In fact, al-Qaeda operatives are trained to self-inflict injuries for the sole purpose of accusing US forces of abuse. We've seen many cases of this since the conflicts in Iraq and Afghanistan began.

General, surely you agree that we are in a war that we must win. Our military personnel are putting their lives on the line every day trying to track down terrorists who want to indiscriminately kill Americans. Our troops and your SEALs need to be bold and decisive in combat; not looking over their shoulder, fearing legal jeopardy for every action or gesture.

In this case in particular there is more than enough doubt as to whether these SEALs committed any wrongdoing at all. In our opinion, prosecutorial discretion should have been exercised. Failing that, we respectfully and strongly urge you to exercise your leadership authority, stop the impending court martial, and exonerate these men.

We await your prompt response.

CC: Hon. Barack Obama, Hon. Robert Gates, Adml. Mike Mullen.

It was signed by Dan Burton, the influential Republican representative from Indiana's 5th district, plus forty-one other congressmen. And although none of them thought the president was likely to step in and put a halt to the rumbling juggernaut of legal procedure, it was also obvious that Robert Gates had essentially stepped aside. The four-star Admiral Mike Mullen was, however, a real hope.

As chairman of the joint chiefs and just beginning his second term, he was the highest-ranking officer in the US Armed Services. A former commanding officer of the guided missile cruiser USS *Yorktown*, Admiral Mullen was a US Navy man through and through. There was nothing he did not understand about the service that wears dark blue.

He had served for forty-three years after graduating from the Naval Academy, Annapolis, rising to command the US Second Fleet in the North Atlantic and subsequently holding the office of chief of naval operations. Now aged sixty-three, Admiral Mullen was every sailor's champion.

In the opinion of Congressman Hunter there was a genuine chance he might declare from his exalted position that, in the interests of the Navy's public reputation, and its duty to provide proper anonymity to its front-line operators, these courts-martial should not proceed.

The letter was dispatched to the great offices of state and to the Florida offices of Major General Cleveland, who replied swiftly, as indeed anyone would, after receiving a letter from the US Congress. His response read,

Dear Representative Burton,

Thank you for your letter expressing your and your colleagues concern regarding the pending Courts-martial of Petty Officers Gonzales, McCabe and Keefe. I understand your interest in these cases and can assure you that I am committed to protecting the rights of the Sailors who have been accused.

Regrettably it appears that your perception of the incident is based on incomplete and factually inaccurate press coverage. Despite what has been reported, these allegations are not founded solely on the word of the detainee, but rather, were initially raised by other US service members.

Additionally, the alleged injuries did not occur during actions on the objective, as is also being widely reported in the media. A medical examination conducted at the time the detainee was turned over to US forces determined that his alleged injuries were inflicted several hours after the operation had ended, and while in the custody and care of the US at Camp Schweidler's [sic] detainee holding facility.

While the assault and resulting injury to the detainee were relatively minor, the more disconcerting allegations are those related to the Sailor's attempts to cover up the incident, particularly in what appears to be an effort to influence the testimony of a witness. All of these allegations were fully investigated by the Naval Criminal Investigative Service (NCIS).

As you have likely read, I chose to deal with this incident administratively via non-judicial punishment pursuant to Article 15 of the UCMJ. However, Petty Officers Gonzales, McCabe and Keefe elected to exercise their UCMJ rights to refuse such a hearing. I have attached previously released, redacted copies of the charge sheets in the hope that they will clarify the allegations surrounding this incident. These charges were drawn from information disclosed during the course of the investigation. The release of any further information at this time would be inappropriate as it might prejudice the outcome of the trial.

I take my military justice authority and responsibility for maintaining good order and discipline very seriously, as I have in six commands previously. Discipline and integrity are primary factors that make our US Special Operators such an effective fighting force. The abuse of a detainee, no matter how minor, creates strategic repercussions that harm our nation's security and ultimately costs the lives of US citizens.

I must ensure that the service members under my command abide by the laws passed by Congress and follow the lawful orders of their superior officers. When there are reasonable grounds to believe that an offense has been committed, and that a specific individual in my command has committed that offense, it is my duty to take appropriate action to not only ensure justice is done, but also to maintain good order and discipline.

It is these factors that led me to refer these charges to Special Courts-martial. I assure you that the rights of these Sailors are being protected and they will have all of the facts of the case presented and reviewed fully by an impartial panel.

Sincerely,

Charles T. Cleveland MG, US Army Commanding

It was, of course, an enormous disappointment, not least because neither the president, the defense secretary, nor the head of the Armed Services seemed inclined to lift a finger to support the three accused SEALs.

Also it would have been reassuring if the Major General had at least known how to spell Camp Schwedler, named for another decorated Navy SEAL, Petty Officer Clark Schwedler, who died with the utmost heroism in combat in Iraq and was, somewhat coinidentally, the son of a Michigan trial court judge.

Major General Cleveland's response was very weak, packed as it was with trite aphorisms and military cliché, very much a letter from a senior officer to a someone of a lower rank and studded with references to his own command seniority.

It also made a few seriously shaky assumptions—repeated references to Al-Isawi's "injuries" when even the prosecution was offering only the slightly cut lower lip, which he probably did himself.

The general also referred to the allegations against the SEALs being "initially raised by other US service members"—plural. If there were anyone else making the same allegations as Brian Westinson, he or she was not yet known to either the defense or the prosecution.

The general also did not see fit to mention the several SEAL Team 10 members standing by to flatly refute Westinson's statement. And as for General Cleveland's assertion that "the more disconcerting allegation" was the "Sailors' attempts to cover up the incident" and their "efforts to influence the testimony of a witness," that was not much short of a wild, inaccurate guess.

Indeed, in Westinson's sworn statement under oath in Ramadi made on September 4 in the presence of a naval lieutenant commander, he asserted that "the three SEALs" had not threatened him and that he thought they were "professional and exemplary sailors"— not precisely the impression Major General Cleveland was handing out to Congressman Dan Burton.

Neither was it altogether fair that he claimed that the SEALs merely exercised their rights when they refused a nonjudicial hearing. The unmentioned truth was that a nonjudicial hearing would have required from them an admission of guilt, which they could not provide because they were entirely innocent.

It could not possibly be deemed unreasonable to suggest that the man who convened the courts-martial, Major General Charles T. Cleveland, quoted what he saw as the "facts" to Congressman Burton in a subtle but somewhat opportunistic manner.

And certainly no one in the highest command of the US military wanted anything to do with a devastating document, produced on December 10, the day the congressional letter was sent to the general. It was written under the letterhead,

DEPARTMENT OF THE NAVY

SPECIAL COURT MARTIAL

NAVY AND MARINE CORPS TRIAL JUDICIARY

CENTRAL JUDICIAL CIRCUIT

To the left was the title, UNITED STATES V. MATTHEW V. MCCABE (the sight of which, incidentally, almost broke his heart, and he never really got over it). But this document was helpful. It was the WITNESS PRODUCTION REQUEST, prepared by the Navy Lieutenant JAG, who right now was detailing the SEAL's defense.

One by one it listed the men who would stand witness for Matt, although it began with an assessment of what might be expected from Ahmad Hashim Abd Al-Isawi, the alleged victim.

Section (a) read,

His allegation of abuse is the basis for the charges against SO2 McCabe. He told the Navy Special Agent that he was kicked in the stomach and hit in the shoulder and head. His statements serve as the backbone of the Government's case. He is simply the most relevant and necessary live witness in this case.

The rest were listed in the document along with an assessment of what each one would testify in support of Matt: his platoon lieutenant; SEAL Team 10's lieutenant; SO1 Eric, the rocket scientist from Georgia Tech who had walked across the pitch-black desert in front of Matt; SO2 Carl Higbie, the air comms chief the night of the raid; Matt's lieutenant from his months in Germany; Matt's troop commander, a very senior SEAL; SEAL Team 10's troop senior chief; two SEALs, one a lieutenant who had trained with Matt, and another platoon chief, both of whom had known Matt for years; and the SEALs' combat camera operator. The list also included three witnesses who would testify concerning Westinson's military character and disposition toward Navy SEALs: MCI Lynn Friant, the SEALs' combat camera operator; a petty officer who served with Brian; and his immediate supervisor, lead master-of-arms.

Matt's JAG wrote at the end of the document that if the government refused to produce any of the above-listed witnesses, then the defense respectfully requests detailed written statement of the reasons for refusal so as "to insure complete litigation of the issue."

He also asserted that witness production requests were likely to continue.

Of the eleven men prepared to stand in a military courtroom and speak on Matt's behalf, there was a decorated naval commander plus four more serving Navy SEAL officers, a senior chief, a platoon chief, and a couple of leading petty officers—the kind of lineup one might have expected if General MacArthur had been court-martialed for whacking the murderous Japanese Admiral Yamamoto in the gut in 1945.

As legal ammunition for an extremely tenuous military trial, that was most certainly impressive in the extreme, for it required hugely respected servicemen to put their own treasured reputations on the line for a well-liked and trusted member of Team 10.

One might reasonably have thought this would have set off about a thousand alarm bells ringing in the Pentagon. But apparently not. There was a kind of angry silence. And the great wheels of "justice" rolled ever onward.

8

—

THE OUTRAGE OF
THE AMERICAN PUBLIC

A destruction of brave men's lives was right now in the forefront. It was in the unfathomable malice being directed at Matt, Jon, and Sam. And for what? Was this political? Was the military being ordered to court-martial these men?

Thursday, December 10, 2009, was a critical day in the court-martial proceedings. It was almost five weeks since the defense counselors had filed their formal request for discovery, those sworn legal statements made by all the SEALs who had been involved with Objective Amber and, for that matter, anyone else who had been near the holding cell where Al-Isawi was held prisoner.

Two weeks had passed since the government had filed written response on the subject of discovery, warning that the documents may be classified but assuring the lawyers "that a 'review' was being expeditiously conducted at that time to determine classification status of any information appertaining to the case."

They checked. And perhaps in response to the burgeoning public uproar, on that Thursday the government was now forced to make a decision: to proceed or not to proceed against these American fighting men, each one of whom wore the flag of the United States both on his battle dress and on his heart.

To proceed would be to expose them both to the public and to the United States' enemies. For the enemy to recognize these men is plainly dangerous for them.

And now the military had a critical decision to make, because to proceed with these courts-martial would thrust the names of the three accused into the public domain. Worse yet, their names would practically go up in lights.

Obviously all combat SEALs loathe and detest any form of publicity. They hope and pray that when their days in the frontline of US offensive forces are finally over, they will be free to live their lives in peace and privacy with their families. God knows that if anyone deserves this, they do.

But the situation surrounding Matt, Jon, and Sam was one of the worst ever. So far as America's Middle Eastern enemies were concerned, these were the men who had grabbed the legendary Al-Isawi and then apparently beaten him while he was handcuffed and defenseless. If these turbaned gangsters could knock down the World Trade Center, they might have a passing interest in the identities of the men who grabbed the Butcher.

This was the dilemma that the US government and its military high command faced. And that Thursday afternoon found many people who occupy many high places pondering whether to release to the defense lawyers the SEALs' handwritten statements, knowing it would effectively throw the three SEALs into the public wilderness, thereby destroying their God-given anonymity.

Lieutenant Paul Threatt, who was concerned only with the SEAL combat warriors' reputations and safety, thought privately: *This could end today. I don't think the Pentagon is going to allow this to happen.*

These were his seriously troubling thoughts. Threatt's business involved the lives of these individuals—their sorrows and fears, their characters and their honesty. He was massively concerned about the welfare of his client, Jon Keefe, and no less so about Matt and Sam. He believed the Navy had an obligation to protect their identities, specifically from sly and cunning Al-Qaeda killers.

"Nothing the US Navy did could possibly justify revealing precisely who the men were—the combat warriors who grabbed the Butcher," he said months later. "I was certain in my own mind the military too would be fully aware of that and drop the charges."

But they did not. And Threatt never quite forgave them for that. The following afternoon, Friday, December 11, presumably after many hours of thought and discussion, the Navy elected to let matters go forward. They confirmed the classification review had been completed and had the newly unclassified documents hand carried to Greg McCormack's law offices in Virginia Beach.

This was such a drastic step, allowing for the first time the innermost core of the proceedings to be seen beyond the frontiers of the US military. The die was surely cast. By releasing this information, the government had thus decided to come against Matt, Jon, and Sam with the full and majestic power of military law—to hell with the consequences.

And they had done so with the full knowledge that a chain of high-risk events would now be set in motion. This also meant that now, at last, the defense lawyers were able to pore long and hard over the written statement made by the young master-at-arms, Brian Westinson.

And before the end of that day the growing battalion of attorneys lined up for Matt, Jon, and Sam were preparing to load weapons to start blowing gaping holes in Brian's wavering recollections of that early September morning in the Camp Schwedler holding cell.

To most of the experienced legal minds it was inconceivable that the military would have condoned this. Uniformed US commanders do not take plain and obvious risks. That level of caution is ingrained into their DNA, particularly when dealing with the lives of men under their command.

And if ever the destruction of brave men's lives was right in the forefront, it was right now—in the unfathomable malice being directed at Matt, Jon, and Sam. And for what? Was this political? Was the military being ordered to court-martial these men?

What other explanation was there? Except that politicians, occupying the great offices of state not to mention chauffeured limousines and tables at the most expensive restaurants on earth, must have been calling the shots. Were they quietly ordering the ruthless sacrifice of the three SEALs in order to pave the way to a better political dialogue with the Middle East?

Perhaps they were. And a nationwide quasi-demonstration of US fairness to its prisoners was all very fine. Unless you happened to be Matt, Jon, or Sam, all of whom stood to be ruined if found guilty of prisoner abuse, failure of duty, lying, scheming, plotting, and God knows what else.

And at this point everyone remotely involved in the project to protect the three SEALs was, in a word, confounded. The lawyers began to find discrepancies in Westinson's statements, and many, many SEALs were declaring they did not see anyone attack Al-Isawi. In their opinion no one had hit Al-Isawi; indeed, none of them would dream of hitting any prisoner—never had, never would. And some of them had been *with* Matthew McCabe and were prepared to stand up in court and swear to God he'd never lifted a finger against the jihadist.

Over in the great hall of the Capitol, Dan Burton was nothing short of mystified. In his view it was impossible that a Major General would dare to write a letter suggesting that the elected Congress of the United States did not really know what it was talking about, that it was relying on inaccurate press reports, and to follow all of this with a short, rather lofty lecture on the general's perceptions of fact and duty.

The thought was inescapable: someone of immense authority may have been standing in the general's corner. There were some seriously heavyweight signatures on that congressional protest, and they had been dismissed out of hand. The question was: Who had done the dismissing? For in this wildly inflammatory instance it was surely a far superior being than a two-star Army general based way down on the west coast of Florida.

This had become an issue of momentous importance, with a ripple effect currently lapping at the Pentagon's E-Ring, where the most senior officials sat, and in the highest echelons of the US media. Everyone was talking about it. The courts-martial of the three SEALs had made the front pages of influential publications in America, all of them indignant, most of them incredulous.

The very reputation of the US Armed Services was being kicked around. The military could not possibly have wished this to continue, unless they were as dumb as their detractors suggested. Which, incidentally, they most certainly were not.

Burton, who was only just on the north side of outraged at the treatment Matt, Jon, and Sam received, decided to give himself a cooling-off period through the Christmas vacation before drafting a reply to the major general. He knew he had to be calm and collected, statesmanlike. But with every passing hour he was handed massive evidence that the country was with him.

The Indiana congressman launched a website along the same lines as that of Graham Ware's "Support the SEALs," and in just a couple of weeks it had thirty thousand followers. Responses were cascading in at more than two thousand a day, every one of them appalled at the way three Navy SEALs, all decorated in combat, were being treated.

And the avalanche of press coverage was by no means restricted to tabloids and sensation-seeking daily publications. This had already hit the pages of the *New York Times,* the *Washington Post,* the *New York Daily News,* and the *Boston Globe,* not to mention the 174-year-old *Toledo Blade* and the almost-as-venerable *Cleveland Daily Gleaner* (Matt McCabe's hometown area in Ohio). Among the national wire services the members of the Associated Press were huge supporters of the accused men.

Among the news organizations, all of which informed influential minds across the United States, were Cybercast News Service (CNS) based in Virginia, a conservative website that was swiftly on top of the story, detailing the two congressional letters to Robert Gates and General Cleveland, with particular emphasis on the opinions of Congressman Rob Wittman, who represented Jon Keefe's hometown area of Yorktown, Virginia.

CNS quoted Mr. Wittman thus: "One of these SEALs is a constituent of mine, and I and many of my colleagues are concerned with the message this sends to our soldiers, sailors and airmen, who serve in harm's way every day. They risk their lives in dangerous and uncertain situations—I am eagerly awaiting the Secretary of Defense's response to the letter I signed in defense of these three SEALs ... I do not believe the prosecution of these men is warranted."

The *Navy Times* was another highly regarded publication that plainly disapproved of the courts-martial. A weekly newspaper also based in Virginia, it provides information and analysis to active, reserve, and retired US Navy personnel, including distinguished former commanding officers.

And the editorial team was swiftly into its stride the moment the story broke, immediately going to Matthew's lawyer, the esteemed Neal Puckett. He told them, "The SEALs are being tried, essentially, for allegedly giving the detainee a 'punch in the gut.'

"They are all together, and they all maintain they are innocent of the charges," he said, before adding, "In a combat environment the handling of a detainee ... these things happen all the time, and can easily be justified as maintaining control."

These military *Times* newspapers are the most widely purchased publications in all Army and Air Force Exchange Service (AAFES) shops on US military bases worldwide. A measure of the enormous size of this franchise is, perhaps, its forty-five thousand employees and thirty-one hundred shops in more than thirty countries.

They run the largest military-base post office in the world in Fort Campbell, Kentucky, and in the US base at Ramstein, Germany, they run probably the largest store on earth. In any one of them the *Times* military newspapers easily outsell national magazines like *People* and *Time.*

This adds up to a spectacularly influential news distribution operation constantly promoting the editorial opinion that the US military really ought to think again on this one. And that was especially true of the *Navy Times*, not only because of its circulation of fifty-five thousand but also because of precisely who that number may include.

Particularly as the largest newspaper publisher in the United States, Gannett Company Inc. of Tysons Corner, Virginia, owns the *Navy Times*. They also own *USA Today, USA Weekend,* the *Arizona Republic,* the *Indianapolis Star,* the *Cincinnati Enquirer,* the *Tennessean,* the *Courier-Journal* (Louisville, Kentucky), the *Democrat and Chronicle* (Rochester,

New York), and the *Detroit Free Press,* not to mention twenty-three television stations—NBC's largest group owner of affiliates.

And on Christmas Eve another deep, dark conservative voice came crashing into the fray. Jed Babbin, editor of the revered conservative weekly *Human Events,* which was for years President Reagan's favorite reading, let fly with both barrels when he unleashed a blistering editorial and began a Save-the-SEALs petition that pulled in ninety thousand supporters in the first week.

Babbin, once President George H. W. Bush's deputy undersecretary of defense, forwarded his petition directly to the Pentagon, to Secretary Gates on behalf of *Human Events.*

Excerpts included:

> We at Human Events hereby request your personal intervention to dismiss the charges against the SEALs ... they captured and detained Ahmad Hashim Abd Al-Isawi, one of the most barbaric and dangerous terrorists in Iraq. ... You are next in line, above General Petraeus in the chain of command ... you can, legally, intervene ... and direct they be returned to duty. We respectfully request that you do so forthwith. To stake the honor and fighting future of these three men ... is manifestly a gross injustice.

Right before Christmas and with almost gleeful abandon, another widely respected conservative publication, the *American Spectator,* joined the fight. This important right-wing monthly, which has published authors such as Tom Wolfe, P. J. O'Rourke, George Will, Patrick J. Buchanan, and the late Malcolm Muggeridge, launched forth with an editorial by the magazine's eminently respected founder and editor, R. Emmett Tyrrell Jr., under this headline:

THE CURRENT CRISIS

WAR IS HELL—NOT LITIGATION

Among the carefully worded prose of a very fine writer were the following statements:

Are these trials really necessary—it is, I think, pretty well established that terrorists do not always tell the truth. General Cleveland had it in his power to tell lower level commanders simply to avoid bloody lips in future—but he set in motion a destructive process. Secretary Gates can end this abuse of power by simply doing what Cleveland failed to do.

Let us get these courts-martial canceled. The guy who should be appearing in the dock is Ahmad Hashim Abd Al-Isawi, whose lip has doubtless healed.

The *American Spectator,* when roused, has earned the reputation of a doughty fighter. Its controversial article in 1994 concerning Clinton-accuser Paula Jones was the basis for a sexual harassment lawsuit that started the chain of events resulting in President Clinton's impeachment. Why in the world the military was happy to cross swords with so many irate and distinguished wordsmiths will, perhaps, remain forever a mystery.

Meanwhile the furor in the US media continued. The fourth-largest circulation newspaper in the United States, the *New York Daily News* (a half-million a day), thundered into print with a damning editorial headlined,

SAVE THESE SEALS: NAVY COMMANDOES RATE HONORS,
NOT COURTS-MARTIAL FOR TERROR ARRESTS

And this newspaper—America's first tabloid—is enormously respected in New York, where its old art deco skyscraper headquarters, the Daily News Building, still towers nearly five hundred feet above East 42nd Street. Beneath the black glass domed ceiling of the lobby stands the world's largest indoor globe.

Its opening tirade, concerning Matt, Jon and Sam, shook the place to its granite foundations. Anyone who did not know about the three SEALs before the end of the year, 2009, most certainly did now. The *Daily News* editorial dripped with outrage and scorn toward the military.

They opened with a demand:

Defense Secretary Robert Gates must intervene to prevent an injustice that turns the world on its head.

It continued in fighting mode:

How can those who opened an official investigation of this trifling matter sleep at night? … It is bad enough that these men have been subjected to the indignity of formal criminal charges. Even an acquittal at trial would be a travesty. Why must they answer the charges of a terrorist?

It is perhaps worth noting that the *Daily News* did not get into the issue of "guilty or not guilty." They wrote the editorial assuming the worst-case scenario:

EVEN IF THEY WERE GUILTY: SO WHAT?

And that was the message they trumpeted to their estimated 2.5 million readers all over the city. On that cold winter weekend, in every one of New York's five boroughs, the issue of these three Navy SEALs eclipsed all others. In fact, the courts-martial seemed for a while to be a New York story, even though it was rooted more decisively in Washington, DC.

But the *New York Daily News* carried a big stick, and it was fresh out of carrots. The voice of the city had spoken—well, bellowed—from the top of that 42nd Street skyscraper. The editors wanted action, a thorough military rethink. The US Navy SEALs belonged to the nation, not to a few yellow-braided officers. They were America's platoons, every father's supermen. And big people better start listening, or else the *Daily News*, winner of ten Pulitzer Prizes, would most certainly want to know why. Loudly. And they were by no means alone.

The fact was that the courts-martial of Matt, Jon, and Sam had become a silver-plated, coast-to-coast national scandal. In a sense it united the entire country. Because only the most flagrant, human-rights liberal could possibly have sided with the powers that sought to humiliate the men from Camp Schwedler. The nation wanted the charges dropped.

And the media onslaught was relentless. And it was not just the printed word that was being aimed with such venom at the Pentagon. The story broke on FoxNews, and that organization had already allowed one of its biggest hitters, radio/television host Sean Hannity, the best-selling author and conservative political commentator, to conduct a major live interview with Neal Puckett.

During the exchange the interviewer, trying to clarify his thoughts, asked, "The al-Qaeda training manual says that members must complain of torture and mistreatment inflicted on them. It's part of their training, correct?"

Puckett replied, "It's to be expected in every situation in which they're captured."

HANNITY: How do we even get ourselves in this situation?
PUCKETT: *By listening to the Iraqi complain, taking his complaints seriously, investigating our own people, America's fighting men, and taking a terrorist's word over theirs.*
H: So we handed over this terrorist, this murderer to the Iraqis, and then he's given back to the Americans—then all he has to do is accuse the Navy SEALs, and they get put on trial for doing the job they're supposed to do?
P: *Look, seems like this guy had blood on him. Someone just had to say, if any of you guys are responsible, knock it off. I don't want to see this happen again. That assumes they think the SEALs did it, which they actually didn't.*
H: Taking the word of a murdering terrorist over our Navy SEALs. It just doesn't make any sense to me.

Generally speaking it was a tough call for the broadcast media because they, by the nature of their business, need live principals on the screen at all times. But there was zero chance of bringing in the three future defendants. Fox and their rivals would have to press on with lawyers and experts, with camera crews and reporters "door stepping" both the Navy base and the Virginia SEAL HQ.

Christmas in 2009 was a worrying time for the families. But Jon did his best to make light of the potential disaster that he faced. The biggest problem was he had no answers for his parents, brother, and girlfriend. No one had yet shown him the other SEALs' statements. The lawyers were still poring over the discovery documents, but no one had yet shown him anything significant.

Matt, who faced a far more serious situation, made his way home to Ohio, but he did not feel much like skiing. Congressman Burton was concerned about the lack of cooperation that General Cleveland was showing toward Congress. This weighed upon him throughout the vacation as he agonized about the content of the letter he must write back to the SOCCENT commanding officer at MacDill Air Force Base.

But he was determined "to convey the American people's perception that the General was unfairly prosecuting three heroes, based, at least in part, upon the word of an inhumane monster."

His letter, dated January 4, 2010, ultimately read,

Dear General Cleveland,

I received your letter of December 15th 2009, regarding the pending courts-martial of Petty Officers [McCabe, Keefe, and Gonzales]; and I appreciate your office's attempting to set the record straight, and clarify what you describe as the "incomplete and factually inaccurate" press coverage of the situation. Having reviewed all of the material you provided, I still have to strongly disagree with the decision of your officers to pursue punishment of these Navy SEALs.

Ahmad Hashim Abd Al-Isawi was one of the most wanted terrorists in Iraq; responsible for the murders of innocent American civilians and numerous attacks on American and coalition forces. The injuries to Mr. Al-Isawi were, as you readily admit, relatively minor, and certainly pale in comparison to the brutality of the crimes he helped perpetrate.

While Petty Officers [McCabe, Keefe, and Gonzales] may have been wrong to not fully cooperate with investigators, it seems to me that the punishment still far exceeds the crime. In my opinion, prosecutorial discretion should have been exercised.

Beyond the fates of the three individual sailors, I have some general concerns about this case that are only reinforced by your letter. First, the fact that fellow US service personnel initially raised the accusations … strongly suggests that we have created a culture within our Armed Forces where our military personnel are now more concerned about protecting themselves from legal jeopardy for every action or statement, than they are about fighting the enemy.

Our troops and these SEALs need to be bold and decisive in combat; not hesitant and over-thinking every action for fear of prosecution. We are in a war that we must win against a determined and patient enemy, who already believes we do not have the will to do what is necessary to defeat them.

Second, because of the intensive media coverage of this case—even if it is incomplete and factually inaccurate as you describe—this is the public perception of the case: the American people are outraged by the courts-martial of individuals who should be hailed as heroes.

In fact over 30,000 Americans have signed my online petition calling for an end to this prosecution.

Perhaps even more alarming than the decline in morale this case has caused the country, is the boost in morale and confidence that this case gives to al-Qaeda terrorists, who, as I said, already believe America does not have the will or stomach to do what is necessary to defeat them.

General Cleveland, you are a distinguished soldier and former Special Forces operator yourself. I have the utmost respect for you personally. But in this case the American people's perception is that you are unfairly prosecuting three heroes, based, at least in part, upon the word of an inhumane monster. Al-Qaeda's own handbook instructs their operatives to allege abuse if detained by American forces.

In fact al-Qaeda operatives are trained to self-inflict injuries for the sole purpose of accusing U.S. forces of abuse. We've seen repeated cases of this since the conflicts in Iraq and Afghanistan began. In my opinion, carrying forward these courts-martial will do our Nation and our Armed Forces more harm than good.

I respectfully and strongly urge you to exercise your leadership authority, stop the impending trials, and drop the charges against these American heroes.

I await your prompt response.

It was signed by Dan Burton, with copies to Hon. Barack Obama, Hon. Robert Gates, Admiral Mike Mullen. And, of course, it never even tackled the most likely possibility—that none of the three SEALs were guilty of anything.

In essence, the trials of the three SEALs were still all military: the court-martial, the major general, the SEAL base, the Navy JAGS, the Special Forces, the commanders, the master chiefs, and the Armed Forces' term for a prisoner: "detainee."

But politics was shouldering its way into the fight with every turn in the road. Representative Burton had rightly marched into the debate some of the most influential men from the Capitol. And the names Gates and, occasionally, Obama were part of the conversation.

Leading conservative writers were in there, swinging hard at military leaders, and conservative publications were making their stand against what they recognized as injustice. Even liberal US newspapers were taking a swerve en masse to the right, demanding fairness for the SEAL heroes.

And Puckett, Matt's civilian lawyer, albeit a former US Marine lieutenant colonel, suddenly ratcheted everything upward by writing a thoughtful but tough article in the most revered conservative publication in the country, *Reflections* magazine, the voice of the new conservative movement of the twenty-first century.

This beautifully written monthly stated its case with passion. And it quoted William F. Buckley Jr., founder and editor of the *National Review,* claiming the same mission statement: "To stand athwart history, yelling stop."

And onto this shining platform of right-leaning intellect stepped Puckett, welcomed by one of the most demanding editorial boards in the world, one that was avidly pro-military and absolutely not in favor of court-martialing courageous and patriotic Navy SEALs.

Indeed, in this rapidly developing uniformed farce, the high commanders fell right into the magazine's catch-all of "sporadic and weak resistance preferring power to principle," perhaps even floundering under the "ideological juggernaut of liberalism," which, in the end, is wrong about just about everything.

Like most of the country, *Reflections* saw the military condemnation of the three SEALs as nothing short of disgraceful. And they reminded the Washington lawyer of the words of their patron saint, the father of Western conservatism, Edmund Burke, who once memorably declared, "All that's necessary for the forces of evil to win the world, is for good men to do nothing."

The Edmund Burke Institute, for which *Reflections* is the flagship publication, was firm in its general resolve: "We refuse to do nothing. We will fight for what is right, true and good. This is the rock upon which we take our stand."

Thus, their team endorsed Puckett to help them make that stand, explaining to an important readership precisely what was at stake. When he filed his thoughtful prose, they headlined it:

NAVY SEALS DENIED JUSTICE

And after he briefly described the circumstances that led to the accusation and the dangers that Matt, Jon, and Sam now faced, he characterized the military's response:

> The commanding general decided to take stern, formal disciplinary action, which would have ended the career of all three of the SEALs ...
>
> Rather than thinking through all of the other alternatives available, the senior legal advisor recommended the general refer these cases to prosecution by court-martial. This action ensured that the public would become aware of the case.

The significance of this arched piece of writing was that Puckett was both a Marine officer and a trial lawyer. Who could possibly be more qualified than him to make this judgment? And therein lies the rub of this puzzling legal conundrum: so many wise and experienced people were thinking in perfect harmony and urging General Cleveland to rethink and cancel all charges against the SEALs.

But somehow there was an obdurate and irrational determination at work here. It was a strange obsession to nail them at all costs, with no obvious benefit to anyone, certainly not to the reputation and public standing of the US Armed Forces.

Right now, in the brand-new year of a brand-new decade, in a relatively new century, half the country was waving angry fists directly at the Pentagon. It was a very long time since that much public rudeness had been hurled at senior officers and officials, a long time since the military had conducted any operation with such a chilling lack of common sense.

And because the public was not having it, Jon Keefe's lawyer, Greg McCormack, decided that one sensible move might be to have his client take a polygraph test, which, though not always admissible as evidence in court, would nonetheless provide substantial validity to Jon's known character and truthfulness.

Greg's staff hired a well-known licensed Virginia polygraph examiner, Andrew M. Casey, to conduct the tests on Jonathan, who readily agreed to undergo them. Examiner Casey's report says,

The main issue under consideration was whether or not KEEFE was truthful when he stated he did not lie to NCIS Special Agent Stamp concerning the alleged abuse of detainee Al-Isawi. During the pre-test interview, the facts of the case were discussed, and all questions were reviewed by him.

RESULTS: Throughout each polygraph chart there were no apparent physiological indications of deception when KEEFE answered "No" to the following questions:

Did you lie when you told Special Agent Stamp that you didn't see anyone abuse or mistreat Al-Isawi?

Did you see anyone abuse or mistreat Al-Isawi?

Was Al-Isawi abused in your presence?

OPINION: Based on the above, it is my opinion that NO DECEPTION WAS INDICATED.

McCormack immediately fired off a request to General Cleveland at Special Operations Command Center, MacDill Air Force Base. It asked that the Naval Criminal Investigative Service at the NCIS Norfolk Office administer a new, more expansive and thorough polygraph examination to SO2 Keefe.

The general wrote back that he hereby granted that request, but in addition to the three questions indicated, the polygrapher would ask Jonathan questions concerning his knowledge of the source of Mr. Al-Isawi's injuries and about his efforts to influence the investigation.

This was a fascinating clash of viewpoints. McCormack understood with 100 percent certainty that Examiner Casey was equally sure that Jon was telling the absolute truth. In the lawyer's opinion there was not a cat-in-hell's chance that any polygrapher on the planet could possibly trap his client into revealing he had told a lie.

General Cleveland may or may not have grasped this. Because if the military wheeled in one of the country's best polygraphers and put Jon Keefe through the ringer, employing every known technique in the book to trap him—and then come up blank—that would surely do the government's case no good whatsoever.

The military and the intelligence services, especially the Navy, have a tempestuous and sometimes embarrassing history with this curious little electronic device, which, while the subject undergoes some kind of fourth-degree interrogation, records physiological activity, blood pressure, heart rate, pulse rate, respiration, and skin conductivity.

There had been many great triumphs and a few perfectly cringe-making failures. The US government had its own grandiose name for the lie detector test: a psychophysiological detection of deception (PDD) examination. And prosecutors love to have it tucked in their brief file so long as it proves the defendant has told a few whoppers.

In a way they could not afford to polygraph SO2 Keefe, but they could also not afford not to. The memory of the horrendous trial of former US Navy Chief Warrant Officer John Anthony Walker, a communications specialist who spied for the Soviet Union from 1968 to 1985, is the reason for this dichotomy.

During his time conducting this profitable enterprise, Walker helped the Soviets decipher more than one million encrypted naval messages. He organized a spy operation involving several Navy personnel, an operation the *New York Times* reported in 1987 as "the most damaging Soviet spy ring in history."

After Walker's arrest Caspar Weinberger, President Reagan's secretary of defense, stated that Walker gave the Soviets information that allowed them access to weapons, sensor data, naval tactics, and terrorist threats as well as surface, submarine, and airborne training, readiness, and tactics. The Soviets essentially knew where every US submarine was patrolling at all times. In the event of war Walker's treachery would have resulted in enormous loss of American lives.

And a simple lie detector test could have stopped the whole thing. Because Walker, despite certain people's suspicions, never took a polygraph test. His Soviet masters had instructed him never to accept any form of promotion that required one. He actually refused promotion because of this.

Walker, the bearded former crew member in the nuclear-powered fleet ballistic missile boat USS *Andrew Jackson*, was badly short of cash, so he simply walked into the Soviet Embassy in Washington one afternoon and sold a top-secret document for several thousand dollars, and this in turn led to a permanent salary from Moscow of up to $1,000 a week.

He was judged responsible for the North Korean capture of the spy ship USS *Pueblo* in 1968. And as a critical supervisor in the comms center for the US fleet's Atlantic submarine force, he betrayed the entire US Sound Surveillance System (SOSUS) underwater surveillance system to the Soviets, who immediately altered their submarine propellers to reduce cavitation and, thus, detection.

Naval experts estimated that Walker and his team provided enough code-data information to sway the balance of power between Russia and the United States during the Cold War. When he was finally arrested—exposed by his angry ex-wife for nonpayment of alimony—

he observed, rather jauntily, that "K-Mart has better security than the Navy."

And the US Navy never quite recovered from that, regularly reaching for the lie detector at the slightest suspicion of espionage inside their warships or dockyards. Walker, after plea-bargaining, got life in jail, but his right-hand man received a sentence of 365 years in a Californian state penitentiary.

The polygraph played some role, either positive or negative in most of the big US espionage cases of the past fifty years. The grotesque and drunken CIA double-agent Aldrich Ames admitted being "terrified" of the lie detector while he was spying for the Soviet Union. But the KGB kept him straight, told him to relax, and Ames beat the polygraph twice in 1986 and 1991. The Wisconsin-born traitor did not, however, beat the US court system, and he was jailed for life in 1994, having fatally betrayed many, many US agents.

Another lethal CIA spy for the Soviet Union, Harold James Nicholson, suddenly failed an agency polygraph test in 1994, and this led to his immediate arrest and jailing for espionage against the United States.

One of America's worst traitors was the Chicago-born Robert Hanssen, who spent twenty-two years working for the FBI but simultaneously spying for the Soviet Union and, later, Russia. They caught him in the end, and Hanssen pleaded guilty to thirteen counts of espionage.

He was sentenced to life imprisonment, without parole, in a high-security Colorado penitentiary. He told his captors that no one *ever* asked him to take a polygraph test. If they had, he confirmed, it might have made him think twice about spying, even though he earned an estimated $1.4 million from Moscow Station.

Thus, the US military has a love-hate relationship with that demonic electronic apparatus. They dared not ignore it for fear of the same torrent of abuse that hit the CIA and the FBI over Walker and Hanssen, both of whom were never required to take one. And then there was Ames, who beat it, and Nicholson, who was trapped by it.

When Greg McCormack made his request on behalf of Jonathan Keefe, General Cleveland had to risk it. But the lawyer rightly understood there was no danger whatsoever to his client, and he welcomed the opportunity despite the extra questions the government was preparing in order to try to trap the big SEAL from Virginia.

Meanwhile almost all of the other lawyers involved in the SEALs' defense had spent much of the Christmas and New Year vacations poring over the sworn statements to which they now had access. And the one that truly preoccupied them was the long NCIS interview with Brian Westinson, made on September 15 but kept under wraps for three months until the government delivered it to their legal offices on December 15.

This statement was made during a re-interview. Westinson had made an earlier report on September 5 in which he stated, in writing for the first time, that he had witnessed Matt strike the detainee on the left side of his abdomen with a closed right fist, and this caused him to fall to the floor onto his right side, with his legs pulled up in the fetal position.

Westinson wrote that he was shocked and scared at seeing this happen, and the three SEALs, Matt, Jon, and Sam, noticed his surprise.

Westinson had recorded that Jonathan said to him: "Don't feel bad for this guy. He killed a lot of Americans and two team guys." Westinson had added that he personally picked up Al-Isawi from the floor and set him in a chair. "He was still bound with his hands behind his back," the MA3 wrote. "And he was wearing a mask covering his eyes and nose. I observed blood coming from his lip."

So far as the defense lawyers were concerned, this was all very well. But their clients had also provided them with accurate accounts of the "incident" from the very beginning, right from the opening meeting at Danny's. And it was stark in the minds of all three accused SEALs that on that morning Westinson had never admitted to seeing anything of the kind and never once even suggested he had seen Matt punch the terrorist.

And both Matt and Jonathan remembered something else: at first Westinson admitted he had been absent from his guard post twice, but later stated it had been three times. In the SEALs' opinion this was because he considered, momentarily, it was more favorable for him to have been missing for as long as possible, during which time someone else may have thumped Al-Isawi in the stomach. The longer the absence, the wider the range of Westinson's alibi.

And now, set before them, the lawyers could read Westinson's rewrite, rethink, rehash statement, made in the camp at Ar-Ramadi when he was not in front of a group of hard, disciplined SEALs who were listening to every word. There, while he worked on that September 15 rewrite, he had free literary rein.

And boy! Had that account ever changed from those stammering accounts he gave in front of everyone in Danny's recreation room. Under intense interrogation from NCIS Special Agent John Stamp, Westinson's re-interview was based on a specific set of questions:

1. How long were you gone from the screening facility before you observed McCabe, Keefe and Sam?

   I left once to go get medical paperwork, once to put the rifle away. I was away from the detention facility approximately five to 10 minutes before returning, to find Sam, McCabe and Keefe inside with the detainee.

2. What did you first see?

   I saw Sam, McCabe and Keefe standing three feet away from the detainee. The detainee was facing them, standing up against the wall. He did not appear to be in any distress.

3. What did you first hear?

   I did not hear anything out of the ordinary when I returned to the detainee facility.

4. Is there a sign in the log book?

   No. No video either.

5. Describe the exact positioning of McCabe, Gonzales, and Keefe when you entered.

   Al-Isawi was standing up, facing McCabe, Gonzales and Keefe, with his back to the wall. He did not seem distressed. Gonzales, McCabe and Keefe were three feet away from him.

6. What did they say to you when you entered?

   I don't remember anything being said.

7. What did you say to them?

Nothing.

8. Did it appear like something was going on? What did you first think when you entered?

   Yes, because I saw Sam looking out of the door, as if making sure no one saw, that would report what they were doing. When I walked in I didn't think anything was going to go on, as if me being there would deter them from doing anything to the detainee.

9. Why would they be in there?

   They had no reason to be in there. With past detainees the Team guys would poke their heads in to look at a detainee but I'd never seen them abuse detainees before.

10. What was Al-Isawi doing?

    He was just standing there.

11. Was he sitting or standing?

    Standing.

12. Did Gonzales, McCabe or Keefe have their hands on Al-Isawi in any way? Helping him stand?

    No, I didn't see anyone touch him until McCabe hit him.

13. Did you ask Gonzales, McCabe, or Keefe what they were doing?

    No.

14. Where were Gonzales, McCabe and Keefe when McCabe struck Al-Isawi? Were they holding his arms?

    They were in the same position I pointed out earlier. McCabe just reached out and hit him.

15. How long were you standing next to McCabe before he struck Al-Isawi? Did McCabe say anything before he struck Al-Isawi? Did Gonzales and Keefe say anything either right before or after the punch?

    I was standing next to McCabe less than a minute before he hit Al-Isawi. McCabe didn't say anything before he hit him. After the punch, Gonzales and Keefe laughed, and Keefe yelled at the detainee, like a roar. As they were walking out, Gonzales said, "That's enough. He'll get more later."

16. Was there any other conversation that took place in the screening facility, other than what you have already told me about?

No.

17. Has anyone attempted to influence your statement? Has Mc-Cabe, Gonzales or Keefe spoken to you since you observed the assault? If so, what did they say?

    Sam wanted to write my sworn statement with me. That's what was the breaking point, what led me to report it. He also told me, "That guy fucked himself up, you're being very unprofessional right now," after he saw me hanging around the TOC. And after the meeting with the Lieutenant the day this happened, Sam said to me, "Get in there with those guys and get your story straight." Sam was referring to the entire SEAL Team, and to the medic, Paddy.

18. What did you think when you saw blood on Al-Isawi's lip? Did you tell anyone about it?

    I was scared but I didn't think it was from McCabe's punch. I don't think that injury could have happened from a blow like that. I thought that before I got back from putting my rifle away one of those three did something to Al-Isawi to cause the injury to his lip.

19. Did you ever speak to Al-Isawi? Did Al-Isawi ever say anything to you?

    I yelled at him to wake up once, when he was trying to fall asleep.

20. When the Lieutenant and Sam returned to clean up Al-Isawi, what did they say about the blood? Did they speak to Al-Isawi? Did Al-Isawi say anything to them?

    When the Lieutenant mentioned the wound to Sam, he said, "Do you think this could have happened on extract?" meaning during Al-Isawi's capture. Sam was acting like he was feigning ignorance of the injury.

21. Is there anything else I should ask you about?

    I think he was abused by other SEALs but didn't see any other abuse.

22. Did you see anyone else walking around or toward the detention facility while you were leaving to get your medical paperwork or put your rifle away?

    When I left the detention facility the first time to get the medical clipboard, I saw SO2 Higbie riding on a quad runner in the direction of the screening facility. I did not see him go to the screening facility though. When I was coming back with the clipboard, I noticed Higbie leaving the facility. He said to me, "Nothing happened back there. Relax," as he was leaving. At that time I looked in on the detainee, and he seemed to be in no distress. Also, Paddy was there, and I don't think he would have let anything happen to the detainee. I didn't see anyone coming or going from the detention facility when I went to put my rifle away. When I was coming back I did not see anyone coming or going from the detainee facility. When I got back to the detainee facility is when I saw Sam, Mc-Cabe and Keefe in the room with the detainee. Paddy was right outside the door to the detention facility when I went inside. He would have heard if the detainee was being abused while I was gone. I only left the detainee twice.

This was the Westinson rewrite. And when the lawyers read it the battle lines were truly drawn. For it contradicted every inch of the other statements that the men of Team 10 had written out under oath. Not one of them had seen anyone harm the detainee, and the medic had declared him unmarked except for, later, the tiny abrasion on his lower lip.

And worse yet for Westinson, none of them believed that any member of a SEAL Team would do such a thing. And no one but no one thought it possible that any SEAL would deliberately lie about such an incident.

Any and all them were prepared to testify to the excellent characters of the three accused. In short, no one thought there was a snowball's chance in hell that Matt McCabe had struck the prisoner Al-Isawi or that Sam and Jon had stood by and then lied about it.

This meant that either MA3 Brian Westinson was lying or the SEALs were lying, as their statements were diametrically opposed. And the jury would have to decide whom they believed.

By this time, with two of the courts-martial already scheduled for January, and with so much more work to do, a two-month postponement was permitted. There was a growing sense that the mighty clash of wills over a minor punch that may or may not have landed on the detainee was shaping up as one of the great legal confrontations of the age and was likely to end up as one of the most expensive.

And already, almost fourteen weeks before anyone was going into court either in Iraq or the United States, there was an enormous point of law that was elbowing its way into the very forefront of the cases: the government's refusal to allow Al-Isawi to be brought to America to testify. However, General Cleveland had approved the defense lawyers' rights to take deposition from the Iraqi prisoner.

But attorneys Puckett, McCormack, and Monica Lombardi, who had recently joined the defense team, were all of the opinion that this violated an enshrined right in a US court of law that the defendant has the right to confront his accuser. And right here the general was wading in deep waters.

In the first week of the New Year Puckett wrote a firm letter under the heading, "Re: Request of deposition of Mr. Ahmad Hashim Abd Al-Isawi."

It read,

Dear General Cleveland,

I received your letter of January 7th, 2010, approving the taking of deposition of Mr. Ahmad Hashim Abd Al-Isawi. I am disappointed that you have approved this request without requiring trial counsel to demonstrate why Mr. Al-Isawi cannot be produced. As the court-martial convening authority, you are the natural arbiter of disputes between the prosecution and defense.

The issue in dispute here is one of serious consequences. It is the right of an accused to confront his accuser. That right is enshrined in our Constitution under the Sixth Amendment. Yet, without any demonstration by the Government of an attempt to produce Mr. Al-Isawi, you have permitted the prosecutors to usurp a fundamental constitutional protection of SO2 McCabe. Ironically, it is a right for which SO2 McCabe was willing and ready to fight, and make the ultimate sacrifice.

If Mr. Al-Isawi is in the custody of Iraq authorities, you could have invited him to attend and coordinated his travel documents through the Department of State. We recognize that such coordination may be difficult, but difficulties do not justify denial of a constitutional right to an accused.

Instead of coordinating his travel, you have decided to depose Mr. Al-Isawi in Iraq. A deposition instead of a live testimony means that court-martial members will not have an opportunity to assess the witness's demeanor, watch his mannerisms, and, most importantly, ask him questions. By denying the court-martial members an opportunity to fully participate in the court-martial process, you are also denying SO2 McCabe a fair opportunity to defend himself and confront his accuser.

In light of your decision to deny our client his full constitutional rights to confront his accuser, and in consideration of SO2 McCabe's right to a speedy trial, we hereby withdraw our request to have Mr. Al-Isawi produced, and agree to enter into a stipulation of his expected testimony.

Puckett signed the letter and had it dispatched to MacDill Air Force Base. This probably delighted General Cleveland and whosoever his political guardians might have been because, at last, they were rid of the threat that some legal curveball might be delivered that would compel them to produce Al-Isawi in the United States, with all the rights and privileges of a regular US citizen, including the ability to plead the Fifth.

It cannot be overstated how seriously US law enshrines this right of the accused. In 2004 the Supreme Court made a decision in the CRAWFORD V. WASHINGTON case that rewrote the standard for determining when the admission of hearsay statements in criminal cases is permitted under the CONFRONTATION CLAUSE of the Sixth Amendment.

This means, broadly, that no lawyer can walk into a US courtroom with a prepared, written, sworn statement from a witness. Because it can be deemed hearsay. The person who made that statement has to be present, right there in the witness box, to utter his words before the judge and jury, prosecution and defense.

Those words are deemed sacred in the search for truth. And no matter how fastidiously any statement has been prepared and sworn and witnessed, it simply will not do. Because nonappearance means the words may be interpreted as hearsay.

This 2004 decision was a momentous change to the law, one of the most defense-friendly decisions in many, many years. It underscored the right to cross-examine witnesses and potentially disallowed hearsay evidence, which courts had permitted for the past twenty-five years.

The ruling astounded attorneys all over the country.

It was such a legal milestone that it brought a brand-new word into the lawyer's vernacular. From that moment on, March 8, 2004, attorneys, when faced with sworn statements from potential no-shows, would thunder, "*CRAWFORD!*"

And even General Cleveland had to pay attention to that. Though standing on the government's decision to keep Al-Isawi in Iraq, he had absolutely no choice about letting the defense lawyers loose on him to conduct a cross-examination. And making matters infinitely worse was the fact that as this legal quagmire was proceeding, there was a newly released statement from Al-Isawi.

All of the defense lawyers, JAGs, civilians, and paralegals were studying this new statement. The recorded first exchange between the prisoner and his military interrogators was the first sight the lawyers had at the direct accusations being leveled against their clients, the SEALs.

In the hours immediately after the incident two special agents from the Camp Cropper Criminal Investigation Division (CID) Office, Military Police Battalion, Baghdad, had sat Al-Isawi down and proceeded to have their linguist/interpreter fill out seven pages of Arabic writing, as dictated by Al-Isawi.

The typed-up account, translated into English, was now presented to the defense lawyers. It read,

September 1st at 2.30AM the American and Iraqi forces broke into my house and arrested me, and then took me to their camp. They interrogated me at one room, and then took me to a different room where I was assaulted and abused by the American forces, by hitting and kicking on sensitive areas on my belly, and shoulder. They were hitting me by the hands and foot.

Questions and Answers: [spelling errors not corrected]

Q: Do you know who hit you?

A: *I don't know because I was blindfolded.*

Q: Do you know what you were hit with?

A: *I was hit by hands and foot.*

Q: Were you hand cuffed?

A: *Yes.*

Q: Do you know you were hit by a man or woman?

A: *A man.*

Q: How do you know?

A: *I can recognize his voice.*

Q: Do you have any injuries from that man who hit you?

A: *Yes. I was hit on my face and shoulder.*

Q: Do you have any other injuries from that man?

A: *Yes. I was kicked so hard on my bellay.*

Q: Were you hit on your bellay by fist or foot?

A: *By foot.*

Q: How do you know you were hit by foot?

A: *Because it was very strong hitting.*

Q: Were you provoked by that man?

A: *No.*

Q: Did you understand what that man was saying to you?

A: *The only word I understood was the f-word, and he said a lot more words that I cannot understand.*

Q: Did you do anything as reaction while that man Was hitting you?

A: *I did not do anything because I was hand cuffed, but after I was fell to the ground, that blind-fold moved a little bit so I saw the man's foot in front of me.*

Q: When was the last time you slept before you got hit?

A: *About an hour before the hitting.*

Q: Were you scared after they broke into your house?

A: *Yes.*

Q: Did you get any medical or Madison treatment after hitting?

A: *I was only examined by the doctor and he told me that he will bring some Madison but he did not.*

Q: Can you describe how strong that pain in your stomach was?

A: *It was very strong pain especially for the first three days, and then it's gone with first week.*

Q: Special Agent was ordered to withhold the day and time and location of completion of this statement from you. Do you have any objections?

A: *No.*

There would be a great deal more to come because, as Puckett's letter to the general had so strongly intimated, the defense attorneys for all three accused Navy SEALs would be traveling to Iraq for a possibly revealing chat with the Butcher of Fallujah, who now claimed "prisoner abuse."

9

US GOVERNMENT DENIES IMMUNITY

When I saw the document, which stated, top left, UNITED STATES
V. JONATHAN KEEFE, SO2, US NAVY, I had to leave the room,
because I thought I was going to be physically sick. I was gone
for about twenty minutes. My lawyer probably thought I'd killed
myself.

There are a lot of decks in the US Navy—quarter decks, gun decks, foredecks, flight decks. But in January 2010 there was a brand-new one entering the seamen's lexicon: the stacked deck. Because by now the government was preparing to erect yet another roadblock right in front of the accused Navy SEALs.

The government's stacked deck involved the necessary statements of the five SEALs who were ready to stand in a courtroom, any courtroom, and swear to the innocence of Matthew McCabe, Jonathan Keefe, and Sam Gonzales. They were the platoon lieutenant, Jimmy; Petty Officers 1st Class Rob and Eric; Lieutenant Junior Grade Jason; and SO2 Carlton Higbie.

All five of them had walked across that dark and lethal desert on the fateful night of September 1, walked alongside Matt, Jon, and Sam, not knowing whether they were headed into a quiet, sleeping al-Qaeda camp or into the jaws of hell. Eric had walked alone, out in front of Matt, wide to the right of Jon, point man for column two.

Carlton had walked close to Sam, who had a hair-trigger grip on the comms. Jimmy was right there with them, armed to the teeth and in command. And now the US government was ranged against them all, seemingly determined to ruin Matt, Jon, and Sam. The government was preparing to deny immunity from prosecution to the other five if they dared to stand in court and speak up for their blood brothers in combat.

This was a truly shameful episode. The five SEALs not being charged—yet—had, through their lawyers, requested immunity during any court appearance, as none of them wanted an aggressive prosecutor, steeped in the tricks and wiles of the courtroom, to trip them up.

All five of them were smart as hell, but they knew little of the law; however, they knew only too well the treatment so far meted out to Matt, Jon, and Sam in the long weeks while the military was attempting to wring confessions out of them. Most of them knew, blow by blow, how government legal officials had spent hours threatening and promising, doing anything they could think of to get an admission, almost forcing the SEALs to sign documents that would confirm that Matt had whacked the murderer and that the other two had lied, cheated, and schemed to get him out of it.

The request for immunity from prosecution was normally routine, so no one expected the requests to be denied. But this case was different, way different. The government appeared to believe there were no holds barred.

And soon, they would learn, the government was prepared to deny their routine request for immunity. The lawyer representing the five SEALs, however, would make it plain: the Team 10 witnesses were not going anywhere near a courtroom until they were given guarantees that they too would not end up in the same boat as the three accused.

As the lines were drawn over the immunity issue, there was a weird and angry silence from the government. And all three defense teams were left to reflect on the inordinate set of circumstances that had dominated this case from the very first moment Ahmad Hashim Abd Al-Isawi had opened his mildly damaged mouth with his poisonous accusations against US Navy SEALs.

And from then on the SEALs had been up against it. There was the alacrity with which they had effectively been determined guilty, removed from their base, stripped of their armor and weapons, separated from their teammates, made to live with the Iraqis, do menial work, act as servants to other SEALs, and be disbelieved at every turn in their road.

There were the countless times when Jon Keefe had been asked to turn against his friend Matt McCabe and admit he had watched him strike the prisoner. There were the failed attempts to get them all to sign documents admitting to their "crimes." And there were the absurdly long delays in providing the defense with routine discovery documents essential for any trial.

And what about the sudden refusal to bring Al-Isawi to the United States so that Matt McCabe should have his constitutional right to face his accuser and confront the "evidence" against him? How about the government's obvious ploy to ensure that defense counsel could not cross-examine this known liar in an American courtroom witness box?

And how about the public uproar? The heavyweight legal opinions being flung at Major General Cleveland? And what about the demand from the US Congress that this entire prosecution be abandoned? And the obvious wish of the American people to have this case thrown out, regardless of whether Matt had walloped the terrorist. There were hundreds of thousands of cyberspace messages evoking nothing but fury and suggesting that no one in the entire country would have given a short damn if Matt had shot the terrorist and been done with it.

Thousands of ordinary people were contributing thousands of dollars to finance the three SEALs' defense. But all to no avail.

The government seemed determined to find them guilty. And now there was this latest hurdle—nonimmunity for the five Team 10 SEALs who wished to testify on their brothers' behalf.

Was this a ruthless attempt at stacking the deck, or what?

If the court-martial convener, General Cleveland, stuck to his guns and refused to grant that immunity, Matt and his teammates could suffer a huge blow to their courtroom strategy. It was, after all, essential that men who had fought alongside them, relied on them, and could testify to their character be present at the trial, standing tall in the witness box and swearing to God that Matt, Jon, and Sam had done nothing wrong.

And now the government's lawyers appeared to have found another way to stop that from happening. Stacking the deck is one thing, but using obvious legal tricks to rob the defendants of even a semblance of a fair shout was quite another.

One of Sam's principal defense attorneys was Lieutenant Guy Reschenthaler, a skilled and thoughtful Norfolk trial lawyer. He was a man with substantial experience prosecuting terrorists, insurgents and other reprobates in Baghdad courtrooms.

"And never," he stated several months later, "never in all of my career, have I known the government's prosecutors so utterly determined to win a case. They seemed prepared to do anything on this earth to nail down convictions against these three American heroes. And God knows why. I'll go to my grave wondering."

For a lawyer still in his twenties, Reschenthaler had a formidable record. In 2009 he had volunteered for deployment to combat environment in Baghdad, where he was assigned to Task Force 134, the unit responsible for detainee operations and prosecutions in Iraq. He served as prosecution liaison in the Central Criminal Court of Iraq, responsible for all cases arising from Special Forces capture-and-theater-internment facility crimes.

His life there was spent among Iraqi attorneys and judges in the Red Zone, with the goal of criminally prosecuting terrorist and insurgents under Iraqi law. He handled nearly one hundred cases, securing convictions in all but two of them. He obtained the death penalty for fifteen detainees responsible for murder.

What Reschenthaler did not know about Iraqi prisoners and their breathtaking deviousness was, generally speaking, not worth knowing.

He'd seen it all before. But he had never seen anything like the US government's determination to convict Matt, Jon, and Sam.

The issue of immunity for the SEALs who would be willing to stand witness for the accused grew more pressing. All through the last days of January and early February a skilled military lawyer from Middletown, Virginia, Charles W. Gittins, worked on statements from the five SEAL witnesses that would be presented to the US Navy trial judiciary, via Greg McCormack.

These "proffers of summarized truthful testimony" that the men would provide if they were granted immunity consisted of full statements, which, by definition, illuminated the necessary and even critical nature of their evidence.

But the government lawyers would not confirm that the immunity would be in any way forthcoming. As a result, Matt, Jon, and Sam felt utterly defeated; none of them could sleep through the night as the specter of ruin and disgrace crowded in upon them.

All three of them lost weight. They were worried about everything, including the rising legal bills, the concern that there would not be sufficient money to pay for their defense. And now they faced the truly chilling possibility that none of their teammates would stand in the courtroom and support them because the government had found a way to scare them out of it.

"I was almost sick with worry," said Matt. "and I could not get that document out of my head—the one that said THE UNITED STATES V. MATTHEW MCCABE, SO2—US NAVY. It would almost have been better if I had knocked down this terrorist dude because that way I'd have had personal clarity. But I'd done nothing, absolutely nothing, and it sometimes seemed even the SEAL authorities had turned against me. It nearly broke my heart."

And through all of this Paul Threatt and Greg McCormack were watching the terrible, wearing effect the case was having on Jon Keefe, who had also been shown a judicial document that stated, top left, UNITED STATES V. JONATHAN KEEFE, SO2—US NAVY.

"At first I could not believe it," he says. "The words seemed to blur right in front of me. How could anyone have leveled that against me?

Was the whole country somehow against me? Not just the Navy—the entire United States?

"I was in Greg's office when I saw the document, and I had to leave the room because I thought I was going to be physically sick. I was gone for about twenty minutes. Greg probably thought I'd killed myself."

It took that long for the mighty breacher from southern Virginia to compose himself—strange how this is so often the way with the bravest of men. But like Matt and Sam, Jon never could comprehend what he was supposed to have done wrong. He still can't.

And all anyone could do at present was to hope to hell the supremely erudite Charles W. Gittins could compose a powerful case for immunity to be granted to the big five waiting in the wings to speak up for their three buddies.

Gittins understood that if the government was going to deny immunity, they would probably announce it from out of the blue, suddenly, and with no real reason. Thus, he had to be ready with an unanswerable reply.

He prepared the proffers of testimony for Lieutenant Jimmy, SO1 Eric, and Lt. JG Jason. And then he worked on the submission for SO2 Carlton Milo Higbie IV, who was currently at the Naval Amphibious Base, assigned to one of the revered SEAL instructor positions. Carl, the massively built, six-foot SEAL who could bench press 450 pounds six times, was enormously well regarded by the Special Forces High Command.

The tactical air controller had previous experience on an Iraqi deployment and was regarded as a vital member of the platoon that had captured Ahmad Hashim Abd Al-Isawi.

His proffered statement would detail the times of duties at the base after they had returned, beginning from "wheels down" in the early hours of the morning, with their prisoner. He would attest that he first called the air officer to discuss some minor coordination problem during the mission and then prepared his e-mails for the mission debrief.

Carl and Jason rode the four-wheel ATV from the TOC to the kitchen, trying to find Paddy. The three of them often ate together, usually with

Eric as well, but the giant medic was not there, so they went down to the detainee facility in case he was still examining Al-Isawi.

When Carl arrived he did not see anyone present with the detainee, so he and Jason waited outside the door. Pretty soon Westinson showed up, and the two SEALs then left. Carl had spent just a few seconds at the holding facility, and although Paddy was not there, he had time to notice that the detainee was seated with his hands behind his back, wearing the mask. Carl stated that everything looked in order, except there was no one guarding the detainee.

The only SEAL he saw was Jason, and his statement confirmed that he, of course, saw no American strike "Amber"—as the SEALs called Objective Amber's target. He himself definitely did not strike Amber, and, subsequently, no one told Carl they had hit or struck Amber at any time.

It should be remembered here that this was the account of a SEAL instructor, one of the most trusted and respected members of the entire US Armed Forces. If Carlton Milo Higbie IV said something was so, then it was so—no ifs, ands, or buts. And right now the government was trying to dissuade him from even entering the courtroom on his friends' behalf.

Like everyone else, a few hours later Carl was awakened and told to report to the meeting at Danny's, where he learned of the allegations of prisoner abuse. The lieutenant outlined Al-Isawi's complaint to the twenty to twenty-five people present. Carl had no idea what the lieutenant was talking about and, anyway, did not believe anyone in that room would abuse the detainee. So he spoke up, stating, "Nobody hit the guy." Others also spoke up, echoing Carl's opinion. When the meeting ended he went back to bed.

In his proffered statement Carl also described how they were then ordered to fill out individual statements, and because of his seniority, he remained with them and assisted several men complete their forms.

His statement to Charles W. Gittins concluded with the following passage:

As Team 10 was transitioning with Team 1, Higbie had occasion to eat with Command Master Chief Lampard, at the Task Force West Camp.

CMC Lampard was apparently unaware of who SO2 Higbie was, because Higbie was not wearing his uniform at the time. Chief Lampard told SO2 Higbie that he was very disappointed in the SEALs for abusing a prisoner, and even more disappointed that they had tried to cover it up, or words to that effect.

SO2 Higbie told Chief Lampard very candidly that no one did anything to the detainee, and no one was covering anything up. And that Higbie thought it was ridiculous that the CMC would say that without any knowledge of the facts. Chief Lampard became quiet, made sort of a grunt, and changed the subject.

END OF PROFFER. Respectfully submitted, and signed by Charles W. Gittins.

On January 29 trial counsel was provided with the proffers of testimony for Jimmy, Eric, and Jason. The submission argued that the testimony of each witness was relevant, necessary, and "in many regards, constitutes exculpatory evidence toward the defense." The issue remained, however, whether the government would grant testimonial immunity.

On February 4 the defense submitted its request that the government grant each of the witnesses immunity. Two weeks went by, and on February 19, 2010, the government denied the request for testimonial immunity for all five witnesses.

Two weeks after that the two additional proffers for Carl and Paddy were also presented on the grounds that these were the unique observations of each witness during the significant time on the morning of September 2. All three had observed the detainee and interacted with SO2 Keefe, SO2 McCabe, SO1 Sam, and MA3 Westinson. They would also add their opinions regarding the military character for Jon Keefe's truthfulness and duty performance.

McCormack then took over this battle with the government, acting on behalf of Jon, who was slotted to appear first before a court-martial. He submitted that each witness had a unique role in the facts of the case. With lawyerly restraint, he did not elucidate his true opinion— that it was insanity not to grant these five SEALs the immunity they deserved. And he made out the case for each of them:

Lieutenant Jimmy: A crucial witness because he was the Platoon Commander, and the first person to observe blood on the detainee's clothing. He alone made the initial report. He conducted the initial investigation, as SO2 Keefe's superior officer, and he had the responsibility of advising SO2 Keefe of his rights, which he failed to do on repeated occasions.

Additionally, he will relate MA3 Westinson's multiple denials of any knowledge of, or role in, the detainee's injury, as well as his demeanor. Furthermore, Lieutenant Jimmy will testify to SO2 Keefe's character for truthfulness and honesty, as well as outstanding military character.

Lieutenant JG Jason: A crucial witness because he was Assistant Officer in charge, and as such observed the detainee at a time when no other witness observed him. LTJG Jason also has knowledge of a motive for MA3 Westinson to lie. Furthermore LTJG Jason will testify on SO2 Keefe's character, for truthfulness, honesty, and outstanding military bearing.

SO1 Eric: A crucial witness because he conducted the initial evaluation of the detainee's medical condition. SO1 Eric's testimony is also necessary to establish the chain of custody of the detainee. SO1 Eric also has knowledge of who was alone with the detainee, and would have had the opportunity to injure the detainee.

SO1 Eric will also testify that after the allegations of abuse surfaced, he examined the detainee, and found "no such indications." Furthermore SO1 Eric will testify on SO2 Keefe's character for truthfulness, honesty, and outstanding military qualities.

SO2 Carl Higbie: Crucial, because he was a witness to Lt Jimmy's interrogation of the personnel connected with the detainee. SO2 Higbie's testimony is also necessary in corroborating the statements spoken by MA3 Westinson (words to the effect that he had a bad reputation and could not afford to get into trouble again) in response to that interrogation.

Furthermore SO2 Higbie was present when MA3 Westinson stated that if he were to be punished for detainee abuse, he would be unable to gain employment with the Highway Police when he separates from the Navy. SO2 Higbie was present when MA3 Westinson stated that he did not witness any aggressive act committed against the detainee.

HM1 Paddy: A crucial witness because he observed the detainee, when he went to the screening facility in Baharia, Iraq. He also conducted the required medical and visual inspection of the detainee, and did not notice any injuries. In addition, HM1 Paddy saw that the detainee was left unguarded by MA3 Westinson for a period of time, during which he could have easily intentionally injured himself.

All of this detailed reasoning was a part of a formal request from Greg McCormack that the military judge direct the appropriate convening authority—General Cleveland—to grant testimonial immunity to the five defense witnesses "And that in the event that testimonial immunity is not granted by the Government, the Military Judge abate the Special Court-Martial proceedings against SO2 Jonathan Keefe."

McCormack summarized the facts of the case, in which he highlighted inconsistencies with grim accuracy, quoting Westinson as saying, "I don't know, I don't know." And then again, "I don't know … a lot of guys were in there."

The lieutenant specifically asked MA3 Westinson: "Did anyone do anything to the detainee?" To which Westinson responded, "No, I do not know." And then, a couple of days later: "I saw something." He then asserted to Lieutenant Jimmy that he saw SO2 McCabe punch the detainee in the stomach "while SO1 Sam and the accused were present." McCormack noted archly that "the specific factual assertions to the alleged assault, provided by MA3 Westinson, are markedly different from those of the detainee."

A brilliantly argued summation of the situation dominated the second page of McCormack's motion. It read, in part:

MA3 Westinson is the key Government witness in this case, and without his testimony, the Government would have no evidence to support the accusations against either Keefe, McCabe or Gonzales. MA3 Westinson acknowledges his attempts to be separated from the Navy early, in order to pursue a career with the California Highway Patrol, and that a conviction by a court-martial would destroy his efforts to secure that career in civilian law enforcement.

To this date, MA3 Westinson has never been charged in connection with his failure to protect the detainee as was his duty, nor with failure to report the injury to the detainee, nor with false official statement for his initial denial of any knowledge of how the detainee was injured.

Although MA3 Westinson has not been granted testimonial immunity by the Government, it is the position of the defense that the Government has, in effect, secured the cooperation of Westinson by giving him the belief and expectation that he will not be prosecuted, so long as he cooperates, and testifies as a Government witness in all three cases. The defense submits this situation is the equivalent to *de facto* immunity.

On page five of the motion McCormack wrote the headline Discussion, and underneath he quoted the Rules of Court-Martial (RCM) 704(e) that pointed out that the decision to grant immunity is a matter within the sole discretion of the convening authority.

However, if a request has been denied, the military judge may grant appropriate relief by directing the convening authority to grant immunity to a defense witness, or he may abate proceedings against the accused upon finding that the following three requirements have all been met:

1. The witness intends to invoke the right against self-incrimination to the extent permitted by law if called to testify.
2. The Government has engaged in discriminatory use of immunity to obtain a tactical advantage, or the Government, through its own overreaching, has forced the witness to invoke the privilege against self-incrimination.
3. The witness's testimony is material, clearly exculpatory, not cumulative, not obtainable from any other source, and does more than merely affect the credibility of other witnesses.

In applying RCM 704(e) the court of appeals for the Armed Forces found that all three prongs must be met. In his motion McCormack reminded the trial court that, according to Gittins, all five witnesses intended to invoke their right to remain silent if called to testify, which satisfied the first prong of the RCM 704(e) test.

He then pointed out that the government had *de facto* granted immunity to MA3 Westinson by not pursuing charges for his admitted dereliction of duty and false official statement. These protections, informally afforded to MA3 Westinson, allow the government to secure the testimony of the only person claiming to have witnessed the detainee's injury.

By denying the defense request for testimonial immunity of each witness, the government simultaneously eliminates four essential, relevant, and material witnesses who exculpate SO2 Keefe with specific factual evidence and undermine MA3 Westinson's credibility. They provide evidence of his conflicting statements and his motive to lie. They also present crucial testimony as to SO2 Keefe's general military character for truthfulness.

The government's actions amount to discriminatory use of immunity, thus satisfying the second prong of the RCM 704(e) test.

Finally, the attached proffers clearly indicate that these material witnesses would provide crucial testimony that can be utilized in the defense of SO2 Keefe, that because each witness had a unique role and perspective, none of their testimony is cumulative or obtainable from another source, and that they offer specific facts tending to establish SO2 Keefe's innocence as well as to impeach MA3 Westinson's expected testimony.

All three prongs of the RCM 704(e) test were met. Consequently, the defense motion to direct a grant of immunity or abate the trial should be granted.

Almost every defense lawyer involved in any of the forthcoming three trials thought that was probably game, set, and match to the defense. The facts of the issue were indisputable: the Rules of Court-Martial were not only clear; they were also carved in stone.

McCormack had blown apart any sense of fair play in this trial, and he'd exposed the government's nearly naïve attempt to dance around the rule book by granting immunity to Westinson but not actually admitting it. As discriminatory actions go, this one was right up there.

But it was still up to General Cleveland to grant the immunity, and he was not required to offer an explanation if he decided not to. As things now stood, the courts-martial against Jon and Sam would take place in Iraq because the US government had flatly refused to allow Al-Isawi to set foot in the United States but could not deny the two accused SEALs their right to confront their accuser in court.

The government did not, of course, offer to contribute a dime toward the enormous cost of flying the defense lawyers halfway across the world to Baghdad, leaving that to the SEALs and their thousands of supporters to make their own wildly expensive arrangements.

And out in the great wide world of the United States, those supporters were continuing to raise their voices in protest at the court-martial proceedings. In addition to the huge website Graham Ware ran, all kinds of organizations were emerging, all of them complaining as well as gathering financial contributions to try to cover the endless bills such trials invariably generate.

From the mighty to the humblest, thousands of blogs and tweets came zipping through cyberspace. From the cold slopes of Alaska, Sarah Palin, the Republican Party's nominee for vice president in 2008, in a characteristically forthright editorial, commanded Americans to "Stand up for the SEALs who are standing up for us!"

There was a rising sense of pure indignation in the United States, as Americans raged against the image of the "lawyered up" jihadist murderer accusing the god-like Navy SEALs of "police brutality." No one believed him. All that people understood was that the US military was falling over itself to prove how Muslim-friendly it was. At least that's the way it seemed to the average person, including about eight zillion bloggers.

The SEALs' trials were being compared to the 2005 "massacre" in Haditha (referred to in chapter 1), when US Marines—who had been fired upon, murdered, and bombed—were accused of being murderers themselves after retaliating. In that travesty of military justice the Marines were all acquitted, but the public saw it as just another grotesque example of the US Navy trying to look "nice and politically correct."

Experienced US military veterans were angrily pointing out that if the prosecution really did have the SEALs dead to rights, they would have gone straight to a "showpiece general court-martial" in order to assuage their fervent desire to be seen as the fairest of the fair.

To many Americans this was the mind-set of the damned, because the United States was involved in an undeniably brutal shooting war in Iraq, where troops were grappling with a cold-blooded jihadist enemy whose chosen currency was bombing, gunfire, executions, torture, and the daily killing of US troops, wherever and however they were serving in that hot, benighted, tribal country.

And by this time the Islamists had learned that the United States would rather suffer any indignity than honestly admit to themselves how much they were hated in the Land of the Two Rivers. The United States was just pretending, and the courts-martial of the SEALs merely caused veterans to write hundreds of dark tweets, warning that a great price would be paid for this cowardice.

"And that price will only go up," warned one former Marine officer. "It always does."

In Arizona, Ware almost lost count of the times he was sent one of the more famous quotes regarding the military's place in society, such as:

> People sleep peaceably in their beds at night, only because rough men stand ready to do violence on their behalf.
> —*George Orwell, author and former unit infantry commander,*
> *Spanish Civil War, 1937*

One highly respected educator from Virginia, the daughter of a "decorated combat veteran who gave his life in the service of this country," sent a moving letter to Major General Cleveland; Admiral Gary Roughead, chief of naval operations; and the Honorable Ray Mabus, secretary of the US Navy. It read,

> My nation is on the slippery shore of very dangerous waters and we are currently engaged in the act of assisting our sworn enemy. I respectfully request your assistance in stemming this tide.

After begging them to stop the courts-martial, the writer added how "deeply concerned" she was for the nation. And there were, literally, tens of thousands of letters in this vein being written in the United

States during that early spring, expressing not so much anger as bewilderment. But this lady had said it particularly well: "Are we supposed to believe that these three men—the smartest, fastest, best-trained, strongest and most capable, are going to engage in a cover-up over such an incident? This simply does not make sense ... to this mother's ears."

She concluded her communication with a final couple of paragraphs aimed directly at the three authorities she named at the head of her letter, General Cleveland, the CNO, and the secretary of the Navy. She said that she felt the three SEALs "would be quicker to leap to our defense, more diligent and self-sacrificing in protecting us, than you would be; certainly less concerned with self-protection." And she added, tellingly, "Politicos and journalists do not secure our safety, nor protect our civil and Constitutional rights, soldiers do."

She sent copies of her letter to the three principal defense lawyers, hoping, correctly, that they might share her view that in this instance the military had effectively gone off its rocker. And every one of the lawyers read it thoughtfully, gratified in so many ways to read the well-presented opinions of an educated, rational, and concerned American citizen.

These middle days of March were bringing the ground rules of the courts-martial into very sharp focus. General Cleveland gave no indication that he was considering changing his mind about granting standard immunity to the five witnesses for the defense, Carl, Jason, Eric, Lieutenant Jimmy, and Paddy. Thus, having been implicitly warned they too might end up being prosecuted, none of them would appear in court for Matt, Jon, or Sam.

But there was by this time a new and powerful force in the arena. And just as Shakespeare's soothsayer mentioned to Julius Caesar a couple of thousand years ago to "beware the Ides of March," so the court-martial judge might have alerted General Cleveland that he ought to beware the consequences of the obviously tricky ploys from his fiercely determined military prosecution team.

On Friday, March 12, the judge who would preside over the two courts-martial in Iraq for Jonathan and Sam made a ground-breaking decision. He informed Major General Cleveland that he categorically did not understand his decision to not grant immunity.

He then simplified the entire issue by stating that General Cleveland had until March 24 to change his mind and grant all five witnesses the immunity their lawyers requested or else the judge would throw the entire case out of court, and that would be the end of that.

This was something of a bombshell to all the commanders who had a hand in this curious prosecution. But it came as no shock to many Navy personnel who were acquainted with the judge. For he was Commander Tierney Carlos, a New Yorker and former assistant district attorney with a very obvious hard edge and an accent straight out of the Lower West Side. One of his favorite descriptive phrases for those he considered less than well briefed was "knuckle head." He was also inclined to fire out the word "dopey" with impressive venom.

He had left civilian law, apparently tired of endless murder cases, and elected to join the US Navy JAG corps in Southern Virginia, where he rightly foresaw a "cleaner" practice and a better quality of life.

Commander Tierney, since then promoted to naval captain, was a vintage New Yorker—a five-foot, seven-inch lean and muscular lawyer with well-cut gray hair and a sharp and decisive manner that concealed a kind and reasonable spirit. Rumors abound, though never confirmed, that he generously mentored several young attorneys who he believed showed real talent in litigation. There were many counselors who had fallen foul of the high standards of his courtroom, and yet the word most associated with Judge Carlos was "fairness." He particularly disliked big, powerful organizations bullying defendants or witnesses.

And from the very start of the SEALs' prosecution there was a kind of controlled exasperation in the judge's demeanor. All of the lawyers suspected he was content to hear the case and to make any decisions required of him. But there was something in his attitude, as though he were slightly impatient with the prosecution, as though, like most of the country, he considered the three SEALs should be believed, that they had somehow earned the special places they occupied in the American people's hearts.

It was as though Judge Carlos recognized that the SEALs did have special license that sometimes empowered them to kill their enemy, no questions asked, because the mortal dangers they so often faced were too great to tolerate anything less.

And on this Friday afternoon in Norfolk in March 2009, he listened carefully to the outline of the case—how a sailor guarding the detainee in the hours after his capture claimed to have seen Matt McCabe punch a terrorist while Jon and Sam watched. And now the distinguished petty officer 1st class, Sam, stood accused of dereliction of duty, impeding an investigation, and making a false official statement.

The defense stated that four other SEALs, including the detachment commander and a Navy corpsman present on the day of the alleged assault disputed the guard's claims. And now, five months into the investigation, they learned that they too could face prosecution. As a result, they hired a lawyer and requested immunity before testifying in the three cases that had gone forward. And now, without giving any reason, Major General Charles T. Cleveland had denied those requests.

Judge Carlos responded by confirming he did not understand that decision. He said the testimony of the five witnesses would shed doubt on the guard's allegations. Not granting the immunity, he ruled, is either an attempt to gain tactical advantage over the defense or evidence that the government is overreaching.

Just as important, Judge Carlos ruled, is that the expected evidence would be exculpatory—that it would clear the defendants of guilt. Documents the men submitted about what happened between 5 a.m. and 8 A.M. the day after Al-Isawi's capture, Judge Carlos said, make clear that the guard was occasionally left alone with the detainee.

The men's refusal to testify under their Fifth Amendment right does not mean they have anything to hide, stated the judge. And he cited Supreme Court rulings, noting that one of the Fifth Amendment's basic functions "is to protect innocent men ... who otherwise might be ensnared by ambiguous circumstances."

Judge Carlos gave Cleveland until March 24 to provide immunity to the five witnesses. He added, "If this does not happen, this court-martial will be abated"—the legal term for indefinite postponement.

It was, of course, the second time Judge Carlos had made a significant ruling in favor of the defense. In January, after the government indicated it would not bring Al-Isawi to the United States to testify in Sam Gonzales's court-martial, the judge moved the trial to Baghdad on the grounds that the petty officer had the right of confrontation—to face his accuser.

And now, by the second week in March, SO1 Gonzales had his court-martial set for Baghdad at a similar time to that of Jon Keefe. Judge Carlos would preside over both of them. Matt McCabe's much more serious court-martial would take place afterward in Norfolk, Virginia, in May, in front of a different judge.

That Friday evening, March 12, the court papers were forwarded to the convening authority, General Cleveland at MacDill, Florida, as well as to various officials in the Pentagon. There were, subsequently, many tortuous conversations on that following Monday morning all over the US military's legal departments. But the decision was already made. Denying the requests for immunity was now pointless, because without this there would be no court-martial. Judge Carlos had ensured that.

And Monday was the day of the Ides of March, the fifteenth day, the date when the great Caesar was stabbed in the back twenty-three times right there in the Roman Senate by men he believed were on his side. Somewhat wryly, Matt said later he understood more or less how Julius felt.

And now the cases did appear to be turning in the SEALs' favor. And several things happened—all pretty good—in quick succession:

1. General Cleveland, with no options whatsoever, granted immunity for the five SEALs, freeing them to testify on their brothers' behalf.
2. At a fundraiser in Scottsdale, Arizona, Graham Ware's organization to support the SEALs raised almost $20,000 for the SEALs' defense fund.
3. In case anyone thought that Matt and Jon had "tricked" their first polygraph, they both took a new supercharged lie-detector

test—not military, but nonetheless the last word in polygraph technology, said to be the only modern test ever devised—virtually unbeatable.

The test was administered by the Virginia Polygraph Service (VPS), located, appropriately, in Fairfax County, home of the one man for whom a polygraph would have been strictly irrelevant, George Washington. The VPS designed a very specific test, made especially to show whether Matt whacked Al-Isawi.

One of the finest lie-detector men in the country, Jerry F. Shockley, a twenty-one-year veteran of the Alexandria Police Department, was in command. A man with more than forty separate qualifications in technique and advanced developments plus innumerable awards from the Virginia/Maryland areas, the former detective lieutenant concentrated on two no-nonsense questions:

1. Did you strike Ahmad Al-Isawi in the midsection?
2. Last September 1 did you strike Ahmad Al-Isawi in the midsection with your fist?

To both of these Matthew McCabe answered a blunt, firm "No." And in conclusion Detective Lieutenant Shockley wrote,

The above questions were asked on three polygrams utilizing the Backster Zone Comparison Test technique. At the conclusion of the examination there were no significant physiological responses. It is my professional opinion that Mr. McCabe was being truthful when he answered those questions.
   —*Jerry F. Shockley*
   (March 17, 2010)

SO2 Keefe, who was equally as open and straightforward as Matt had been, had a slightly more torrid time at the hands of the lie-detector team. He had already taken and passed two nonofficial tests, but this was a modern power-polygraph.

They fitted electronic wires all over Jon and placed him in a chair with special butt pads and motion sensors, never telling him that one sharp clenching of the butt signified a bare-faced lie. They told him to sit still, restricting all movement. Thus installed, he moved only his eyeballs, scanning his interrogation room, looking up at the high one-way glass windows through which he knew a full squadron of agents and "detectives" were observing him.

One of his only two comforts was the presence of his two lawyers. Paul and Greg were right back there somewhere with their own window, watching for the slightest hint of unfair tactics. The other was the fact that he never told lies. Whichever way anyone looked at this scenario, it was one hell of an expensive way to establish something that obvious.

Afterward Jon's lawyers felt polygraph analysts were treating him with suspicion. In the NCIS test he was polygraphed three times for two hours, and each time was accused of trying to trick the machine.

"They told me I was trying to slow down my heart!" he remembers. "Accused me of being very calm! Told me I was trying to beat the system. I had no idea what they wanted from me. I just gave them the complete truth in answer to their questions. How could there possibly be any suggestion of a lie?"

In the end they sent Jonathan's results to the FBI in Washington. One opinion stated he was trying to control his breathing, and one paragraph claimed he was taking only four breaths a minute instead of the average human rate of thirteen. "It was a good thing I didn't slow down my heart at the same time," he said. "I'd probably have dropped dead right there next to the polygraph."

The final conclusion caused the military to infer they could not trust the results. Nonetheless, the officer gave the same conclusion as the one for Matt: "It is my professional opinion, that Mr. Keefe was being truthful when he answered those questions."

The findings of the ex-Virginia policeman arrived in time for Graham Ware's rally for the SEALs in Scottsdale. Matt attended, and the lie-detector exonerations were announced eight times by elected Republican Congressman John Shadegg, the lawyer son of Arizona's

Steve Shadegg, who managed Barry Goldwater's 1952 and 1958 US Senate campaigns and organized the Draft Goldwater Movement in the 1964 presidential campaign.

Congressman Shadegg, former chairman of the Republican Study Committee, like so many other SEAL supporters, was a distinguished politician. And he spoke for all three of the accused men, asserting that the American public must know the findings of those lie-detector tests.

He also told the large gathering: "The prosecution of Matthew, Jon, and Sam sends the most terrible message to young men and women across our nation who may be thinking about serving their country, that we would second-guess them in the performance of their duties. I believe the charges should not have been brought, and they should be dismissed.

"This whole incident is an outrage!" shouted the Arizona congressman to the cheering crowd. "Rather than being charged, these young men should be *thanked*."

In the annals of these forthcoming, drastically expensive trials, March will go down as a pivotal month—the days when the military judge made plain his intolerance of certain prosecution tactics, when the revelations of the killer lie-detection system were announced, when the prosecution realized that there were important members of Team 10 who would flatly refute the allegations of the government's star witness not to mention those of the terrorist himself and, of course, that the laws of the United States would not allow them to be bullied and frightened out of making proper courtroom appearances.

March was the month when it was settled that Jon and Sam would be court-martialed separately in Baghdad in late April. Matt's trial would be a few weeks later in Norfolk, without Al-Isawi being present. His attorney, Neal Puckett, had agreed the terrorist need not be called.

But March heralded the emergence of a new and significant force in the trial of the senior petty officer Sam Gonzales of Blue Island, Chicago. Sam was a dedicated Special Forces warrior who harbored only one wish: to prove his innocence and then to continue climbing the ladder of command in the Teams. This new fighting force—lawyer Guy Reschenthaler—had, as the weeks went by, developed a determined devotion to Sam's cause.

Reschenthaler was only twenty-seven and had just returned from his six-month tour in Iraq, where he had spent most of his time in the middle of knock-down-drag-out courtroom battles in which the authorities were trying to jail or execute some of the most dangerous terrorists in the Middle East.

And now, stranded in the Navy's legal department, he was just facing up to a new career—defending sailors, Marines, and Coast Guardsmen on charges of DUIs, theft, and sexual assault. For the former lion of the Baghdad prosecutor's desk, this stacked up especially drearily against the desert dramas of beheadings, mass production of illegal explosive devices, mass murder, and acts of terrorism.

Perhaps there were those who sensed that Reschenthaler was becoming steadily more bored by his new life, despite many courtroom appearances. But someone, somewhere in the Navy Legal Service Office decided he had better get into a case that would spark his interest and talent.

When he was added to the defense team, it had already included one member of the JAG corps, Lieutenant Commander Andrew Carmichael, who was working with the other defense attorney, civilian lawyer Monica Lombardi, out of her private practice in Virginia Beach. The case file was presented to Reschenthaler, containing all the known details about the three SEALs accused of abusing a star detainee plus lying, dereliction of duty, and false statements.

"Yessir," muttered the Pittsburgh-born Reschenthaler to himself, "I could get seriously into this."

Thus, the heavily built, slightly bored graduate of the renowned Duquesne University School of Law became embroiled in one of the most high-profile courts-martial in recent memory—and at a huge cost.

"Resch," as he was inevitably known, shed a penetrating light on Sam's character when he recalled the moment they first met. Armed with his case brief, the young lawyer called his new client over at the SEAL base and says he spoke to him with unrestrained awe. "He was a Navy SEAL, right? And around here that's about the closest anyone gets to being a superhero."

Later that day the phone rang, and the front desk told him: "Lieutenant, I have SO1 Gonzales here to see you."

Resch recalls giving his shirt an extra tuck, sharpening himself up, and walking down to the waiting room, where he pushed open the door and said, "Mr. Gonzales?"

At which point a short muscular man stood up and put down his newspaper. He was not in uniform and wore a long-sleeve shirt with a navy pullover, jeans, and old flip-flops. He grinned, offered his hand, and said, "Hi. Just call me Sam, Lieutenant."

They walked back to the office, where the automatic lights had already gone out with politically correct efficiency.

"You don't need to turn 'em on, sir," said Sam, in a low voice. "I'm a SEAL, and we're used to working in the dark. Just leave 'em off, Lieutenant. I like it better this way."

The lawyer already knew the SEAL Teams operated permanently on first-name terms, and he asked quietly for the petty officer to relate his side of the prisoner-abuse story.

But at this point he did decide not to tell the SEAL this was his first true criminal case in the United States, unless he counted a pre-Iraq trial in which the even younger Resch defended a sailor who managed to get drunk and passed out at the wheel in a Burger King drive-through. On reflection he also decided not to mention that he lost the case by offering some outlandish excuse that the guy's psoriasis medication was to blame!

"No problem, Lieutenant." replied Sam. "Because it's really simple. Look, we rolled this guy up, took good care to make sure nothing happened to him in the helo on the way home. Then we put him in the box—that's the big shipping container we have rigged to temporarily hold a captured target.

"Next morning the guy spits blood and says the Americans did it. The general wanted us to take a slap on the wrist with a General's Mast nonjudicial punishment. But that sounds like a 'guilty' to us. And we said, 'No, the hell with that.' And now we're all here."

It was an instant alert for Lieutenant Resch: this sudden switch from the Navy to the Army, the slightly jarring sound of the word "general" as opposed to lieutenant commander or captain. And right there Resch tuned in to an issue: the term Admiral's Mast, meaning an appearance on a disciplinary matter before a commanding admiral, had its entire roots and ethos in the Navy.

Over the years the term had been used to apply to the Army, a General's Mast. But to the legal mind there was a difference. In the Navy an Admiral's Mast is deadly serious, going back to the days of sail, when some critical mistake or careless action might have endangered the ship.

In the Army, however, it's somehow considered in a lighter mode, signifying a slap on the wrist and finished. But these SEALs were not in the Army. They were in the Navy, and the very term Admiral's Mast signified the admission of a serious crime. They could not face that. Right here there were crossed wires, and Lieutenant Resch was the first lawyer to tune in, and he was sitting right across from the senior accused SEAL.

In Reschenthaler's opinion this switch from naval discipline, this handing over of the prosecutors' torch to the Army was a very significant occurrence. The two services are related but different. And there is ageless folklore involved in both. The Navy marched to the beat of a sometimes-stricter drum.

And in this case the dogged independence of the SEALs served only to cause the Army commanders to dig in to their entrenched positions ever deeper. Sometimes the SEALs' wills seemed to irritate the Army authorities unnecessarily. Perhaps the Army should never stand in charge of judgments that involve Navy personnel.

There were a thousand dichotomies in the air, and Reschenthaler, like any halfway-decent defense lawyer, needed to clarify in his own mind the guilt of the accused SEALs. And the question always rears its head: Did they do this? Or is it just circumstances ganging up on them?

It took him a very short time to decide that it was impossible for Sam Gonzales to have stood by and then deliberately lie about the issue. SEALs of his experience simply do not behave like that. Sam was an ambitious man. He had received a Bronze Star for valor in combat. Would he put his entire career on the line and risk standing in a court-martial telling a pack of lies?

Couldn't happen, was Reschenthaler's opinion. And the lawyer's father, a Pittsburgh doctor, supported him in that. His father interpreted the slightest sign of doubt crossing his son's mind as strictly un-American.

"You gotta be kidding me, Guy," he would say when his son started thinking about the case from the government's point of view. "That Iraqi was a murderer, a terrorist and a threat to society, and even if it was true our guys punched him, he deserved it. You better get your head screwed on straight."

The fact that Reschenthaler's analysis came from careful legal examination of the facts and a natural tendency toward playing the devil's advocate cut no ice with Reschenthaler Senior. And Guy still finds it interesting that his father's views entirely echoed those of the vast majority of the American public.

Meanwhile a close camaraderie developed between Resch and Sam, who came to the legal office sometimes just to talk. The Navy had all three SEALs in some kind of a holding pattern. Every morning they checked into Team 10, and every morning they were dismissed and sent home. Sam found time to lay an entire hardwood floor at his home.

Exasperated and a little scared of the great unknown that lay ahead, he settled into a routine of brutally hard workouts and home improvements—a considerable waste of the million bucks it cost the US government to develop him into one of the world's elite fighting troops.

And the more time the young lawyer spent with him, the more certain he was that Sam could not possibly have seen anyone punch the terrorist or conspired to cover it up. Sam had an aura of naval professionalism about him, and this cried out to Resch that the government had this one all wrong.

Willingly, Reschenthaler took on more and more of the workload for the team, particularly regarding the coming motion being prepared to support the CONFRONTATION CLAUSE. Hour after hour he combed through the discovery documents, telephoned potential witnesses, and researched for the legal team's motions that might end this nightmare for the tough, rather ingenuous SEAL leader.

And the situation pleased everyone. Monica Lombardi was very busy building her private practice, and Drew Carmichael was loaded down with command leadership responsibilities. The fact that young Reschenthaler was prepared to work eighteen-hour days was a blessing.

And this gave him time to make the CONFRONTATION CLAUSE motion his pride and joy. As the junior defense attorney, he needed to tread fast, firmly, and carefully, skills long ago perfected by the hefty former Thomas Jefferson High School wrestler, whose Duquesne Law School was situated just a few hundred yards from the Pittsburgh Steeler's end zone along the wide Monongahela River.

Although built like an M1 Abrams tank, at five feet seven inches, Reschenthaler was never destined to join the Rooney family's black-and-gold warriors up there at the confluence with the Allegheny River, combat was still his instinct. And the courtroom suited him perfectly, especially the cut-and-thrust of criminal litigation.

And he picked up the CONFRONTATION CLAUSE motion and researched it as though he were on his way to the Supreme Court rather than a court-martial. He had agonized over every word and nuance. In Reschenthaler's mind this was the key to the case. His youthful optimism told him that victory was not only essential; victory might also blow this case right out of the water. If his team could win Sam's right to face his accuser but the government would not bring Al-Isawi to the United States, it had to be all over, right? No court-martial.

Well, nearly. Before a courtroom packed with journalists and spectators, Lombardi, the most experienced of the defense team, was armed with a motion largely written by Reschenthaler but also packed with skilled and experienced opinions written by Lombardi herself as well as Drew Carmichael.

To Reschenthaler it felt a bit like his own work, but he knew that it was a team effort and that Sam's two more senior lawyers had made a major and mature contribution. All the necessary research, pertinent precedents, and solid argument were there for Lombardi. And everyone remembers the moment. With Sam sitting tense and white-faced between her and Reschenthaler, Lombardi stepped up and began: "May it please the court ..."

What followed was a masterly presentation of the newish law to which the Supreme Court had delivered such a crystal-clear precedent, articulating not so much a bedrock principle of the Anglo-American judicial system but a cry from the very heart of the gods of law—that every defendant has the right to face his accuser.

Lombardi did not care whether Al-Isawi was in Baghdad or Timbuktu, and she did not care how difficult it would be for the US authorities to get him to the Norfolk Naval Base. She coldly pointed out that according to Antonin Scalia, associate justice of the Supreme Court, the court-martial of Sam Gonzales and the other two SEALs could not proceed legally if the terrorist was not in attendance.

Her case was unstoppable. And a few days later the judgment of the military court was handed down: victory for the defense. The Supreme Court's CRAWFORD decision had mandated that Sam and his codefendants, Matt and Jon, had the constitutional right to face Al-Isawi in court.

"Case over," muttered Reschenthaler. "Because there's no way they'll bring this crazed jihadist into a US Navy yard."

Right, but wrong. Paul Threatt came visiting, and he chuckled in his deep southern accent: "You guys gotta hear this one. I just found out we're all flying to Baghdad!" And they were going to hear Al-Isawi's testimony directly.

"*WHAT?!*" Carmichael and Reschenthaler exclaimed in unison, astounded at being virtually ordered to spend time in a heavily guarded courtroom in the most dangerous part of the most deadly city in the most lethal country in the Middle East.

"They're just about to make it clear," said Threatt. "if we want a piece of Hashim, they're gonna fly us to Baghdad. I don't know what's going on, but our SEALs must have really pissed off some people in DC."

Threatt was not crazy about it either. And neither was the lead defense attorney for Jon, Greg McCormack, who in many ways had only himself to blame. For it was he, McCormack, who had insisted that Al-Isawi was a crucial witness and that there could be no sworn deposition used in court in lieu of the terrorist's live testimony.

McCormack had taken a firm position against any such suggestion— he was adamant that Al-Isawi was a necessary witness and that the trial should not proceed without his live, personal testimony in court that would allow members of the jury to see him and ask questions of him during the trial.

The argument was too good. The government's lawyers began to splutter, and McCormack won the day. He was nonetheless taken aback when the judge suddenly resolved the issue by ordering the trials of Jon and Sam to be moved to Iraq, where the terrorist prisoner was now in Iraqi custody.

"I admit I was not real thrilled about it," said the lawyer. "Iraq was a very dangerous place. And because of this, I had for several years refused multiple cases that were taking place over there. And now here I was, heading to Baghdad for this trial."

Nothing, however, would have persuaded Jon's attorney to withdraw from the case. He believed in the big SEAL's innocence with missionary zeal. And in a series of dazzling legal maneuvers, he had succeeded in removing two of the three charges against his client.

The last triumph took place in the courtroom in Norfolk before Judge Carlos in late March. And right here, finally, the special agent who had mercilessly conducted the alleged abuse investigation out of Ramadi came face to face with someone who could answer back. The agent, an ex-sheriff from South Carolina and an ex-FBI agent, had been especially antagonistic at Jon's interrogation, and he was still was no pushover.

But McCormack had filed a motion to suppress, and he had a critical point of law to prove, and this soon left the agent stuttering for words. In the end the attorney from Virginia Beach forced him to admit he had failed to read SO2 Keefe his proper rights when he had him in that room at Ramadi.

The issue was Jon's second statement, which he was coerced into making despite the existence of the first. In these cases it is mandatory upon the government to inform the accused of the "cleansing warning," when he must be told that that first statement will not be used against him in a future court-martial. The special agent had issued no such warning, and McCormack left him swinging in the wind.

Judge Carlos granted the motion, threw out the charge involving Article 107, that Jon, asserting that he did not see anyone abuse or mistreat Al-Isawi, had made a "totally false" statement that was known by

Jon to be so false. The judge's ruling was firm: There was "no cleansing warning"—and that made it unfair and against military law. Goodnight Vienna.

"Right at that moment I knew I had a chance," says Jon now. "Greg was awesome. I'd always been told I had one heck of an attorney. And now I'd seen it firsthand, right there in that courtroom. He was right up there, fighting for me, arguing, acting like the charge against me was a crime against humanity.

"I remember sitting there watching him and thinking, 'Jesus! I'm glad he's on my side.'"

When McCormack was all done with the charge that Jon had deliberately made a falsified statement and Judge Carlos was all done with the accusation he would not allow on a point of law, all that was left was the charge that Jon had somehow committed a "dereliction of duty."

Above all other things McCormack understood how much Jon was counting on him. So despite Baghdad bombs, high explosives on desert roads, suicide attacks, and ambushes, he would have walked barefoot to Iraq to protect Jon.

And by now he had become a genuine expert on the case. He had interviewed Westinson in what was probably the most demanding two hours and twenty minutes of the young guard's life. McCormack had probed, demanded, questioned, and reminded as he pieced together all that had happened in the half-light of Camp Schwedler in the hours right before the sun had risen above the eastern horizon of the Syrian Desert on that ill-starred September morning.

And while McCormack, Puckett, Threatt, Reschenthaler, and Lombardi were all pulling the legal documents together, all three SEALs continued in the no man's land into which they had been cast. Almost daily they attended their lawyers' offices, with Matt driving to Washington and the others to Virginia Beach.

Sometimes the cases seemed to swing their way; other times the obdurate mind-set of the government's prosecutors made life very tense. The SEALs were uncertain how soon they would have to sell their homes to help pay for their counsel. And they all found it impossible to accept that they were no longer active members of SEAL Team 10 and must soon face living in quite badly reduced circumstances.

One particular visit to McCormack's office stands out in Jon's mind. It was a midweek afternoon, and he arrived to be introduced to three more members of the prosecution team, none of whom he had ever seen before.

"I do not remember the precise words they used," he says now. "But the meaning was as precise and focused as anything could be. They told me, 'We want to cut a deal with you.'"

At this Jon looked blank. And then they told him that if he would rat on Sam and Matt, and say he saw Matt hit the terrorist, then he would be given "a clean slate and sent on his way."

The SEAL breacher tried to gather his thoughts as he wondered, *Who are these guys?* His mind raced, and then he looked at the silent Greg, sitting behind his desk.

Jon just blurted out: "This is a total waste of time."

McCormack spoke slowly and said, "This is your decision. If you want to say 'Okay' and rat on your buddies, then I will also make you a promise … you will not have to pay me one dollar." And he pointed to the legal documents, which the new prosecutors had placed on the desk, and added, "Sign those, and it's over."

SO2 Keefe, Echo Platoon's heavyweight combat operator, said nothing. And the prosecutors' lead man further extended the hand of quasi-friendship. "Jon," he said, "you can move to the West Coast, far away, in a place where you would not be hated for ratting on your buddies."

"This guy had to be either dumb or insane," recalled Jon. "But he obviously had no idea what it meant to be a combat member of a SEAL Team. I thought then of telling him I would allow someone to cut off my right arm before I would say one word against any of them. And I believe they would have done the same for me.

"Was this guy nuts?" he went on. "If I, or any other SEAL, ratted on a teammate, he would be hated from one coast to the other and all points in between. Besides, they were asking me to lie. Matt never hit anyone."

SO2 Keefe continued with his grim, blank stare, slowly allowing it to evolve into one of pure contempt. And he still relives the moment, when representatives of the US government "asked me to lie about my buddies who'd done nothing wrong."

He just stood there. And then he said, "No."

The prosecutors picked up their papers and left. It had lasted all of ten minutes. But in Jon Keefe's mind it was an everlasting ten minutes.

McCormack was, of course, not surprised. He had been obliged to act impartially, and he had done so, evenhanded to the end. But he later admitted, "I could have told them it was about seven billion to one against Jon betraying Matt and Sam. But I had to let it play out. It was such a monumental offer, I knew the decision had to be his. I also knew what that decision would be.

"If they'd offered Jon Keefe all the world, he'd still have turned them down. You had to know him well to fully appreciate what kind of a guy he was."

Jon himself remembers leaving McCormack's office and thanking God for the presence of the tough, relentless attorney in his corner. McCormack had served in the US Army as a military prosecutor and knew what it would take to win this case—three decades of experience had taught him that.

But Jon was just learning, though he'd already experienced the sheer weight and numbers of men who were against him. He never again met or even saw the three negotiators who had visited McCormack's office, "which I guess showed they must have an unlimited supply of people working to convict us," he said.

"I knew I could count on Greg. But those new guys, I didn't know where they came from. All I knew was the Army was leveling the charges, and they had naval JAGs to make sure they got it done.

"I guess I knew, from here on, it was me, Matt, and Sam—us against the United States military."

10

DENIED IN FAVOR OF THE DEFENSE

The major first reported the alleged beating to the chain of
command. Now here was this enormous group of people,
seven thousand miles from home, to fight a court-martial—
"I guess he had a lot to answer for. If he'd shut up, this all
might never have happened."

The US Navy's Little Creek Amphibious Base on the Virginia coast is
possibly the most absurdly named stretch of real estate in the country.
It should, of course, be called the Massive Creek Base or even Gigantic
Amphibious, as it comprises twelve thousand acres of real estate in
four locations in three states—the largest base of its kind in the world.

Little Creek is home to fifteen thousand naval personnel and
twenty-five home-ported ships. This is the assault-landing HQ of the
US Navy, the specialized warships, and the even more specialized warriors. Any time the greatest oceangoing force on earth decides to hit
an enemy hard, driving an attack through shallow ocean waters, this
is where it begins.

Unsurprisingly, Little Creek is home to four Navy SEAL Teams—
2, 4, 8 and 10—invariably the first men to hit the surf and charge. They
live, train, and work here on a base constructed around two major

naval highways, Guadalcanal and Midway—stark and permanent re-
minders of what can happen when you drop your guard in peacetime.

It was to this great, sprawling citadel of warfare that two of the
lawyers representing the senior SEAL, Sam Gonzales, traveled on a
rainy spring morning in 2010. With special permissions granted, documents signed, and offices reserved, they arrived to speak to the men
who would soon line up alongside them and attempt to fight back
those who would try to discredit three of the bravest men on the
base.

Sam's naval JAG, Lieutenant Guy Reschenthaler, and civilian lead
counsel, Monica Lombardi, turned up on time and immediately ran
into their first Special Forces operator of the day, a classic associate
member of the warrior Teams, built like a Mack truck, hard muscled
and tattooed from wrist to shirt sleeve, with slightly wild hair.
Reschenthaler recalled, "He looked like a Caribbean pirate, just the
way you'd expect one of these extraordinary characters to look."

They settled into a conference room, and the first SEAL who had
volunteered to support the three accused brothers stepped through
the door—another hulking, big man with defined arm muscles but
clean-cut and free of tattoos. With a deft lightness of touch, he pulled
back a chair, sat down, and said quietly, "I'm Higbie."

Faced with the SEALs' ground-to-air comms expert as well as one
of the strongest men in the platoon, Lombardi began their questioning. Carlton Milo Higbie IV confirmed he was more than prepared to
stand up in any courtroom to defend Matt, Jon, and Sam. And he
spoke quietly of the atmosphere in Camp Schwedler—slightly bored
men trying to wrap up terrorists, the overworked support staff, and
the constant need to be on high alert right out there in what he called
"Indian Country."

Carl was flawless in both his recall and recounting of the night of
September 1. He told how they "wrapped up" Al-Isawi but did not
strike him or get rough with him at any time during the capture. The
big SEAL described how they painstakingly walked the prisoner across
the desert to the waiting helicopter, which had been circling a mile
away.

Reschenthaler made a note of Carl's cool assessment of the following events: "And then this Westinson either lied or beat the guy up himself!"

Immediately he reverted to the SEALs' usual way of naming the prosecution's key witness, Brian Westinson, or "Weston" as he was called: "Weston struggled to fit in. He was always talking about P90X workout videos or becoming a CHIP [California Highway Police]."

"You could have considered Carl a loose cannon because he was so smart and droll," said Reschenthaler. "But then best remind yourself this guy was a highly educated Navy SEAL who had occupied a position of supreme importance on that night mission, single-handedly standing ready to call in air support. SEALs don't have loose cannons. They only have tightly coiled professionals, and you look at Carl Higbie—that's exactly what you've got."

Next man in was the SEALs' chief medic on the mission, the man who would have stepped right into the front line as the platoon doctor if anyone had gone down. A big surprise here: Paddy turned out to be the huge Caribbean Pirate whom Lombardi had seen in the corridor, still unkempt and tattooed but with a brilliant recall. His account of the pertinent events absolutely matched Carl's.

He confirmed he had screened the prisoner on arrival. And then coldly announced that Westinson was alone with Al-Isawi when Paddy left the holding cell.

Next, Reschenthaler and Lombardi interviewed Lynn Friant, the camera operator, and as the one person Westinson had befriended, she was important. But Lynn had a sense of justice and was plainly concerned about the state of mind of the young master-at-arms. She believed he had real issues but looked upon her as a big sister or mother or some kind of confidant.

He had admitted to her that he was having problems at Camp Schwedler. He had stressed himself out by refusing to delegate his duties and insisting on undertaking long, sometimes twenty-four-hour watch cycles.

Lynn painted a graphic picture of an immature, self-stressed young man desperately trying to justify his existence at the hot, dusty Forward

Operating Base (FOB) in Iraq. She described how he came to her after the incident, and Reschenthaler carefully recorded her opinion that Westinson was having some kind of mild nervous breakdown.

She stated that Westinson told her: "I gotta do something. I gotta tell somebody what happened. My Dad will never love me. My parents will hate me. I'm the only son. My life is over. I'll never be a CHIP. I gotta tell. I gotta tell."

Lombardi and Reschenthaler were concerned by this, and they were both aware that it could hurt their case. Talk of a nervous breakdown could elicit major sympathy for Weston rather than point out an obvious unreliability factor.

They closed the meetings thoughtfully, unsure what might lie ahead when they finally met Westinson in the very near future.

This was not long in coming. Reschenthaler and Lombardi now joined Sam's lead JAG defense lawyer, Lieutenant Commander Andrew Carmichael, a graduate of the US Naval Academy, Annapolis, and former surface warfare officer in USS *Laboon*, one of the Navy's nine thousand–ton twin-shafted Arleigh Burke destroyers, which carry the deadly 530mph Tomahawk Block IV SLCM (ship-launched cruise missile) with a thousand-pound warhead.

Carmichael had also worked for the chief of Naval Operations Legal Staff in Arlington, Virginia, while graduating from Boston College's Law School. He now joined Reschenthaler and Lombardi in a pretrial attempt to interrogate Westinson, who was still the only government witness accusing Matt McCabe of striking the terrorist.

The three naval attorneys arranged to meet him in the conference room at Lombardi's office. And they sat patiently, waiting for Westinson, who was running late. This gave them much time for speculation: What was he like, this nervous young man who had turned his hand against these decorated SEALs? Did he understand his importance, that he was the government's only chance? Would the lawyers, like or hate him? Would he have a nervous breakdown under questioning?

There was a tense atmosphere in that conference room when Westinson finally made his entrance and apologized for his lateness. Reschenthaler's own recollection of that moment was solid: "Tell the truth," he told him. "I quite liked him, although I'm not sure any of us trusted him."

With the natural authority of a retired Thomas Jefferson High School wrestler, Reschenthaler added, "He seemed like an all-American kid who could have been a pal on your football team, a good kid, but one who took himself just a little too seriously, maybe trying too hard to be older, more mature than he was."

His story, however, was graphic, maybe too graphic. Brian outlined his own plight: working hard, dealing with long hours, trying to run security on this tough FOB. He liked the SEALs and enjoyed working with them. And he recounted how, when Al-Isawi was "rolled up," Paddy took some processing photographs after his examination while he, Westinson, guarded the "box"—the holding cell converted from the shipping container.

Al-Isawi had then been placed in a chair, blindfolded, and his hands were tied. According to Westinson, Sam Gonzales then came in and said, "I gotta take a look at this guy." Soon after that, Jason arrived.

And right here the master-at-arms moved into brand-new territory, at least it was for the lawyers. "Sam stood up and kneed the prisoner in the gut," he said. "Jason stood by and laughed. They worked him over. Then Higbie showed up and 'roared' at Al-Isawi, scaring him, since he was blindfolded.

"Higbie then went outside, grabbed a stick and started beating on the walls, and running that stick against the metal, to scare the blindfolded captive.

"Next McCabe and Keefe came in. One struck Hashim from behind, knocking him to the floor. Someone kicked Hashim while he was down, striking his ribs. He was helped up, only to receive a swift punch in the gut from McCabe."

He added that the SEALs eventually left, and Westinson then tried to clean Al-Isawi, wiping blood from him. But the dishdasha was stained, and the terrorist's lip was bloody. The prisoner was given a new dishdasha to wear, but when the Iraqis came to pick him up, according to Westinson, the prisoner began to spit blood and said, "The Americans beat me, the Americans beat me."

The master-at-arms admitted "freaking out" when he understood that the SEAL officer who was handling the exchange, Lieutenant Jimmy, started asking questions, and that's when Westinson stated that he needed to make a report.

Brian recalled going to camera operator Friant and saying that something needed to be done. And Lieutenant Jimmy confirmed he would be taking statements. Westinson then said that Sam Gonzales told him, "We gotta get this straight. This is bullshit."

And right then Reschenthaler knew this entire story was suspect, "because by then I knew Sam pretty well, and this sudden outburst and rough language was just not his style. But Westinson pressed on with his account, explaining how he balked at fabricating a story and how Sam once more approached him and said he better get on board."

"I just want justice," Brian concluded. "I want to do the right thing."

And that essentially wrapped up the interview. Westinson had demonstrated credibility. "He was sincere," said Reschenthaler, "and his words seemed heartfelt. But he was lying and we all knew it. The problem was, would the jury agree? I'll admit it. We had big concerns."

By the time they were all scheduled to leave for Iraq, the attorneys had interviewed Westinson three times, including once by McCormack, who was probing for inconsistent statements to use against him at the trial.

Right now it looked as though Jonathan Keefe would be the first of the three to face the court-martial, and that was precisely what McCormack wanted: the opening shot at the master-at-arms and the prisoner in the witness-box, in front of the court. Sam Gonzales's trial would be up next, immediately after the court had decided whether Jon had been somehow derelict in his duty.

And in the final few days before departure there was heavy activity in the Navy legal department, as cases were brought up to date prior to the defense attorneys' departures.

Nowhere was busier, however, than the office of Guy Reschenthaler, who was organizing the case files, drafting questions, both cross and direct, for each witness, and sending them over to the senior attorneys, Drew Carmichael and Monica Lombardi. The point was that

Carmichael and Lombardi had a lot of other work, whereas for Reschenthaler, Sam's court-martial was an absolute priority.

It was his first real US case, one that looked certain actually to end up in court. Above all else, he did not wish to screw it up. Thus, Reschenthaler's preparation on behalf of his team was meticulous. "I didn't mind, he said. "I was working all the hours God made for Sam because I did not want to let him down. And I really did not want the government to win."

Running concurrently to all this detailed documentation was a whole string of requests from lawyers who had not served before in Iraq. Reschenthaler and Matt McCabe's JAG, Lieutenant Kevin Shea, were the resident experts, so they fielded all of the questions: *What do we bring? Are there showers? Should we bring food? Can we drink the water?*

There was one task, however, that faded almost completely from view: the endless number of inquiries usually made by command, wanting to know about status, motions, strategy, and prospects. But in this case there was nothing.

"Command treated it as if the court-martial did not exist," says Reschenthaler. "Kinda like the red-headed stepchild. No one in our leadership structure ever talked to me about it. Even the executive officer and the CO never mentioned it to me."

Reschenthaler thought this was a wise strategy on the part of command; after all, anyone who wanted to stage this court-martial on the combined word of Brian Westinson and a wanted Iraqi terrorist might be well advised to say as little as possible.

The large naval court-martial group flew first from Norfolk to Washington/Dulles International Airport, twenty-six miles west of downtown Washington, DC. Almost everyone involved in any way was traveling on the same commercial flight to Iraq, and this caused a rather unusual atmosphere.

This began at the main airport itself, where a whole conglomeration of SEALs, men who had served together in combat many times, were joshing and joking, recalling times past and trying not to appear too frivolous in front of the judge and, for all they knew, the jury. Because this was a major gathering of defense attorneys, support staff, witnesses, and prosecutors all flying halfway across the world for a truly bizarre pair of court-martials, at God knows what expense, in the same aircraft. Even Westinson was there.

Jon was with his buddy Matt, who was traveling with his two JAG attorneys. Neal Puckett, his civilian counsel, was unable to attend, though his presence was not essential because Matt would be there as a witness for the defense, to stand up whenever he was called upon to speak for the excellent character of either Jon or Sam.

Jon recalled, "I think the defense outnumbered the prosecutors by about five to one. There must have been thirty of us, all headed to Qatar out of Dulles. In one sense it was fun to meet my old buddies, guys we'd fought alongside in Iraq, all of them ready to stand up for me in court.

"But I felt kind of strange. Waiting in line to board the aircraft, the judge was in front of me and the prosecutors behind me. In the aircraft Westinson was two rows ahead of me. Can you imagine how awkward that was? Especially being surrounded by a dozen hard-trained, beefy SEALs, dressed in smart civilian clothes, trying not to laugh."

For Jon the whole scenario seemed unreal. "Just looking ahead at Westinson, sitting there, saying nothing, refusing to make eye contact with any SEAL throughout the entire flight," he remembered. "Here was the guy who was accusing us of beating up a terrorist. I'm telling you, it was weird. Really weird."

"It was not so long ago," said Jon, "that a Navy commander and a SEAL master chief wrongly thought someone had kidnapped him when he'd gone missing."

And here they all were, every one of them, attack and defense, plus the judge, hour after hour on this seven thousand–mile journey to Qatar, through seven time zones. And all to decide whether the devoted SEAL and patriotic Virginian Jonathan Keefe had been derelict in his duty, and whether the senior SEAL petty officer, Sam Gonzales, already decorated for valor, had been equally derelict.

Not to mention the guilt of a cover-up, impeding the investigation. No wonder the rest of the SEALs were laughing. They must have been thinking, *Could this be real? I have to be dreaming.* It was as though the military, in particular the US Navy, had totally forgotten who these people were.

The flight to Arabia took almost fifteen hours, and they came in from the east, over the blue waters of the Gulf in the early morning, with the wheels of the Boeing reaching out for the near-three-mile long, sand-swept runway, the largest in the Middle East.

For those who had not been to Qatar, Doha International Airport, gateway to the fabulously wealthy desert kingdom, was something of a shock, particularly if they were expecting a few Bedouins propped up against some ramshackle Arab hut, jammed between the date groves at a dried-up oasis.

Doha has parking bays for forty-two airliners, with sixty check-in gates and parking for a thousand cars. The court-martial special came howling out of the hot morning skies with the sun directly astern of the tail's plane. And the US military were waiting to move the Americans on, through the baggage hall with practiced speed before transporting them west by bus across the desert to the Al-Udeid Air Base, home to a major forward headquarters, US Central Command.

On arrival the lawyers and witnesses began to get organized. And there were a lot of them. Lynn Friant was there to give her evidence, as was Paddy, the medic who looked like a pirate. Paul Franco, a Navy reservist who had once worked as a New York firefighter, was there as Westinson's boss, and he intended to stand up in court for Jon and Sam to confirm what everyone now believed about the nerve-wracked young master-at-arms. Paul was a very formidable ally for both accused SEALs: in 2010 he was on the short list for Sailor of the Year... that's the entire US Navy—nothing local.

There were all kinds of SEAL officers, one a naval commander, plus the command XO and Special Agent Stamp, with a senior man from the West Coast to speak up for the military character of both Sam and Jon. They also flew in another master-at-arms who worked alongside Brian. He was there voluntarily to validate that, in his opinion, Brian was unstable.

The group stayed in Qatar for two days, during which they may have appeared like one big happy family. But this they were not. The tensions were sometimes unbearable. The SEALs did everything together—ate, slept, and lifted weights, but Jon sat near the judge in the dining room, and this felt extremely awkward.

Perhaps anyone would feel this way—sitting a few places away from the man who would soon determine his fate militarily and, perhaps, for the rest of his life. Much of the time the SEALs spent with the defense JAGs—Reschenthaler, Shea (observing on behalf of Matt), Carmichael, and Paul Threatt. They became friends during this time, and in a sense this probably heightened the attorney's determination to clear their names. The guys from Team 10 were nothing if not a close fighting unit.

When they finally left, bound for Baghdad, the SEALs were dressed in their field cammie uniforms. And they traveled, as they often did to a combat zone, in one of those huge Boeing C-17 aircraft.

"It was all very familiar to us," recalls Jon. "But it was again darned awkward for me. I was sitting five feet away from the people who were trying to throw my ass in jail."

The seven hundred–mile journey north to the Iraqi capital took a couple of hours, as they flew up the Gulf and then over the desert. They arrived late morning and touched down at Camp Victory on the western side of Baghdad, hard by the International Airport.

It's rather a gaudy place in some ways, built as it is around Saddam Hussein's grandiose Al-Faw Palace, which still stands in all its splendor, its thousands of lights glittering nightly over a large ornamental lake, which was all suitably ostentatious for the murderous old Lion of Babylon.

Of course, the gaudy part was somewhat diminished by the twenty-seven miles of concrete barriers surrounding the vast US military complex, which at the peak of the war with Iraq housed forty thousand troops and thirty thousand contractors. There have been moments of great triumph here behind these barriers and great speeches delivered in the marble halls that the Americans commandeered.

But for Saddam the glory of conquest swiftly faded. He was incarcerated in a cell at Camp Victory for three years and then tried and executed there, within sight of his once-lavish presidential lifestyle.

For the two accused SEALs coming into land, this was a place of military folklore, but they had many more pressing things on their minds. For here they would be stationed for more than two weeks while two veritable armies of lawyers prepared to thrash out the gigantic mystery of whether Matt McCabe, from Perrysburg, Ohio, actually did thump Al-Isawi right in the gut.

If he did not, then it would be over as suddenly as it had begun. If he did, however, anything might happen. Judge Tierney Carlos had a lot on his mind. And he strived to keep to himself throughout these fiendishly unusual pretrial days.

In the opinion of the SEALs and the defense lawyers, however, Judge Carlos, the straight-talking, pragmatic New York lawyer, had always looked askance at this prosecution, especially at the government's rather eccentric stand against three of its most elite warriors.

During the long, hot days when the court-martial personnel were in residence, Brian Westinson hardly ever showed his face, nor did the other master-at arms he had brought along in order to put a more positive slant on his character than the rest of the witnesses would.

Weston and his "minder" were both mostly missing, believing—and with good reason—that the SEALs did not include either of them among their favorite people.

Also missing were Greg McCormack, Jon's lead civilian counselor, and Monica Lombardi for Sam. Both these ultrabusy attorneys were arriving a couple of days later, but not in the same aircraft.

And right there, fate stepped in with an unforeseen hand. On April 14, as McCormack was in a plane racing across the North Atlantic toward a European landfall, an unbelievable incident broke out some five hundred miles north of his aircraft. Clear of the Labrador Sea, the plane was approaching the earth's 20-West line of longitude, southeast of Greenland's Cape Farvel, when a gigantic volcano almost blew itself apart in neighboring Iceland.

No one can pronounce its name, but the power and wrath of Eyjafjallajökul in the south of the ice-bound country was suddenly unleashed. The glacier-topped volcano hurled thousands of tons of molten rock clean through the ice cap, hurling a gigantic wall of ash, dust, and steam six miles into the air.

It slowly formed a vast cloud of dust, ash, and cinders, which climbed into the North Atlantic jet stream, producing a satanic darkness that was instantly capable of clogging aircraft engines on one of the world's busiest flight paths, south of Greenland. And the eruptions kept going, so steadily that no one knew when they would stop or whether another of Iceland's twenty-two highly erratic active volcanoes would also erupt.

At this point the world's airlines went into a collective flat spin. Dozens of flights were diverted and ordered to return from whence they came. Airports were closed and twenty countries shut down their airspace, stranding millions of passengers all over the world. It was only the third time since the Vikings showed up in the ninth century that Eyjafjallajökul had blown. But two centuries ago it blew intermittently for fourteen months!

Jon put the whole thing down to the obvious displeasure of an even greater power than General Charles Cleveland: one of the largest black clouds ever witnessed was drifting over northern Europe and heading directly southeast toward Greece and then Baghdad. "It's an omen," he muttered. "We could be here for a year. They'll have to cancel it! God is on our side!"

Meanwhile McCormack's flight was diverted to Amsterdam, stranding him there without luggage, waiting for the cloud to disperse. And in turn this caused havoc back at Camp Victory, where McCormack's client, Jon, was scheduled to face the court-martial first, six days from then, April 20. This was when McCormack, with his meticulous preparation, would have been first in line to tackle Westinson and the shackled terrorist in the witness box.

The unavoidable delay of Jon's lead civilian counselor now made this questionable, because no one knew how quickly the ash cloud would disperse to allow the attorney to get out of Holland. Indeed, the court may be forced to reschedule and instead bring forward the Sam Gonzales case. Sam's lawyers—Monica Lombardi, Drew Carmichael, and Guy Reschenthaler—were by now all in Iraq, but right now the issue was very much up in the air (unlike McCormack).

And right here in Camp Victory this very expensive group had to somehow find their own level, passing the days by working long hours, brainstorming, planning, strategizing, and, in the case of

Threatt, poring over the highly variable statements made by Westinson, who was, in company with the crazed jihadist, public enemy number one to Jon and Sam.

Threatt had long realized that the conduct of the master-at-arms held the key to the entire operation. So he made a study of any circumstances surrounding Westinson's activities.

He noted that after the Marines left the huge Baharia Base, the Schwedler Camp was left to defend itself, and their departure had unnerved Westinson.

To improve security, Westinson had managed to get an elevated camera installed. And once it was in place, he watched the camera-feed obsessively. Although he was often told to take only a three-hour shift, he had been watching the camera feed for twenty hours when Echo Platoon arrived with their prisoner. Threatt concluded, "He was exhausted, agitated, and extremely nervous."

As he searched through various statements, Threatt was certain that Westinson was not at his peak when the lieutenant handed over the prisoner to him alone, an action that required him to walk Al-Isawi across the camp to the detention cell.

Now according to Al-Isawi's testimony, he was struck as soon as he entered the detention cell, or Conex Box. This was the one lie about which the detainee was consistent through all his statements and testimony.

"This is important," noted Threatt, "if you believe the detainee at all. Because there is a lot of other evidence establishing that MA3 Westinson was the only person with Al-Isawi when he first entered the cell."

In fact, based on all the statements and the medical report, Threatt's theory was that MA3 Westinson himself had kicked the detainee into the chair, which caused him to fall, hurting his lip. The prisoner then aggravated the damage to his lip and spit blood onto his dishdasha to create the impression of abuse. "There is," he noted, "simply no evidence of the kind of vicious beating that Westinson and the detainee allege." And then he added, "When the officer in charge initially questioned MA3 [Westinson], he claimed ignorance. But after it became apparent that the damage to the detainee happened while he was alone with Westinson, then [he] concocted the story of McCabe's punch. Which then evolved into a story which had every special warfare operator in the camp beating on the detainee."

Threatt supported his opinion of Westinson's unreliability by noting that Westinson himself had admitted that he "was bored" and felt he was "wasting his life" at the camp. And in a later statement, Westinson admitted to not "patting down" Al-Isawi when he was being processed.

Lieutenant Threatt also noted conflicting evidence from the medical evidence: "MA3 says the detainee was struck on the left side. The detainee says he was hit in the face and kicked while on the ground. The photos indicate slight discoloration on the right side."

And he concluded, "Basically it appears the government cannot firmly establish damage to the detainee beyond the sore on the inside of his lip. And a dentist asserts that was unlikely to be the result of blunt-force trauma to the lip, due to the absence of a clear cut. Rather the damage of a fever blister."

Reschenthaler also took the opportunity to get close to the SEALs and, slightly to his own surprise, swiftly discovered that Sam was their undisputed leader. "Everyone looked up to him," he recalled. "I could scarcely believe that this respected and blunt-spoken assault warrior, twice decorated for valor, was being charged by his own side with dereliction of duty and with covering up an alleged flagrant assault on a prisoner by another decorated SEAL. I guess you had to know Sam to understand the pure futility of such charges."

The young lawyer from Pittsburgh was also glad to speak more to Carl Higbie, the iron man from Connecticut who was also deeply respected in the Special Forces community. "At first, you could have thought Carl a bit of a wild card because he did have an eccentric side to his nature, at least intellectually," said Reschenthaler. "But he was rock solid when it mattered, a totally dependable member of the platoon in the times when it really counted. The guys thought the world of him."

Paul Franco, the ex-firefighter, also made a major impression on Reschenthaler. "He was one of our witnesses, and I knew right from the start he intended to speak of Westinson's unstable nature and occasional breakdowns," he said. "Paul was smaller than the Team guys, but all personality, light blond hair and blue eyes, looked like a member of a boy band!

"But the SEALs really liked him, and that was the acid test. I'd trust their judgment any time. As I got to know him more, sometimes had a beer with him, I knew it would be a blast to have on the stand one of the proven top sailors in the US Navy speaking of Westinson's shortcomings. Because when Paul Franco spoke, the jury would listen. It was terrific to have him on our side."

Back in Qatar the various lawyers had been flung together. It was not unusual to find Threatt and Reschenthaler in company with Matt's legal observers, Kevin Shea and Kristen Anastos, plus Drew Carmichael, having a beer with an important government witness, whom I shall refer to as "the Major," a man who was intensely proud of rising from enlisted soldier in the first Gulf War to his present commissioned rank in the second.

The Major turned out to be the man who first reported the alleged "beating" of Al-Isawi to the chain of command. "Looking around at this enormous group of people assembled seven thousand miles from home to fight this court-martial," said Reschenthaler, "I guess he had a lot to answer for, discretion-wise. If he had only just weighed the evidence, this all might never have happened."

To the lawyer, the Major was an anathema. "It was he who made that report that Hashim had 'bruising' and a 'bloody lip.' We were all here because of him. And he was a real dinosaur. His heroes were guys like Genghis Khan. He even lent me a book about that old Mongolian conqueror.

"Ironic, right? He admires the most bloodthirsty warriors in history yet makes an unfounded claim of abuse on this terrorist for fear of running up against the politically correct military culture."

Anyhow, as the days went by, with McCormack still grounded beneath the ash cloud, it was becoming increasingly apparent that the two trials were probably going to reverse order. If the ash, which was falling all over Europe's mountains, would not billow its way out of the stratosphere, then McCormack might be seriously late.

And at this point Reschenthaler, with Carmichael and Lombardi, began to make plans to go first on the basis that the judge could not possibly waste everyone's time waiting for McCormack. This huge circus was costing sufficiently already, without court time being sacrificed.

Carmichael convinced Lombardi that Reschenthaler should handle the terrorist. The younger defense JAG had easily the most experience with litigation through an interpreter, and he knew the most about terrorists and how they would act on the stand. Reschenthaler had, after all, prosecuted those ninety-two cases in Baghdad the previous year.

Lombardi quickly grasped the sense of this and gave the green light to the junior. The government then made Al-Isawi available in a small building on Camp Cropper, Baghdad's top-secret military holding prison, which was surrounded by razor-wire and concrete and was where Saddam Hussein spent his final days.

Reschenthaler noticed a photograph of the late Iraqi dictator still on the wall of the room where he would conduct his first interview with the wanted al-Qaeda terrorist, the man who had caused this gigantic upheaval—indeed, fracture—in the US military.

Shea and Anastos, on behalf of Matthew McCabe, went into the room first, because their task was to prove that the leader of Objective Amber had not laid a glove on Al-Isawi. They were in there for about a half-hour, and when they emerged, Reschenthaler was waiting.

"Get anything?" he asked, hoping that the prisoner had cracked and admitted that Matt had never touched him.

"A little, not much," replied Shea. "But c'mon, the photos tell us all we need to know."

Threatt, who was still officially scheduled to go first if McCormack could get there in time, went next and stayed with Al-Isawi for almost an hour.

"Get anything?" asked Reschenthaler when Threatt emerged.

"Oh, boy. You gotta get in there, Resch."

As it happened, the junior JAG was not quite ready. For the past half-hour he had been busy with a pair of nail scissors, cutting and picking out the threads that held all of his military insignia, patches, medals, and decorations.

"One thing you must understand," he said later. "These terrorists are not stupid—at least, not their commanders, like this Al-Isawi character. He'd have taken one look at my uniform and known I'd served in Iraq previously, and that would have put him on his guard.

"They know our insignia. They can 'read' a uniform. And I needed it to be stripped of all clues before I faced him."

Immediately Al-Isawi was at a disadvantage, facing an American lawyer who knew his kind well, understood the almost-irresistible Iraqi inclination to exaggerate, sometimes wildly, and to lie about something so often they end up believing it to be true.

Reschenthaler had one overriding aim through this impending interview: not to dominate the prisoner nor intimidate him but, rather, to make the Iraqi terrorist like and trust him. That way he could coax him into exaggerating his injuries and making some attempt to elicit sympathy from the American attorney, lulling him into the sense he was dealing with a friend.

If he could just get the terrorist to trust him and describe the fantasy of his wounds and how he received them, then Reschenthaler could spring the photographs on the jury, the medical snapshots that showed not a mark except for the cold sore.

"I knew if I could just pull that off, the government's case against Sam Gonzales could implode right there," he said.

"Look," he told Carmichael, "I'm going to say some things in there to get this guy to open up. Don't think that I believe what I'm saying. I have a plan. Trust me."

Carmichael nodded. And Reschenthaler walked through the door of the interview room, wearing the widest, least sincere smile of his entire career. He was Al-Isawi's friend, not his enemy, and he just wanted him to tell his own truthful side of story. Yeah, right.

But as he opened the door, almost before he uttered a lighthearted greeting to Al-Isawi, he saw a pretty bad strike against him. Sitting there and scowling at him was someone who, in Reschenthaler's opinion, was just about the world's worst Arab translator.

"You gotta be kidding me," muttered the lieutenant attorney.

Reschenthaler was acquainted with an excellent linguist in Iraq, an American citizen who had advanced degrees in the United States. This man was a true international Arab—raised in several countries, several capitals, from Somalia to Saudi Arabia, with his father a global financier, a senior banker.

Reschenthaler had requested the government, through the formal channels, to make this friend available because he was the best he'd ever seen in Iraq. But right now, at this very moment, Reschenthaler knew his request had been refused, and for no reason that he could see.

"Must have been out of spite, anything to get an advantage over the defense," he said. "There could have been no other reason. We were all now at the mercy of whatever linguists were around. And I had this guy."

Reschenthaler was familiar with the translator assigned to help him interrogate the jihadist and thought he was a slacker. And now here he was, slouching in his chair, mumbling his words, and acting as though he were doing everyone a favor by translating. The lieutenant was furious, even more so because it had become increasingly obvious to him that the government would do *anything* to roadblock the accused SEALs' defense.

Reschenthaler had to think quickly. He immediately tested the mumbling translator and thought to himself that he had either been born profoundly dumb or he was pretending. After testing his interpreter a couple of times, noting the slowness of his replies, he turned his attention to the silent Al-Isawi, who was just sitting there.

Reschenthaler tried his level best to look pious, which was not a natural expression for any former wrestler. And then he started in on the terrorist: "I want first to say, sorry. What happened to you pains me. This is not the American way. Please forgive us. I am here to get your story straight. Justice must be done."

Reschenthaler spoke in short sentences, using small words, making sure nothing got muddled in translation. But Carmichael was looking uneasy, and Reschenthaler could not help feeling ashamed at what he was saying. But he had a plan, and he understood the components of that plan. And the main one was to get this darned terrorist on his side.

Al-Isawi muttered in Arabic, "Na'am, na'am"—that's "Yes, yes." And he placed his hand on his chest and bowed his head, a Bedouin gesture of honesty and submission.

Reschenthaler did his best to pretend he did not understand the translation, asking for a repeat, feigning noncomprehension, yet another of the morning's great American falsehoods. Reschenthaler had an excellent grasp of Arabic, the result of six months working in Baghdad's Central Criminal Court.

He turned to Al-Isawi and told him, "Please tell us your story." Which, again, was part of the plan, avoiding the appearance that the American was "pushing the envelope," leading the witness, steering him into areas he did not wish to go.

No need for that. Reschenthaler had already done his work. Now he sat back and waited for the handcuffed terrorist to give a graphic account of his vicious beating and shocking wounds, a blow-by-blow description of the demonic SEALs, the very incarnation of the American Satan.

"I was trying to look deadly serious," said the attorney. "But inside I was smiling. This character was about to give me all the rope I needed to tie a noose."

Al-Isawi said the SEAL Team broke into his house and smashed jars, pottery, and dishes. He said they stole his money, a claim that Reschenthaler understood as referring to the $6,000, which Matthew McCabe had confiscated and immediately handed over to the authorities when they arrived back at Camp Schwedler. In Iraq this was a king's ransom.

"How did you get the money?" asked Reschenthaler.

"My mother saved for years and years, to send me on the Haj," he replied.

BA … BAM! Reschenthaler had the sentence that would shred Al-Isawi on cross-examination. Because he knew that each one of those bills was consecutively numbered, which meant they were either stolen or forged.

They were certainly not the pittance earnings of an Arab woman in war-torn Fallujah, carefully stored to send her son to the Haj, the Fifth Pillar of Islam, the largest annual pilgrimage in the world, when hundreds of thousands of Muslims converge on Mecca in Saudi Arabia. Not even a maestro of untruths like Al-Isawi could duck his way out of that one.

"Please, go on."

"The Americans then ..." And he talked about how they captured him and escorted him to the helicopter, and his story more or less matched that of the video tape, recorded on one of the SEALs' mini-night vision cameras attached to his helmet and that had been shown to the defense lawyers.

Al-Isawi's account was solid. Which Reschenthaler regarded as bad news, because it meant the prisoner was getting credible. So he swiftly switched the interview to the events in the holding cell.

"I was blindfolded, with no water," he said. "Then I was struck from behind, falling from my chair to the floor, then kicked swiftly."

Darn, thought Reschenthaler. *That matches Weston's story.*

"Hear any voices?"

"Yes, yes. I heard one loud voice."

Could be Higbie, could have been Weston, taking out his frustrations ...

"See any feet, or anyone's face?"

"No faces, but I could see a set of boots."

BA ... BAM! The SEALs were wearing flip-flops. They always do when they're off duty in the desert. No one was wearing boots. Except for one man—Brian Westinson.

"Tell me about the beating."

"I got kicked hard, so hard. I then was punched over and over."

"How hard was the kick?"

"So hard. I could tell they wanted to hurt me."

"I bet they had steel-capped boots, huh?"

"Yes, yes. Steel boots. So hard."

Reschenthaler almost burst out laughing as he thought, *Steel-capped flip-flops, right? Way to go, Hashim!*

"Now, what about the punches?"

"So hard." And from here on, Reschenthaler kept coaxing him to reveal all. And the terrorist quickly warmed to the task, describing how he could not eat for two days because his mouth was so swollen from the beating that he puked blood, he lost a tooth, and his shoulder was so badly damaged during the beating that he still could not raise his arm, more than seven months later.

Al-Isawi did not have the slightest clue that the SEALs' defense teams all had the pictures that showed him virtually unmarked.

Reschenthaler allowed him to continue to embellish the beating out of all proportion. He supported him, looked suitably pained at strategic moments. And at all times looked concerned over the savage treatment the terrorist claimed had been inflicted on him.

It all took about an hour. And at the conclusion Reschenthaler asked, "Is there anything else I can do for you?"

"Yes, yes," said Hashim. "Can you please, sir, get me my money back, or give it to my mother? She worked so hard for it, selling jewelry for all those years."

Reschenthaler told him he would contact the prison JAG on his behalf. And he told him: "Yes, I'll help. Stealing is stealing, and Americans do not do that. Also I'm going to bring you back to show you the courtroom the day before the trial. I know the American system and the Iraqi system differ greatly. But I want you to be comfortable, so you can do a good job as a witness. Is that okay with you?"

"Yes, yes. Thank you," he replied, and he again placed his hand on his chest and lowered his head in that polite and, well, pious way.

Reschenthaler thought, *Am I actually outfoxing this fox? Is he actually buying this … ?*

The American picked his words carefully. And he chose: *Astad*—an Arabic term for "Sir," one that conveys respect, and to his joy, the translator picked up on it.

"With your help, sir, I want to see justice done," said Reschenthaler.

"Na'am, na'am. Shukran [Yes, yes. Thank you]," said the Butcher of Fallujah.

Reschenthaler's own thoughts were more along the lines of: *I'll give you "thank you," you little sonofabitch, once I get you on the witness stand.*

Meanwhile Carmichael had very possibly lost his nerve. He was disgusted with Reschenthaler's performance and saw it as unpatriotic, somewhere on the south side of treason, and he encouraged the junior JAG to apologize to the American soldiers.

The two men stepped outside the interview room, and Reschenthaler shook his head at the sudden emergence of the literal mind and responded, "No way. I'm doing my job and I have a plan. You'll all have to trust me. The soldiers are here to guard the killers. I'm here to get my man Sam acquitted."

Carmichael came back with: "Look, I know you've got your plan. But you made us look bad."

"We'll look great once we win this case," said Reschenthaler. "What do you care what the guards think?"

Carmichael, however, thought otherwise, and he said again, "Please, Guy. They think we're a bunch of leftie attorneys."

And Reschenthaler could tell he was genuinely troubled. "Okay, okay. I'll talk with the guards' sergeant."

And he walked over to the senior man on guard duty at this US Alcatraz of the desert and said, "Look, my colleague and I want you to know we were putting on a show in there. We don't like the guy ..."

But the sergeant cut him off. "We know who he is," he said, grinning from ear to ear, "and we know who you are." This referred to the fact that many of his crew had seen Reschenthaler prosecuting in Baghdad before.

"Keep up the good work, sir. You got this bastard right where you want him."

This demonstrated, even in a private conversation, that the sentiments of the regular US military were totally out of step with the establishment. Even this hard-eyed sergeant of the guard, on duty in a viciously dangerous Iraqi environment, thought precisely nothing of the word of a terrorist who was trying to discredit US Navy SEALs.

And the fight went on, with McCormack still stuck fast in Amsterdam. The worst of the ash cloud was now about a thousand miles across and threatening to cast the northern hemisphere into semidarkness. Fresh eruptions were hurling even more volcanic debris into the sky, with ash and dust blasting out of the crater, the color of spent fire.

This was the highest level of air travel disruption since World War II. And McCormack was spending half the day on his cell phone talking to Jon's JAG, Paul Threatt, and more or less accepting that his plan to be the first to nail Westinson and the prisoner in the witness box was going up in smoke, as it were.

There was, of course, nothing anyone could do about it. Even a fast boat would not have solved the problem. McCormack was stuck in the land of windmills and tulips. And unless there were imminent gale-force winds in the European weather forecast, that was where he'd remain.

For the next couple of days the ash cloud's obdurate lack of progress dominated the Baghdad courtroom. Would McCormack get here or not? And Sam's team of Lombardi, Carmichael, and Reschenthaler was already working on the theory that he would not make it. They had to assume this, because that would require them to go in first, with Sam Gonzales, maybe at an hour's notice.

Two days after his interview with the Butcher, Reschenthaler brought Al-Isawi to the courtroom. This was the eve before trial, and the same slacker linguist was there, and so were the guards.

Reschenthaler was polite. "Mr. Hashim, I can call you that, correct?"

"Na'am, na'am."

"I want you to sit in that chair. It's the witness chair."

Al-Isawi sat and looked around, muttering again, "Na'am, na'am."

"This is an American-style courtroom. I understand it is much different from your system."

"Na'am, na'am."

This was, thought the attorney, *truly awesome. The guy said "yes, yes," to everything I said.*

"The judge will sit there," he told him. And he carefully explained the layout of the court and who would be seated where. Al-Isawi plainly felt comfortable, and he was extremely warm to the man who would cross-examine him ruthlessly, probably tomorrow.

Carmichael brought him water, and Reschenthaler confirmed he had asked around about the money, which excited Hashim to no end. And the Pittsburgh attorney then assured him he had spoken to the JAG and was very much on the case.

"I've filled out the paperwork," said Reschenthaler. "I know it's a slow process. But I'm trying."

Al-Isawi was very obviously thrilled. *He's mine*, gritted Reschenthaler. *This bastard's all mine.*

And he once more went over the questions he'd asked the day before. And to Reschenthaler's near-ecstatic joy, Hashim exaggerated even more wildly. He said his injured shoulder hurt to this day, that his gut was still sore from the beating, and that there had not been one or even two kicks; there had been dozens.

When Al-Isawi was done Reschenthaler thanked him again and warned him that another attorney would question him in the courtroom before Reschenthaler stepped up. "That's our system, I'm sorry," he added.

And then he pointed to the podium and said, "Once the other attorney is done, I'll stand right here, and we'll get the truth out. We'll make sure justice is done here tomorrow."

"Shukran, shukran [Thank you, thank you]."

It had been a brilliant morning's work, and despite the uncertainty about McCormack's arrival, the two men who would fight in Sam's corner returned to their apartment to strategize further.

By now Reschenthaler was counting on the ash cloud and counting on going first. If that happened, he would catch Al-Isawi unaware and not ready to face a perceived friend suddenly emerging as a relentless enemy. "I now believed my plan would only work if I could just get to Hashim first," he said. "Drew knew it, and I knew it.

"The one thing on this earth I did not need was for the friggin' ash cloud to disperse and for Jonathan's team to get in first. That would put another attorney in there in front of me, placing a very cunning terrorist immediately on his guard. And that would really work against me in my current role as Hashim's brand-new best friend."

The Gonzales team took a firm position about Al-Isawi's sad little lip injury: if anyone had struck him, that someone must have been Weston, who had the opportunity and, as the prisoner was effectively bound and gagged, the ability.

Now, Brian Westinson was a perfectly normal well-built young serviceman, but that is not the same as being a SEAL. By their standards

Weston was on the weak side, and a swift punch from him would not really mean much. However, in the utterly unlikely event that Matthew McCabe had banged the prisoner, that would probably have taken his head off or, at the very least, inflicted serious damage.

These were the conclusions of Carmichael and Reschenthaler as they prepared to put both Al-Isawi and Weston under intense cross-examination to try to show that both men had every reason in the world for blaming the Iraqi's very suspect injury on the US Navy SEALs.

For the moment, however, the defense rested. At least they took time off to go for lunch, carefully skirting around the American counter where processed hamburgers and hot dogs were being prepared. The attorneys headed directly to the India counter, where the home-cooked, curried food was nothing short of world-class.

Generous plates of chicken and lamb vindaloo, shashlik, and rogan josh set them up for big decisions, and the biggest one was not whether to call Carlton Milo Higbie IV as a witness for Sam Gonzales. In Reschenthaler's opinion, Carl was just too big a presence—larger than life in every way, massively built, "like a goddamned man-mountain, super-bright and funny as hell."

"There's just a chance," he told Carmichael, "the jury might take one look at this guy and decide he could easily have given the prisoner a light clout across the mouth as he left the holding cell and then got the other SEALs to join in."

Reschenthaler knew it was a long shot. "Nonetheless, it could happen," he said. "Carl is just too big a deal, and he could be judged a wild card. He does not add much to our case because the SEALs are all united in their accounts. But the one thing he does give us is the chance for the case to go south." That did it. Petty Officer Carlton Milo Higbie IV was on the bench for this one.

Meanwhile the accused SEALs occupied their own space and shared their own concerns principally with each other, although the enormous support for them could be sensed in just about every corner of this US military complex.

Later that night, after dinner, Jon and Matt took the half-hourly bus over to the Army Exchange, the troops' little store on Camp Victory.

Waiting outside for the return bus, they were given a ride from a couple of the SEAL Team 8 guys in their Toyota HI-LUX truck.

All the way back the Team 8 SEALs told them that everyone was in their corner. In their considered view the charges against the three Team 10 SEALs were nothing but bullshit, and that was what everyone in the platoon thought. They said if they had no mission tomorrow, then every last one of them would be in that courtroom in support of Jon.

It was a fast journey home. Team 8 was about to leave on a mission, a night raid in a bad part of Baghdad, and the driver was under pressure. Worse than Jon, in some ways. Because the Team 8 Platoon was expecting a firefight tonight, and they were going in with heavy machine guns.

That same evening, in the final hours before the first trial, Lombardi arrived to take charge as senior counsel. She was really tired after that long trans-Atlantic journey, and all three members of the Gonzales defense team were surprised to be summoned to an 802 judicial conference with the judge at nine o'clock at night.

They hurried over to the main courtroom building on Camp Victory and found Judge Tierney Carlos close to boiling point.

"Okay, you're up tomorrow ..." he began.

"But I've only just got here ..." protested Lombardi.

"Look," he snapped. "I'm getting tired of this. I've been listening to it since January, and I've been right here for three days waiting for either you or McCormack to show up. I'm running this courtroom, and tomorrow you three, and your client, better be ready."

Lombardi had never seen the normally affable Judge Carlos so irritated. For the first time she now knew the trial of Sam Gonzales, the first of the three, would go ahead tomorrow, Thursday, April 22. Reschenthaler was so pleased to have the opening shot at the prisoner, and they returned to their temporary home base and started work.

Because McCormack was still unable to take off from Amsterdam, Jon's trial would be pushed back a couple of days. After all the long months of legal maneuvering, trying to persuade the government to drop the case, Sam and his team prepared for battle. And it was no less serious now than it had been when the SEALs were first accused.

Tomorrow Sam's life and beloved career as a Navy SEAL was on the line. Alone in his little on-base cabin, he never slept for even an hour. His friendship with Reschenthaler helped, because he understood the amount of work the attorney from Pittsburgh had put in. But he was very frightened.

Reschenthaler, Carmichael, and Lombardi would either save him tomorrow, or his life as he knew it was over. Ahead would lie only disgrace—*the expelled Navy SEAL who had lied to his superiors.* And still, all through that longest of nights, Sam could not understand why they were doing this to him.

But before the trial began, there was the highly contentious procedure of motions when the lawyers for both sides go before the judge and attempt to lay down agreeable ground rules that would work in their favor, prosecution or defense.

And here the defense team ran into a characteristic blocking tactic that the government had committed: first of all, none of the government's motions had been presented for the defense to study and prepare to counteract—there was no copy paper for them, and there was no printer.

Carmichael, who had hard firsthand experience of the art of blocking, put it down to straightforward "dirty tricks" deliberately done to prevent Lombardi and her team from making thorough and well-prepared responses.

Stuck out here in this third-world country in a first-rank desert where even the defense conference room was never cleaned up from one day to the next, the chances of getting ahold of a decent printer were remote. Carmichael actually had to write one critical motion for the judge by hand.

This was the Motion in Limine—that the terrorist's tactical handbook, the *Manchester Manual,* be entered through judicial notice.

This meant Carmichael was requesting the *Manchester Manual* be included as part of the evidence and asking the judge to read the salient parts to the jury. The term "Limine" is from the Latin for "from the start." And they had half-expected the prosecution to put up some kind of strong objection, but nothing much occurred, and Judge Carlos agreed with Carmichael. The motion was granted.

In the great scheme of things this was a small victory. But to the defense it really mattered. That diabolical little handbook instructed all al-Qaeda operators to lie categorically about being abused by Coalition Forces if captured. And as Reschenthaler mentioned more than once: "If that's not significant, what is?"

The upcoming jury selection was also critically important to the defense. "We wanted personnel who were already stationed in Iraq," Reschenthaler said, "because each one of them would know all about the *Manchester Manual* and the lies of terrorists."

And then there was a new Motion in Limine from the prosecution, handled by the youngest member of the team, Lieutenant Nick Kadlec. He and the prosecution's senior counselor were now supported by a cool, blonde, pale prosecutor, previously stationed in Norfolk but now flown in from Italy to help.

Carmichael and Reschenthaler had previously been concerned about them having three against the government's two counselors, thus increasing the possibility of bullying witnesses and giving an unfair advantage to the defense. But now the numbers were even, and the new arrival was perfect—for the defense.

She was rather cold in manner, calculating, and Reschenthaler hoped she would become the memorable face for impersonal government, that overwhelming legal machine that cared nothing for the valorous Sam Gonzales, this outstanding Navy SEAL and obviously nice man.

Meanwhile the ambitious Kadlec went to bat for that government, standing up before Judge Carlos to plead his motion that the defense attorneys not be allowed to "badger" Weston. The prosecutor wanted that set in stone—that Lombardi, Carmichael, and Reschenthaler refrain from harassing the witness and that the judge would step in and order them to desist.

Reschenthaler thought that would be a mortal blow, because if ever anyone was going to be harassed, it was undoubtedly Weston, who may just have been responsible for this entire catastrophe.

The defense counselors need not have worried, however. Judge Carlos slapped down the prosecution's motion in short order. He was even visibly angry with Kadlec, admonishing him: "Nick, Nick. This is my courtroom. You can't dictate whether you'll sit still while your witness is harassed. If you object, I'll make the call. *Got it?* The motion is denied."

The last motion involved the slightly fraught subject of evidence, which involved good military character. The accused may only present opinion, or reputation evidence, *not* specific acts. The government may only rebut with specific acts. For example:

Mr. Witness, how long have you known Sam, the accused?
Five years.
How do you know him?
He works in my department.
Are you his supervisor?
Yes.
Have you observed him perform his military duties?
Yes.
How often do you see him a week?
Five days, maybe five hours a day, give or take.
And do you know others who observe him?
Yes, officers superior to Sam, and his peers.
And what is Sam's reputation for military character in the
   community?
Excellent.

That's what's allowed. It cannot be specific. And right here, Reschenthaler had a problem with a motion he considered vital to Sam's defense. What's more, he anticipated the prosecution would try to stop it.

The issue was Sam's combat medals, specifically his Bronze Star, with a "V" (for valor), the fourth-highest combat decoration in the US military, awarded for heroic or meritorious achievement and only to those engaged in action against enemy forces.

Reschenthaler put it to Judge Carlos that the distinction of having earned that medal was significant and should be included in evidence.

The government immediately objected, claiming the Bronze Star with its combat "V" was neither opinion nor reputation, as required by the codified Rules of Military Evidence.

It was too singular, a specific act, as the combat "V" suggested the medal recipient had performed some heroic act. For a few moments this threw Sam's defense team for a loop, especially as there were only minutes left before jury selection began.

But Reschenthaler came back, more determined than ever, and argued that the jury would see the medals anyhow, as Sam Gonzales was permitted to wear his uniform and display all of his ribbons. Furthermore, he pressed, no one would know what act Sam had undertaken, only that he must have had a reputation as an excellent SEAL to earn that medal in the first place.

Judge Carlos had heard enough. He stepped in and snapped, "Enough! That's enough. Guy, just get me a list of his awards and I'll read them to the jury."

Lieutenant Commander Grover for the prosecution was on his feet immediately: "But sir ..."

Judge Carlos would have none of it. "I would say," he stated, carefully, "that a Bronze Star with a combat 'V' is evidence of a good military character. It's coming in."

He turned back to Reschenthaler and asked, "Can you get me the list?"

"Sir," replied the attorney, frantically looking for copy paper, "we do not have any paper, and we cannot get set up with a printer."

"You mean the government has not provided you with any of that?"

"No, your honor."

"Well, what do you have? Anything?"

Reschenthaler dived into his jacket pocket, trying not to laugh. "I have these napkins from the DFAC [dining facility—cafeteria]."

"Fine, fine," said Judge Carlos, casting his eyes heavenward. "Write them on there, and give the list to the clerk, and we'll get the awards on the record."

Reschenthaler scribbled away on the napkin and then handed it to the judge directly, with an appellate exhibit number. And so passed into the official court-martial record the formal list of Petty Officer Sam's combat decorations, right there on the napkin.

"That was important," said Judge Carlos. "Thank you, Guy."

Jury selection took place immediately afterward, and six "good men and true" were sworn in. And once more, things broke well for the defense. Every juror had been serving in Iraq. Every one of them knew the creed of the *Manchester Manual* by heart and understood what it meant to every al-Qaeda prisoner, trained as they were right from recruitment to lie flagrantly if captured.

Reschenthaler and Carmichael had both considered that manual—what it meant and its clear and obvious dishonest creed—to be of such importance that in preparation for this trial they had recently taken the trouble to attend a conference focused exclusively on the little book.

The junior attorney from Pittsburgh had long considered his JAG mentor, Lieutenant Commander Carmichael, the finest litigator he ever met in the US Navy's JAG corps. And he listened carefully to one of Carmichael's lifelong certainties about courtroom know-how: "If you're going in there with even the slightest chance you may end up in an argument on any subject, no matter how apparently insignificant, make sure you know a whole lot more about it than the guy on the opposite table."

Thus, Carmichael and Reschenthaler were experts on that manual. And when the time came to fight for its inclusion in the trial, they both knew they had to win. It took no time at all to convince the judge they were right; it rarely does when two attorneys understand precisely what they are talking about.

In this case the trick was to get the *Manchester Manual* entered into evidence via judicial notice so that no authentication would be necessary in court—no proving, for instance, that the defense hadn't written the book themselves.

And when, finally, the Lombardi team left the grim legal building in the desert, with its blast-wall defenses against the possibility of an al-Qaeda bomb, they were able to look back at several months of quite-notable pretrial victories. Six times, on either side of the world, they had pleaded with Judge Carlos for a decision in favor of Sam Gonzales. And each time they had come away with precisely what they wanted.

There were the two Norfolk motions: (1) the request for immunity from prosecution for the five witnesses who would stand up in court for the accused SEALs and (2) the rights of the three accused SEALs to confront their accuser in open court.

Both granted.

Then there was in Iraq (3) the *Manchester Manual* and its judicial inclusion and (4) the argument over the definition of good military character and Sam's medals on the napkin.

Both finding for the defense.

And there was (5) Lieutenant Kadlec's failed plea on behalf of the government that the defense team should not harass his star witness.

Denied in favor of the defense.

And finally (6) the undeniably skilled work of Reschenthaler when he demonstrated, to the judge's obvious consternation, the prosecution's unreasonable behavior in not providing the defense with even basic office supplies.

The defense had not lost one yet. And, to misquote Commodore John Paul Jones, they had not even begun to fight. Because the real enemy was not yet over the horizon.

11

TWO VERDICTS IN THE IRAQI COURTROOM

Ten Navy SEALs will swear by all that's holy that Matthew McCabe did not strike the prisoner, not one of the SEALs struck the prisoner, no one lied, no one threatened, and no one covered up any aspect of the evidence.

Seven months and twenty-two days had passed since those fateful hours in the dark, small hours of September 2, 2009, when the men of Echo Platoon had frog-marched the handcuffed al-Qaeda murderer Al-Isawi out of his desert stronghold.

Seven months and twenty-two days since Petty Officer Sam Gonzales had stood alone, beneath the sinister watchtowers of the terrorist garrison and quietly called in the three SH-60 Seahawks to airlift the Team and their prisoner out of this menacing jihadist outpost.

And now he was still on the outer reaches of that very same nine hundred thousand–square mile Arabian Desert, and the sand on his boots was identical, light and blowy. But this was not quite such a wasteland. Before him was an American military courthouse, and he must cross a wide main road to get to it.

He was not armed, yet to him the building was about a hundred times more dangerous than Al-Isawi's quarters had ever been. Because inside that building there were people trying to destroy him personally.

Three highly trained military attorneys were prosecuting him, Sam, on behalf of the government of the United States of America.

Sam Gonzales of Chicago, Illinois, had given up trying to work out precisely why. Or what he had done to deserve it. The problem was that this particular Navy SEAL was not like the others. For him there was no life beyond the Teams, only blackness.

The SEALs were his lifelong ambition, his reason for living, his pride, his happiness, and his love. If it all suddenly ended, he had no idea what would become of him. In truth, he did not really care. He kept going because he believed that Reschenthaler, Lombardi, and Carmichael would somehow get him out of it. And to that end, he was already hoping for a new deployment when he returned to SEAL Team 10.

For the others, that was a possibility. But there were many, many people involved in this case who were about ready to quit the US Navy and head for the hills. Lawyers and combat warriors alike were mortified by what was happening to the three accused men, and some of them were, albeit subconsciously, considering civilian life.

Sam was different, though. For him there was nothing else. To resign from the SEALs was beyond his comprehension. He lived—and always would—for the discipline, for the sound of a new magazine snapping into the breach of his rifle, the planning, the stealth, the defeat of his country's enemies.

And the sight of the Stars and Stripes right there on his battle patch sent a shiver of patriotism through him every time he pulled on his body armor. He wore that patch next to his treasured Trident—his symbolic badge of honor, which he slept with, under his pillow, every night of his life. Sam Gonzales was not like the others.

He understood as well as any of them what a guilty verdict would mean, if these strangers somehow decided he had been "derelict" in his duty and had indeed lied to his superiors to cover up some crime that he knew perfectly well had not been committed.

It was the disgrace that mattered to him most. And in the end he was at their mercy. Now in the burning heat of this Baghdad spring day, he walked across the street, flanked by Lombardi and Reschenthaler, like a nineteenth-century French nobleman headed for the guillotine.

A fusillade of machine gunfire or even a flying bomb was all part of Sam's job description. And he could deal with those. But the treacherous ambiguity of the courtroom, the insinuation and inference, would probably prove beyond him, and he gripped Lombardi's arm as they walked through the corridors of the US military's Baghdad legal building.

The case began shortly before 2 P.M., and as promised, a contingent from SEAL Team 8 was present. Whatever had happened on their night mission, it had not stopped them showing up in support of Sam Gonzales, and they sat shoulder to shoulder in the gallery.

Judge Tierney Carlos, presiding over the large courtroom from a somewhat majestic raised dais, sat at the head of a wooden staircase.

The prosecutors' table was placed on the left of the courtroom looking at the judge, closest to the jury. And there, Lieutenant Commander Jason Grover would be seated next to Lieutenant Nicholas Kadlec, with the lady Reschenthaler referred to as the "Ice Maiden" on the right.

Lombardi's table for the defense was set on the right-hand side of the courtroom. And as soon as they arrived, she placed Sam at the far end. Lombardi herself sat between Reschenthaler and Carmichael. None of it was by accident. This was courtroom strategy, and it ensured that when members of the jury looked across at the uniformed Navy SEAL, they would see him face-on.

They would also quickly grasp that Sam was seated right next to a stand-up, decorated lieutenant commander, a graduate of the US Naval Academy, who quite plainly believed in him. And also in his innocence. Everything counts in these highly combative courtroom clashes.

And already the defense counselors had to make a knife-edge decision. They would not call Sam Gonzales to the stand. SEALs are not famous for their guile except in battle. They are trained to fight hard, with maximum cunning and ruthless execution. When they speak they speak plainly—no innuendo, no confusion, and no economies with the truth.

That's what a SEAL is: uncompromising in his views, unbreakable in his personal code, and, unhappily in this case, inclined to think that everyone else is like him—with the exception of the enemy, none of whom can be trusted one yard.

Because of this, a skilled and devious prosecutor would trip up Sam Gonzales, trapping him into one of these all-too-familiar courtroom techniques:

You mean you don't know?
Well, not really ...
Then it could be true?
I suppose it could ...
But you just said you thought it could not be?
Well ...
So you weren't really telling me the truth, were you, Petty Officer
    Gonzales?
Well, I believed I was ...
Do you mean you're uncertain of the difference between the truth
    and lies?

That's what is known as a brutal cross-examination. It has nothing to do with right and wrong; it has to do with the courtroom skill of the attorney and the inexperience of the witness. It's harsh, often unfair, and Lombardi was not going to have it inflicted on Sam. Like his great buddy, Carlton Milo Higbie IV, but for different reasons, Sam would spend this trial on the bench.

Lombardi arranged the court papers in front of her, and some she pushed over toward Carmichael. Sam averted his eyes when he saw the top one, headed "THE UNITED STATES V." and then his own name and rank. This was the one with which he could never come to terms. Because throughout his working life he had been prepared to die, any time, any day, for the United States of America.

And now it seemed he was up against his own side. It was the only part of this whole trouble that more or less reduced him to rubble. And his lower lip tightened as he caught sight of it again: THE UNITED STATES OF AMERICA V. SAM GONZALES. He guessed it was not much different for the other two, Matt and Jon. They too were perfectly willing to die for their country. Otherwise none of them would have been SEALs in the first place. For all three of them, those words on the official charge documents were a never-ending dagger through the heart.

The courtroom rose as Judge Tierney Carlos made his entrance and took his place on the dais. When everyone was once more seated, the prosecutor Lieutenant Nicholas Kadlec rose and briefly outlined the case against Sam Gonzales: that having watched Matthew McCabe strike Ahmad Hashim Abd Al-Isawi, Sam proceeded to lie about the incident and then indulged in a SEAL cover-up of the issue, falsifying the evidence.

Lieutenant Kadlec indicated to the jury that Al-Isawi would stand before them and inform them personally about the abuse he had suffered and that the Navy master-at-arms who had been guarding him in the holding cell, MA3 Brian Westinson, would testify to support his statement.

Attorney Kadlec told Weston's story and made the significant point: Why would he lie about this, when the whole world wants it not to be true? There is only one answer—that it was true. And he is not lying.

Carmichael had already overcome one major setback this morning: he had arrived at the courtroom without his wedding ring and, assailed by superstition, had prevailed upon another JAG, Paul Threatt, to set some kind of an all-comers sand record across the desert to retrieve it. Threatt had made it back with moments to spare.

Carmichael's opening statement had taken until 2 A.M. to perfect. He, Lombardi, and Reschenthaler had gone over and over the facts, especially that Brian Westinson had made many statements, four of them to the trained NCIS agents. He had also been subjected to four different interviews and, the defense would argue, there had been serious differences among them.

The Navy JAG would communicate to the jury that ten Navy SEALs will swear by all that's holy that Matthew McCabe did not strike the prisoner, that not one of the SEALs struck the prisoner, that no one lied, no one threatened, and no one covered up any piece of evidence.

"Ten Navy SEALs," he would remind them. "But the government has decided to believe the word of this one man, Westinson, the one man who we know with 100 percent certainty has not been telling the truth."

And now Carmichael rose from his chair in this otherwise silent courtroom and began with a short introduction. "The prosecutor," he said, "just told you the story of two witnesses. Now I will tell you the story of everyone else. Because every other witness you are going to hear tells the same story. Only the two government witnesses say something different.

"And who are these two government witnesses? A scared, immature MA3 with a huge motivation to lie ... [long pause] ... and a terrorist."

Carmichael now walked back across the well of the court to the table allocated to the defense. He stood by Sam Gonzales, then turned to the jury and said, "Hi, I'm Lieutenant Commander Drew Carmichael. And I am proud to represent this man. He is a United States Navy SEAL, winner of a Bronze Star with Valor, a Navy Commendation Medal with valor, and acting leading chief petty officer for a forward-deployed SEAL platoon."

The essence of the defense strategy was to talk the jury through the mission, to take them back to that strange desert and walk with the SEALs over the rough ground in the dead of the night until the moment when they located the building and Matthew McCabe led the guys in.

Carmichael reminded everyone that the SEAL leader identified and subdued Al-Isawi. "He could have roughed him up right there," he said. "But he did not. He was completely professional at all times. He found much evidence—various IDs, a lot of cash, weapons and ammunition. And they brought the terrorist in, removing his handcuffs for the walk back to the helicopter, making sure he did not fall."

Sam's senior naval counsel then reconstructed those early morning hours of September 2, laying out for the first time all in one sequence, chapter and verse, the timeline of events from the moment the SEALs handed the prisoner into Westinson's custody.

It now came out that Westinson watched Al-Isawi for about fifteen minutes and then took him over to the Iraqi section and left him in their custody for ten minutes. It was not yet 0500, and it was certainly not yet light. And that was when Weston had stumbled into the first of his many problems. This was right in the middle of Ramadan, the most holy month of the Muslim year—thirty days of prayer and fasting, lasting from August 11 to September 9—thirty days when Muslims are virtually forbidden from eating and drinking from dawn to dusk.

Weston's Iraqi Muslims mutinied because right now they needed to eat before facing the long hot daylight hours when they denied themselves food. They volubly complained to Lieutenant Jimmy about this sacrilege of one of the Five Pillars of Islam, the ninth month of the year, Ramadan, during which no one should request any Muslim to work during darkness.

Lieutenant Jimmy was furious and personally accompanied Weston to collect Al-Isawi. He then yelled at the young master-at-arms for daring to turn his prisoner over to the Iraqis without asking permission.

They walked the blindfolded Al-Isawi back to the Conex Box holding cell, and at 0500 Lieutenant Jimmy entrusted Westinson once again to guard him. Everyone else from Objective Amber was either eating breakfast or showering.

Lieutenant Commander Carmichael then informed the jury that his client, Sam, had decided to go check on the master-at-arms to make sure he had everything he needed. And he asked McCabe and Keefe whether they wanted to come with him, after which the three of them rode over on a four-wheeler.

"All three of them say the same," said the attorney. Weston said he was okay and didn't need anything. "The whole encounter lasted not much more than one minute."

He also told the jury that Carl Higbie and Jason had walked in to check on Weston and the detainee. Carmichael stated, "Weston said he was fine, and neither Carl nor Jason noticed anything wrong with Hashim."

At 0545 HM1 Paddy, the big medic, arrived at the Conex Box to do a medical inspection of the detainee. He passed Carl and Jason on the way, just as they were leaving. The medical inspection lasted around fifteen minutes, Westinson having helped by lifting the prisoner's arms to check for bruising. Paddy noticed no medical issues with Al-Isawi.

"From this point on," continued Carmichael, "MA3 Westinson was left by himself with the detainee for two hours, although he admits to abandoning his post twice. And at around 0730 he moved the detainee to another Conex Box, closer to the camp, where he could try to flag someone down to allow himself a break."

It was just before 0800 when Lieutenant Jimmy came by to check on Weston and saw blood on the front of Al-Isawi's dishdasha, spots about the size of a Nerf-foam football. "More a spatter than a pool," said Carmichael.

"What the hell happened?" demanded Lieutenant Jimmy.

"I don't know," replied Weston.

And that was when the SEAL officer and Westinson walked the prisoner off the base to hand him over to the Iraqis. Both men remembered how Al-Isawi's demeanor changed as soon as he saw his countrymen—bending over and crying out in pain, sucking on his lip, trying to spit blood.

The meeting was called, and the lieutenant confronted the SEALs with the problem. And then he reported everything to a higher authority.

"What follows," Carmichael told the jury, "is the story you will hear from everyone, from all the SEALs. Though not just from them but also from the techs [the name SEALs give other enlisted ratings who work with them]. And not just enlisted men, but officers.

"In short," he added, "*everyone* besides MA3 Westinson and the terrorist will tell you this story."

Carmichael paused and moved to the center of the courtroom. And here he began what was undeniably the first lucid account of all the many statements made by the witnesses for the prosecution. So many of them had been heard, fragmented, opportunistically selected, and, indeed, sometimes presented out of order. That was all about to end.

Carmichael, aided by his experienced and diligent team, Lombardi and Reschenthaler, was about to blow MA3 Westinson's words into the stratosphere.

"You have heard from the prosecutor a version of MA3 Westinson's story," he said. "But what he did not tell you was, that was Version Six! Yes, MA3 Westinson has told six different versions of his own story."

And in grim, metronomic sequence, he laid out publicly for the first time, the words of the master-at-arms that he, Lombardi, and Reschenthaler had traveled halfway across the world to refute on behalf of Sam, Matt, and Jon.

"Version One, uttered on that infamous morning at 0800, September 2, when Lieutenant Jimmy first discovered the blood on the prisoner: 'I don't know what happened.'

"Version Two, told and repeated only a couple of hours later in the general meeting called by Lieutenant Jimmy: 'This is all my fault. I left my post and he got hurt. This is all going to come on me.'

"Version Three came two days later, when MA3 Westinson began to test out his story. He tells the camera operator, MC1 Lynn Friant: 'I may of [sic] saw something. I was out of the room, but when I was walking about, I saw the detainee recoil as if hit. Then I saw McCabe standing as if he hit him. I didn't see what happened, but I think it was a sort of half-punch.'

"Version Four came the next day, September 5. MA3 Westinson goes to Lieutenant Jimmy and tells him he saw 'McCabe hit the terrorist in the side while he was sitting in a chair. Both Gonzales and Keefe were watching. Keefe cheered. Sam said, 'Don't feel bad. He deserved it.'

"Version Five came ten days later. Having already made a sworn statement on September 5, where he told investigators 'everything,' he now reports a new 'secret meeting' that occurred about an hour later, 'where all the SEALs sat around and got their stories straight.'"

Carmichael told the jury that in this Version Five, Petty Officer Gonzales is now directing everyone to get their stories straight. "This," he said, "is a follow-on meeting which MA3 Westinson had never even mentioned before. And everyone else denies ever happened."

It was from this meeting that the charge of obstruction of justice was leveled at SO1 Gonzales. And Version Five also contained another mystery: the detainee is "standing" while being "punched" despite "sitting" in Version Four. "And all of a sudden HMI Paddy is in the room," stated Carmichael. "And he's witnessing the whole thing. So MA3 Westinson has moved back the timeline by one hour."

Again the naval defense counsel paused before adding, "And then came Version Six. This is where it gets really interesting. Because after charges have been brought and the story is being covered by the media, suddenly the entire SEAL platoon is involved in the assault. Now McCabe is hitting on the terrorist while Sam Gonzales cheers and Keefe 'roars' in approval. Keefe goes out to get a stick so he can pound the terrorist.

"MA3 Westinson says HM1 Paddy has to go outside so he is not a witness," said the attorney. "And in a new twist he claims SO2 Higbie and Lieutenant Jason are now involved, and each takes a turn striking the terrorist."

With an expression betraying nothing but astonishment, he adds that according to MA3 Westinson, he and HM1 Paddy could now see this five-thousand-pound Conex Box rocking because the SEALs are wailing on the helpless detainee that hard.

"And now comes Version Seven. And I must ask you to wait," said Carmichael, "to wait until MA3 Westinson walks through that door and sits in the witness stand. What's it going to be? I don't know. But we're all going to find out." And, should we forget, let's remind ourselves of government witness number two. He's the Blackwater Bridge terrorist, Ahmad Hashim, who killed four Americans, burned their bodies, and hanged them from a bridge for all to see.

"He's a jihadist who was just playing by the al-Qaeda handbook, the *Manchester Manual*, the guide for all members of this terrorist organization, how to conduct virtually all operations—blending into a foreign country, recruiting, fund-raising, and how to behave in a coalition prison.

"Let me offer you rule one: at the beginning of any trial, once more the brothers must insist on proving, before the judge, that torture was inflicted on them by state security.

"Rule two: complain to the court of mistreatment while in prison."

Carmichael concluded with a flourish: "At the end of the day this is what the government has with which to prove its case:

"Master-at-Arms 3rd Class Westinson—with his seven versions.

"And the terrorist—with his *Manual*.

"SO1 Sam Gonzales has everyone else."

And it was already clear that the jury thought much the same. Both Lombardi and Reschenthaler recall them looking laser-eyed at the master-at-arms when he was finally called as the first witness for the prosecution and took his place in the witness box in order to raise his hand once more against one of America's beloved SEALs.

That initial address to the jury stuck in the minds of all who heard it. Months later, Reschenthaler said, "Drew's opening was fantastic. He never raised his voice, never slagged off the MA3—just stated the facts. It was completely captivating. To this day I've never heard better."

Reschenthaler still has a picture in his mind of the opening hour of the trial: "Sam in his dress uniform, sitting quietly facing the jury, with a four-square, decorated naval officer standing next to him, refusing to hear a word against him. They were a study in everything that's good about the US Navy, top-class people—unafraid, honest, and straightforward. The charge sheet against Sam Gonzales was, in my opinion, a travesty."

Nonetheless, the prosecution called MA3 Westinson to the stand and carefully walked him through his part in the events of September 2, 2009. Both naval officers, Grover and Kadlec, were probably not loving the prospect of Lombardi's forthcoming cross-examination.

Lombardi then rose from her chair and began her interrogation of Brian Westinson. Her position in this part of the court-martial was calculated. She would appear softer, less inclined to intimidate the witness than either Carmichael or Reschenthaler, and she began in a steady, deliberate, and not unfriendly way.

Lombardi talked to Brian about his background, his hopes, his ambitions, which included his aim to become a California Highway Patrol officer. But slowly she proceeded to the timeline that she and Reschenthaler had drawn up—the interlocking of Westinson's various versions and the times and places he had specified. Hardly any of them seemed to dovetail properly.

And Lombardi kept "looping"—walking him along that line, establishing his version, and then flashing back to another version, a conflicting account. In short order Westinson was all over the place, and

Lombardi, with a touch of characteristic flamboyance, was marching around the courtroom, pacing, demonstrating her anguish at these contradictions.

One of Lombardi's favorite comments is, "C'mon, I'm a typical New York Italian—we speak with our hands!"

And right now her hands were working overtime—sometimes spread wide apart in mock bewilderment, sometimes pointing to the document in her hands, sometime gesticulating to emphasize a decisive point. And like all experienced trial attorneys, she was swift to pounce upon the dramatic. When Westinson began to elaborate on the viciousness of the beating Al-Isawi had taken at the hands of the SEALs, especially Matthew McCabe, she was at her best, muttering, just loud enough: "Oh my God, how awful."

By the time Lombardi was all done with Brian Westinson, this case had swerved away from the government, and it would never really swing their way again.

Grover then called the terrorist Al-Isawi to the stand, and immediately the three defense lawyers thought he had this one all wrong. Because of Reschenthaler's experience in the interview room, they all knew the interpreter was hopeless—an elderly Egyptian who was a bit deaf and spoke in a remote Egyptian dialect.

Grover, an excellent litigator but with a courtroom arrogance about him, quickly began using big words and long-winded sentences to impress the jury. Defense counsel thought it was a disaster because the translator could not understand much of it and was thus unable to communicate with Al-Isawi.

The jihadist in the witness box, dressed in a bright yellow jumpsuit with his hands bound in front of him, was plainly lost at sea, particularly as he somehow believed Reschenthaler was not only his best friend but also his lawyer. Twice he looked over to Reschenthaler, seeking guidance. Both times the young Pennsylvania attorney averted his gaze and lowered his head so the jury would not catch on he had buttered up the mass murderer now standing in the box.

Al-Isawi's obvious confusion was a triumph for the defense. The terrorist had been telling lies on a world-class scale for more than seven months, adhering to the doctrine of the *Manchester Manual*, and

Reschenthaler was relentless in his thoughts. He believed the government had refused him his excellent translator out of pure spite, and now they were paying for it with this Egyptian. Reschenthaler thought it entirely likely that Judge Carlos might in the very near future use one of his favorite words: "Dopey."

Finally the prosecution was finished with Al-Isawi. And Reschenthaler stepped up for the cross-examination. He was careful to call him "Hashim," his surname, at all times—no "Mr.," as he was careful to show this killer no respect whatsoever.

And then in stark contrast to Grover, Reschenthaler began to speak in short, deliberate sentences—no long words, nothing to confuse the translator: "Let's go back to the beginning, shall we? And get out the entire story."

And from there he moved to the long story of the "horrible" beating that Al-Isawi claimed he had suffered. Reschenthaler coaxed out of him the whole graphic description—the barrage of kicking while he was on the ground, the steel-capped boots, and the blows to the head and stomach. The jury sat stunned by this tale of cruelty.

Reschenthaler had been sympathetic, trying not to look at Lombardi, who virtually winced at every detail of the pounding Al-Isawi claimed he had received. Reschenthaler guessed she probably looked like Lady Macbeth right then, but he kept his eyes on the terrorist.

And then he pulled out his trump card. He produced the photographs taken in the couple of days following the "horrific beatings." The clear shots that showed Al-Isawi had hardly a mark on him except for the cold sore.

"May it please the court, I would like to publish these photos to the jury."

He personally handed them to the president and, for the record, stated, "I am now handing the jury the photographs which depict that 'horrific' beating."

"OBJECTION!" Grover was on his feet. "Counsel is commenting on the evidence."

Reschenthaler was waiting for that one. And he answered quickly and loudly: "Your honor, excuse me, I am showing the jurors the photos."

The judge ignored the objection and allowed the defense to proceed. And by the time anyone could make further comment, the jury was looking at the pictures. If anyone had been badly beaten up, it was surely not Al-Isawi, who was unmarked. Lombardi saw at least three of the jurors roll their eyes in disbelief.

It was one of those courtroom moments. The government's case had taken a body blow. The terrorist, who everyone hated anyway, had been proven to be a liar of the highest ranking. His entire evidence must have been a total fabrication. His allegations against the Americans were palpably, obviously false.

And the old Jefferson High wrestling star came rumbling in for the kill, pressing home the point about the "dishonest" SEALs.

"And I believe the Americans stole money too?" he said, his voice redolent with sarcasm.

"Yes, yes. Six thousand dollars."

"Was this your money?"

"No, my mother's. She was saving it for the Haj. She worked hard, selling jewelry for years, to send me on the pilgrimage."

"Are you aware that the money found at your home was all numbered, marked consecutively?"

The jury picked up on it. But the interpreter was confused, and Al-Isawi did not get it: it was counterfeit money, used to fund acts of terror.

Reschenthaler asked the question again. "Are you aware ..."

"No ..."

Reschenthaler walked over and showed the jurors pictures of the money. He knew he was pushing the rules of evidence, leading the jury with the close-ups. But he desperately wanted Grover to object again on behalf of the government while he was laying into the terrorist.

Reschenthaler looked young, very young, and the plan was to entice the big, bad government to object, show them beating up on a young American attorney while protecting a terrorist. Because if they did, Lombardi's team scored major points. And if they didn't, Reschenthaler was about to run roughshod over the prosecution in this courtroom.

As it happened, Grover and his team did not take the bait, so Reschenthaler was free to question Al-Isawi at will, nailing down the pure farce of the beating and proving beyond a doubt the colossal lie about the money.

Reschenthaler had always planned to conclude the cross-examination with a significant flourish, and now he asked the question that might, ultimately, seal Al-Isawi's fate and would almost certainly save Sam Gonzales.

"Isn't it true," he asked, "that you, Hashim, are the mastermind behind the Blackwater Bridge Massacre?"

Like Carmichael, he'd renamed the Fallujah bridge over the Euphrates in the interest of expediency, but almost everyone in the courtroom knew precisely what he meant. He said it quickly in order that the translator could not possibly follow. Reschenthaler was still determined that the government would pay for hiring a different translator.

To hell with you, government, he thought. *You give me this guy instead of my linguist, well ... we'll just see how that works out.*

At this point the translator threw his hands in the air and said in broken English: "Sorry—I ... I no, I don't hear good."

Grover himself had been the man who had very cheerfully denied the request for the top translator, and now Reschenthaler stared hard at him before replying, "That's okay. I'll repeat it slowly."

And he turned to the jury, looked at them squarely, and asked, "Isn't it true ... [paused for translation] ... that you were ... [pause] ... the mastermind ... [pause] ... behind the ... [pause] ... Blackwater Bridge Massacre?"

By now the jury were hanging onto Reschenthaler's every word, and he walked back, theatrically, to his chair before Al-Isawi could respond. The translator finished, and the well of the courtroom was empty. Everyone was seated, and Al-Isawi said, "No. No."

"Thank you," said Reschenthaler politely. "No more questions." After a forty-five-minute cross-examination by the youngest lawyer in the room, the terrorist now stood before the court forever branded as a thunderous liar.

The government's case against Petty Officer Sam Gonzales was, by any standards, in desperate trouble.

And the SEAL knew it. He only just suppressed a smile as he leaned forward and said to Reschenthaler, "Nice job, sir," which is just about the highest praise SEALs hand out to anyone.

And nothing much improved for the prosecution as SEAL after SEAL came into the witness box and swore under oath that none of them knew anything about Matthew McCabe striking anyone. Each one of them attested to the exemplary character of Sam Gonzales, and most expressed admiration for the quality of his military conduct and competence.

The longest testimony next to that of Westinson was from Lieutenant Jimmy, who provided detailed background to the mission and a well-constructed timeline for all events that morning and beyond.

Also in the witness box was Lieutenant Jason, who had walked in the left flank that night and then joined the heavily armed rear guard while Matt and the guys stormed the Al-Qaeda stronghold.

Jason, who had stood in the shadows with his fire Team, with his machine gun ready, would not utter one word against Sam Gonzales and had nothing but praise for the senior petty officer who had walked across the desert carrying the critical comms in Objective Amber.

As for the allegation that Matthew had attacked the terrorist and that Sam had lied about it to his superiors, well, Lieutenant Jason found it difficult to dignify that with a straight answer. But his smile and contemptuous shake of the head said a thousand valuable words to the jury.

He might just have well have asked the prosecutors: "Are you guys actually nuts?"

Carmichael next called HM1 Paddy, knowing that this was a vital witness because he was not a SEAL but a corpsman, and he too disputed the theory that the SEALs had somehow gotten together and lied.

He stood on the stand and stated flatly that the SEALs had already gone to bed by the time he examined Al-Isawi, so any injury must have happened after they had vanished for sleep.

The SEALs last saw the prisoner at 0500, and Paddy himself had examined him at 0600, when he was most certainly not injured. Therefore, it must have happened after that, and the only person with Al-Isawi after 0600 was Westinson. So, as far as this senior medic could see, that minor injury on the lip was either caused by Weston or had been self-inflicted.

There was even more evidence in support of the self-inflicted theory, as seen when Carmichael called the base's oral surgeon, a US army captain, to the stand. The doctor said flatly the wound on Al-Isawi's lip looked like a canker sore, an aphthous ulcer, and the terrorist had bitten the top off it and then sucked at it to make it bleed.

The prosecution came back with a good cross-examination, asking whether it could have come from any other way. And the doctor replied that it could have come from a "fall from a chair, where you hit your lip on the way down."

But Carmichael immediately recrossed and asked whether the wound could have come from a severe blunt-force trauma, like a punch or boot to the face. The doctor said definitely not a boot and very unlikely a punch, because this would have caused much more severe damage, with bruising around the mouth. This was not in evidence.

Carmichael's final question was decisive: "Doctor, in your professional expert opinion, was that mysterious gash on the terrorist's lip self-inflicted?"

"Yes."

But the battle to prove whether Westinson was reliable swayed back and forth. The prosecution, somewhat surprisingly, called MC1 Lynn Friant. Reschenthaler thinks Grover's strategy of calling up a defense witness was designed to keep the other side surprised. And, indeed, Friant testified for the prosecution that Westinson was concerned about the incident from the very beginning. However, under cross-examination by Reschenthaler, she was able to elaborate, saying that Weston told her: "My parents won't love me anymore." There were several other slightly bizarre comments emanating from the master-at-arms, who was claiming his future was already ruined.

Reschenthaler then asked her: "Isn't it true that Westinson looked up to you as a mother figure?"

At this Friant blushed and replied, "Well, I'd like to think more of an older sister figure."

Reschenthaler chuckled and said, "Fair enough."

Both judge and jury laughed at this one light moment in what had been hitherto a deadly serious court-martial. But once more, the case swung for the defense because that moment made Friant likeable, so the jury responded to her well.

The prosecution could not allow this less-than-flattering assessment of Weston's character to go unchallenged, so they swiftly wheeled in Westinson's supervisor, MA1 Dotson, who valiantly tried to build up the case for Weston's reputation for truthfulness. But this was tough going, as it was just hours after Carmichael and Lombardi had painted a different picture.

And just to press home their advantage, defense now called Paul Franco, the ex–New York City fireman, to rebut this rebuttal. And the boy-band look-alike let no one down. As Weston's ultimate boss, he testified that, of all the people he had ever supervised, the master-at-arms was at the bottom of the barrel.

This was the last witness before closing arguments, and Grover had his work cut out for him from the moment he stood up to address the jury. But he rose to the occasion and delivered a powerful speech. He was succinct and to the point.

Grover reminded the jury that two of the Blackwater guards killed in the Fallujah ambush were former Navy SEALs, and this could have been a motive to attack the infamous Butcher.

And then he brought up the fine balance and high moral code all SEALs must develop. "We give them training and much power and responsibility," he said. "And with that we assume they will uphold American values and the values of the SEAL community. None of us must ever forget this is why we are better than terrorists."

Some closing speeches by the prosecution are hard for the defense to immediately follow. And this was one of them.

Lombardi's closing was a calm and considered reminder to the six-man jury of all that they had heard: the obvious honesty of every one of the SEAL witnesses; their unanimous voice, their certainty that no military rule had been transgressed; and their loyal, admiring assessment of the accused man, Petty Officer 1st Class Sam Gonzales.

She further reminded them of the inconsistencies of the government's star witness, MA3 Brian Westinson, with his swerves away from the timeline and his plain motive for not telling the truth—that, indeed, he was the only one who could have whacked the terrorist.

As for the terrorist, Lombardi spoke of him with thinly disguised scorn. He was, she believed, a man of such evil and deviousness that to accept his word against those of the US Navy SEALs was, more or less, beyond her understanding and, she assumed, that of the members of the jury.

At the end of her closing speech Judge Carlos announced a recess for lunch, after which he ordered the jury to chambers to deliberate. And in such moments as these, preconceived ideas and theories are apt to disintegrate. What had seemed blissfully simple and encouraging half a day ago now seemed fraught with peril. A thousand "what ifs" cascaded through the three defense attorneys' minds, not to mention the hopes and fears of Petty Officer Gonzales.

No sooner were the members of the jury out of sight than Reschenthaler slipped firmly into negative mode. What if they find Sam guilty? Reschenthaler thought the prosecution had done a good job making Brian credible, and he thought his appearance on the stand had been effective. But *Jesus!*, he thought, *you never know how a jury will decide.* Just in case, Lombardi had already asked the accused SEAL to write down very carefully his thoughts about why he became a SEAL, what the Navy meant to him. And Sam had come through with a wonderful, moving piece of writing in which he laid bare his soul.

Lombardi almost wept with sadness and frustration at what the government might still do to him. But the plan had to be there: if he were found guilty, Sam would read out before the court what he had written.

Reschenthaler thought it imperative that the many heroic deeds that Sam had undertaken be told to the judge before he passed sentence. But Sam would not agree. He said simply: "I am not allowed to speak of these things. No SEAL would."

And in a truly heartbreaking moment, right there in that Baghdad courtroom, facing ruination, he just reminded Reschenthaler that SEALs are silent professionals and do not discuss their trade.

"I can't do it, Guy," he said. "I just can't."

"Not even now, perhaps to save yourself?"

"Not even now," said Sam. "Not even now."

Carmichael and Reschenthaler moved outside to get on the phone to call Matt McCabe's right-flank point man, Eric, who had left the Navy and became a medical student. Over the phone he regaled the two attorneys with anecdote after anecdote about Sam, and they both thought that, if their luck held, they had a chance to get him off with a letter of reprimand.

In less than two hours they returned to the courtroom, where Sam was sitting stoically awaiting his fate. And then the jury returned. Everyone arose from their chairs. And when the jury was seated, Judge Carlos asked, "Does the jury have a verdict?"

The senior member stood up and replied, "Yes, sir."

And now the bailiff stood up and walked over to collect the "findings worksheet," a set of directions on which the jury had checked either "guilty" or "not guilty" to the various charges against Sam.

Judge Carlos read them and said, "Very well, bailiff. Hand this back. And now, when you're ready, the senior member may stand and read your findings."

The jury leader immediately stood. And so did everyone involved in the case. By his own admission Reschenthaler recalls a state of grace with which he was not normally accustomed: "My legs felt like Jell-O," said the former marauder of the mat.

And now the juryman spoke: "On all charges and specifications, we find the accused ... not guilty."

Reschenthaler and Lombardi froze. Sam almost went into shock with relief. And Carmichael leaned over and shook his hand. Sam reached out for Lombardi's hand. And behind them the room erupted—as near as possible to an outburst of joy from a court-martial as traumatic and cruel as this one had been.

Even Judge Tierney Carlos smiled as he congratulated the jury on a job well done and then dismissed them.

By now everyone was shaking hands. The entire courtroom was ecstatic. Even Weston just sat there and clapped his hands, nodding his head. And then strangely, when the courtroom was emptying, he grabbed a broom and started to sweep the gallery.

Sam Gonzales, with gigantic understatement, said quietly, "This is a big weight off my shoulders."

The only man on the entire base who was still in the throes of fear and depression was Jonathan Keefe, who had been in his room alone all day, staring at the ceiling. But within a few minutes of the verdict there was a loud knock on his door, followed by the excited voice of Matthew McCabe trying out one of the worst jokes in the history of the world: "*JON! JON!*" he yelled, "They've found him guilty. They're talking about a firing squad."

At which point Jon read straight through his buddy's antics and began to laugh. Then Matt went real and told him: "Sam's been found not guilty. Not one juror voted against him. The lawyers crushed it. All the defense witnesses did a fabulous job. We've had a blow-out victory!"

"When he finally opened the door, he couldn't find me," said Jon later, "because I was way up there, on cloud nine. And God was in his heaven."

They were, however, denied much of a celebration, because Jon was due in court on similar charges the very next morning. But two major clouds had been lifted: the one of almost permanent injustice that had hung over them all since last September, and the one that was full of ash and cinders that had now veered east and allowed McCormack to take off from Amsterdam and finally make it to Baghdad.

Jonathan Keefe and Paul Threatt borrowed a vehicle and drove out to the airport to meet him, and they conducted a detailed strategy session in the hours before Sam's celebration dinner, such as it was.

This took place in the on-base Army cafeteria, and all of the defense team and witnesses were there. But it was quiet and calm, because the defeated prosecutors were also there at a nearby table in the chow hall. And no one wanted to indulge in obvious triumphalism. Besides, this was a victory that needed to be repeated on the morrow.

And now McCormack prepared to take over the helm, as he was

completely up to date with the proceedings in the first trial and had given due consideration to Judge Carlos's mind-set.

McCormack understood that for many hours the judge had sat through the SEALs' evidence, and by this time he understood that he could show that Westinson was unreliable and that Al-Isawi was at least as big a liar as everyone had suspected. Those were the official opinions of Sam's jury, who believed neither of them in their unanimous "not guilty" verdict.

Judge Carlos had heard it all and, in McCormack's opinion, had agreed with it all. And in the back of his mind there was a feeling of disquiet, the long road ahead that would involve making a case for Jon and wheeling out all the witnesses the judge had already heard, explaining everything to a new jury.

However, along the corridor of the building where they were staying Threatt was experiencing very similar doubts. He and Reschenthaler were burning the midnight oil agonizing over that same quandary. Reschenthaler was helping out voluntarily as a well-wisher and adviser, having fought a front-rank courtroom battle with the terrorist the previous day. And he believed to the bottom of his heart that the three SEALs were innocent.

In his combative mind, that road—resurrecting everything to a new panel—was not a good plan because these jurymen, hearing the allegations for the first time, would require an endless amount of "nursing" through the evidence. Threatt, vastly more experienced than Reschenthaler and pretty combative himself, also believed the correct route for Jon and his defense team was to go "judge alone," dispense with the jury, and throw themselves on the mercy of Judge Tierney Carlos.

And now, long after the midnight hour, both Threatt and Reschenthaler trooped along to McCormack's miniscule bedroom to find him with about four thousand documents all over his bed. Threatt explained his thoughts, and the veteran courtroom warrior from Virginia Beach immediately agreed.

As the paid civilian lawyer and lead counselor, he would, in the final reckoning, make the formal call to remove the jury. But he stressed that Jonathan himself had to be on board and in agreement.

"Well, he's asleep," said Threatt.

"Wake him up," replied McCormack.

At which point Threatt and Reschenthaler walked over to Jon's room and did just that. And soon all four of them were in McCormack's overcrowded bedroom, sitting on the bed, surrounded by trial documents, and explaining to the big Navy SEAL why they wished to make this sudden last-minute swerve from the traditional path of a court-martial defense team.

The six-foot four-inch breacher listened carefully and then said, "Let's go for it." He might have been about to storm a terrorist stronghold.

Once this was clarified there was still much to decide. And here McCormack made a brilliant call: he elected to call no witnesses. In short, he decided not to present a case to the court but to let the prosecution get on with it and try their luck at presenting to the court a case that had been shot full of holes less than twenty-four hours previously.

Both Threatt and McCormack considered the difficult position of the judge. If they presented a strong case for the defense, he would be in a situation in which he personally had to find against the prosecution and would thus be compelled to rule against the military brass who had continually allowed this case to proceed.

By going "judge alone" and not presenting any case for the defense, they offered Judge Carlos the strong and correct procedure of finding that there was not sufficient evidence to sustain a guilty verdict, not enough evidence to cast aside the issue of reasonable doubt, and little alternative except to uphold the universal assumption of "innocent until proven guilty."

By allowing the prosecution to stand or fall, McCormack and Threatt made an awkward issue for the judge into a relatively simple one—provided, of course, that Al-Isawi presented his customary volume of lies.

It was, of course, an unusual step—electing to be heard by the judge only. Indeed, it was only the second or third time out of hundreds of military trials in the past twenty-eight years that McCormack had taken such a route. At least it was in a trial as fiercely contested as this.

But Judge Tierney Carlos had been looking skeptically at this court-martial for many weeks. He had found for the defense over and over in various motions and points of law. And yesterday, in his own court-room, a six-man naval jury had delivered a "blow-out" verdict of not guilty, which more or less put the US Navy in line with hundreds of thousands of Americans who believed the case against the SEALs should never have been brought.

McCormack was a renowned jury lawyer—a silver-tongued, passionate advocate, adroit at swaying any jury to his point of view. But this was different. He was sure of his ground, and Petty Officer Keefe and Navy JAG Threatt were with him.

They would leave it to the judicial expert on the case, Judge Carlos, who had not let them down in any way thus far.

McCormack decided not to disclose this change in forum until the morning of trial, and as expected, it threw the prosecution off base, as they found themselves now trying to persuade a senior JAG that the previous trial had been "unsafe" and that Jonathan Keefe, the breacher from Virginia, was guilty as charged. And they were extremely pressed for allies.

And McCormack had his heavy guns primed. When Jonathan Keefe's trial began in the morning, McCormack would reserve his most telling barrages for Westinson. In his opinion Reschenthaler had so utter discredited the terrorist that he scarcely mattered. Whatever he said, it no longer counted.

The specific task of Jon's defense team was to remove once more the master-at-arms as a dependable voice for the prosecution, as Carmichael and Lombardi had done for Sam Gonzales. And the decision to go with Judge Carlos quickly proved to be a master stroke. The prosecution were instantly on the back foot, forced to shelve speeches designed for a jury.

And McCormack was about to give one of his finest military trial performances in the court of a judge who had not yet shown *any* significant sympathy to the men who sought to ruin the three SEALs.

On the morning of the trial he was accompanied by Lieutenant Paul Threatt, who had stood so doggedly alongside Jon from that very first phone call from Norfolk to the Qatar Base. Neither attorney had ever doubted Jon's innocence, and McCormack in particular, after his long wait in Amsterdam, was fired up for confrontation.

As for the prosecution, there was an understandable lack of steam, at least it seemed so to McCormack. Their situation was simple to understand: the jury in the previous case had not believed what Al-Asawi had alleged and had not believed Westinson. That jury believed both of them were lying. In fact they probably thought that everyone in the courtroom believed both of them were lying.

And here they were again, trying to convince the very same judge that yesterday's not-guilty verdict for Sam Gonzales was actually a mistake and that Al-Isawi and Brian Westinson were, after all, shining beacons of truth.

Tough call. And in McCormack's opinion there was a distinct lack of zing in the prosecution's opening attempts to inform Judge Carlos that Navy SEAL Jonathan Keefe, a striking figure in his dress blues and combat decorations, was a liar and was derelict in his duty.

There was an irrelevance to Al-Isawi's appearance, but when Westinson took the stand, here was the real target. And when McCormack rose to begin his cross-examination of the young master-at-arms, the crowded courtroom took on an entirely new atmosphere.

Armed with a crisp legal summary of all prior statements, McCormack came out swinging from the opening bell, and he wanted to know precisely why Westinson had denied seeing anything when Lieutenant Jimmy first questioned him. He rapid-fired questions at MA3 Westinson, not being particularly interested in what he had to say in response.

How come you saw nothing that time, and then saw every SEAL on the base banging away at Al-Isawi?

I think we've established you were lying—I just want to know when? Which time?

Could you just explain to me how you went from seeing nothing, knowing nothing, to witnessing this apparent gang of Navy SEALs all attacking the detainee, one after another, abusing him, right before your eyes?

Sarcasm almost enveloped the courtroom as McCormack reminded MA3 Westinson that he'd claimed the two-and-a-half-ton holding cell was "rocking when the SEALs were beating up the detainee."

And then the classic line from the previous day was of course repeated: Al-Isawi had no marks, with the only minor injury being the
abrasion on the inside of his lip, which the oral surgeon had said, categorically, was self-inflicted. If this had been a championship bout, the
referee would have stopped it. Either that or the government's corner
men would have thrown the towel into the ring.

By the end of that cross-examination McCormack was confident.
The master-at-arms, he believed, was suitably discredited. McCormack
stressed the probability that Westinson had essentially made up his
story to cover his own rear end. He had, after all, been alone with the
detainee, and when Lieutenant Jimmy finally saw the small cut on the
Iraqi's lower lip, Weston had decided to give himself a custom-made
alibi.

McCormack's presentation of this theory was relentless. And although spectators, both media and Iraqi officials, might have thought
they were seeing a skilled and pugnacious American attorney merely
bullying a witness, they were not. Instead, they were witnessing the
pent-up fury of a veteran lawyer who believed to the bottom of his
heart that Jon, Matt, and Sam were the innocent victims of an enormous error of judgment and a virago of lies and false accusations. He
believed the military had treated them all disgracefully.

And he was fighting for them with all he had. This was not the
venom of a professional trying to win a case; this was a cry from the
heart, a demand for Judge Tierney Carlos to put this right. And there
would be no mercy for anyone trying to stop him. McCormack was
ruthless with MA3 Brian Westinson, and he did not care who witnessed his performance.

He bounced his questions forward and then back, keeping MA3
Westinson off his guard and wanting to know, above all else, why the
story changed over time, from knowing nothing to the final version.

He was particularly vehement over Westinson's account of how Jon
and Sam had started laughing, and how Jon had gone outside for "a
big log," which later became a "little stick." And how the SEAL
breacher had stood over the detainee, making a "growling, roaring"
noise trying to "psyche out" the detainee.

He demanded definitions for the words "growling" and "roaring." He wanted to know how big the log/stick was, to the inch. He bounced back to the times the detainee was without a guard, when Weston had left for short periods. He wanted to know if anyone else *could* have committed an assault.

That was one very confused master-at-arms when McCormack was all done with him. And the attorney was so confident that he immediately told Jon that there would be no need for him take the stand and testify. The defense would rest without presenting any substantive evidence, just as they had planned in the small hours of the morning on the cluttered bed of the lead counselor.

They would not even call on the hero of the hour, Petty Officer 1st Class Sam Gonzales, who was in attendance, wearing full dress blues and ready at a moment's notice to step up and swear to God that Jonathan Keefe had never once in his military life been derelict in his duty and neither would he have dreamed of telling a lie to his superior officers.

The prosecutors could struggle on all alone. And Judge Carlos would have the option of confirming what had been established yesterday: there was insufficient evidence to eliminate the possibility of reasonable doubt.

There was, however, one significant turn this case would still take, and the Judge himself activated it. He had seemed slightly on edge over the nonappearance of any defense witnesses. Suddenly, when it became official that defense would offer no more, Judge Carlos elected to call witnesses of his own. It was the first time in a long career that McCormack had seen such a development in any courtroom.

And Judge Carlos, as he had always done, operated close to the heart of the matter. He called up the camera operator MC1 Lynn Friant and quizzed her about the somewhat eccentric opinions that Westinson had confided in her. This was understandable, as the highest military authorities, who had, jointly and severally, condoned this ill-fated court-martial, would doubtless scrutinize his verdict.

It was essential that the weakness of Westinson's character and evidence be fully exposed, and Friant could surely shed light on that, speaking as his surrogate elder sister. And she was particularly illuminating about his fears of a lack of love, both parental and otherwise, subsequent upon this trial.

The judge also called Carl Higbie IV as well as the medical officer who had confirmed there were "no contusions" visible on the detainee. Summoned once more to the witness box, PO1 Paul Franco repeated, as his immediate boss, that Weston was near the bottom of the barrel of all the sailors he had ever supervised.

Paul Threatt cross-examined all these witnesses. But he had no requirement to be combative because they were all on the side of the defense, each and every one of them certain that Jonathan was entirely innocent of the charge against him, whatever the hell it was.

And together the four of them provided a big turning point in the case. And when Grover rose to make his closing argument for the prosecution, McCormack and Threatt were confident in their position.

It was another good speech, making many of the same points he had made the day before: Why would Westinson lie? What about those two former SEALs killed in Fallujah? But the government's case had been established on a quicksand of inconsistencies, exaggerations, and lies.

McCormack then stepped forward to close for the defense with a speech in the same class as Carmichael's opening in the Gonzales trial.

He justified nothing, as he had presented no case. But he concentrated on the utter unreliability of the prosecution's case, with lightly veiled references to the fact that this was a court-martial that should never have been convened, leveled as it was against these upstanding, brave, and loyal members of America's elite fighting force.

Once more the prosecution rose to make its rebuttal, their final closing argument. This took little time, and Judge Carlos probably felt by now he had heard enough. And he immediately called a recess while he retired to consider his verdict. The time was shortly after nine o'clock in the evening, and everyone knew they were there for however long he took.

The judge was under orders to get this thing settled just as quickly and inexpensively as possible. And that did not include another day in this courtroom. It might drag on until the small hours, but tonight Judge Carlos would pronounce his verdict on Petty Officer Jonathan Keefe.

As the judge retired to his chambers, reporters and broadcasters rushed out of the windowless courtroom into the heat of the desert night, cell phones ready, camera crews on high alert. No one knew how long the judge would take, and the media pack scrambled for satellite connections to the United States.

McCormack remained with Jonathan, but Threatt headed for the exit, just to stand outside in the air, to break from the claustrophobic courthouse and gather his thoughts.

A couple of hours earlier he had been as confident as his fellow attorney, but Judge Carlos's unorthodox decision to call witnesses on his own account had cast mild doubts in his mind—not whether Jon was guilty but rather whether the learned judge had other ideas. Either way he recalled later that he was feeling slightly uneasy, standing out there in the media scrum and listening to them dictating their stories.

He found this disconcerting. Everyone he could hear was sending a story that sounded like a verdict of guilty was more or less automatic. There were endless phrases about abuse, about the SEALs beating up the terrorist, and about how they had closed ranks against the prosecutors.

"It was as if they had heard nothing," Threatt recalled. "As if they had never even read or listened to the evidence of two of the most unreliable prosecution witnesses ever to set foot in a military court of law."

The defense's refusal to present a case meant the media had not received the benefit of a group of larger-than-life SEALs marching through the witness box, assuring anyone who would listen that this was the most absurd prosecution ever brought and that all of the accused SEALs were among the best of the best.

In a sense that military tradition of saying nothing had, at this stage at least, somewhat backfired, and thousands of words were flying through the stratosphere, offering lurid accounts of every last act the SEALs were alleged to have done wrong.

It sounded to Threatt as though his client had already been found guilty. And though logic was telling him this was legally impossible, his heart was listening to those journalists, and they were trained not to be right but to be persuasive. And they had about a zillion dollars worth of electronic camera equipment helping them to start spreading the news.

And this would hold up for the immediate future, until Judge Carlos either shut it all down or agreed with the prosecutors.

The time passed slowly: one hour . . . two hours . . . and almost three before the court officials summoned everyone inside. Judge Carlos had reached his verdict a few minutes after midnight, and the courtroom fell stone-silent as he spoke.

"Upon reviewing the evidence," he said, "and considering the testimony given by Ahmad Hashim Abd Al-Isawi and Master-at-Arms 3rd Class Brian Westinson and, indeed, MC1 Lynn Friant and PO1 Paul Franco, I find there is insufficient reliable evidence. And therefore I find Petty Officer 2nd Class Jonathan Keefe . . . not guilty."

Jon showed not a flicker of emotion as the verdict was delivered. He offered a tight, curt little nod of approval and turned to shake the hand of the faithful Paul Threatt. But from the crowded courtroom, packed with SEALs, there erupted one of those collective outbursts of "Y-E-E-E-SSS!" as the accused SEAL finally walked free, innocent of every charge that had been leveled at him over the previous eight months.

Because now he was found not guilty of the lies they said he'd told, of the allegations that he'd conspired to cover up the punch Matt never threw. Innocent of being derelict in his duty. Innocent of every darned dishonest thing they said he'd done in the hours after he'd led the platoon forward in the darkness of the desert, machine gun in firing position, and through the wire in search of the most dangerous terrorist in Iraq.

Right now there was only one question left: Could he ever forgive the US Navy for what they tried to do to him? What about the days, weeks, and months of torment as he'd confronted the possibility of personal disgrace and dishonor for crimes he'd never committed?

Could he ever feel the same about the US Navy and the command-ers who had presented him with a bound legal file that was headed: THE UNITED STATES OF AMERICA V. SO2 JONATHAN KEEFE?

Did anyone have any idea what that had done to him, just the sight of it? How could they? How could anyone understand what those most terrible words could do to a US Navy SEAL, a man who had sworn before God to defend his country with his own life any time he was asked to do so?

Sweet Jesus, could anyone ever understand what they had put him through? And could he now regain faith, when for so long there had been no cause for faith? Could he really return to the cause to which he had dedicated his life?

Like General Douglas MacArthur, Jon Keefe would always hear in his mind the "crash of guns, and the mournful mutter of the battle-field" in the strife-torn rubble of Fallujah. The issue was that from now on, could he cast aside the deep wounds of this court-martial and answer once more the everlasting call that summons a Navy SEAL to battle stations to fight against the enemies of the United States of America?

Neither the US Navy nor the SEALs have an official motto, nothing formally written down or carved into a marble slab. But what they have is probably less destructible. And it's engraved on the soul of every SEAL: Courage, Honor, and Commitment. Jon Keefe still had his soul, but he no longer knew whether the nobility of those words was still intact. He only knew he would try his best and rejoin his pla-toon, wherever that might take him.

12

THE GREEN LIGHT FROM HIGH COMMAND

SEAL combat leader: "I have no idea why Matthew is sitting at that table accused of anything. That's a future SEAL leader right there. And he would never lie to anyone in his command. Not in a thousand years."

The US government's case against its own Navy SEALs was laid spread-eagle across the sands of Arabia. And now the disparate armada of attorneys, witnesses, freed men, and court officials prepared to embark on the aircraft that would airlift them all seven hundred miles south, back to the old Bedouin lands of Qatar.

The outward journey, less than one week and about ten thousand light years ago had been, at best, incongruent—the thirty-four-strong court-martial touring party had been divided politely but academically almost down the middle. There were those who saw this persecution of the SEALs as disgraceful and those who saw it as a necessary proceeding to show the world that the United States was always superior to lawless terrorists—politically correct, that is.

The homeward journey, however, brought a new dimension to the word "polarize." Because now there were two distinct camps, divided not by civil and intellectually well-chosen phrases but rather victory and defeat, the triumphant and the vanquished.

There were prosecution lawyers who had been unusually hell-bent on securing convictions for the government. And then there were the iron-souled US combat warriors who had traversed half the globe just to stand in that courtroom and swear that the two accused men, their brothers-in-arms, Jonathan Keefe and Sam Gonzales, were innocent.

There was the judge himself, Commander Tierney Carlos, who as a hard-eyed beacon of common sense and justice, had brooked no unfairness against the defendants. And there were the defense attorneys, a large team of both civilians and Navy JAGs, who had fought tirelessly, night and day, for men they sincerely believed had done no wrong.

For the civilians, Greg McCormack and Monica Lombardi, there was, inevitably, the warm glow of courtroom success. But for members of the Navy JAG Corps there was a special private sense of disquiet.

For the prosecution, Lieutenant Commander Jason Grover, a senior and distinguished naval attorney, had worked with the extremely capable Lieutenant Nick Kradlec, and they had done everything possible for a near-impossible case, featuring two prime prosecution witnesses who no one believed, one of them a killer and an al-Qaeda terrorist who had murdered Americans.

And the Navy defense victors, representing Sam Gonzales, included the youthful and aggressive Lieutenant Guy Reschenthaler, working with Lieutenant Commander Andrew Carmichael. For Jonathan Keefe, Lieutenant Paul Threatt was his lead Navy JAG, and Matthew McCabe's two Navy JAGs, Lieutenant Kevin Shea and Lieutenant Kristen Anastos, further supported them all.

All of these lawyers essentially worked in the same office in Norfolk, Virginia. A combination of brilliance, passionate belief, and a darned shaky case to begin with had defeated the senior prosecution attorney. It was perfectly obvious that a few commanding officers in both the Navy and the Army were by now looking at these court-martial results with a somewhat jaundiced eye.

General Charles Cleveland and his staff were likely not happy about the outcomes. No one likes to bring a failed prosecution, certainly not one that had been cast so ignominiously upon the drifting sands of the Syrian Desert.

This applied particularly to any case in which there was not only relentless public pressure to have the proceedings stopped but also advice from distinguished military lawyers, eminent commentators, and many important members of Congress, all suggesting that these prosecutions against Navy SEALs were approaching the very heights of judicial folly.

Although General Cleveland and his legal assistants had been thoroughly alerted to the dangers of their prosecution, they had nonetheless pressed on in an obdurate way. The question that had baffled every lawyer involved, not to mention the defendants and very probably the judge was: Why?

What advantage could there possibly have been to charging SEALs with an offence that no one in the United States cared about? So many Americans thought, *Banged a terrorist in the mouth or wherever? So what? Whack him again for all I care.*

But the most bewildering aspect of the case was the obvious flimsiness of the prosecution's case. Everyone knew the unmarked terrorist was likely to be torn apart on the witness stand, and everyone knew the honest, straightforward SEAL witnesses, not to mention the medics, were going to cast doubt about Westinson's validity as an assistant to the prosecution.

Plainly these doubts had been in place since the very first statements had been taken. Why then, had a former Special Forces officer like Charles Cleveland risked going ahead when the apparition of failure lurked around every corner?

And now the SEALs' prosecution had been discredited. The jury did not believe Westinson or Al-Isawi, and neither did the judge.

So why? Was there something these very smart attorneys had missed? Was there some ulterior motive attached to this entire case? Were the men of SEAL Team 10 under some kind of a cloud?

Well, that last question was bothering at least two, maybe three, of the attorneys on that long journey home. And slowly they were putting together some kind of a theory, mentally lining up the administrative strikes against the SEAL Team, the kind of small incidents that might have added up to a general exasperation with the bearded American tigers of the Iraqi desert. And there were, undeniably, several possibilities:

1. A lot of US servicemen, most especially in the Army, quietly resent the SEALs because they march to the beat of a different drum. They are allowed to wear their hair longer than everyone else, and often wear beards to fit in better with local tribesmen. They often address their officers on first-name terms. Also, that steel-edged brotherhood stands supreme; they place their lives in each other's hands most days. Officers rarely if ever pull rank on their devoted warriors.

2. Team 10 had a battlefield incident in the not-too-distant past, and there was the normal inquiry. Certain military bureaucrats had almost fallen over themselves generating volumes of red tape connected to the incident.

3. Carlton Milo Higbie had built a "catapult," meant to infuse some levity into the very serious wartime atmosphere, but not everyone found it funny. Working from some ancient Roman battle manual, the irrepressible, superintelligent SEAL managed to construct a huge siege weapon capable of hurling a hefty rock several hundred yards. The SEALs all thought this was hysterical, but there were those in authority who very definitely thought otherwise.

4. And somehow or another, a couple of big cans of diesel fuel intended for the generator were accidentally poured into the Camp Schwedler water supply, instantly poisoning it. Team 10 was not in any way responsible, but the camp's problem of water, which now had to be brought in from the main Marine base, was just another pain-in-the-ass problem involving the iron men from Virginia Beach.

5. And now there was another problem: prisoner abuse, this time just a few miles from Abu Ghraib. You could almost hear the collective groan emanating from commanding officers at the mere

sound of that career-busting phrase, and they must have thought, *TEAM 10! Jesus Christ! Not them again!*

Because, although this was now 2009, only four years since the Abu Ghraib disaster, the mere mention of the words "prisoner abuse" caused an almost neurotic reaction among US service chiefs seen only rarely since the fall of Saigon in 1975.

No one would ever forget the crushing reaction of the US Defense Department when Abu Ghraib came to light—seventeen soldiers and officers removed from duty, eleven of them court-martialed, resulting in a couple of heavy jail sentences, one of ten years, another of eight.

Abu Ghraib saw the demotion of a brigadier general to colonel. It also saw the powerful Defense Secretary Donald Rumsfeld offer his resignation. And it all started with *prisoner abuse*. And Matt McCabe's alleged bang to the guts of Al-Isawi had, in the opinion of several lawyers, triggered a drastic overreaction.

In truth, there could have been but three takes on why General Cleveland persisted with the courts-martial when it was plainly risky to do so:

1. Someone very senior was telling him to follow the international politically correct line, no matter what.
2. The words *prisoner abuse* had caused an entirely uncharacteristic loss of nerve at several high levels in the US military.
3. There was a strong feeling that Navy SEALs were getting too "untouchable," and here, at last, was the occasion to teach them a short, sharp lesson, to show them that even they, the gods of US combat, were not above regular military law.

It was quite surprising how many of those defense attorneys were inclined toward option three. And there was one further point with which every last one of the defense counselors was in unanimous agreement.

The military authorities had jumped onto the wrong side of this argument very early on—too early—before they had even examined the facts or listened to the SEALs. And once the commanders had crossed that line, determined to establish "prisoner abuse," there was no way back.

Because everyone had immediately jumped all over the accused SEALs, treating them as though they were guilty. Master chiefs, commanders at every level, legal officers—everyone was trying their best to please their respective masters and, it seemed, paint Matt, Jon, and Sam in the worst possible light: bullies, conspirators, and liars.

It would have been downright impossible for the military authorities finally to say, "Oh, we probably got this one wrong. Al-Isawi is an obvious liar, Brian Westinson is ... well ... unreliable, and Matt, Jon, and Sam can go free." It had all gone too far, too quickly. And there was no way to retreat.

The road ahead led directly to that famous SEAL combat zone, known colloquially as an "Oh shit! scenario." And unlike the SEALs, the high command was not yet prepared to "engage the enemy." That would have to wait for a courtroom, and in there, under the US Constitution, every accused person has a right to absolute fairness.

And that was, after all, the only thing each one of the three charged SEALs had ever requested—a lawyer and a proper hearing.

And when push came to shove in that Baghdad trial room, the government finally saw what it was up against—a half-dozen legal-armed attorneys, carrying sledgehammers of the law with which to obliterate the charges against their innocent clients.

Thus the soured atmosphere between the various factions on the aircraft home to Norfolk. Thus the polarization of the entire court-martial fraternity—those who believed that justice had most certainly been done and those whose judicial noses had been put very badly out of joint.

Jon and Sam slept soundly through much of the seven thousand–mile journey from Qatar to Washington. It was the first time either of them had slept soundly for more than seven months.

Behind them, sitting with his naval JAGs, Lieutenant Kevin Shea and Lieutenant Kristen Anastos, was the one man for whom the endless ordeal was not yet over. Petty Officer Matthew McCabe was still only twenty-four years old and, in his own mind, still with a mountain yet to climb.

Despite the two acquittals in Iraq, Matthew was still charged with the actual whacking of the terrorist. He alone had to face trial; he alone was charged with three separate counts—assault, dereliction, and lying. He alone may face military jail if found guilty.

Moments like these, when your two buddies are free and cleared of wrongdoing, peace of mind hard to achieve. And all the old dreads and fears came crowding in on Matt, no matter how many friends and well-wishers were with him on that aircraft home.

Right now he was as alone as he had ever been. No one else would face what he must face. No one else would stand before a military court and hear the satanic words, the UNITED STATES OF AMERICA V. MATTHEW MCCABE. No one else would feel the stark, helpless chill of accusations when none was deserved.

The great rallying points of the US Navy's slogan, "Honor, Courage and Commitment," were hollow to him now, his short years of service no longer calling him to the flag. Matt's questions were searching: Am I brave enough to face myself when I am so afraid? Can I stand up in this storm that I now must face? Or will these great forces, lined up against me, in the end prove too strong?

On the aircraft he could see the prosecutors' frowns. Anyone could tell they were less than happy. Where would they go from here? Would they somehow rally their own troops and charge back into the fray with new evidence and testimony to be used against him? Who else was there? Who might now step forward and swear before God that they had seen him thump the terrorist?

Right now nothing would have surprised Matt. And not too far away sat the strange and silent figure of Brian Westinson, whose actions, to Matt at least, were beyond comprehension.

There was some comfort for him in the two Baghdad trials' outcomes. No one had believed Westinson in Iraq, and there was a fighting chance they would not believe him in Norfolk either. But Matthew had now seen justice at work. In the beginning he had thought it would be a simple task to tell the truth and make it obvious the charges were absurd.

But this, his first brush with the law, had already taught him differently: all the guile, study, and aggression the attorneys could gather were required just to prove the obvious. The dark forces that walked the horizon had to be stopped, and that required a courtroom bludgeon, for they would not retreat on their own. That was the way of adversarial law as it is widely practiced in the free world.

Matt needed every one of his four-man legal infantry. His lead JAG, Lieutenant Kevin Shea, was a tough courtroom advocate, a New Yorker, one of five brothers—two of them SEALs and two of them US Marines. Lieutenant Kristen Anastos had worked tirelessly on his behalf, and they would now join forces with Puckett's law firm in Virginia, bringing another new fighting force into play.

He was Puckett's law partner, Major Haytham Faraj, a twenty-two-year veteran of the US Marine Corps, an enlisted man who had come up through the ranks—mortar section leader, Fifth Marines, platoon sergeant (weapons); deployed to Operation Desert Shield and Desert Storm, and distinguished staff sergeant.

Major Faraj then attended the Military College South Carolina (the Citadel), where he graduated magna cum laude and was commissioned in 1995, later to be assigned to Third Battalion, First Marines, becoming a company commander. He received his juris doctorate degree (cum laude) from the American University College of Law in Washington, DC.

A fluent Arab speaker, Major Faraj began his career as a trial attorney in the Marine Corps, rising to senior defense counsel at Camp Pendleton, California. By the time he came on board for Matt's trial, he was Puckett's partner, slightly outranked by the former lieutenant colonel but nonetheless a formidable defense counsel force in any court-martial.

"My kind of guy, right?" muttered Matt to himself on that long, largely sleepless journey home. And even as his worst dreads churned in his subconscious, the bayonet-sharp mind of Faraj, a military weapons expert, was preparing the first of his legal missiles, and this one was aimed straight at the heart of SOCCENT on MacDill Air Force Base, Florida, home of Charles T. Cleveland, major general, US Army, commanding.

In short, the ex-Marine major was suggesting that the Major General, who had convened these trials, do himself and everyone involved a huge favor and dismiss these "untrue allegations" against SO2 Matthew McCabe.

It was a personal letter written on the headed paper of the Puckett and Faraj Law Firm on Jamieson Avenue, Alexandria, Virginia, exquisitely timed to hit while the US-based brass were still reeling from the results of the failed courts-martial against Sam Gonzales and Jon Keefe.

The letter was argued immaculately, as would be expected from an attorney as battlewise as Faraj. It sought not to trap the general in a corner from which there was no escape but rather to appeal to his long experience as a Special Forces commander and a lifelong leader of men—American men, that is.

After so many triumphs in the bear-pit of a criminal courtroom, where he'd delivered so many pleas couched in harsh, confrontational terms, Faraj also knew how to take his foot off the gas pedal when the occasion demanded.

His private letter, in full, to the general, read,

Dear General Cleveland,

I write to plead the case of SO2 Matthew McCabe. This is not mere posturing, and it is not lawyering. It is a former serviceman pleading the case of a current service-member. It is one warrior pleading the case of, and to, another warrior.

Indeed I am a lawyer; and it is true that I represent Matthew McCabe, and have an interest in seeing this case resolved in his favor. However, before I became a lawyer, I served 16 years in the infantry as an enlisted Marine, and then as an officer. I have deployed numerous times, served in combat and held several leadership and command billets.

I have analyzed this case from every angle in as detached and objective a manner as I could; given my connection to it. I went so far as to have Matthew McCabe submit to an independent professional polygraph exam, the report of which I attach.

The polygraph confirmed what I concluded, and what Matt McCabe has said all along. He did not hit anyone. I cannot answer why the detainee says he was abused, I cannot explain MA3 Westinson's version of the facts. But one thing remains certain: Matt McCabe is innocent.

SEALs and other Special Forces have no need to abuse. They are too disciplined and too professional. You know this. By my count you have commanded six different Special Force commands and units. You know these types of men better than anyone. They are aggressive, tough, dependable, and, most importantly, honorable. They are serious men, doing serious business. They would not betray the trust you placed in them.

I am asking you not betray the trust Matt McCabe has placed in you. He became a SEAL knowing that he was joining the ranks of a very few special men. He knew he would be exposed to harm on the battlefield. He willingly volunteered. He understood that he and his brothers may at times come under scrutiny, and criticism, for doing their job. But he believed that you, and his other officers, would protect him, for so long as he did what he was supposed to do.

Matt McCabe was doing what he was supposed to do. He arrested, and transferred a very bad person to the authorities. He did not abuse him, or in any way act in an unprofessional manner. Yet today, he finds himself facing serious charges that may end his career, take his liberty and ruin his life. Will you protect him?

I recognize that as a commander, you have a duty to investigate allegations of misconduct, but you also have a duty to prevent frivolous prosecutions, and unsubstantiated charging. Two of your sailors, Keefe and SO1 Gonzales, have been acquitted of the unsubstantiated charges; another remains. He loses sleep, suffers from the hurt of betrayal, and feels confused about why he must go through this process, because he has done nothing wrong. He has a talented defense team, but that guarantees nothing.

At the end of his trial, he may very well stand guilty of an offense he did not commit. He would have a federal conviction. He may go to prison. He may be discharged, with a bad conduct discharge, in spite of his honorable service. He may lose his rank, and have to return home dishonored and betrayed.

Has it not become clear that these SEALs did nothing improper? A jury and a military judge, in the cases of Gonzales and Keefe, respectively disbelieved the version of the facts sponsored by the detainee and MA3 Westinson.

And I believe you will find the conclusions of the two courts, that no misconduct occurred, persuasive enough to move you to dismiss the charges against SO2 McCabe. I also attach the polygraph examination we gave to Matt. It was administered by a certified polygrapher, but if you continue to have doubts, I invite you to speak to Matt personally.

As a former Marine, former warrior, and officer of the court, I want to assure you that Matt has maintained the same version of the facts all along: he never abused the detainee.

It is my sincere hope that you will end this matter by dismissing the charges against SO2 Matt McCabe. Protect your Sailor from the untrue allegations, and end his nightmare.

Semper Fidelis,

Very respectfully,

Haytham Faraj, Major, USMC (Ret.)

Faced with that and with the flat-out rejection of the two courts-martial, General Cleveland nonetheless elected to ignore the onrushing judicial tide. He told Faraj he was allowing Matt's trial to proceed. The twenty-four-year-old Echo Platoon Team leader would face the jury in the next two weeks, in Norfolk, under the guidance of the senior judge, Captain Moira Modzelewski.

This would be a very formidable courtroom. Judge Modzelewski had recently been appointed to serve as the presiding officer of the Guantanamo Military Commission that would sit in judgment over the detained al-Qaeda suspect, Noor Uthman Muhammed. Captain Modzelewski was a world-class authority on terrorists as well as US law. Generally speaking, hers would not be the ideal forum to convince the judge that Al-Isawi was anything but a vicious little desert murderer and about as trustworthy as Colonel Gaddafi.

Captain Modzelewski had studied at the University of Virginia Law School and at the Naval Justice School. In 1989 she was appointed as an assistant professor at the US Naval Academy in Annapolis. She was also pretty adroit at nailing down trained liars, and when she finally had the heavily guarded Noor Uthman in front of her at Guantanamo, she subjected him to a grim two-hour grilling just to establish that he understood the meaning of the word "guilty."

She fired a barrage of questions at him, all starting with the phrase, "Do you understand?" Finally he was allowed to plead guilty, thus averting a sentence of life imprisonment. But Captain Moira had established one lifelong rule for her courtroom: do not lie to this judge, because you will, judicially, be hung out to dry.

This was not at all good news for Ahmad Hashim Abd Al-Isawi. But it was an almighty plus for Matt, his four lawyers, and the tight-knit platoon of SEAL warriors who would stand shoulder to shoulder in unshakable support of their Team 10 brother.

There was barely a week between the arrival home of the court-martial aircraft from Iraq and the start of Matt's trial. And before it began Puckett and Faraj came charging in with an instant motion to dismiss, both attorneys plainly indignant with General Cleveland's short, sharp refusal to even consider stopping the trial.

Their case for the defense was based on a report on the *O'Reilly Factor* on FoxNews, presented by Geraldo Rivera, in which he quoted sources "very close to" General Charles Cleveland alleging that he was pressured to continue with the trials despite public outrage and two not-guilty verdicts in the cases of Petty Officers Gonzales and Keefe.

Puckett and Faraj thus demanded the case be dismissed because of "unlawful command influence," the inference being that an even higher authority had leaned on the general and told him he was expected to allow Matt's court-martial to proceed.

This particular possibility in US military law is heavily frowned upon, categorically banned from happening. In some cases the merest suggestion of this kind of "insider trading" has been resolutely dealt with in the defendant's favor.

This one, however, was more evenly weighted. And the prosecution countered strongly, arguing that FoxNews had not provided sufficient objective facts in their report to warrant the dismissal of the case.

Judge Modzelewski accepted the prosecution's argument, agreeing that television stations need only rumors to allow them to run the story. That is not good enough for a US court of law, where evidential requirements are about one hundred times more stringent.

She dismissed the defense motion not for the lightweight methods of modern journalism but because she held that General Cleveland could not be held responsible for the continuation of the trial and because Matt himself had been given the option of nonjudicial punishment but chose instead to go to court-martial.

Just how little the military judiciary had played this angle was actually quite alarming. A naval nonjudicial punishment carries the assumption of guilt and is almost certainly a career wrecking ball. The three SEALs were admitting nothing, so the court-martial was their only option to establish total innocence. And for them nothing less would suffice.

Anyway, on Monday morning, May 3, Judge Modzelewski threw out the motion, rejecting the FoxNews report.

Puckett and Faraj were back on their feet in a flash, bringing a second motion that asked for a new transcript of Al-Isawi's deposition, the one taken in Baghdad that would constitute his testimony in absentia in McCabe's trial.

Al-Isawi was a prosecution witness, and the government had provided the translator. Urged on by Reschenthaler, Puckett and Faraj understood only too well the critical nature of any Arab translator who might have been either dumb, deaf, or crooked, and they wanted a new one to listen to Al-Isawi's audio testimony. And this might have taken another day.

But defense did not care how long it took, because both lawyers realized that the Arabic translator might have said anything. Faraj had already suspected that in pretrial depositions the translator seemed to be asking his own questions and ignoring those that the attorney posed. He told this to the judge, protesting that it was against the rules, and he provided a totally unreliable and untrustworthy deposition.

The defense wanted a brand-new linguist, with no prior knowledge of the trial and with an unbiased way of presenting the answers from the shatteringly dishonest terrorist.

Judge Modzelewski agreed with that and instructed the prosecution to provide a new translator to listen to Al-Isawi's audio testimony, even if it did take extra time, before jury selection the following day, Tuesday. This meant that the trial would probably now take up the entire week.

This was the most likely outcome, because all of the battle lines had been hard won. Prosecution and defense had been, effectively, daggers drawn for months on end. And when the trial finally began on Tuesday, May 4, after jury selection, the pure tension of these long, argumentative proceedings could be seen.

An eight-man US naval jury was duly selected—four enlisted men and four commissioned officers. None of them were SEALs. The panel comprised various grades of seniority: one Navy petty officer 2nd class (equivalent Army sergeant), one Navy petty officer 1st class (equivalent Army staff sergeant), one Navy chief petty officer (equivalent Army sergeant 1st class), and one Navy senior chief petty officer (equivalent Army master sergeant).

The officers were a lieutenant JAG, a lieutenant, a commander, and a captain—every one of them was male except the captain.

At eight o'clock that morning Matthew McCabe, in company with his father, Martin, his mother, Pam, and fashion-model sister, Megan, arrived at the Norfolk Base, where a large protesting crowd was assembled at the gates, holding banners aloft and chanting his name. Some had been there the entire night. Tents were still erected, a speakers' forum had been established, and Matt could see a banner that demanded, STOP THIS WICKED COURT-MARTIAL. And he could hear the voice of the American public chanting his name, over and over: "MATTHEW... MATTHEW!"

It was a chorus that had echoed across the country in a hundred meetings and fund-raisers and in the great halls of the US Congress. And it was a chorus that refused to be stilled. And even with the military's iron clamp on the release of information, that voice could still be heard echoing in the early morning quiet of this vast naval dockyard.

They drove past the security guard, and Matt hunkered down in the backseat and tried not to be recognized as reporters, broadcasters, and cameramen swarmed toward every incoming vehicle, trying to catch a glimpse or perhaps a even a word with the SEAL whose prosecution had enraged so many ordinary US citizens.

The media, though resolutely on the side of all three of the accused SEALs, had not quite lined up their ducks correctly. Their overall view remained steadfast: *If Matt had walloped the terrorist, so what? The terrorist deserved it. And who cares anyway?*

Curiously this was gratifying but by no means acceptable to the SEALs. Months later Sam Gonzales mentioned to his legal team that people had missed the point. The three accused did not wish for approval nor indeed support for a stray punch landing on Al-Isawi; rather, they wanted it plainly understood that none of them, Matt, Jon, nor Sam, had punched the detainee, that no SEAL would ever dream of punching a detainee.

That was why they had all gone to court-martial. It was also why a large group of SEALs were all lined up ready to march into that courtroom and stand with Matt against the forces of doubt and dishonor.

It was also why Matt was very gun-shy about the press. He was never quite sure how journalists would present this case to the public. And his lawyers understood they were not seeking dismissal on some technical point of law; Matt wanted total exoneration, just as his two teammates had been granted.

He did not want the question of the punch to be somehow held up in the air: *even if he threw it, how could it matter?* He wanted three things established and then hammered into a marble tablet: no punch, no punch, and no punch. Because there was no punch.

So the car left the chanting crowd behind and headed for the US Navy courtroom, a four-story granite stronghold that stands guard over military law in the Dark Blue section of the US Armed Forces.

Smartly dressed in his dress blues, Petty Officer McCabe walked with his family into the building and down the corridor into the courtroom where the charges against him would be heard and disputed, again and again, during the next four days.

The room itself resembled every courtroom in a thousand Hollywood movies: about a dozen rows of benches left and right, with a three-foot-high balustrade and a swinging gate in the center. The long table for the prosecutors was set to the left-hand side of the well of the court, closest to the jury, with the defense table on the right.

The judge, Captain Modzelewski, sat on a raised dais, directly ahead, and she greeted the SEAL from Ohio with noticeable respect. He replied succinctly: "Yes, ma'am."

Matt sat between his four attorneys. The two Navy JAGs, Lieutenant Kevin Shea, and Lieutenant Kristen Anastos, were both wearing dress whites. On his other side were his civilian attorneys, the ex-US Marine officers Neal A. Puckett and Haytham Faraj, both wearing immaculately tailored business suits.

This represented a whole of lot of legal muscle for one possible whack. But right now Matt understood, perhaps above all other members of the Armed Forces, just what it might take to stop a shocking accusation once it had been given an unexpected green light from the high command.

He glanced back once to the now-full public gallery, and he could see Jon Keefe's parents sitting close to his own. He caught his mom's eye, and in a strange way that meant all the world to him. Pam smiled at him just once—a fleeting confirmation that she was still in his corner, right to the end, just as she always had been.

He could also see Echo Platoon's senior chief, a very influential SEAL whose presence was highly significant and represented vital support for the accused man.

Katie Helvenston and Donna Zovko were also seated. These were the mothers of two of the murdered Blackwater security men who had been mutilated and strung up from the Fallujah bridge over the Euphrates. Jerry Zovko had been a former Army Ranger, and Scott Helvenston had been a former SEAL. Eight years after their barbaric murders both mothers still wept for their slain sons. Donna was still inconsolable as the full name of the Butcher of Fallujah was read out in open court.

Both men had been laid to rest in US military national cemeteries—

Jerry, thirty-two, in the Western Reserve, near Akron, Ohio, and Scott, thirty-nine, in the Florida National Cemetery in Bushnell. But there was something so appalling in the manner of their murders that no one associated with either man ever fully recovered.

And no one ever forgot Katie's remarks after the fifth anniversary of that notorious Fallujah ambush, when she finally blurted out that Al-Isawi's men had decapitated her son and then cut out his heart. "How could anyone, how could they be so cruel?" she whispered, adding that DNA samples had to be gathered from Scott's children in order to identify his body because he had been mutilated beyond recognition.

And now she would live through it all over again. And once more tears streamed down Katie's face as Lieutenant Nick Kadlec rose to present the case for the prosecution of Matthew McCabe.

He explained to the jury that this was a prosecution that they did not want to hear. "But as the evidence unfolds," he said, "it becomes a story you must believe."

Matt never flinched as Kadlec added that Matt had failed to live up to Navy standards when he struck the detainee in the abdomen and walked away, leaving the prisoner on the floor, bleeding.

Almost as a parting shot, Kadlec confirmed that the detainee had his hands tied behind his back throughout his ordeal. "I urge you to do the right thing," he told the jury, "and summon the moral courage to hold McCabe accountable."

Puckett conducted the opening submission from the defense, and he immediately contended that Petty Officer McCabe was only doing his job, doing what all SEALs are trained to do, serving an Iraqi arrest warrant. He quickly added that the detainee's mouth injury had begun as a canker sore and that any subsequent bleeding was self-inflicted and had nothing to do with McCabe.

He told the jury they would not be convinced beyond a reasonable doubt, "but you will believe he is innocent," he said, "because Petty Officer Matthew McCabe is innocent."

The prosecution then deployed the three-hour audio deposition of Ahmad Hashim Abd Al-Isawi, who by now had been charged by the

Iraqis with masterminding the 2004 slayings of Jerry Zovko, Scott Helvenston, and two others.

And during this the court heard him deny any involvement with al-Qaeda or Hamas. He stated simply that US and Iraqi forces had raided his home and then taken him to a US base, where he was attacked "for five minutes."

He claimed he was standing with his hands tied behind his back when he was hit in the stomach. He described how he fell down from the force of the punch and hit his face on the floor. He said he felt "pain in my face" and later tasted blood in his mouth. While on the floor, he said, he had been kicked several times with a boot-covered foot in his shoulder and back.

He said that even though he was blindfolded, once he hit the floor he could see enough from beneath his eye cover to realize his attacker was bare-legged and wearing shorts. At no time did he identify any SEAL as his assailant.

At the conclusion of Al-Isawi's electronic deposition, there was of course no cross-examination, as he was approximately seven thousand miles away in a Baghdad military jail, and Matthew had waived his right to confront him in the courtroom. But the defense lawyers were well up to pace with the savaging that Reschenthaler had handed out to the terrorist during the Sam Gonzales trial.

And the jurors understood, like everyone else, that the terrorist had not been believed in either of the Iraqi trials. The still-contentious issue of his nonappearance remained immovable. The US government was never going to bring Al-Isawi into the United States; therefore, the case had needed either to be moved to Iraq, where he could appear in court, or it would stay in Norfolk, and defense would have to do without cross-examination.

The attorneys had decided there was no sense taking Matt back to Iraq to stand trial in a hostile environment. They would proceed in Norfolk without "crossing" Al-Isawi, whose total unfamiliarity with the truth was, after two trials, now an established fact.

This left the government with only one other card to play: the MA3 Brian Westinson. Again the prosecutors presented Westinson as a credible and reliable witness. But this was swimming against a flood tide of testimony to the contrary. So piece by piece Puckett dismembered his statements in the witness box. He pointed up the inconsistencies, the clashes on the timeline, the differences, great and small, in Westinson's several statements and interviews.

As soon as the Washington attorney stood up to begin the cross-examination, well, the writing was on the wall for the prosecution.

Q. You're nervous today, aren't you?

A. *Yes, sir.*

Q. You're nervous because you've testified twice before and weren't believed?

A. *No, sir.*

Puckett compelled Westinson to outline the initial events of that morning, when he left the holding cell in search of the medical paperwork, and then,

Q. When Lieutenant Jimmy began his inquiry after the detainee was found to have a bloody lip, you told him there were some Team guys back there, but you did not tell him any names, is that right?

A. *Yes, sir.*

Q. So even though you knew Carl was heading over to the detention facility you did not tell Lieutenant Jimmy? Is that right?

A. *Yes, sir.*

The attorney then established Westinson's somewhat-persecuted state of mind:

Q. You felt all eyes were on you, correct?

A. *Yes, sir.*

Q. You were also worried because you thought the detainee would run his mouth?

A. *Yes, sir.*

Q. You were worried to be found derelict in your duties, correct?

A. *Yes, sir.*

Q. Because, in fact, no SEALs should go back there to see the detainee, correct?

A. *Yes, sir.*

Q. And then you were interviewed by an agent?

A. *Yes.*

Q. You told him you saw a half-punch thrown by McCabe?

A. *I saw McCabe do what he did.*

Q. You said it was McCabe, someone on your own Team?

A. *Yes.*

Q. These guys were your friends?

A. *Yes.*

Q. It's hard to do the right thing, isn't it?

A. *Yes.*

Q. It takes courage, doesn't it?

A. *Yes.*

Puckett, having established the actions of the young master-at-arms, now switched to Westinson's official role as a Navy policeman.

Q. How was everyone dressed that morning?

A. *I was wearing pants. I don't remember what the others were wearing.*

Q. Did you wear a badge on this deployment?

A. *No. I never wore a badge.*

Q. But, by training, you are a law enforcement officer?

A. *Yes. But I was not trained in detainee ops.*

Q. And you did not immediately report the misconduct you watched?

A. *No, sir.*

Q. And in fact you are guilty of dereliction of duty, as well as failure to report an offense under Navy regulations?

A. *Yes, sir.*

Q. And, as a law enforcement officer, you have a duty to stop and prevent crime, don't you?

A. *Yes, sir.*

Q. Yet you did not tell Petty Officer McCabe to knock it off when you saw him throw a punch?

A. *No, sir.*

Q. You never said a word?

A. *No, sir.*

Q. You did not even threaten to report Petty Officer McCabe?

A. *No, sir.*

Q. But you say you had a conversation with the medic about the incident?

A. *Yes, sir.*

Q. And you say that Petty Officer Keefe had a stick?

A. *Yes, sir.*

Q. So the medic would have seen Petty Officer Keefe with that stick?

A. *He should have, sir.*

Q. And you said Petty Officer Keefe was banging that stick to scare the detainee?

A. *Yes, sir.*

Q. But you have not been charged with making a false official statement?

A. *No.*

Right here Puckett took a spell to demonstrate the utterly astounding fact that, despite the obviously doubtful conduct of his duties, no one had charged Westinson with anything. And Puckett continued harshly:

Q. Or false swearing?

A. *No.*

Q. Or perjury?

A. *No.*

Q. Or dereliction of duty?

A. *No.*

Q. Or failure to report an offence?

A. *No.*

Q. And you have not been charged with assault?

A. *No.*

And at this point Puckett switched back to the scene of the alleged crime.

Q. So the detainee is delivered?
A. *Yes, sir.*
Q. Then Petty Officers Sam, Keefe, and McCabe show up minutes later?
A. *Yes.*
Q. Then the medic needed paperwork and departs?
A. *Yes.*
Q. He is gone a few minutes—over five minutes—and you decide to go look for him?
A. *Yes, sir.*
Q. So you abandon the detainee, and both of you are looking for medical paperwork?
A. *A lot of that stuff is foggy.*
Q. Then you return to see Petty Officer McCabe strike the detainee, and you said in one of your statements, "I froze."
A. *Yes, sir.*
Q. But we also know from your statements that Petty Officers Carl, McCabe, Sam, Keefe, Jason, and Rob all were in the presence of the detainee without supervision?
A. *Yes, sir.*
Q. And Petty Officer Eric came in an hour later?
A. *Yes, sir.*
Q. So six or seven SEALs had direct contact with the detainee?
A. *I suppose so, sir.*
Q. But you did not accuse all of them, did you?
A. *No, sir.*
Q. But there was no reason for them to go back there?
A. *No, sir.*
Q. But you saw Petty Officer McCabe punch somebody?
A. *Yes, sir.*

Q. And you are a law enforcement officer?

A. *Yes, sir.*

Q. And you did not report that?

A. *No.*

Q. From the "abuse" around 0800, you never reported it?

A. *No, sir.*

Q. Well, why did you not report this crime?

A. *It's the command climate. I felt I couldn't do my law enforcement job. The master-at-arms means nothing in their community.*

Q. Did Lieutenant Jimmy scare you?

A. *No, sir.*

Q. But you chose not to report this to him?

A. *I'm not happy I saw it. I wouldn't have reported it if it didn't happen.*

Q. But in failing to report it, you lied to the lieutenant?

A. *Yes, sir.*

"No more questions," replied Puckett.

With the Washington attorney finally through, Westinson's testimony was once more seriously discredited. And now began the long parade of witnesses who would walk through the courtroom to present the defense position that Brian Westinson was a confused young man.

Everyone felt a bit sorry for him in many ways. But not in one way—he had graphically described the beating handed out to the terrorist and said he saw Matt do it. Many people would never forgive him for that. Because too many people believed it was not true.

First came Paul Franco, the Navy reservist who held the rank of petty officer 1st class and had been overall supervisor of all non-SEALs at Camp Schwedler, the men who provided the deployed SEAL Teams with backup work in logistics, construction, coordination, and so forth.

He explained to the court how Westinson's immediate superior, MA1 Philip Cimino had left after a controversy over a force protection plan that left Westinson with a heavy workload, one with which he plainly could not cope. Some of Franco's testimony was colorful, and he mentioned how he noticed Westinson, a few days after Objective Amber, walking through the camp "in tears, unshaven and disheveled."

He asked what was the trouble, to which Westinson responded, "I hate this fucking place. This is a shitty deployment."

"Well, what's wrong?" asked Franco.

"Nothing's wrong."

But Petty Officer Franco swiftly found out that Westinson was ignoring some of his tasks in order to sit and watch the closed circuit camp protection system, and this was plainly "stressing him out."

On the following day Franco again discovered the MA3 in tears, visibly upset. And again he asked him: "What's up?"

This time Westinson responded, "This is all going to come back on me. This guy is going to make a claim that something happened to him."

The conversation continued for a short while, and in Franco's opinion Westinson "started to become unglued." He made a few weird statements, like "Who's going to marry me. ... I'm never going to get a job with the California Patrol."

Petty Officer Franco advised him to tell the truth and to report whatever it was he knew to the lieutenant. At that time Franco had no idea there was an allegation of prisoner abuse.

Asked about Petty Officer Matthew McCabe, Franco replied, "I've worked with him. He's an awesome guy."

Defense then called the combat camera operator, Lynn Friant, who confirmed her several previous statements, particularly that Westinson was very stressed out both prior to and immediately after the mission, "stomping around like a child at times."

She stated that when he was in this tearful and emotional state it embarrassed her, and she tried to get him to speak to one of the senior petty officers.

She explained that when the Marines finally pulled out of the camp, Westinson was the only MA3 on the base. And rather than have others assist him with the watches on the surveillance cameras, he stood many of them on his own.

Friant could not remember his precise words, but she did recall that sometime after Al-Isawi's capture, Westinson came to her "in a state of upset, crying and emotional." He told her he was the apple of his mother's eye, "and now I have destroyed everything." She asked him what he was talking about, and he replied, "Everything. You know, the statement."

Friant echoed Franco in that, in her opinion, McCabe was one "awesome Navy SEAL."

MA1 Philip Cimino had been Westinson's direct supervisor throughout the deployment until he left two weeks prior to the operation. He took the stand and stated that Westinson was young and believed that SEALs consider themselves "better than everyone else."

In Cimino's opinion, McCabe was a "great guy, and an awesome SEAL."

In direct contradiction, the prosecutors called another MA1 who had worked with Westinson between the time he returned from Iraq and the court-martial. He said that Westinson was a good guy, and he never had a problem with the young master-at-arms.

The SEALs then proceeded to line up for Matt, speaking on his behalf. Commander Hamilton came first, the senior officer from TEAM 7. He was the man who had taken the decision to push this case higher toward prosecution and, ultimately, to this courtroom, taking advice en route from the determined Master Chief Lampard.

He said nothing against Matt but instead quoted from a very thorough deployment guide he had authored, and this book stated categorically that prisoner abuse would not be tolerated. He read out that part of his work to the jury in an inevitably self-congratulatory way, but he had nothing to say about Matt's character.

Hamilton had never been a friend. But in this building that scarcely mattered. Matt had heavy backup. His distinguished troop commander took the stand and stated categorically that Matt was a great Navy SEAL with a tremendous work ethic who had never been in any kind of trouble before.

He added that Matt had an enviable reputation and had been given much responsibility, more than most SEALs of his age, and had handled it all perfectly. In the commander's opinion, Matt would *never* lie to a superior. "And," he added, "he's not lying now."

They then called to the stand Sam Gonzales, whose acquittal two weeks earlier could now be introduced into the record. Sam was the leading petty officer on the platoon and second-highest ranking enlisted man in the entire Iraqi camp. His trial and acquittal had made Sam, if anything, even more highly regarded in the SEAL community, and he took the stand for Matt. He told Puckett flatly that Matthew McCabe was known to be a great Navy SEAL, with a deep, natural sense of honor.

As one person who was there, Sam confirmed the events of the morning of September 2. "I did visit the detention facility with Matt McCabe and Jon Keefe that morning," he said, "but there was no assault. We dropped by just to see if Westinson needed anything. No other reason."

For the record, Sam stated there was no one on that base with whom he would rather work on a dangerous mission than Matt McCabe or Jon Keefe.

Next up was Carlton Milo Higbie IV, the brave and intellectual SEAL who was, pound for pound, probably the strongest man in a brotherhood of proven iron men. He stood tall in the witness box, making little effort to hide the underlying disdain he felt for the court-martial of his friend and colleague Matthew McCabe.

Carl was one of those people who had neither the intention nor necessity to lie to anyone about anything. Ask him a question, and you'll get a straight answer, probably resembling a metaphoric pile driver. He was a SEAL who would never stab his enemy in the back, simply because that enemy would never have even a split second to turn around.

"Matt McCabe?" he said, "He's just a really great guy. Any of us would trust him with our lives. He has an outstanding reputation, based on his clear and obvious honor. I have no idea why he's sitting at that table accused of anything. That's a future SEAL leader right there. And he would *never* lie to anyone in his command. Not in a thousand years."

Matt's close colleague in the mission, Petty Officer 1st Class Eric, the rocket scientist from Georgia Tech, stepped up next. And the sight of this very brilliant SEAL standing gun-barrel straight in the witness box, speaking on behalf of Matt, was hugely impressive.

Eric, the point man on the mission, who had moved alone, quietly over the night desert right out in front of Matt's right-hand assault column, was the trusted voice that Matt heard constantly over the comms all the way into the al-Qaeda stronghold.

And now that same SEAL was standing in a courtroom, eyed by the prosecutors, men who may not believe what he says. And his task on this day was to tell everyone attending this court-martial that Matthew McCabe was an honorable man.

And the two SEALs glanced at each before Eric spoke. God knows what they were thinking, these two highly trained combat warriors who trusted each other to the death, as Eric tried to show that Matt was a man of honor.

"This man is one awesome Navy SEAL," said Eric. "And he has a reputation which I have never before heard challenged." The men had worked together on many lethal night missions in Iraq, missions in which their roles had been reversed—Matt out there manning the communications, with Eric the lead sniper.

And the bond between them was there for all to see in that room. Neither would ever speak about their camaraderie, but there were a hundred memories between them from dust-filled hellholes around Fallujah, when each had relied upon the other and death had threatened them both around every pile of street rubble.

And now here was Eric standing in a witness box in Norfolk, Virginia, telling people he considered Matt a thoroughly decent and outstanding colleague, a man of honor.

It was noticeable that in all cross-examinations of the SEALs the prosecution was apt to tread softly. And they made no exception with Petty Officer Eric, whose words went virtually unchallenged.

Defense also called the non-SEAL medic, HM1 Paddy, the "pirate," who confirmed everything the SEALs themselves had mentioned about Matt, including, once more, a statement under oath that he was a man of honor.

It may seem unusual for a group of Special Forces to persistently use the word "honor," but that word is a bedrock of SEAL culture. It's impressed upon them right from start of the BUD/S course, after which the outstanding graduate is awarded the title Honor Man. The word is contained in the SEAL Creed: "My Trident is a symbol of honor."

And the many meanings of the word are consistently demanded throughout SEAL training: integrity, decency, righteousness, principle, character, pride, and morality. In the SEAL community to cast doubt upon a SEAL's honor represents an insult that once caused men to fight duels. To call him a liar is probably worse.

So many men who had worked with him were now defending Matt's honor. And even more men were standing by on the far side of the world to help. The oral surgeon in Iraq who had argued for Jon Keefe and Sam Gonzales, stating that the detainee had caused his own lip injury, was right by his cell phone when Puckett called from that Norfolk courtroom.

The jury heard the surgeon's words, via satellite from Baghdad, confirming that in his view Al-Isawi had bitten his own lip ulcer, thus creating his own blood wound.

Puckett jumped all over this, raising his voice to stress that this validated their position that no assault had ever occurred. Once more he reminded the court that all al-Qaeda detainees are trained to injure themselves and then claim abuse.

By this time Puckett and Faraj were beginning to feel confident they were out in front in this argument, and they considered it unnecessary even to ask Matt to take the stand. Neither did they call Jon Keefe, who was sitting quietly outside, waiting to step in, if required, to defend his best buddy's honor.

Before the closing arguments on this sunlit May afternoon the prosecution called one more witness, who, it was planned, would support their position that two SEALs, Matt and Jonathan Keefe, had colluded immediately after the alleged assault to get their stories straight in writing, because their statements appeared to be identical.

And right here that witness really let the prosecutors down, testifying instead that the statements of SEALs who were on the same mission very often coincided in every detail. But the real body blow in this particular clash came when the prosecution added that the statements of Matt and Rob were, in fact, not the same, and, they contended, they should have been, as the two men had attacked the *same* building after the walk-in to the al-Qaeda garrison on the night of September 1.

And the defense thought this represented a mistake by the attorneys. Yes, they countered, Rob and Matt had moved into the attack simultaneously when they reached the building where Al-Isawi was hiding out; however, that apartment block was divided into two parts—Matt took the one on the right, and Rob took the one on the left.

The apartments were almost identical, with very similar layouts, but the personnel were different. And so Rob's statements did not dovetail with Matt's because they were in two separate places.

At this point in the trial the jury was been permitted to retire for a break while the attorneys battled the point. And seemingly right on cue, Lieutenant Jimmy came on the line from his deployment at the SEAL base in Hawaii.

With no jury present Lieutenant Jimmy spoke clearly about the statements that were now the subject of a legal altercation. Yes, it was correct that Matt's and Jon's statements were the same, standard because they were headed toward the same place. Matt's words and those of Rob were different, however, because they marched forward across the desert in two different columns, aiming for two separate apartments.

So of course they were different, and Lieutenant Jimmy, the officer in charge of the entire operation and on the line all the way from Hawaii, was swift to point out the logic of this. It all had the effect of making the defense look the wiser of the two legal teams.

In Matt's mind, even months after the trial was over, he still considered the clear and lucid words of Lieutenant Jimmy to have been a focal point of the court-martial: testimony from the other side of the world confirmed, once more, the obvious—that US Navy SEALs do not lie to their commanders. Ever.

From here on out Matt thought the jury listened rather more intently to the words of Puckett, Faraj, Shea, and Anastos than they did to those of the prosecution. And then it came down to the closing arguments.

Lieutenant Commander Jason Grover rose from his chair to present the case for the government. "This is a simple case," he said. "But not an easy one. Because nobody wants to believe a decorated Navy SEAL would assault a detainee."

But he returned to his only real witness, MA3 Westinson, who, he said, "had no reason to lie when he testified that he saw McCabe punch the prisoner in the stomach."

He then asked the jury: "What's Westinson's motive to blame his shipmates? If he was looking for an explanation for something that happened on his watch, he had an easy one right in front of him—he could just say the terrorist did it to himself. He said no such thing."

Grover dismissed the way the SEALs had refuted the testimony Westinson provided. He considered the SEALs were trying to protect one of their own. "They circled the wagons," he said. "They do not want Petty Officer McCabe to be held responsible for this."

He concluded the prosecution's case by stating that the military has zero tolerance for detainee abuse and that all members of the services are duty-bound to follow the law. "We uphold the rules," he said. "And we're better than terrorists. That's why we're here."

He then gave way for the defense's closing argument, which Faraj, who had been extremely busy during the overnight hours of recess, would conduct.

The former US Marine Corps major had been shopping, purchasing a brand-new white T-shirt and a small bottle of bright red food dye, the stuff used to enhance coloring. It comes in various forms—liquid, powder, gel, and paste. Faraj wanted liquid only, and not much of it.

And now, with his backup equipment on the table before him, he recapped the case, mentioning Westinson's unreliability and the obvious lack of motive for Matt McCabe or any of the other SEALs to walk into the detention facility and punch the prisoner.

"Why," he asked, "didn't McCabe just shoot Al-Isawi in the first place?"

"These accused SEALs," he continued, "are professionals. And for the government to be believed, every last one of them has to be lying."

At which point he produced his final plan of attack. Referring to the bloodstain on the terrorist's dishdasha, he wondered how many members of the jury realized how little blood it actually took to make a considerable mess of a white garment.

And he poured a small amount of the food dye into a spoon that was no more than a half-inch across and sprinkled it down the front of the brand-new T-shirt. The subsequent stain was more or less the same as that on Al-Isawi's garment.

"That's all it took," said Faraj. "And you may think this apparent injury was not nearly so severe as that original bloodstain suggested."

Faraj also resented the prosecutors' statement that the SEALs had circled the wagons to protect one of their own. "Absolutely untrue," he told the jury. "I disagree with the concept that the SEALs are covering up. I actually find it pretty offensive."

He formally requested that the jury find Matthew McCabe not guilty on all charges and to "finally free this innocent man of these accusations." With the closing statements complete, the prosecution requested additional time to prepare a rebuttal.

The attack on Westinson's character that a string of defense witnesses made required the prosecution to find a way to rehabilitate him. But this was very late in the day to resuscitate a key witness.

There really was no way back for the prosecutors. And at 4:15 P.M. on Thursday, May 6, Judge Modzelewski handed the case over to the jury. They were gone for just one hour and forty minutes, and when they returned the foreman announced that they did indeed have a unanimous verdict.

"We find Matthew McCabe not guilty on all counts," he said.

Brian Westinson, the only man who claimed he saw Matt strike the terrorist, yet again had not been believed.

And Matt, the last of the three SEALs to stand trial, was finally exonerated of all wrongdoing. The third court-martial had agreed with the first two: no Navy SEAL had punched Al-Isawi.

The three trials had cost the government in excess of $2 million. The SEALs' legal expenses topped $250,000.

Like a true SEAL, Matt accepted the greatest victory as though he were used to it, showing little emotion at the reading of the verdict. But before he could even shake hands with his attorneys a well-dressed lady walked swiftly out of the public benches, muttering, "Thank God, thank God" as she threw her arms around Matt's neck, thanking him for capturing her son's murderer.

Donna Zovko still clutched her rosary beads in perhaps the most famous picture of the trials, taken on someone's cell phone. Donna's eyes were closed as she clung to Matt and fought back that ever-present apparition of her son's body strung up on that Fallujah bridge. And in her heart were a thousand words that would never be spoken. To Matt she only murmured, "Thank you" over and over. Just a very private thank you in a very crowded courtroom.

One involved person was, however, missing from this final triumph: Katie Helvenston. Distraught almost beyond tolerance, she had left in the middle of the trial and flown home to the Midwest. Her exit was one of high courtroom drama because it happened when the recorded voice of Al-Isawi was heard during the trial. The stress of listening to these people trying to attack Matthew followed by the sound of this mass murderer lying to the court simply overcame her, so, in floods of tears, she went away, still thanking Matt for dragging the murderer of her beloved Scott into captivity to face trial.

In the moments after the verdict Matt turned to his attorneys and embraced each one of them in sincere thanks for everything they had done—although, in truth, this had not been the knock-down-drag-out battle of the first two trials. This one had the inestimable advantage of the two not-guilty verdicts established in Baghdad.

"To be honest, this was far more straightforward," said Faraj, "because right here we had two very definite villains, who were not telling the truth, and one very definite hero. That quickly laid it right out for the jury."

With the court-martial concluded, the press stampeded to their phones, relaying the major story that the last SEAL had been found not guilty on all counts.

The website "US Navy SEALs," unaffiliated with the United States' armed forces, fired out a release of the good news they wished to share, mentioning the very poor view everyone took of the prosecution's insinuation that the SEALs had circled the wagons. And they quoted Faraj's "pretty offensive."

They also stated the following: "Try as we might, not to make biased judgments, it is certainly difficult to consider allegations given by a suspected terrorist over the testimonies of Navy SEALs, who risk life and limb for what their country believes in."

Their e-mail release ended with their own verdict: "An expectant public has heaved a sigh of relief."

And boy, were they ever right about that. It was 6 P.M. on a Thursday evening, and the words "acquittal," "decision," "verdict," and "trial" were flashing through cyberspace. The name Matthew McCabe was heard more often than that of Barack Obama.

Outside the courtroom there was something approaching pandemonium. The correspondents for Al-Jazeera, the Arab television station out of Qatar, were ducking and diving, trying to find Iraqi sympathizers and, perhaps, someone who would say that it was impossible for any Arab to get justice in the United States. They had almost no luck.

But when Matt and his lawyers stepped outside there was a scene of genuine joy that transcended even the reporters' duty to report the most objective story for their publications and broadcasters.

Matt kept saying he was "ridiculously happy," and all the principal characters, who had been swept up for so long by this dubious court-martial, were mingling together in the Norfolk Navy Yards: Jon and Sam, Puckett and Faraj, Anastos and Shea, the SEALs, Eric and Carl, and Reschenthaler and Threatt, and of course, Donna.

Journalists besieged Matt's parents, and Martin McCabe told them: "My son and his friends are the guys who preserve the American dream. You start prosecuting them, that American dream is going to go away, because everything will fall apart." He added that there had been support for Matt, Jon, and Sam not just nationally but from all over the world.

Matt's mother said, "I'd just like to say I believed from the first day that Matthew was innocent. Because he would never lie to his SEAL commanders. That's what we knew, and that kept us all going. It's been very stressful, and we are very glad it's finally over."

Almost two hundred miles north, in Washington, DC, Congressman Dan Burton, who had helped immensely in collecting thousands of signatures in support of dismissing the charges against the SEALs, moved immediately into his office.

He had made it clear to McCabe's lawyers that he had been perfectly prepared to attend the court-martial and testify to the full extent of public outrage and national opinion. He would confirm that a motion to this effect had been raised in Congress.

As the media swept the airwaves with the breaking news of the verdict, Representative Burton released a statement that very night, offering "Heartfelt congratulations to Petty Officer McCabe and his family."

He added, "With all three Navy SEALs now cleared of all charges in this case, I believe this sends a very positive signal to the men and women in uniform who are fighting for America around the world today.

"I join the many thousands of Americans who cheer for SEALs McCabe, Keefe and Gonzales tonight, and on behalf of the 35,000 who signed my own petition for these three heroes, I thank them for their honorable service and welcome them back to duty."

FoxNews, which had stood resolutely by the SEALs from the day the story broke, had Matt on the air, live from the Norfolk Base, interviewed by anchorman Bret Baier.

"It's been troubling at times," said Matt. "Having your career and your life on the line is not an easy thing to handle. But everyone's been pushing for us, and that's made it a lot easier."

Bret ventured that people at home were "really upset you had to go through this ... people who said this should not have happened. ... What do you tell them today?"

Matt answered right there on national television: "Tell them I thank them, but really, not to worry about it anymore. I mean, we're all acquitted of these charges. And we're all going to move on with our careers, put it behind us. It's done, over with. I'll try not to think about it ever again. Just move on and live a happy life."

"Thank you," said Bret. "Thank you for your service to our country." And that pretty much encapsulated what most people felt. Except for one man, the convener of the courts-martial, General Charles Cleveland, whose office announced he would be making a statement on the following day.

Apparently the major general needed to sleep on this one, as well he might, as the man who could have stopped it months ago, when it became evident that Westinson was unreliable and that the mass murderer Al-Isawi was just about as unreliable as you can get.

As it happened, the general released a rambling essay on his views, and it lacked even one single shred of humility for putting three exemplary, patriotic members of the Special Forces through hell, despite so much learned opinion to the contrary.

Unsurprisingly his opening paragraph was about himself: "I take my responsibility as a commander and convening authority very seriously, and did not make the decision to refer these charges to courts-martial lightly."

The general then obliquely blamed the three SEALs for requesting court-martial even though he, Cleveland, "would have preferred to handle the incident administratively." Apparently he did not realize that no incident had occurred for him to handle administratively—and that he was relying on the words of a murderous terrorist and a discredited sailor.

He mentioned that the evidence presented reasonable grounds to believe that offenses had been committed and that the three petty officers had committed those offenses. He failed to mention that the evidence presented even more reasonable grounds to believe no offences had been committed at all. And the best legal minds in the country were telling him so.

With pompous military bureaucracy, he concluded his opening section with these words: "In the interests of justice and to maintain good order and discipline, I chose to proceed with the courts-martial."

He then rambled on, thanking the jurists and the lawyers for pursuing the interests of justice, protecting the sailors' rights. The general appreciated their examples of dedication to "protecting and defending our Constitution."

He added that in the face of some opposition, he allowed these charges to go forward because "I truly believe that the best process known for uncovering the truth, when the facts are contested, is that process which is found in our adversarial justice system."

In the general's view, "There is no better way to discover the truth than by presenting evidence to an unbiased panel of members, having witnesses testify under oath, and having that testimony subject to vigorous cross-examination."

He concluded with a high-handed overview: "Incidents such as these carry strategic implications for US forces and US National Security, and ultimately cost the lives of Americans. I will continue to take allegations such as this seriously, investigating them whenever they are brought to my attention, and acting on them when the evidence so dictates."

He greatly looked forward to the SEALs returning to their Team "and continuing their duties in defending our great nation."

A lieutenant colonel for SOCCENT added, "General Cleveland is satisfied that the military justice process has been executed fairly, and that thorough due process was carried out during these trial proceedings."

"Well, that's a relief," said one of the three SEALs (forbidding his name to be used on pain of death). "Thank God he didn't take it lightly. Now he's not only satisfied, but he maintained good order and discipline. Wow!"

The general might have received more universal acclaim had he said what most people thought, something like, "Sorry I authorized the blow-out of over two million dollars of taxpayers' money on these three trials. And I will never again accept the known lies of a rabid Iraqi terrorist against the words of my decorated US Navy SEALs. I accept my shuddering limitations in this instance."

That would have been acceptable. As it was, the US military was not applauded for its actions in court-martialing their own heroes; instead, it left many throughout the Navy and the general public with a very bad taste in their mouth, and it led many active personnel to resign from the Dark Blue branch of the armed forces.

And the Butcher of Fallujah, Ahmad Hashim Abd Al-Isawi?

The Iraqi authorities hanged him for murder.

EPILOGUE

For several months after the trials Matthew McCabe and Jonathan Keefe tried to pretend nothing had happened. They accepted new appointments to join Team 10 on deployment in Afghanistan. But in the twenty-first century, for the fighting man, this was a sinister place, where death lurked menacingly around every inch of the dirt-brown scrubland.

Insurgents, Taliban, and al-Qaeda were often unrecognizable. Friendly tribesmen turned out to be bitter enemies. Men whom the Americans had trained suddenly turned their weapons on their instructors. Nothing was what it seemed. The danger was never-ending. And US Navy SEALs needed to be always at the top of their game because they, above all others, were most often ordered into harm's way.

Matt and Jon realized at more or less the same time they were not able to produce their usual peak performance. Both men held platoon positions of immense responsibility. But that old hair-trigger reaction was missing—the lightning-fast instinct for danger, the sure and deadly aim-and-fire, the quivering antennae for the presence of an enemy, the instant grasp and communication of combat alertness.

The two SEALs shared a mortal fear that someone would get hurt or killed because of them. And both men strived to find once more that edge of combat readiness that sets a SEAL Platoon leader apart from all others. It was not a matter of fitness, as they both were tuned to a peak of physical strength and excellence.

In truth, neither of them knew precisely what it was. But something was gone. Those courts-martial had, somewhat insidiously, invaded their Special Forces psyche. No two men ever tried harder to regain whatever it was they had lost. But they were somehow fighting for a lesser god.

And it was no use, because a flame deep within them had flickered. It had not died; after all, they were both supremely well trained and dedicated special operators. But it would never burn quite so brightly again.

Matt's determination to become a SEAL officer was missing. Jon's devotion to the cause was diminished. Those terrible months when they felt the US military had turned against them for no reason whatsoever had taken a grim toll.

Nothing was the same. Long before they embarked on the big Navy transporter to fly them home from Afghanistan, they both knew it was over. They were two young men in their midtwenties who needed to seek out a new beginning.

And they both allowed their US Navy contracts to run out without ever indicating they wished to re-sign for the fighting force they both still loved but could no longer serve at the supreme level they had always attained.

By the spring of 2013 they had left the Teams. And even in these testing economic times, new employment was not too difficult to find. Half the country remained appalled at what had happened to them, so many a helping hand was offered.

Matt moved to another part of the United States to begin a career in finance, aided by a major businessman who had been outraged by the court-martial of the young SEAL.

Like many SEALs, Jon considered a position with a security firm where his SEAL training was regarded as near priceless against an irritating and ruthless twenty-first-century enemy. But three months later he was still undecided.

It would be impossible to assess how great an effect those military trials had on the ambitions of other young Americans hoping to serve in the US Armed Forces. But there was an effect, and many elite personnel already serving began to look elsewhere, perhaps to a less harsh and less politically correct form of employment.

Others, who were directly involved in the long legal battle to prove the three SEALs' innocence, also experienced this sorrowful dying of the light. Lieutenant Jason, who on that night had stood shoulder to shoulder with Jon, blocking the rim of Al-Isawi's stronghold, was severely shaken by the Navy's action against his teammates and left the service to go to law school.

Carlton Milo Higbie IV, who some thought might end up as a SEAL commander, also quit to pursue a career as a political writer.

More than two years later Lieutenant Jason also left the Navy to study law. As an officer of Echo Platoon, the courts-martial of three of his men had not enhanced his future prospects.

The superb Lieutenant Paul Threatt left the US Navy to set up a private practice dedicated to serving military service members. What happened to Jonathan Keefe affected him for a very long time. Threatt remained active in the Naval Reserves.

Lieutenant Guy Reschenthaler also resigned, returning to his native Pittsburgh to practice law and admitting, "I love the US Navy, and I cannot say anything against it. But I can also say that the court-martial of Sam Gonzales played a large part in my decision to leave the service."

Lieutenant Kevin Shea, who had worked hundreds of hours with Lieutenant Kristen Anastos, preparing Matt's defense, also resigned from the Navy to become a New York police officer, working Westchester County north of the city and close to his picturesque hometown of Nyack on the Hudson River.

For Petty Officer Sam Gonzales, there was no life beyond his Trident. And he slipped back into his Team as though he had never left, still the dedicated and meticulous senior enlisted man, still a Navy SEAL to his fingertips.

Brian Westinson left the Navy and returned to California.

In July 2012 US Secretary of Defense Leon Panetta announced that President Obama had nominated Major General Charles T. Cleveland to be promoted to a three-star Lieutenant General, Commanding US Army Special Operations, Fort Bragg, North Carolina.

George Washington was a lieutenant general. So were Ulysses Grant, William Sherman, and George Patton.